Helping Clients with Special Concerns

Helping Clients with Special Concerns

Sheldon Eisenberg
Cleveland State University

Lewis E. Patterson
Cleveland State University

Rand McNally College Publishing Company
Chicago

To Marge, Jerry, and Danny Eisenberg
Janice and Elizabeth Patterson

And to the memory of
Earl and Elizabeth Brubaker

Sponsoring Editor	Louise Waller
Project Editor	Teri M. Ludwig
Designer	Kristin Nelson
Cover	Ken Kenniston

Contents

Preface

While there are a variety of texts that discuss the general processes and theories of effective helping procedures, *Helping Clients With Special Concerns* is among the first to deal with specific problem areas for special populations. This book provides students in the helping professions with a conceptual understanding of various problem areas and then uses this psychological base to explore specific approaches to treatment.

In trying to establish the scope of this text the authors concerned themselves with those problems or client groups that are most frequently encountered in community and school counseling facilities. In a sense, the authors wish to provide vicarious clinical experiences for the novice counselor so that he or she can map the way through the helping situation with a client. More than that, the material of the book is well-suited to helping experienced counselors extend and deepen their knowledge of clinical problems and populations.

The book is divided into three main categories: personal concerns, of which depression and shyness are examples; family concerns, which are exemplified by divorce and bereavement; and special populations, which examines such groups as adults and young children.

After drawing up the table of contents, the authors realized that a better book would result if persons with special skills, knowledge, and experience would develop and write some of the chapters. The final contributors come from a variety of theoretical backgrounds and have experience as psychologists, counselors, and social workers (see *About the Contributors* at the end of the book).

In order to ensure the overall consistency in the treatment of each chapter, the authors developed specific guidelines for including an *understanding* section and a *helping* section. Each chapter was also written to demonstrate a relatively broad spectrum of ideas about helping with a specific problem or population. Contributors were given considerable latitude in expressing their own views, provided that they also touched base with the mainstream literature in their particular areas. Each chapter reflects both the theory and practice associated with a particular concern, as viewed by a skilled helping professional, who brings both practical skill and scholarship to this task. Without exception the authors believe the contributors will agree that we were demanding and challenging editors.

Whether you are being trained as a professional helper, are a new member of the profession, are looking for some insights into helping your clients, or are an experienced professional looking for some fresh thoughts, we think you will be stimulated by the chapters that follow.

We wish to acknowledge our very patient and skilled support staff at the Cleveland State University who helped with the production of the manuscript. We also appreciate the help of Louise Waller and Teri Ludwig of the Rand McNally editorial staff. Their good humor made the transition from manuscript to text a smooth process. We are particularly grateful to Linda Nichols, whose language skills helped us to smooth the words (our own and our contributors), and to Donna Magri, whose secretarial skills were essential in communicating with the contributors and in preparing a readable manuscript.

S. E.
L. E. P.

Fundamental Precepts of Effective Helping

SHELDON EISENBERG
LEWIS E. PATTERSON

The search to identify those common elements that form the basis for *effective helping* continues. As the following chapters of this book were developed, the editors had an excellent opportunity to study and understand the components of effective helping as presented in considerable variation by contributors of different theoretical backgrounds. In this short introduction we shall summarize a set of precepts that form the basis for our understanding of the helping process. These principles have emerged from five sources: our experience as helpers; our experience as counselor educators; our knowledge of the counseling theory literature; our editorial work with the drafts of the chapters in this text; and our discussions with each other. We think the contributors to this work will agree with most, if not all, of the precepts to be presented.

Precept One: Understanding

To be truly effective, the counselor must have a thorough understanding of human behavior and be able to apply that understanding to the particular set of problems or circumstances of each client.

Diagnosis and hypothesis-generating are critical and inevitable parts of the counselor's work. The process of diagnosis has two interrelated functions: first, to describe significant patterns of behavior or affective experience; and second, to provide causal explanations as to why given patterns of significance are happening. The process is one of developing tentative hypotheses, questioning their validity, and using supportable hypotheses as the basis for making critical decisions concerning the focus, process, and direction of the counseling experience.

To understand human behavior means to have a set of concepts and theories that help to account for and explain significant human reactions and relate them to experiences. These concepts and principles provide the core for the counselor's diagnostic and hypothesis-generating work. Counselors use their understandings to talk to themselves about their own behavior as well as the concerns, actions, perceptions, emotions, and motivations of their clients. With no theory, counselors have nothing to say in their conversations.

This first precept has been crucial at the very inception, and in the subsequent development of this text. Each chapter has been developed to provide the practitioner with a set of principles that will help him or her to understand the specific concern or specific client population being discussed. Each has been written to help the practitioner account for and hypothesize about significant human patterns that would be unexplainable without the theory. Each chapter has also been structured so as to help the reader use these hypotheses as the basis for effective helping practice.

People often point out two dangers involved in the diagnosis/hypothesis-generating process. One is that the process often becomes a game that applies labels of best fit to clients, thus putting them into categories. Once categorized, the client is stereotyped and all the "therefore" statements that apply to people in general in the category also apply to the client. As a result, the client's uniqueness as an individual is often lost. Worse, other important client attributes are missed because categorizing creates perceptual blinders for the counselor.

A second danger is that helping professionals often make mistakes in their diagnoses and these mistakes often result in ineffective and sometimes counterproductive helping efforts.

We agree that these dangers are real. But they are not dangers inherent in the diagnostic process itself; rather they are dangers of the misuse of the process. Counselors who comprehend the role that an understanding of human behavior serves in their work, and who recognize the proper function of diagnosis, will work very hard to avoid these dangers. It is part of their ethical responsibility.

Precept Two: Client Change

The ultimate purpose of the counseling experience is to help the client achieve some kind of change that he or she will regard as satisfying.

Virtually every significant theory of counseling states that creating some kind of client change in a growth-enhancing direction is the ultimate intended outcome of the counseling experience. Some say overt behavior change is the *sine qua non* of the experience. Others say that behavior change is simply symptom change; real and lasting change comes when the client develops new perceptions about self, significant others, and about life. Further, some counselors take a remedial orientation; their efforts are to help the client change dysfunctional behavior to more functional patterns, such as overcoming shyness, reducing debilitating anxiety, controlling counterproductive anger, or reducing interpersonal conflicts. Others believe that the change goal of counseling is to help people make important life decisions; the counselor's role is to help the client use a rational thinking process at life points of confusion and conflict. Still other counselors view their work as that of stimulating favorable personal and interpersonal growth. As they see it, remediating dysfunctionality and assisting in decision-making may become important contributions to the overall growth experience of the client. For these counselors viewing people in the process of becoming and having an in-depth picture of the healthy or fully functioning individual are crucial perspectives on the counseling process.

Client change is often difficult to document. Behavior change, if it occurs, is probably the easiest to observe because it is the most tangible. However, clients may also change their views about certain behaviors that they previously regarded as undesirable—or they may change in the extent to which they experience stress related to an unwanted life situation—or they may change in a variety of other ways that involve internal experiencing. In spite of the difficulties of assessing some kinds of change, it seems to us that a counselor who cannot describe the changes that the client has undergone has no basis for knowing when counseling has reached an effective conclusion.

Precept Three: Quality of the Relationship

The quality of the helping relationship is significant in providing a climate for client growth.

As each human being meets a new human being, he or she makes judgments about how much of self to share with that other individual. Before sharing deeply we all assess the risk in terms of what we think the listener will do with our personal thoughts and feelings. If trust is experienced, we share more and grow more; if trust is not experienced, we remain closed and go away from the experience unchanged.

The critical elements of the helping relationship that promote openness are described often in the literature of the field: respect vs. rejection; empathy vs. shallow advice-giving; congruence/genuineness vs. inconsistency; facilitative self-disclosure vs. counselor closedness; immediacy vs. escapes to past or future; and concreteness vs. abstract intellectualizing. The counselor must communicate respect for the client as a person with rights who is trying to live the best life he or she can for self. Genuine caring is communicated when a counselor tries to understand the client's world as if it were his or her own and gives the client verbal cues about that understanding. The effective counselor shares self and offers the experience of his or her relationship with the client as a way of opening communication to deeper levels of understanding. He or she will respond openly with a here and now immediacy to provide feedback and to help the client understand the immediacy of his or her own experiencing.

In some ways a brief discussion of the facilitative relationship of counseling may seem trite, and for that reason we would urge that the reader depend upon other sources for an in-depth treatment of the nature of the helping relationship. We would be remiss if we did not signal our belief that the counseling relationship makes communication at a deep level possible and is therefore a *sine qua non* of effective helping.

Precept Four: A Sequential Process

Counseling is a process that occurs with a fairly predictable sequence and which is characterized by movement toward identifiable outcomes.

Counseling has a beginning, a middle, and an ending. At the outset the client and counselor mutually discuss the concerns of the client. The counselor attempts at this point in the process to learn as nearly as possible what the client is experiencing and what has brought him or her to counseling. As the counselor listens to the client he or she works to develop an appreciation of the client's phenomenal world: how the client perceives self, significant others, and surrounding life space. This stage of counseling involves more than just identifying a problem or concern; it also includes developing a knowledge of how the client experiences that concern in the world as he or she sees it. Understanding the client's phenomenal world enables the counselor to offer constructive confrontations that can lead the client to greater self awareness, an essential quality of the middle stage of the counseling experience.

In the middle stage of counseling the client undergoes an in-depth exploration process in which the counselor tries to help the client understand self and the conditions of his or her life that relate to the concern(s) that the client has chosen to work on. Intense listening, careful reflecting, and occasional confrontation characterize the counselor's contribution to this stage of the process. For the client, goals that have been implicit in the way he or she has construed life experiences now begin to become explicit. The counselor helps the client to put these wishes (goals) into words that describe as clearly as possible what the client wants to make happen. New insights, discoveries, and awarenesses about self characterize the client's experiences during this stage of the process. The experience is exciting for some, uncomfortable for others.

Still later in counseling, client and counselor work together to consider the means that may lead to the accomplishment of desired goals. Finally there is an assessment of whether the means are sufficient to the goals, often after attempts at implementation.

On the surface this model may appear simple, to some perhaps oversimplified. Effective, in-depth counseling is a highly complex art form. Indeed, people who have watched films and video tapes of highly skilled counselors at work have often noted the parallels to a good abstract painting. With each viewing new observations and new discoveries are made, exciting fresh insights occur, and there is excited controversy about the quality of the effort. The artistry of the skillful counselor becomes especially apparent during the second stage of the process when the interaction moves from talk to work, from surface to depth, from defensive to more open, and from confused to insightful. Simulating that process is exciting, invigorating, exhausting, and sometimes frightening, but not simple.

Precept Five: Client Self-Disclosure and Self-Confrontation

The counseling process consists primarily of self-disclosure and self-confrontation on the part of the client, facilitated by interaction with the counselor.

In order for counseling to take place, the client must disclose personal material to the counselor, who in turn tries to understand the client's world in a context of what he or she knows about how people respond to life situations. While clients may reveal significant personal materials in their nonverbal behavior, the primary medium for counseling communication is verbal. Clients reveal their thoughts and feelings to a perceptive counselor by what they say, the affect with which they say it, and by what they choose to obscure in their verbal material. The more fully self-disclosure takes place the more fully the counselor can serve to help the client discover new ways of coping.

Self-confrontation by the client is a process of looking at self with an expanded perspective that allows for the development of new perceptions about self. The counselor assists the client to broaden his or her perspective on self by providing honest feedback. At the simplest level that feedback may just be restatements of the client's own words—restatements which cause the client to consider once more a thought just expressed. As the counselor becomes more confident of his or her understanding of the client, he or she may choose to move to a more comprehensive form of feedback which helps the client see self in a situation from alternative viewpoints. Since such feedback comes from the counselor's frame of reference, it frequently confronts the client with a view that he or she has not previously experienced. It is important for the counselor to be as free of vested interest as possible in using confrontation as a counseling tool.

Whether the counselor's feedback is at the low-risk restatement level or the higher-risk confrontation level, the client must confront self with new ways of seeing and understanding self in life situations. Through this process, a new understanding of personal needs, desires, perceptions, and assumptions emerge, and new coping skills are discovered and refined.

Precept Six: Intense Working Experience

Counseling is an intense working experience for the participants.

For the counselor, the related activities of attentive listening, information absorption, message clarification, and hypothesis-generating require intense energy. Beyond these largely intellectual activities is the emotional experience of caring for another enough to be affected by that person's emotions without allowing self to become lost in those emotions and debilitated as the facilitator.

For the client, the hard work comes with an effort to understand what is difficult to understand; in the endurance of confusion, conflict and uncertainty; and in the commitment to disclose to self that which is painful to think about. The effort and commitment require a level of concentration that may never have been experienced before. For all clients there are the added stresses of revealing one's personally felt inadequacies to another and the experiencing of emotions that disturb one's life. The work of producing growth through counseling is always demanding on the client, often painful.

Counseling is not the same thing as conversation. In conversations two or more people exchange information, ideas, and viewpoints. The experience is usually casual and relaxed. People leave a conversation and move easily to other things. Counseling is characterized by a much deeper level of intensity. Ideas are developed more slowly, encountered at a deeper personal level, and considered more carefully. People leave a counseling experience mentally and emotionally depleted, yet still thinking about what was discussed. If the experience of working has not occurred during the session for both client and counselor, then counseling has not happened. Conversation may have occurred, but counseling has not.

Precept Seven: Ethical Conduct

Offering to provide professional people-helping service obligates the helper (counselor, social worker, psychologist, etc.) to function in an ethical manner. Codes of ethics published by the relevant professional associations will serve to set some needed parameters.

Ethical practice may be defined as providing a helping service, for which one has been appropriately trained, with care and conscientious effort. Unethical practice occurs under three conditions: when the professional helper becomes involved with clients whose problems are beyond the scope of his or her training; when the helper exploits his or her position to collect fees or salary for incompetent service; and when the helper fails to understand his or her obligation to respect a client's rights to privacy and to free choice.

It is fundamental to professional services of all kinds that the client must trust the practitioner (lawyer, C.P.A., medical doctor, as well as counselor, social worker, psychologist) to provide competent service. It is this trust that allows the client to share his or her personal concerns in a way that goes beyond casual conversation and which makes effective helping possible. As with all professions, it is a violation of trust to offer a service which one is incompetent to deliver, or to exploit the public by offering less than the service one knows the client needs.

Respecting a client's right to privacy includes the maintenance of a confidential relationship within which the client is free to reveal important personal information as he or she becomes ready to do so. The client who hears his or her private thoughts revealed to another by his or her counselor has been betrayed, unless the nature of the words suggests a credible threat to life or limb. A client who is manipulated by a counselor to reveal information he or she is not yet ready to reveal has also been the victim of an invasion of privacy. The line between facilitative leading by the helper and prying into personal matters can be a fine one, and the distinction is often in terms of timelines and context.

Respecting a client's right to choose freely is also troublesome to some counselors. If one begins with the assumption that rational persons will ultimately arrive at the same set of conclusions about a given problem or circumstance, it is easy to conclude that the client who does not arrive at an answer that the counselor values is thinking irrationally. At times that may be true, and the disagreement serves as evidence that counseling has not yet been carried to an appropriate termination. In other instances the disagreement may signify that the client has values which differ from those of the counselor and perhaps from those of the society at large. In such instances the counselor may help the client to understand the logical consequences of the view he holds to be certain that the client is making a fully informed choice. Having accomplished an exploration of alternatives and consequences, the counselor has fulfilled his professional responsibility and has no further right or obligation to attempt to impose a particular choice.

PART I

Effective Helping With Common Personal Concerns

The seven chapters in this section represent common clinical concerns for which people are apt to seek a counselor's help. Each represents an important area of human dysfunctioning, which if not alleviated can cause personal unhappiness, a fixation in growth, and a block to effective personal functioning. The authors of each chapter provide a theory base to understand the problem area and develop guidelines for helping people with their concerns.

Eisenberg points out that the perceptions people hold toward self powerfully affect personal decisons, interpersonal functioning, ways of coping with stress, emotional control, and the scenario one builds for his or her personal future. Changing one's perceptions from self-disgust to self-respect can result in a variety of concomitant changes, including increased ability to cope effectively with stress, a greater tendency toward rational problem-solving and decision-making, more realistic and optimistic thoughts about one's personal future, more effective interpersonal relating, including assertiveness, and a reduction in frequency and intensity of episodes of anxiety, depression, and anger.

Anxiety, depression, and anger are among the most distressing of human experiences. When experienced in proportion to the events that trigger them, they serve an instrumental function in helping us respond to danger, overstimulation, and aggression. Out of control, each of these emotions becomes a tyrant that saps energy from productive living and can evoke danger to life and limb. Taken together, the chapters by Bocknek, Trembley, and

Schuerger explore the sources and origins of these emotions and subsequently provide a variety of approaches for helping people manage their emotions.

Alienation is often said to be a common experience of persons living in our post-industrial society. Living, as we do, in a complex world with large numbers of other people, it is easy to become confused about our relationship to our fellows. Few of us are employed in work that is directly related to sustenance. The family is a less predictable support than it was in earlier times. Johnson, in his chapter on alienation, suggests that the socialization process often occurs in a defective or incomplete way, leaving the individual out of touch with the complex world in which he or she lives. Socialization is the process through which we learn value, attitudes, roles, competencies, ways of perceiving the world, and a sense of identity. In the chapter on alienation Johnson describes the process of identification and role-learning that affects the nature and direction of a person's socialization experience and discusses a variety of ways that a counselor can combat an individual's defective socialization.

In a complex world intrapersonal and interpersonal conflicts are inevitable parts of life. Maslow suggests that important and significant growth occurs as a result of a person's efforts to resolve internally felt conflicts. The way people deal with interpersonal conflicts has a powerful and long range affect on our relationships with others. Poor interpersonal conflict management efforts based on winner-loser approaches are likely to result in interpersonal alienation. In contrast, efforts based on the premise that conflicts can be resolved without somebody losing are likely to lead to greater interpersonal respect and perhaps closeness amongst the conflicting individuals. In her chapter on conflict, Frey presents a variety of models for understanding different kinds of conflict and describes a model for helping people resolve specific intrapersonal as well as interpersonal conflicts. She also suggests programs educators can use to help students learn effective conflict resolution approaches.

Finally, Loxley's chapter discusses the nature of shyness and the approaches for helping people overcome their shyness. Since the healthy alternative to shyness is assertiveness, much of her chapter focuses on the recent ideas that have come from the assertiveness development literature.

Understanding and Building Self-Esteem

2

SHELDON EISENBERG

Helping people learn to like, accept, respect, and trust self has been a goal of counseling at least since the early writings of Rogers (1942) and probably well before. It has always been a goal of parents and of teachers who view education as preparation for life. Yet, we are a long way from being as effective as we would like in achieving this goal for people who have learned not to like or respect themselves.

There are four purposes for this chapter: To propose a definition for self concept; to discuss the implications of the definition; to identify some of the behavioral correlates associated with high and low self-esteem; and to describe and analyze several approaches to helping clients learn to like themselves.

The Self Concept Defined

Most of the theories of personality, counseling, and psychotherapy propose a definition of self concept as a central part of their theoretical framework. Although there are some differences, there is also considerable congruence. We shall use concepts from attitude development and systems thinking to define self concept as "the total set of information, ideas, perceptions, assumptions and beliefs a person has about self." The self concept system consists of a set of elements, in the form of beliefs or perceptions, all of which are connected directly or indirectly to the other elements within the system. Some core elements within the system are central to keeping all the other elements organized and intact. Other elements are peripheral; they are connected but not core to a person's total understanding of self. This definition can be presented pictorially from a figure developed by Purkey (1970).

The core elements of a person's self concept system consist of a set of beliefs about basic adequacy and self-liking. At this level self-focused beliefs include statements such as "I'm O.K." or "I'm not O.K." (Harris, 1969) and "I like me" or "I don't like me." A person whose basic attitude or life stance is "I'm not O.K." and "I don't like me" will clearly be miserable, unhappy, and highly anxious. More specific behavioral correlates of the "I'm not O.K." stance will be discussed further in the chapter.

Figure 2–1   Model for Self Concept

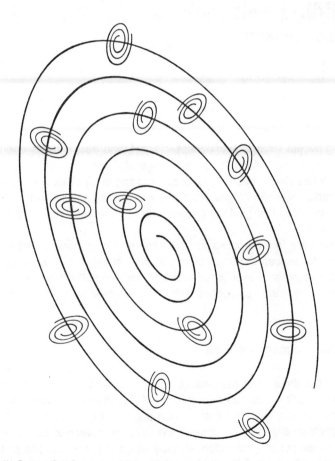

Source: W. W. Purkey, *Self Concept and School Achievement.* New York: Prentice-Hall, 1970.

At a more specific level the belief elements of a person's self concept will include a set of competency-specific appraisals (I-can-do-its and I-can't-do-its). Attached to these appraisals will be a set of value loadings: positive, negative, conflicting, and occasionally neutral. For example, a person may say, "I have excellent secretarial skills and that is important to me. I am not comfortable in relating to people and I am unhappy about that. I am taking college courses and I have real difficulties in math. Sometimes that bothers me and sometimes it does not. I also have a good memory for telephone numbers, but this skill does not matter to me very much."

A person's self concept also includes perceptions about interest and activity preference patterns. "I enjoy watching football on T.V. but not playing it. I like small group conversations but hate big parties."

A fourth set of self perceptions within a person's total belief system is the attributions or reasons people provide to account for their own behavior. "I get really nervous when I have to take tests, especially essay tests." "I am a high level executive and enjoy my work because I like being in control. I work very hard because success is important to me."

Although people have many self-focused beliefs most people are not fully aware of all the beliefs they hold about self. Some have highly developed self-images. Others have only a rough, inarticulate picture of themselves. The "Who am I" structured activity illustrates this observation very nicely. The activity requires two participants—an inquirer and a responder. The inquirer simply repeats the question "Who are you?" With each inquiry the initiator must provide a new description of self. Most people describe themselves by the family and career roles they perform: wife, husband, sales representative, lover, etc. Relatively few people can respond to more than ten inquiries and many cannot provide self-descriptions beyond their roles.

Although some aspects of a person's beliefs and perceptions about self are not easily available in awareness, beliefs about self still appear to act as powerful determinants of behavior. As will be described in further detail, people who dislike self are often motivated to avoid failure while people who like self are often motivated toward success experiences. Most theories of counseling emphasize that increasing a person's awareness of, and knowledge about self is a key to stimulating growth, effective decision-making, and behavior change.

While the definition provides a useful base for understanding the meaning of self concept, it also points out some thorny questions about self concept development and change. One is, what is a healthy self concept? While basic self-liking and self-respect are important ingredients, the person who *appears* to like and respect self does not automatically have a healthy self concept. Some people display the patterns of self-confidence as a coverup for underlying feelings of self-doubt, which are sometimes the core of their total belief system. Second, not all self-doubt is unhealthy. In the self-actualization models of Maslow (1968) and Rogers (1961) the healthy individual is in the continuing process of trying to understand the feelings, perceptions, and motivations for personal behavior. Paradoxically, for healthy individuals this self-questioning process happens within the context of a basic context of personal adequacy. Their life stance seems to be, "Basically I like myself even though I am not perfect. My growth efforts are to improve upon my personal effectiveness. I am not perfect, but it does not follow that I must dislike myself."

A second question is, what is a "realistic" self concept? How can individuals know when their self perceptions are realistic or accurate? Agreement between self perceptions and some source of external data is the criterion most often used. Thus a person's self views are generally considered to be accurate or realistic when his or her self descriptions fit the descriptions made by significant others or when his or her self descriptions agree with some kind of test data. For example, the individual who can accurately predict his or her interest profile on the *Strong-Campbell Interest Inventory* is often said to have an accurate picture of self; the person whose predictions about SCII scores are inaccurate is said to have an inaccurate, undeveloped, or unrealistic view of self.

Clearly there are some problems in using external validation as a standard for assessing the accuracy of a persons set of self views. Two examples will suffice. The first is the physically underdeveloped adolescent from the ghetto whose career aspirations are to become a professional basketball player. At least outwardly he appears to believe he is capable of this career goal. Very few who have this career aspiration really succeed. Yet, who is to say this boy is one who will not.

An even tougher example lies with the teacher who gets mixed evaluations from students. Some students like the teacher; others do not. The classroom is highly controlled and students show evidence of learning on typical achievement indicators. The teacher perceives herself as excellent. The administrators agree. The students do not think she is excellent because she gives too many assignments and is a hard grader. Some of the external information is consistent with the teachers self view; other information is opposite her self view. Who is to say the teacher's self perceptions are inaccurate? Who is to say they are accurate?

Since having an accurate picture of self is an important indicator of self-regard, the question is important. Often an inaccurate picture of self is an indicator of basic defensiveness and self-dislike. Yet without valid criteria to assess the accuracy of a person's self view, we are left floundering. Until we have better methods of appraisal, the counselor must remain very tentative in coming to the conclusion that a client has an unrealistic self concept. It may be that the counselor's picture of the client is more inaccurate than the client's picture of self. The counselor can be wrong in such judgments as often as he or she is right.

The definition also points to many of the difficulties related to doing research for which self concept is a variable, either antecedent or consequent. The essential problem is that we have not yet developed reliable and valid ways of measuring the concept a person has of self. There are several reasons for this. One is that a person's total self concept is a complex set of many interconnected elements.

The complexity defies any simple assessment procedure. Second, self concept is a set of private or covert beliefs, some of which are not even clear to the person. Any assessment procedure, whether it is based on self-report, projective testing, or standardized personality inventories provides a set of data to the counselor or researcher. However, the data only provide overt clues about private experiencing. The counselor or researcher must make inferences from the data, and it is extremely difficult to validate inferences about something as complex as a person's self concept.

Because of the measurement difficulties, research conclusions for which self concept is a variable must be regarded as tentative. In the long run meta analyses procedures, such as those described by Smith and Glass (1977), may help. But right now research studies can only provide suggestions about generalized truths related to self concept. Some research results are reported later in the chapter, but for the reasons indicated they are offered to illustrate tentative hypotheses.

Behavioral Correlates with Self Concept

With problems such as those described above, researchers have understandably become less attracted to self concept as a researchable variable. Because of the measurement problems many have even wondered whether the term "self concept" is a useful construct. Most counselors and therapists believe it is an important concept for practitioners even if good research is difficult. Despite the problems most professional helpers agree with three very basic assumptions about self concept: *It is better to like self than to dislike self; it is better to have a realistic view of self than an unrealistic view of self; and it is generally better to be aware of the beliefs one holds about self than to be unaware of self views.* Definitional problems notwithstanding most agree that the healthy individual likes and respects self, is both optimistic and realistic about personal estimates of personal potential, has a realistic image of personal attributes and abilities, can experience honest pride in achievements, and can accept limitations without guilt, shame, or embarrassment.

In this section some behavioral correlates of both high and low self-esteem are considered. There are two reasons why this discussion is important. One is that the counselor does not see a person's self-esteem. He or she makes inferences about self-esteem from overt behavior. The behavior patterns described provide the counselor with data from which reasonable diagnostic inferences can be made. An important purpose for this section is to help the reader increase his or her diagnostic skills.

The second reason is that often some of the behavior patterns to be described may seem strange at first glance. Linking the behavior patterns to underlying self-esteem helps one to understand the meaning and significance of the patterns. The counselor who can relate extreme risk-taking to underlying feelings of inadequacy will have gone a long way to help the client with personal life choices.

Coopersmith (1967) suggests that persons with high, medium, and low self-esteem have different expectations for the future, differ with regard to interpersonal assertiveness, and have different basic styles for coping with stress.

Persons high in their own estimation approach tasks and persons with the expectation that they will be well received and successful. They have confidence in their perceptions and judgments and believe that they can bring their efforts to a favorable resolution. Their favorable self-attitudes lead them to accept their own opinions and place credence and trust in their reactions and conclusions. This permits them to follow their own judgments when there is a difference of opinion and also permits them to consider novel ideas. The trust in self that accompanies feelings of worthiness is likely to provide the conviction that one is correct and the courage to express those convictions. The attitudes and expectations that lead the individual with high self-esteem to greater social independence and creativity also lead him to more assertive and vigorous social actions. They are more likely to be participants than listeners in group discussions, they report less difficulty in forming friendships, and they will express opinions even when they know these opinions may meet with a hostile reception. Among the factors that underlie and contribute to these actions are their lack of self-consciousness and their lack of preoccupation with personal problems. Lack of self-consciousness permits them to present their ideas in a full and forth-right fashion; lack of self-preoccupation permits them to consider and examine external issues (p. 70).

In contrast, Coopersmith (1967) describes the person with low self-esteem as follows:

The picture of the individual with low self-esteem that emerges from these results is markedly different. These persons lack trust in themselves and are apprehensive about expressing unpopular or unusual ideas. They do not wish to expose themselves, anger others, or perform deeds that would attract attention. They are likely to live in the shadows of a social group, listening rather that participating, and preferring the solitude of withdrawal above the interchange of participation. Among the factors that contribute to the withdrawal of those low in self-esteem are their marked self-consciousness and preoccupation with inner problems. This great awareness of themselves distracts them from attending to other persons and issues and is likely to result in a morbid preoccupation with their difficulties. The effect is to limit their social intercourse and thus decrease the possibilities of friendly and supportive relationships (p. 70).

Locus of Control

An integration of the literature on attribution theory (de Charms, 1968), internal vs. external locus of control (Phares, 1976), and risk-taking suggests that people's self-images influence their perceptions of events, their perceptions of the source of causation for these events, their tendency to take risks, and their expectancies regarding future success and failure. Attribution theory posits that people have an inherent tendency to provide themselves with an accounting or explanation of events that happen to them, to attribute reasons for what happened. Sometimes the attributions people make are attempts to understand; other times they are defensive efforts to avoid responsibility or self-blame. The theory also proposes that students' attributions regarding their academic performance fall into four different categories: ability, effort, task difficulty, and luck. The first two categories are internally based sources. "My academic achievement depends on my personal abilities and the amount of effort I put into achieving." The last two categories are based on explanations that are external to self. "My academic achievement is heavily influenced by forces and factors largely outside my own control: the lectures were too confusing, the exam was too difficult, the instructor graded unfairly, the text was a poor one."

Using Rotter's Social Learning Theory as a conceptual base, Phares (1976) pioneered the research on internal vs. external locus of control. His view is that where people attribute control in their lives (self vs. outside of self) is both a personality characteristic and a situationally determined belief. His contention is that some people are generally oriented to the belief that what happens to them is largely their own responsibility and influenced by their own choices, efforts, and actions. In contrast others generally disown personal responsibility for their actions. They believe that forces and factors outside their lives determine what will happen to them and that they have little or no control over these forces. Phares presents a fascinating case study of Karl S., a young adult male who had completely given up on life because he was convinced that he had no control over his environment and that everything that happened to him was beyond his personal control. From his point of view, life was fated and predetermined for him. The normally effective reinforcement contingencies did not work as a set of therapeutic procedures because Karl believed that there were no causal connections between his actions and the events that followed.

Few people take the extreme position that *everything* that happens to them is totally self-controlled. Most believe they have influence over some events in their lives but not over others. Thus the belief in internal vs. external control is also a situationally influenced matter.

While the relationship between self concept and beliefs about self vs. external control has not been fully researched, a reasonable working hypothesis is that people who deeply like and respect themselves are also likely to believe that their personal destiny is largely within their personal power to control. They attribute both success and nonsuccess experiences (viewed more as mistakes than failures) as dependent upon their personal actions. In contrast, people who feel insecure and inadequate are more likely to take the general view that control of ones life is external to self. For the person who takes the life position "I am inadequate and not O.K.," the position "I have little control of my life" is an almost automatic corollary.

Externally oriented individuals often have either a "victim" or failure identity. People who take on the victim identity (as developed by de Charms, 1968) believe that their life is not their own; it is shaped and determined by forces, conditions, and people outside themselves over which they in turn have little control. There is an absence of any sense of personal agency or potency in their thinking and, concomitantly, an absence of any sense of responsibility for the events that happen in their lives. To the internally oriented person victim-thinking sounds like rationalization. To the person with the victim identity the thinking of the internally oriented person often sounds hopelessly idealistic and sometimes absurd.

Fear of Failure

Basing their work on an integration of attribution theory, internal vs. external locus of control, and research on risk taking, Beery (1975), and Covington and Beery (1976), did much work on self concept and fear of failure in the student experience. As a college counselor, Beery noted a surprisingly high number of students were distracted, fixated, and even obsessed by an internalized fear of failure. He hypothesized that these clients equated sense of worth with academic achievement and that the anticipation of a low academic performance created strong feelings of personal inadequacy. People suffering from this pattern would cope with it by trying to avoid a sense of failure. Internal attributors would cope with their inadequacy perceptions through superachievement efforts (sometimes inappropriately described as overachievement). These students study and overstudy and put in far more hours on course projects than other students. Their actions seem to be motivated to disprove the internally held belief "I am not adequate and can be adequate only if my performance is perfect."

The vicious cycle of this pattern is that such persons will perform to the limits of their capacity. Yet, seeing their high level performance, significant others will expect even more of them, thus forcing the individual to put even more pressure on self.

Procrastination is another pattern to cope with a personal sense of inadequacy and accompanying failure-fear. Procrastinators avoid situations in which they will be evaluated because failure is anticipated as the result. Often they contrive conditions whereby if something goes wrong the less threatening external attributions are available as explanations. The vicious cycle of this pattern is that it generally results in the very thing that the individual is so desparately trying to avoid. Assigned tasks are not completed; deadlines are often missed, exams are often skipped; final evaluations are often below the acceptable or downright failures. To the achievement-oriented individual the procrastinator appears lazy, unmotivated, and full of excuses. The underlying fear is often not apparent.

Some procrastinators are very good at developing external justifications for their actions. Developing physical illness is one common pattern. Throwing themselves into other safer activities is another. In the face of a real bind some procrastinators may have accidents. In attribution-theory terms the motive for all these actions is to avoid the internally based explanations (personal effort and ability) for not being successful. The procrastinator does not want to face the idea that the real explanation for his or her pattern is the fear of not having the ability to be successful. Creating these incidents provides a justification for the more tolerable externally based explanations.

The procrastination pattern can be difficult to break because two subtle motives are often involved: avoidance of failure and a passive expression of hostility. The procrastinator who fails can cause intense pain for those who have high expectations and toward whom he or she may be feeling a good deal of suppressed or repressed anger.

As Ellis (1974) points out, people are frequently unaware of the assumptions and beliefs behind their own behavior. People often go through life acting as though these assumptions are true without being conscious of them. The individual with the victim identity may not be aware of his or her assumption that life is beyond personal control. The procrastinator may be totally oblivious to his or her belief in self as a failure. As Ellis further suggests developing awareness of these underlying philosophic views can sometimes stimulate a powerful change in behavior. Application of this principle is discussed more fully in the Approaches section of the chapter.

Risk-Taking

Self-image also appears to be related to risk-taking tendencies and level of aspiration. A risk-taking situation occurs whenever there is the possibility that an action may not result in success, or whenever an action may result in success but also additional outcomes that would be regarded as nonbeneficial. Counselors take risks whenever they confront; clients take risks when they disclose themselves to an unknown counselor; people take risks when they purchase products sight unseen; physicians take risks when they perform surgery. Since uncertainty is a certain condition in our social order people will inevitably have to take some risks every day. But people differ with regard to how often they will take risks and what kinds of risks they are willing to take. Further, a given action that seems very risky for one person will seem only mildly risky to another and vice versa. Self concept appears to be one very important antecedent to risk-taking.

In his efforts to study the achievement motive Atkinson (1964) set up a very nice laboratory analogue to risk-taking which illustrates the relationship. He devised a ring toss game, not unlike what you would expect to see in a typical carnival. Subjects took a few practice tosses and then had the option of standing anywhere from two feet to twenty feet away from the target. They could also change their position after each toss, for a total of twenty tosses. The researchers noted with surprise that some people elected to stand very close, where success was virtually certain, while other people elected to stand far away where the chances of success were extremely low (one or two hits out of twenty tosses). Still others would stand in the middle range, where the chances for success were on the order of twelve out of twenty. Atkinson had gathered previous data about the subjects, including whether they were success oriented vs. fear-of-failure oriented. What the findings suggested is that success oriented individuals tended to take reasonable risks (stood in the middle distance range). However, subjects having a fear-of-failure orientation either stood very close or very far away. (Note that the long distance shooters could attribute their nonsuccess to task difficulty and thus avoid the internal attributions.) The more general hypothesis that studies of this sort lead to is that secure individuals have a stronger tendency to take reasonable risks. Insecure individuals tend to be either very safety oriented or to take extreme risks which do not imply anything about personal effectiveness.

These same studies showed a relationship between self concept and level of aspiration. An individual's level of aspiration is indicated by the kinds of goals he or she sets for self. In the ring toss activity after twenty tosses from the middle range where success rate was ten to twelve, subjects were asked to indicate their expectancies for success for the next twenty shots from the same distance. Surprisingly some subjects (undershooters) projected as low as two hits while other subjects (overshooters) projected eighteen hits. The undershooters set unrealistically low goals where there was virtually no chance of failure. The overshooters set unrealistically high goals where the sense or pain of failure could be avoided through rationalization. One need not perceive self as failure if the goals involved are impossible to achieve.

The more generalized notion is that people who set either unrealistically low or unrealistically high goals regarding both personal achievements and career aspirations may be doing so for the same underlying reason—to avoid experiencing a sense of failure. The fear of failure in turn reflects a basic sense of personal self-doubt.

The relationships described in this section of the chapter provide some useful diagnostic hypotheses for the counselor. The person who perceives the events of his or her life largely within his or her control; who is not dominated by a fear of failure, especially in evaluation situations; who can take reasonable risks; who sets optimistic, challenging, and yet realistic goals; and who is interpersonally assertive (not belligerent) is probably reflecting a basic liking and respect for self. In contrast the individual who attributes the important events in his or her life beyond self control; who perceives self as victim; who is dominated by a fear of failure; who either cannot take risks or else takes absurd risks; who either has no goals for the future or else has a very unrealistic and vague scenario for the future; and who is either interpersonally withdrawn or interpersonally belligerent is presenting a set of patterns that very likely reflect a sense of basic insecurity. The patterns the counselor observes help to make inferences about the self views that lie behind them.

Self Concept and Defensiveness

A basic truth in life is that most human beings want to like themselves. Self-dislike or self-disgust (guilt, shame, embarrassment, or anger turned toward self) is not likely to be endured for great lengths of time. So strong is this human pattern that psychologists with a need-theory orientation, such as Maslow (1968) and Rogers (1961), have postulated that self-liking or positive self-regard is a basic human need. Maslow saw the need for self-esteem as the next most basic of human wants after bodily survival needs had been taken care of. In essence people whose self-esteem is low will behave so as to satisfy their need for self-esteem. Adler

(1957) and his disciple Dreikurs (1964) said much the same thing when they posited a universal striving for uniqueness and superiority. Their contention was that each person strives to find some way to be different from all other human beings. By being unique one could find at least one small way to feel superior to others. (They believe that this motive emerges from the inherent dependency and inferiority of the infant condition).

Thus, people will strive to discover a sense of adequacy and beyond that a sense of competence as White (1973) saw it. At least for adults the affirmation of competency lies in one's achievements and accomplishments. Feedback that one's efforts have not achieved success is painful and is likely to be defended against.

Experienced clinicians have often noted that once developed, a person's basic self-image becomes highly resistant to change. Some clients will function to maintain and protect their views of self regardless of whether their views are positive, negative, or neutral. Even in the face of highly positive feedback and support from significant others, some clients persist in maintaining a negative self-image. This resistance to change is sometimes perplexing and often viewed as a major obstacle to therapeutic movement. Sometimes the defensive barriers seem almost impossible to overcome.

Why on earth would a person want to protect and maintain a negative image of self? Why not adjust one's views of self to fit the realities of incoming information?

Several explanations are available. One is that for anyone self concept change becomes an identity crisis. Earlier, self concept was defined as an interconnected system of ideas about self. Changing core elements of one's self system can have a ripple effect, threatening all the other elements of the system. If one's total view of self were to change, the result would be a loss of identity. There is security in having an identity, even if it is a negative one; loss of identity takes away what little security a self-doubting person possesses. It is better to have a consistently negative view of self than to have no sense of who one is.

A second explanation relates to expectancy theory. The essence of this theory is that there is instrumental value in maintaining a negative view of self. People with basic self-doubt often come across to others as highly fragile and vulnerable. Others treat them softly and in a nonthreatening manner. Little is expected from fragile individuals. They do not have to deliver much. Since little is expected there is little chance for failure. Maintaining negative views of self is a defense against the imposition of higher expectations from significant others. Changing views to a more positive life stance would result in higher expectations. In turn, the person would subject self to greater risks, more stressful interpersonal treatment, and the possibilities of failure. A negative self concept can sometimes shelter a person in the cocoon of babyhood. This is often the basis for victim and inadequacy identities.

Another theory, from psychoanalytic thinking, is that the tendency to protect a negative self concept may be the symptom of yet deeper underlying problems.

Often intense unresolved guilt for some terrible childhood event may exist at a subconscious level. The presence of this guilt can prevent a feeling of adequacy in at least two ways. One is that as long as the guilt is there, even if subconscious, the individual may not be able to give self permission to like self. In essence, "I am guilty, therefore awful and evil, and do not deserve to like self." A second way is that people harboring deep level guilt feelings frequently want to punish themselves. The misery, unhappiness, and deprivation of the joys of life that often accompany self-disgust can clearly be seen as forms of punishment.

None of these explanations can be seen as universals. They serve as the bases of hypotheses for the counselor to use as he or she listens for clues and the hypotheses they support. As the client talks about self, some hypotheses become validated while others are rejected by the client's material. Further, the hypotheses are not necessarily incompatible with each other. Two, and sometimes all three, may apply to the same client.

Freud (1946) was quite intentional in using the term "defense mechanisms" to describe these processes to protect the self. They occur when a person's views of self are being attacked and threatened. They are coping efforts to protect or defend the self from attack, insult, or harm.

One of the ironies of the human condition is that people with low self-esteem are likely to be more defensive more often and in more ways than people whose sense of competency is strong. People whose self-esteem is strong do not feel the need for self-protection nearly as strongly as those whose self-esteem is low. As a result, they are more open to feedback and thus more open to growth-stimulating experiences. In contrast, people whose sense of adequacy is not strong try to protect their vulnerable and fragile self views by distorting and blocking out important information (either from within or from without). By blocking this way, they are closed to the very feedback that can energize growth and change. The irony is that people with healthy self concepts grow; people who do not like themselves continue to not like themselves and their growth becomes blocked.

Persistent defensiveness acts as a resistance to counseling movement and as a barrier to growth. Harrison (1973) explains how:

> defenses block our learning, often dooming us to make the same mistakes over and over again. They make us blind to faults of our own we could correct, as well as those we can do nothing about. Sometimes they make us turn the other cheek when a good clout in the nose would clear the air and establish a new and firmer footing for an honest relationship. They can, in extreme cases, make so many kinds of information dangerous to our conceptual systems that we narrow and constrict our experiences, our feelings, and our thoughts, becoming virtual prisoners of our own protection.
> I believe there is in each of us a kind of counterforce which operates in the service of learning. Let's call it a *need to know,* or a drive toward competence. We are used to thinking about physiological needs, and we recognize there are probably social needs, such as need for love; but we often overlook the need for competence and knowledge. Yet it is in operation all around us. We see it in the baby when he begins to explore as soon as he can crawl;

we see it again in the "battle of the spoon," where the child actually gives up the certainty of getting the food into his mouth for the less effective but exciting experiment of "doing it himself." We see this need again as the adolescent struggles to carve out for himself a life that is uniquely his own; and we see it reflected in continuing efforts to understand and master the world as adults. People who read history for pleasure, who have creative hobbies, or who attend sensitivity-training laboratories are all manifesting this drive to competence and knowledge.

The need to know is the enemy of comfort, stability, and a placid existence. For its sake we may risk the discomfort of examining and revising our assumptions about groups and people; we may expose ourselves to the anxiety-provoking experience of "personal feedback," in which we often learn others do not see us quite as we see ourselves; we place ourselves in groups where we know in advance we will be confused, challenged, and occasionally scared. Some of us expose ourselves to such situations more than once; to me, there could be no more convincing proof that the need to know is frequently stronger than the desire to maintain the comfort and stability of accustomed conceptual systems (p. 121).

Persistent defensiveness is an important indicator of underlying insecurity. Occasional episodes of defensiveness reveal to us our own human vulnerability. Persistent defensiveness signifies behind it a global sense of insecurity and self-doubt.

There is no need to supply the reader with the standard list of classical defense mechanisms; they are easily available. (Coleman, 1974 and Mischel, 1976 have especially nice discussions). The important point is to understand the relationship between self concept and defensive behavior and to see defensiveness as a person's effort to protect self. Dealing with resistance will be discussed in the Approaches section which follows.

Approaches to Helping

In the Introduction to this work the authors acknowledged the importance of the core conditions for making effective counseling happen. Beyond the offering of these core conditions a variety of counseling theories and models are available to the helper. Indeed, in his comprehensive compendium Patterson (1973) identified 14 such theories, and several were not discussed in this resource. To systematically apply each is beyond the scope of this chapter. Instead several approaches will be discussed, each of which has more potential for some clientele than for others. The orientation for this section of the chapter will be to describe each of five approaches and to identify the clientele for whom the approach appears to have promise. The approaches are arranged in order of perceived severity of client self-doubt for which the different approaches appear to have applicability. Discussed in order will be Supportive Counseling and four insight orientations including: client-centered counseling, rational-emotive counseling, ego psychology, and depth therapy.

Three important assumptions are made in this discussion. The first is that clients differ with regard to the level of their self-doubt, and the helping approach chosen by the counselor must be appropriate to the client's level of self-acceptance. Second, all the approaches presented are assumed to be offered within the context of the core conditions described in the introductory chapter. The core conditions provide an experiential framework within which many helping approaches are possible. The third assumption is that the effective helper is a person who can not only provide core conditions in his or her relationships with people, but also has enough personal flexibility to implement a variety of approaches, depending on his or her diagnostic judgment. Thus, this section will describe several different approaches and will aid the reader in diagnosing for whom they are appropriate.

Supportive Counseling Approach

Basing their efforts on the idea that self concept is essentially a theory about self, many counselors, teachers, and parents will use success programming and other support techniques to achieve healthy self concept development in young children and self concept change in older clients. Glasser (1969), for example, has proposed that the school environment be made failure free. The underlying assumption is that success experiences and supportive feedback provide data to the individual which support the basic self-referrent conclusion "I am O.K., competent, and likable." With this basic stance encouraged and nurtured, the young child develops the optimism needed to support further achievement efforts, healthy interpersonal relationships, risk-taking, and openness to new learning experiences.

Examples of this approach abound. Caring parents work hard to provide young children with tasks and toys that create success experiences. Praise and encouragement are offered when a child struggles with a new task and finally succeeds. (When our three-year-old child succeeded for the first time in putting on his own coat, he ran to show us what he had accomplished. He showed all the behavior indicators of feeling proud. He got lots of attention, recognition, and physical affection). Elementary school teachers try to structure as many success experiences into the classroom learning situation as possible. The Montessori approach to preschool learning emphasizes the use of apparatus and materials to teach motor skills and concepts. Some require persistence and effort, but all are designed to be failure free. In counseling groups, strength bombardment is sometimes used as a structured activity. Members give feedback to each other about the qualities they like, respect, and admire.

The supportive approach has potency, especially when used with very young children whose self-image is at an early stage of development. (Notice that the descriptions emphasized structuring the situation so that *effort* leads to success). It also has potential for older children and others who experience transient self-doubt during periods of stress but who like self at a basic level. Encouragement and support during transient self-doubt episodes can provide a needed boost and can motivate initiative in the face of possible withdrawal. The case of Mary

Ellen demonstrates the application of this approach to a counseling practicum student.

Mary Ellen was a 34-year-old high school English teacher and a practicum student in our Counselor Education program. She had an intact marriage with two children. In her teaching role she was assertive and caring: students liked and respected her. As a result of much positive and supportive feedback she had learned to be confident in her interpersonal relationships. Like most practicum students, she started the practicum experience with a combination of excitement about the learning potential of the experience and insecurity about her personal effectiveness. Doing well in practicum was extremely important to her. Early in the experience she demonstrated exceptional effectiveness with some challenging and resistant clients. She had used some daring confrontations which had resulted in important breakthroughs. These experiences, accompanied by supportive feedback from the practicum supervisor, helped her respond to subsequent clients with more initiative and assertiveness.

She was assigned an especially challenging client for whom confrontation was not an appropriate counseling approach. When she confronted, her client became defensive, moving the interaction to safe talk, in effect making the remainder of the session appear unproductive.

She came to the practicum supervisor very distraught, saying, "I blew it." She then described what happened along with a projection of the likely consequences which were presented as disastrous. After listening to the tape for a while, the supervisor said, "Well, I agree that confronting this client was not helpful at this point. But I understand your reasons for it. I'm not sure the effects will be as disastrous as you are anticipating." Some approaches for follow-up were explored and reasonable approach was identified (which subsequently did work out effectively).

After this, the supervisor said, "Mary Ellen, there is something else we need to discuss. I'm hearing you communicate a lot of underlying doubts about your potential as an effective helper. You have shown both you and me that you have very strong helping skills. Even with this client, except for the inappropriate confrontation, your work has been strong. In our discussion you showed some excellent insights. I want you to know I am confident about your potential as a helper."

Mary Ellen: "Thanks, I really did need to hear that from you. I appreciate your support. It helps a lot." Her feedback was honest.

Mary Ellen's work for the rest of the practicum experience remained excellent. She continued to have in-depth interactions and continued to confront constructively. She made mistakes but dealt with them as mistakes and not catastrophies. She no longer took the position, "If I make a mistake, I am therefore inadequate to be a helper."

For people who are functioning effectively with a basic sense of adequacy, feelings of insecurity are most apt to arise in the face of stressful situations where there is doubt about one's ability to cope effectively in such situations. Under these conditions and with such people a combination of support and exploration regarding effective ways to cope with the situation are likely to alleviate the temporary feelings of insecurity.

Insight Orientations

At a time in the development of clinical psychology when there were intense battles between behaviorists and psychoanalysts, London (1964) found it useful to distinguish between action-oriented and insight-oriented helping approaches. Action-oriented approaches emphasized the systematic application of behavior modification principles to achieve change in behavior; they did not emphasize insight development as a crucial part of the treatment process. If the client's behavior changed for the better, the helping efforts were regarded as successful. If desired behavior changes did not occur, helping was not considered successful, no matter what else happened. In contrast the insight-oriented approaches emphasized insight development as the *sine qua non* of the helping process. Different therapists had different ideas about what insights were alleged to be crucial. But what helpers as diverse as Rogers, Perls, Ellis, and Freud all had in common was the assumption that favorable change would occur if client insight could be developed. Lasting change for the better was unlikely to occur if insight did not occur. London's distinctions had some problems (Mahoney, 1974), most notably the view that action approaches and insight approaches are inherently incompatible with each other. Nonetheless, the approaches that follow can be described as predominantly insight oriented.

Both Rogers (1961) and Ellis (1974) have some valuable contributions to offer for counselors who work with clients experiencing mild levels of self-doubt and feelings of insecurity that cut across a variety of situations but do not permeate their entire being.

Client-Centered Counseling Approach   Rogers' view is that in the presence of a helper who feels and communicates unconditional positive regard, a genuineness that is transparent, and high levels of empathy the client who doubts self will develop an in-depth understanding of self. In turn this will lead to a respect for self, a trust in and respect for one's personal capacities and attributes, and a movement from outward directedness to a more internalized locus of evaluation and control. Rather than doubting, a person will come to trust his or her perceptions and feelings. Where perceptions are proven inaccurate the person will come to regard such events as mistakes rather than failures or catastrophies. With a greater prizing of self, anxieties, hostilities, and intolerances will be reduced.

The client-focused process that makes these outcomes happen is self-examination. Rogers believes that self-doubt and its accompanying perceptual, emotional, and behavioral correlates occur because individuals have not done enough introspective work. Self-examination work leads to more awareness of one's internal perceptions, feelings and motivations. In the context of a counselor offering unconditional positive regard, this increase in self-knowledge leads to greater self acceptance. Empathic responses stimulate the introspective work. Positive regard and genuineness provide supportive conditions to make the work happen. Ultimately the difference between empathic and nonempathic responses lie in their effects on the client. High level empathy responses trigger introspective work; low level empathy responses do not.

Cognitive Change Counseling   Ellis bases his Rational-Emotive approach on teaching the client how to think rationally, and using the newly acquired rational thoughts, to behave more effectively, especially in interpersonal situations and in stressful problem-solving situations. To learn to think rationally, the client must first learn to identify and become aware of the irrational assumptions that influence his or her counterproductive perceptions, emotions, decisions, and behavior.

Any assumption is irrational if it establishes criteria that are impossible to meet or if it logically leads to corollaries that are self-defeating by their implication. The person who dislikes self has at least one, and probably several, irrational assumptions behind his or her actions. A dominant one, related to the fear of failure, is "I am not O.K. unless my performance in achievement situations is perfect and flawless." Counselor education students suffer frequently from this assumption which is irrational because it is impossible to accomplish. Perfect performance happens only in storybook situations and not in reality. A more logical set of assumptions might be these: "Mistakes are inevitable. I will make some mistakes. But it does not logically follow that because I make mistakes I am incompetent and therefore worthless. I will learn from my mistakes and improve upon my effectiveness without catastrophizing them as failures." Self-doubting people often catastrophize their mistakes. A large part of Ellis' work is to help clients appraise the outcome of their actions realistically.

Another frequent irrational assumption is "I am O.K. only If I am liked, accepted, and respected by everyone in my environment. If I am disliked, criticized, or rejected then I am not O.K. and that would be awful." (Again, note the catastrophizing and intolerance.) This assumption, too, is irrational because it is impossible to achieve. Realistically, I encounter many people in the course of a day, and not all those people will like me. Some may be neutral and others may dislike me. If an individual does not like me, it does not follow that it is my fault. Nor does it follow that I must dislike me because this other individual dislikes me.

Many self-doubters cope with their self-doubt by withdrawing and behaving passively in interpersonal situations. Self-doubters who have difficulty behaving assertively, often harbor this assumption: "The world is a dangerous place where I could be hurt. I have been hurt before and I could be hurt again. The less visible I am the less likely I am to be hurt. I had better not risk it." This assumption is irrational because in our society to get what one wants from life, one has to pursue it assertively. The self-protecting withdrawal pattern leads to missed opportunities, disappointment, and frustration. A more rational assumption would be this: "While there may be some specific occasions where it would be better to remain silent, in the long run being withdrawn as a consistent behavior pattern does not pay off and frequently is counterproductive. Additionally, as a human being I have some rights, including the right to make sure my other rights are protected. The most logical person to protect my rights is me."

A fourth irrational assumption, held especially by withdrawing self-doubters, is: "Everyone else is better than I am. Therefore I should be humble and subordinate." A more rational life position would be: "Some people may have achieved in ways that I have not. Some have acquired skills that I have not. But it does not follow that I am insignificant, unacceptible, and worthless. I can still like me and be proud of my own skills and achievements."

The essence of Ellis' approach with self-doubting people is to help them identify the present-day irrational assumptions they are making, confront them with the irrationality of these assumptions, teach them rational assumptions, and help them learn how to put these new ideas into practice. When the new assumptions are learned and put into practice, people will behave more effectively, their new behavior will pay off, they will be more successful, and with this success they will like themselves much more. Self-doubt is changed to self-confidence when people discover they do have the ability to get what they want from life as long as their goals are reasonable. With success, the self-expectancies become "I can do it" instead of "I can't do it."

In somewhat larger context Ellis' ideas convey the more general perspective that a person's self concept is a constellation of attitudes about self. Some of these attitudes are healthy, rational, realistic, and functional. Other self-referent attitudes are irrational, unrealistic, and dysfunctional. Self concept development as a goal is a matter of helping clients change attitudes toward self. Whatever social psychologists have learned about attitude change would apply to helping clients with self concept change. Attitudes can be changed by presenting people with data that are discrepant with the originally held attitude, by confronting people with alternative attitudes, by helping people examine the behavioral and decision-making implications of maintaining one attitude vs. its alternatives, and by propaganda techniques. The counselor as a propagandist has long been a controversial part of the counselor's professional identity. Ellis himself has no trouble affirming this identity because the ends (increasing personal effectiveness) are honorable.

Social psychologists have also observed the phenomenon of resistance to attitude change. With his model of cognitive dissonance, Festinger (1957) points out that new ideas represent antitheses to orginally held ideas and will be inherently resisted. The level of resistance depends on the centrality of the original idea to an individual's total belief system; on the centrality of the original idea to an individual's basic identity (peripheral attitudes change more easily than core attitudes); on the instrumental value for maintaining the original idea; on the threat potential of the new idea for the individual's total self view; and on the pressure for change (too little pressure minimizes incentive—too much pressure results in resistance). The counselor working for attitude change must understand and diagnose the centrality and payoff value for the original idea, the threat potential of the new idea, and must find the right balance of pressure to maintain incentive for change while at the same time minimizing resistance.

Ego Psychology Applications   In a very real sense the approaches described to this point may be viewed as elements of the ego psychology approach to counseling (Erikson, 1968; Grossman, 1964; Hartmann, 1964; Hummel, 1962). From this point of view the goals of counseling are to help individuals cope with stress in their lives (including personal and interpersonal conflict); develop wise and sensible scenarios for their personal futures; and to develop realistic plans to bring about these future goals. The functions of the ego are basically the cognitive skills an individual needs to comprehend and assess reality and to plan and make wise decisions. These include the following functions of effective problem-solvers, planners, and scientists: identifying and clarifying a problem; identifying and understanding the various factors and variables that contribute to a problem; pooling this information to develop tentative hypotheses; reality-testing the validity of hypotheses, conclusions, and assumptions; generating alternative problem resolutions; exploring consequences; prioritizing; choosing; and developing implementation plans.

These ego functions apply to various counseling goals ranging from career choosing to daily living effectiveness. Thus, as ego psychologists see it the primary function or process goal of counseling is to help clients strengthen those specific ego functions that relate to the problem and concomitant goal for which they have sought counseling assistance. As the client develops these skills he or she becomes more effective in dealing with reality, resolving conflicts, and making important life decisions. Concomitantly, his or her basic senses of adequacy are enhanced and the self concept is strengthened. The enhancement of self concept occurs when the client acquires those functions or cognitive skills necessary for effective living. He or she has more faith in his or her personal capacity for coping.

Ego psychology is an integration of some elements of psychoanalysis, along with behavioral, cognitive, and social learning theory. In contrast to psychoanalysis, the goals of counseling are not comprehensive personality restructuring that requires long-term, in-depth uncovering. Rather the goals are to help the client cope, adjust, and make decisions. Thus, ego counseling tends to be much shorter (five or six sessions), does not tend toward an uncovering process, and utilizes relatively little depth interpretation. In this approach, the primary counselor diagnostic function is to identify those client ego functions that need strengthening and further development.

The supervisor's approach with Mary Ellen, described earlier in this section, is a good example of one application of this approach. Given the data of the Mary Ellen's counseling experience, she had jumped to an inappropriate conclusion. She overcatastrophized the results, causing her to doubt her essential ability as an effective helper. Essentially the supervisor's role was to help Mary Ellen reexamine the conclusion she had come to, acquire a more reasonable conclusion, and use this new conclusion as the basis for subsequent planning. Along the way, anxiety was reduced and basic faith in personal effectiveness was restored.

Since there are a variety of possible techniques and approaches for which ego strength development is the essential goal, the range of approaches among ego psychologists is as wide as the range among other counselors. What is generally true among ego psychologists is that they tend to devote proportionally more attention to cognitive functions and dysfunctions that relate to client concerns than to affective factors. Within that broad parameter some are oriented to discovery learning techniques, while others are more oriented to a verbal instruction model. While they are not prone to advice-giving (which denies the client an opportunity to learn how to do for self), within the parameters of the facilitative core conditions most are prone to using an instructional model that involves the teaching of specific cognitive skills. The elements of good instruction are usually important ingredients of the counseling process.

The approach would appear to have particular potential for clients who have a basic core of self-caring, but who experience moderate level self-doubt because of some continuing coping problem, the lasting presence of some important un-resolved conflict, or because of some identifiable deficit in one or more specific ego-based functions. A strong core of basic self-esteem must be readily apparent to the counselor for this approach to be effective. If this core is not present, the approach may have the Band-Aid effect of dealing with a symptom without dealing with the underlying problem. The client whose self-doubt is core to his or her being well has great difficulty in mastering and applying the ego functions the counselor is trying to teach.

Depth Therapy Approach   There are some people who have never really had a core liking and respect for self. These are people who are basically insecure and who may express their basic insecurity through various combinations of with-drawal, passivity, hostility, and extreme competitiveness. Some people try to cope with their core self-dislike by devoting extremely high levels of energy to trying to prove to self and others that they really are O.K. Their underlying view is that self-worth equals levels of accomplishment and achievement. The double bind these people impose on self, and project on to others, is that while their sense of worth can only be proven by the quality of their performance, when they do perform well or achieve effectively they discount their own efforts. They desparately want success but cannot tolerate it when it happens because the data of actual success are incompatible with their basic self view. In the face of success they experience cognitive dissonance and react defensively to protect their negative self view. They desperately want, and at the same time resist, changing their views of self. Depending on who is doing the describing, this pattern may be described as irrational, neurotic, unhealthy, or crazy.

For people following these patterns the helping experience must move well beyond the support process. Indeed, such clients often reject a counseling ap-proach built primarily around support giving. In the process such clients may also reject the counselor because he or she does not really understand. At best, for such clients support as the primary level of intervention will act as a temporary Band-Aid to help the client get through a specific crisis. It does little to deal with the essential problem.

Clients following this pattern usually have been denied opportunities to develop a basic sense of adequacy early in their life histories. Often their early relationships with primary adults are characterized by continuing experiences of rejections, put downs, lack of support, indifference and inattention, and the imposition of impossible standards and double or multiple binds. Through childhood their expectancy was to receive ridicule and punishment rather than encouragement, support, and reward. Treatment from primary adults was often erratic, unpredictable, and unstable. As children, such people often expected some kind of painful treatment, but since this treatment was so unpredictable (that is, did not correlate with identifiable childhood behaviors), the child had no clear way to prevent the abuse. He or she knew that some kind of physical or emotional abuse would happen but had no way to prevent it. The results are the development of a sense of helplessness, the anticipation of danger and harm, and an inability to develop trusting relationships (Seligman, 1975).

Such clients can be said to have developed negative and self-defeating scripts or recordings (Berne, 1964; Steiner, 1974). For these clients counseling may be seen as a process of changing unhealthy scripts to those which are healthier and more functional. This goal usually means long-term and depth therapy which includes a process of uncovering repressed material from the past. Repressed anger and accompanying guilt for having the anger, feelings of intense bitterness and disappointment, mourning over what might have been but was not alienation, loneliness, rejection, abandonment, and the finishing of unfinished business are all significant themes that require depth work. Along the way client resistance to working on this painful material inevitably becomes a part of the process and must be dealt with. Since negative scripts are the endowment of primary adults, rejecting a script often includes rejecting the primary adults who provided and installed the script. Clients in this experience often must go through the conflicting, guilt-provoking and painful experience of rejecting parents (at least for a while) in order to reject the script. Often the developmental process is one of temporarily rejecting parents so they can be perceived and understood more clearly. During this developmental period anger, hate, vengeance, a need for retribution, and an unwillingness to forgive may all be expressed, with concomitant self-disgust for having these "unacceptable" feelings.

Beyond this stage, however, is another: the stage of reconstruction and mature acceptance. As the unfinished business gets worked through and finished, parents become people with limitations and flaws, who had their own developmental histories and scripts which caused them to become the way they did. The figure on the pedestal or behind a translucent protective barrier becomes a more visible figure at eye level. Once visible with less distortion the figure becomes more understood, less intimidating, and more acceptable.

Beyond the core conditions, two helper skills become particularly important. The counselor must apply his or her understanding of human behavior to be able to diagnose the material and themes under the surface of the client concerns. He or she must see what the client is protecting behind the defensive facades. Secondly, the counselor must have the resourcefulness and inner strength to confront this underlying material in ways that stimulate nondefensive, introspective work.

For the helper one of the very difficult parts of the process is what to do about client resistance. Traditional psychoanalysis has viewed resistances as obstacles to further growth which somehow had to be overcome. The metaphor was combat; the battle strategies were confrontation, interpretation, verbal desensitization, and patience. More recently Gestalt thinking (Polster and Polster, 1973) had taken the position that while the client must *understand* his or her resistances, it does not follow that the helper must work to remove them. The client needs his or her resistances to protect self; efforts to remove them can result in what amounts to an identity panic. Helping a client understand his or her resistances and exploring with the client the decision about what to do with and/or about them, in itself can become an intensely affirming and thus highly growthful experience. Some clients seem to discover that they can function effectively by learning to use their resistances as creative forces, rather than seeing the resistances as sick parts of self.

Over the long experience of depth therapy the unfinished business is uprooted, old scripts examined and either discarded or modified and new scripts for self are developed to replace them. As this happens, the client learns to stop beating self and others. In the place of self-disgust, self-acceptance can emerge.

A Final Note

Perhaps the world would be a more perfect place if a healthy self concept were a genetically endowed attribute of all human beings. Human anger and violence would be reduced, maybe eliminated. Competition and forms of discrimination would be reduced. There would be less pain. People would do more reaching out and less self protecting. Inner peace would be more than an idealistic scenario.

But we are not born that way and it makes no sense to grieve about what is not possible. It may be possible to teach parents how to raise kids so that they like themselves. Schools can build self-esteem development programs into the early school curriculum. Effective counselors and teachers can work with young children to teach them to like themselves early, so that later on self-disgust is prevented. It will not be easy, and not cheap. But it is possible if that is where our priorities lie.

Questions for Further Inquiry

1. When you experience self-doubt, how does it influence the way you relate to others?

2. What linkages do you see between self-doubt and anxiety, depression, anger, alienation, and shyness ?

3. It has been said that we are all "victims" of our socioeconomic heritage. Do you agree or disagree with this point of view? Why?

4. What differences do you see between a "self-centered" person and a person with a "healthy self concept."

5. How may a counselor know when a client is being defensive? What approaches may a counselor use to help clients face the real issues behind their defenses?

References

Adler, A. *Understanding human nature.* New York: Premiere Books, 1957.

Atkinson, J. W. *An introduction to motivation.* New York: Van Nostrand, 1964.

Beery, R. C. Fear of failure in the student experience. *Personnel and Guidance Journal* 1975 *54,* 190–203.

Berne, E. *Games people play.* New York: Grove Press, 1964.

Coleman, J. S., & Hammen, C. L. *Contemporary psychology and effective behavior.* Glenview, Ill.: Scott, Foresman, 1974.

Coopersmith, S. *The antecedents of self-esteem.* San Francisco: Freeman, 1967.

Covington, M. V., & Beery, R. G. *Self-worth and school learning.* New York: Holt, Rinehart, 1976.

de Charms, R. *Personal causation.* New York: Academic Press, 1968.

Dreikurs, R. *Children: The challenge.* New York: Hawthorn, 1964.

Ellis, A. *Humanistic psychotherapy: The rational-emotive approach.* New York: McGraw-Hill Paperbacks, 1974.

Erikson, E. *Identity: Youth and crisis.* New York: Norton, 1968.

Festinger, L. *A theory of cognitive dissonance.* Stanford: Stanford University Press, 1957.

Freud, S. *The ego and the mechanisms of defense.* New York: International Universities Press, 1946.

Glasser, W. *Schools without failure.* New York: Harper and Row, 1969.

Grossman, D. Ego activating approaches to psychotherapy. *Psychoanalytic Review* 1964 *51,* 65–68.

Harris, T. *I'm o.k., You're o.k.: A practical guide to transactional analysis.* New York: Harper & Row, 1969.

Harrison, R. Defenses and the need to know. In R. Golembiewski & A. Blumberg (Eds.), *Sensitivity training and the laboratory approach, (2nd ed.)* Itaska, Ill.: F. E. Peacock, 1973.

Hartmann, H. *Essays on ego psychology.* New York: International Universities Press, 1964.

Hummel, R. C. Ego-counseling in guidance: Concept and method. *Harvard Educational Review* 1962 *32,* 461–82.

London, P. *The modes and morals of psychotherapy.* New York: Holt, Rinehart, 1964.

Mahoney, M. J. *Cognition and behavior modification.* Cambridge, Mass.: Ballinger, 1974.

Maslow, A. H. *Toward a psychology of being, (2nd ed.)* New York: Van Nostrand, 1968.

Mischel, W. *Introduction to personality, (2nd ed.)* New York: Holt, Rinehart, 1976.

Patterson, C. H. *Theories of counseling and psychotherapy, (2nd ed.)* New York: Harper & Row, 1973.

Phares, E. J. *Locus of control in personality.* Morristown, N.J.: Silver-Burdett, 1976.

Polster, M., & Polster, M. *Gestalt therapy integrated: Contours of theory and practice.* New York: Brunner/Mazel, 1973.

Purkey, W. W. *Self concept and school achievement.* Englewood Cliffs, N.J.: Prentice-Hall, 1970.

Rogers, C. R. *Counseling and psychotherapy.* Boston: Houghton Mifflin, 1942.

Rogers, C. R. *On becoming a person.* Boston: Houghton Mifflin, 1961.

Seligman, M. E. P. *Helplessness: On depression, development, and death.* San Francisco: W. H. Freeman, 1975.

Smith, M. L., & Glass, G. V. Meta-analyses of psychotherapy outcome studies. *American Psychologist* 1977 *32*, 752–60.

Steiner, C. *Scripts people live.* New York: Grove Press, 1974.

White, R. W. The concept of healthy personality: What do we really mean? *The Counseling Psychologist* 1973 *4(2)*, 3–12.

Understanding and Managing Anxiety

3

GENE BOCKNEK

Ubiquity of Anxiety as a Human Experience

Some people pursue happiness; others seek security and peace of mind; a few strive for self-actualization. But whatever the goal of growth may be, everyone encounters anxiety.

Wherever humankind has dwelled, irrespective of time, place, or culture, anxiety has been an inevitable companion. The universal occurrence of this powerful experience argues compellingly for its understanding by the human services practitioner. The discomfort that it creates demands that we also learn all we can about the effective management of anxiety, because anxiety is never going to go away and should never go away. The real issue is, in fact, one of learning effective *management* of it. For reasons that shall soon be made evident, anxiety is useful, and learning simply to control it can be nonproductive or even harmful to the well-being of those we are trying to help.

Manifestations of Anxiety

Anxiety is experienced by everyone, and by everyone in a variety of ways. At times we are acutely aware of its presence. On other occasions its affects us unconsciously. Often we mask or disguise its presence, to others and to ourselves. Ernest Hemingway noted that many bullfighters are prone to frequent yawning prior to entering the bull ring. A client of mine used to complain of being bored at times when she might appropriately have been distressed. Disguising anxiety only helps to keep us from recognizing the cause. The anxiety is still there.

The manifestations of anxiety are limitless. Suffice it to say that all the major pathways of expression—affective, motoric, somatic, and cognitive—are used at different times by all of us in our encounters with anxiety. In the affective realm anxiety varies from a mild form of uneasiness to worrying to nameless panic. Motor experiences include physical restlessness, tics, functional paralysis of a limb, muscular tension or cramp. Common somatic symptoms include headache, dizziness, blurred vision, ringing in ears, blushing, sweating, diarrhea, rapid heartbeat, and a myriad of others. On a cognitive level people experience specific worrisome thoughts—"I don't look well," "I wonder if she got into an accident"—in milder forms to "I think I'm losing my mind" as the feeling intensifies.

Effects of Anxiety

Whatever the immediate experience may be, there are predictable effects of the impact of anxiety on the person. Above all, anxiety is a *noxious* experience. It is somewhat unpleasant even in its mildest forms, and it becomes increasingly unpleasant as it intensifies. The distress eventually becomes unbearable and people will destroy themselves rather than suffer intense and unremitting anxiety.

Left unattended by the psychological regulatory processes of the personality, anxiety becomes *cumulative.* As long as the precipitating circumstances remain, anxiety will grow. And as it grows, its cumulative effect increases and often spreads. The person who started out feeling vaguely nervous becomes fidgety and restless. Disturbing thoughts enter the mind and will not be dislodged. A sense of fear grips the emotions. Sooner or later, the anxiety becomes *irresistible,* demanding confrontation and relief: "I need a drink," or "If I don't get out of here, I'll go crazy!"

Significance of Anxiety

The significance of anxiety's role in human behavior is clear. Whatever its cause, by its very nature anxiety commands attention and relief. It is therefore one of the most determining influences in a person's life. Most of the seemingly inexplicable and irrational reactions we observe in ourselves or others results from attempts to ameliorate, avoid, or obliterate the intolerable effects of anxiety. Must of what is called psychopathology can be understood as incomplete methods of managing anxiety. From the perspective of the helping professions, therefore, one of the most important tasks is in working with clients to find more effective means of managing anxiety—optionally by developing ways of dealing with the conditions that give rise to its occurrence.

Role of Anxiety in Human Behavior

Descriptively, anxiety can be said to inhibit, facilitate, or distort human reactions. Everyday illustrations readily come to mind. The adolescent applying for his first job wants a chance to earn some money. At the same time he fears being rejected.

Instead of walking into the employment office, his anxiety causes him to oversleep or postpone the job interview, his path to finding a job is inhibited by the anxiety engendered by fear of rejection.

But anxiety can also enhance function in a positive way, usually when it occurs in a milder form. A college student wants to do well on her final examinations. But she knows that the test will be difficult. As she reads the textbooks she becomes more focused on what the authors are trying to communicate, how it relates to the larger subject matter. Her concentration is deepened because of the anxiety, and she thinks more carefully about what she is reading.

Anxiety in more severe form can distort functioning as well. The man who recently suffered a heart attack has been traumatized by his narrow escape from sudden death. His world view shrinks to interpreting everything in his life as a potential trigger of a fatal heart attack. He must avoid any exertion that could tax his heart, including going to work and having intercourse with his wife. His intense anxiety reduces him to psychological invalidism.

A Perspective on What Follows   In the succeeding pages the author will first identify his own theoretical biases. This will be followed by a brief review of the several divergent theories of anxiety. Anxiety and the dynamics of human behavior will then be explored. The last section of the chapter will be concerned with intervention strategies relative to anxiety management; ethical and humanitarian issues; and, finally, some beginning steps toward a general theory of anxiety management.

Toward an Understanding of Anxiety—The Author's Biases

After a quarter-century of clinical work I find my thinking most compatible with what may be called the ego/developmental orientation. As its name implies, this approach emphasizes the central role of the ego in organizing behavioral processes over the developmental history, or life span of an individual. As used in this context, ego is a construct referring to those processes in the personality that govern cognition (learning, planning, reasoning, etc.), organize and interpret experience, and regulate response to internal and external stimuli. The ego functions to help the person operate holistically in some consistent and purposeful way. The developmental approach emphasizes the natural, inevitable growth potential inherent in all living things.

For too long, progress in understanding human behavior has been retarded by the chasm separating clinicians studying psychopathology and laboratory scientists studying isolated psychological activities. The ego/developmental approach bridges these two worlds and thus permits the knowledge derived from one sphere to be applied to the other. This is possible because most contemporary theories acknowledge some central organization to behavior and concur that human beings are constantly changing rather than static. Both human natural history and clinical psychopathology are compatible with the ego/developmental orientation.

Unfortunately, neither ego nor development can account for human behavior in the absence of cultural and interpersonal factors. In addition, climate, ecology, history, and geography all play significant roles in human experience. Consequently, I find it necessary to incorporate a position which accepts reliable data of any kind that affects human behavior. In this sense a theoretical bias for eclecticism also colors my views.

The eclectic position acknowledges that most major theories contain elements which are accurate and others which are inaccurate. Eclecticism attempts to select and integrate the most valid components of all theories. As the reader will undoubtedly observe, even the combination of eclecticism with ego/developmental theorizing leaves much that is unknown or incomplete in understanding human behavior. It may well be the case, moreover, that certain truths are overlooked or undervalued—despite my conscious vigilance—because of the subtle operation of theoretical bias.

Theories of Anxiety

A number of writers emphasize the *sociocultural* roots of anxiety in human experience. In *Civilization and Its Discontents* (1930) Freud suggests that society forces people to repress their instinctual drives, thus creating anxiety. Fromm (1947) has long argued that social pressures to develop a "marketable" personality cause alienation from oneself and, hence, neurotic anxiety. More recently, Szasz (1960) has pointed out ways that society stigmatizes and punishes those whose behavior is at variance with social norms.

Another body of theorists focus on the *interpersonal* origins of anxiety. Sullivan (1953) traces all psychological distress to sources in human interaction. Fairbairn (1955) and Guntrip (1961) led a splinter group of psychoanalysts who detail the evolution of anxiety from an object relations point of view. The recent emergence of family dynamics as an approach to the cause and treatment of psychopathology owes much to the work of Ackerman (1958), Minuchin (1965) and Kantor and Lehr (1976).

The proponents of *intrapsychic* theory originate with Freud's (1953) theory of conflict between the personality components id, ego, and superego. Hartmann's (1958) theory of adaptation, and the developmental theories of Kernberg (1972), Mahler (1972) and Kohut (1971) represent latter-day modifications of psychoanalytic theory, the predominant intrapsychic approach.

Anxiety is a learned response to fear-producing stimuli, according to various investigators with a *behavioral* orientation. Miller and Dollard (1941) pioneered this group of theories. Contemporary writers include social learning theorists such as Bandura (1977) and Wolpe (1973).

Cognitive theories of anxiety emphasize the role of ideas and thoughts in promoting psychological distress. Festinger's (1958) theory of cognitive dissonance, Ellis' (1962) focus on irrational ideas, and Beck's (1976) concept of learned helplessness characterize the thinking of members of this group.

Renewed interest in *phenomenology* stresses the experiential aspects of anxiety. Rogers (1951) points to the discrepancy between perceived and idealized self as a causative factor. Perls (1969) emphasizes fragmentation of the person's mode of experiencing. Laing (1959) focuses on the sense of being overwhelmed as a central issue.

Even in this limited review it is apparent that anxiety can be conceptualized and described in many different ways. More strikingly, it is probable that all these approaches are at least partly accurate! Can there be so many different kinds of anxiety? More likely, these varied schools of thought reflect the multiplicity of the sources and the manifestations of one universal, all-important human experience. The most reasonable conclusion would seem to be that anxiety originates from many sources: within the personality, from social pressures, from childhood events, from human relations, from economic and political conditions, from the growth process itself. The sheer amount of attention given to the study of anxiety by so many investigators is the most compelling evidence of its importance. No theory of human behavior can ignore the central role of this omnipresent condition.

Anxiety and the Dynamics of Human Behavior

The Haan–Kroeber Model
As we have seen, many theories account for the ways anxiety originates, develops, and is experienced. Later on in this chapter we will examine a variety of intervention strategies for the management of anxiety. This section treats the complex dynamics of the way anxiety interacts with human function.

Freud's (1953) early contention that anxiety activated defense mechanisms was for years the only substantial explanation of the effect of this noxious experience on behavior. According to this formulation, the ego responds to the dictates of the pleasure principle to reduce tension (i.e., anxiety) by erecting processes (forgetting, diverting, disavowing) which reduce or avoid the unpleasant, threatening experience of anxiety. While this theory accounted for many of the less adaptive responses to anxiety, it failed to account for other kinds of behavior. For example, how does one explain the novice tennis player who accepts repeated frustration or embarrassment while struggling to learn the game? Or the person who risks his or her life to save someone who is drowning? Everyday life offers many examples of people who tolerate, or even increase, anxiety levels while pursuing their goals. In some instances (e.g., driving in rush hour traffic) anxiety actually improves efficiency by making the person more alert, better coordinated, etc. Even the Freudian explanation of objective, or signaling, anxiety which alerts the person to danger fails to explain some of these events.

The most sophisticated and comprehensive theory would have to account for not only the maladaptive defensive reaction but also explain how people handle anxiety in constructive, productive ways as well. Such a formulation was developed by Haan (1963) and Kroeber (1963) and has recently been elaborated further by Haan (1977).

The Haan–Kroeber model postulates that the ego develops three modes of responding to anxiety. The most common mode of response is the coping mechanism. *Coping involves ways of tolerating moderate amounts of anxiety while the person learns how to deal with the circumstances which give rise to the anxiety.* Coping can be understood as a problem-solving approach. The person deals with the anxiety (e.g., by concentrating on the problem) so as to overcome it.

If coping fails—or the individual has not learned how to use coping mechanisms—a defensive mechanism (e.g., denial) may be invoked. As in the Freudian formulation, *defense mechanisms act to reduce or avoid the noxious affect of the anxiety* and allow the person to function, but with less effectiveness. Unfortunately, since the anxiety-producing situation has not been resolved, the situation will again create problems for the person when it is encountered. (The person may have to give up playing tennis or else face the frustration again at the next attempt.)

The third level of response is fragmentation. *In fragmentation the person avoids being overwhelmed by anxiety by resorting to private, distorted, unreal interpretations of the situation* ("I am already a fine tennis player"). Haan (1977) believes that the primary purpose of any of these three mechanisms is to preserve the inner sense of logic and organization of the person. As she puts it,

> the person's intent . . . is merely that he be able to continue with a degree of self-determination, whether he copes, whether he defends, or fragments (p. 49) . . . . The person will cope if he can defend if he must, and fragment if he is forced, but whichever mode he uses, it is still in the service of his attempt to maintain organization (p. 42).

In the past psychodynamics has connoted a neurotic mode of psychological functioning. The Haan–Kroeber model permits a more complete understanding of how anxiety can be encountered, from the most productive to the most destructive patterns.

Anxiety as Dynamic Energy

To continue this examination it is useful to conceptualize anxiety as energy, with its own dynamic properties. An important part of understanding the operation of anxiety is an awareness of what these properties are, and how they can vary.

Since anxiety is energy, it can fluctuate in quantity. The psychological experience of this fluctuation is denoted by its *intensity*. The more intense the experience the more threatening and disruptive it is for the person. An important focus of counseling intervention oftentimes is directed at helping the person to moderate intense anxiety.

Another property is that of *directionality*. While people do experience anxiety as unfocused, usually a counselor or client will detect a locus or direction. Typically, anxiety can be linked with a situation or expectation. Even diffuse anxiety can be linked to one or two body sites where it is most felt. Directionality thus speaks to the purposive quality of anxiety.

Finally, the *content* of the anxiety is significant. Both the pathway of expression—somatic, motor, affective, cognitive—and the description of the subjective experience ("like a band across my chest") can provide important clues about its origin, nature, and severity.

Ego Strength

Implicit to this entire discussion is the fact that anxiety cannot be studied in a vacuum, but only in the human context in which it occurs. A vital ingredient in understanding the impact of anxiety, therefore, is the ability of the person to deal with that impact. The construct which defines that ability is ego strength. Haan (1963) identifies several indices of ego strength:

1. The number and quality of coping and defense mechanisms (fragmentation reactions imply a lack of ego strength).
2. The number and amount of anxiety-laden concerns (these have a cumulative effect on ego functioning which is corrosive).
3. The person's ability to deal with stresses of varying kinds (everyday living provides a wide variety of stresses).
4. Ego resiliency (the ability to "bounce back" after a stressful or traumatic experience).
5. The amount of "secondary process" functioning (the ability to delay response, reason, plan, use judgement).
6. Adequacy of reality-testing functions (the ability to recognize objective reality).
7. Modes of discharge available (how many ways does the person relieve tension).

An assessment of ego strength is one of the central features in considering the most effective way to offer help to someone who seeks counseling services.

Psychodynamics In most clinical settings the term psychodynamics refers to the interacting processes of conflict, anxiety-arousal, and defense. This process is usually conceived as the underlying cause of the problems which bring people for professional help. By incorporating coping, fragmentation, and somatic or motor discharge into such a model, it is possible to extend the notion of psychodynamics into a general explanation of how anxiety affects behavior. More precisely this model can diagram all the options available to the person confronting anxiety.

In this model, any perceived threat (intrapsychic conflict, impending surgery) arouses anxiety. The ego system is mobilized to confront the anxiety, utilizing one or more of the available options: coping, defending, fragmenting, motoric or somatic discharge. *Coping* requires that the anxiety be kept at a threat level low enough for the person to tolerate while attempting to find ways of resolving the threatening conditions. *Defending* involves the activation of processes that lower anxiety by avoiding or reducing the sense of threat. *Fragmenting* reduces anxiety by distorting the perceived threat to conform to subjective wish. *Motor discharge* obliterates anxiety and threat by resorting to a physical fight-or-flight type of reaction. *Somatic discharge* transforms the anxiety into a physiological overreaction and thus gets rid of the immediate psychological distress.

Most people utilize all of these modalities during their lives. But only coping, which most of us use most of the time, permits the person to continue to grow and develop in the healthiest way. Often these processes occur in combinations. Kübler-Ross (1969) notes that the common way of dealing with massive loss is to react at first with the defense mechanism of denial, before coming to accept the reality (coping). While seeking a solution to a stressful problem (coping), one may pace the floor (motor discharge), experience stomach ache (somatic discharge), and get angry at the cat (displacement defense).

Figure 3–1 A Generic Psychodynamic Model

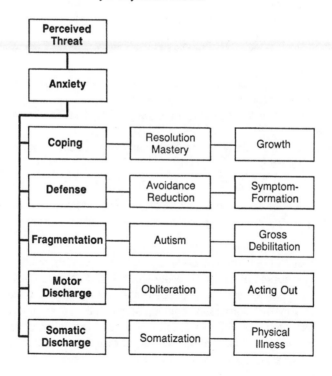

In more chronic and/or severe reactions to anxiety the noncoping options tend to predominate. It is precisely these instances that are most likely to come to the attention of the professional helper.

Approaches to the Management of Anxiety: Types of Intervention Strategy

How does the helping person intervene in the management of anxiety? This question has provoked almost as much study and controversy as the issue of the origins of anxiety. The two are closely related concerns, but with one major difference. Intervention requires the application of theory to practice, and is a much more recent area of professional study.

It is possible to distinguish two major approaches to intervention strategy, theory-based and case-based. *Theory-based strategies* emerge from a more general set of beliefs about the nature of anxiety and its remediation. Typically these are grounded in a theory of neurosis, which in turn, has direct implications for what problems need to be addressed with the client. *Case-based strategies* emphasize specific ways of understanding and encountering the problems presented by a client, whatever the broader origin of the difficulties may be. The difference may often be a difference in perspective rather than technique. For example, the importance of the helper-helpee relationship is disputed by no one. At the same time, different intervention techniques may be applicable in one theory-based approach; or, the same technique may fit two or more different theories. But it is also true that radically different strategies for intervention do exist, often because their practitioners operate from divergent sets of premises.

Theory-Based Intervention Strategy
Sociocultural theorists tend to fall within two broad clusters. Those such as Fromm (1947), Horney (1939) and Erikson (1950) see the origins of anxiety in environmental pressures but view individual psychotherapy or psychoanalysis as the treatment of choice. Others, such as Szasz (1960) and Albee (1968) recommended that social institutions or society itself must be altered when they create conditions inimical to human welfare. *Interpersonal* theorists such as Sullivan (1953) and Guntrip (1961) tend to rely on traditional individual psychotherapy. Family and network therapists (e.g., Minuchin, 1965; Speck and Attneave, 1973) prefer to work with the social unit in which the difficulties arise. Therapeutic and support groups are also recommended often by those practitioners who view anxiety as developing from troubled interpersonal relationships.

Contemporary Intrapsychic theorists tend to emphasize short-term (e.g., Sifneos, 1977) and extended individual psychotherapy (depending upon the chronicity of the anxiety). Increasingly they also make use of group therapy, medication, support groups, hypnosis, and biofeedback techniques as these seem relevant to the individual case. *Behavioral* theorists need to develop reinforcement schedules, conditioning and desensitizing procedures, and the like. While these can be designed as programs for classes and groups in weight reduction or assertiveness training, it is probable that anxiety reduction programs are individually constructed. *Cognitive* therapists such as Ellis (1962) or Beck (1967) are likely to prefer dyadic relationships or group situations, where the ideational manifestations of feelings and attitudes can be explored.

In sharp contrast to most of the previous approaches are many of the radical departures which characterize the phenomenological and somatopsychic specialists. Some proponents of these methods may incorporate traditional counseling interview techniques into their procedures. Within the *phenomenological* group can be found the variety of techniques associated with Gestalt therapy (Passons, 1975). These can include physical activity, "centering" behavior, dream re-enactment, use of body language, "hot seat," etc. Transactional analysis (Berne, 1961) resorts to a "life scripting" process to differentiate the parental, childhood, and adult roles the client adopts. The several meditative approaches (Carrington and Ephron, 1972) focus on helping the person to attain an altered state of conscious experience through chanting, body positioning, relaxing, or concentrating on one's mantra or special symbol.

The *somatopsychic* group is equally diverse, sharing only an emphasis on activating bodily and physiological processes to deal with anxiety. Included here is the use of medication and drugs, by far the most common treatment of anxiety. In addition, massage in its various forms, European or shiatsui (which relies on acupuncture medians) focuses directly on bodily tension. More chronic tensions which affect body posture are diagnosed and dealt with in ways ranging from Feldenkrais (1972) exercises to bioenergetics (Lowen, 1958) and structural integration (Pierce, 1976). Biofeedback, yoga and hypnosis are other means by which the person's bodily processes are "educated" to recognize and deal with manifestations of anxiety.

Strengths and Limits of Theory-Based Intervention   As experience and research accumulate, providing a base for theoretical formulation, a coherent body of knowledge emerges. Theory at its best links explanation to method. This understanding is, of itself, a useful part of any treatment or educational program. When methods are tied to a rationale, improved understanding of either component will usually effect a corresponding improvement of the other, thus providing for continued growth and effectiveness of the procedure. Psychoanalytic theory and practice today (e.g. Blanck and Blanck, 1974) is far different from Freud's original formulations, due to the continuous work of his followers in modifying both theory and technique with the knowledge derived from additional experience.

The primary risk of the theory-based approach lies in a tendency to overvalue the accuracy and effectiveness of the approach. Followers act as though the theory was a fact instead of an evolving set of beliefs. Another risk is that proponents of one theory may try to fit everyone into that model, failing to acknowledge its limits of application. Client-centered counseling is of proven utility with many verbal college students, but can be harmfully misapplied to crisis intervention. A situation calling for concrete action may deteriorate further if the counselor insists on gradual exploration.

Case-Based Intervention Strategy

At the heart of case-based intervention strategy is evaluation on an individual basis. Each person or situation is considered unto itself. The helping person brings to the assessment/intervention process all the theoretical and technical ability that can be mustered, toward an understanding of how to assist the client. The parameters of that assessment usually include the following features:

1. Severity of the anxiety

   a. *Mild to moderate.*   The client's functioning is impaired but not immobolized by the anxiety. Alicia gets restless and nervous every morning on her way to work. The crowds on the train bother her. Coming home is not quite as bad.

   b. *Phobic.*   The client's functioning is virtually paralyzed in a specific area of everyday life. Everytime Jack enters an elevator he begins to sweat. He gets dizzy and nauseous and feels like he will pass out unless he gets off the elevator.

   c. *Panic.*   The client verges on terror, often with no specific cause. No distractions or reassurance are helpful. Sue feels like she's losing her mind. She can't think or concentrate. She keeps having this terrible feeling she can barely describe.

2. Source of anxiety

   a. *Historic.*   The anxiety may be of recent origin or of long standing. Jim reports, "I've had this nervous stomach for as long as I can remember."

   b. *Precipitant.*   Anxiety attacks are triggered by an event or person(s) in the client's life. "I've been like this ever since my marriage broke up."

3. Kind of anxiety

   a. *Focal.*   Anxiety is evoked at particular times, by particular conflicts or conditions, conscious or unconscious. "I don't know why, but it happens every time Hal comes by."

   b. *Diffuse.*   Anxiety is everpresent, widely experienced, unrelated to time, place, or person. "That uneasy feeling is always there. I can't get rid of it."

4. Nature of the anxiety

   a. *Situational.*   The most common cause of anxiety is a situation which is perceived as threatening, whether or not the danger is objectively real. Alex gets sweaty palms and rapid heartbeat whenever someone asks him for a favor.

b. *Developmental.*   Moving from one developmental period to another requires a change and adjustment that is often stressful. The person may be too well-rooted in the present stage and unwilling to change (e.g., the campus hero who is about to graduate). The impending life stage contains threatening elements (e.g., acknowledging that one is no longer youthful). Unresolved earlier issues conflict with developmental demands (e.g., repressed anger at mother inhibits relating to female peers).

c. *Need frustration or deprivation.*   The pressure to satisfy blocked or unfulfilled needs creates anxiety. Linda gets severe headaches whenever she tries to diet.

d. *Incremental.*   Oftentimes a variety of smaller stresses accumulate, erode the person's coping resources, and precipitate an anxiety attack. "My wife is pregnant, my father just had a heart attack, business is bad, I can't take much more of this" (client begins to cry).

e. *Traumatic.*   A sudden or unexpected emotional shock will almost invariably elicit manifestations of anxiety, often severe reactions, "Oh, my god!" (shouting, thrashing arms about) "Help me! He's dead!!"

Thus, while anxiety can assume many forms and many levels of severity, even though each manifestation is different from the next, they can all be assessed by referring to the dozen headings listed above. In addition, anxiety can sometimes be inferred from its apparent absence! Certain situations are of sufficient threat value to justify an expectation of anxiety arousal. When the person acknowledges no awareness or overt sign of anxiety, an alert counselor will look for indications that a defense mechanism has been invoked to dispel the perceived threat. (Joan casually reports, "I just found out my best friend was raped." The listener asks, "How did that affect you?" Joan replies, "In the city those things are bound to happen.")

One suspects that Joan has dealt with her (presumed) fright by the defense mechanism of intellectualization. The (presumed) threatening experience has been transformed into a vague intellectual generalization, thus removing it from the personal realm and into an external condition of urban life. Further exploration of other threatening events in her life may show whether this is her usual response to threat.

Purpose of Intervention

Since anxiety is such a potentially disruptive experience, the helper must be sensitive to any clues which indicate that the client is unable to deal effectively with the experience. More specifically, does the anxiety cause personal fragmentation or activate rigid defense mechanisms? Or, is the person able to utilize coping mechanisms to resolve the conditions giving rise to anxiety? *Intervention, then, can be thought of as a procedure utilized by a helper to assist a client in more effective management of anxiety.* Intervention strategy is the selective use of intervention modalities, based on an assessment of the individual client's needs in managing anxiety. As the counselor tunes in to the client's comments and behavior, he or she will be attempting to make sense out of that material on several levels of understanding:

1. How severe is the client's anxiety—does it *prevent* functioning (e.g., eating, sleeping, studying) or *interfere* with functioning?
2. Is the anxiety focused (on a time, place, person, etc.) or is it more *generalized?*
3. What does the client's reaction to anxiety indicate about his or her ego strength—are *both* coping and defense mechanisms used? Is there evidence of fragmentation of impaired reality testing? Is there evidence of resiliency?

As this assessment proceeds, the counselor's understanding of the client increases. This, in turn, provides the counselor with a better sense of how to respond to the client. The counselor's response then truly becomes an *intervention,* designed to help that client at that point in time. The particular modality chosen is, therefore, a tool used by the counselor in the service of an intervention strategy.

Modalities of Specific Intervention

Each mode of intervention will be identified, defined, described, and its applications and limits briefly explained. But this coverage can only highlight a subtle and complex series of interactions in the helping process. With extended experience and continued study the helping person will achieve increasing skill in applying this process beneficially.

Support

In itself support implies a cluster of interventions. Support attempts to reassure the client of his or her ability to survive the threatening experience. Support may be communicated nonverbally by an understanding nodding of the head. It can be a verbal acknowledgment of the person's distress, "This must be hard for you," or reflecting the person's own words, "You were really frightened." Less preferably, one may even suggest, "You'll get over this."

Support is one of the most universally effective interventions. At its most fundamental level it tells the client he or she is not alone, and that there is hope. When used to excess, there is risk that the client will shirk responsibility for coping with the problem and, instead, retire into a dependence upon the helper. Fantasies of a magical cure, or that the helper will solve the problem, may replace active striving to work it out oneself. Excessive support may also seem patronizing, or suggest to the client that the counselor does not really understand the severity of the problem.

Exploration

Exploration entails probing or expansion into areas associated with the anxious experience. Exploration may examine associated thoughts, feelings, images, impulses, wishes, fears, body reactions somehow related to the original point of departure. Exploratory interventions by the counselor can be open and ambiguous: "How do you mean?" "Tell me some more about that," or "What does that remind you of?" A more focused exploratory comment would be, "What comes to mind when you think of_____?" Structural exploration can also be employed: "Tell me about your sister," or "What do you think he meant by that?" Since much of the counseling is by its nature exploratory, the helper's silence while the client is talking often constitutes a *de facto* exploration in that the client is left free to continue expanding the topic. Nonverbal behavior, such as a puzzled or questioning look may also be a cue for the client to continue probing.

This procedure has important drawbacks, despite its apparent simplicity. Exploration can be a long, drawn-out process. Both the helper and client need to be patient to allow time and space for associative process to work back to the problems sources. Counselor sensitivity and theoretical grounding are also important factors in maximizing the value of exploratory interventions.

Catharsis

In its purest sense catharsis is a venting, or release of emotion. Freud's earliest theory of anxiety was that it resulted from dammed-up sexual energies. With release, anxiety disappeared. Every helper has experienced the beneficial effects people can receive from "getting things off my chest." In the more dramatic forms the client may kick, cry, scream to release pent-up or repressed emotions. This direct affective expression can often produce a great sense of relief.

The perceptive helper may note signs of pent-up emotion from client comments, "I feel like I'm ready to burst open," from client's history, "When we were kids, he always picked on me, he never let up," and from somatic signs or nonverbal behavior such as headaches, fist-clenching, etc.

Catharsis occurs better in a climate of safety and support, where the client need not fear ridicule or retaliation. While emotional release is vivid and often brings dramatic results, the helper should realize that often these benefits are short-lived if they are not integrated with a new sense of strength or understanding. In some cases, catharsis may also become an end in itself, a psychological license to justify temper tantrums rather than a step toward mature integration of emotions into everyday behavior.

Confrontation

When the helper brings the client into direct awareness of some aspect of his or her behavior process, it is called confrontation. People are often ignorant of, or blinded to, the meaning of their actions. Their understanding of their behavior stops at the point where it confirms a belief or satisfies a need. In confrontation the helper faces the client with the meaning and/or consequence of actions. Usually those meanings or consequences are contrary to what the client appears to be intending.

> *Client:* I was feeling nervous, so I had some beers. What's wrong with that?
>
> *Counselor:* What happens to you when you have some beers? (Client had previously indicated that he becomes violent after using alcohol)

As in the example above, the client is commonly faced with the destructive meaning or consequence of his or her behavior. This is of particular importance in working with people who experience little guilt or who avoid taking responsibility for their actions. The helper's purpose is to help the client see that it is the behavior, not someone else's disapproval, that results in unhappy, outcomes for the client. The client's violence, not an insensitive bartender, was what got him arrested.

A somewhat different form of confrontation has also been used effectively by the writer. This variation, *supportive* confrontation, brings the client into conscious contact with strengths or positive attributes.

> (Some months later, with the same client)
>
> *Client:* I was so damn nervous. I went home, watched the tube, and fell asleep.
>
> *Counselor:* You were so nervous. Yet you didn't get drunk, get into a fight, end up in jail.

It is important for the client to see that the same anxious feeling could be handled in a way which did not compound his problem.

The power of confrontation lies in its linkage to visible behavior and/or everyday meaning. Nevertheless, it must be applied with caution. Some clients lack either the capacity or the willingness to tolerate so blunt a look at themselves. Too, the helper's own reaction to client's destructive behavior may result in a moralistic condemnation rather than an objective presentation of the behavior. Confrontation that is aimed at guilt-arousal may jeopardize the counseling relationship.

Interpretation

This intervention explains the person's attitudes or behavior in terms of its underlying causes. Interpretation offers the client insight into the (often unconscious) motives which gave rise to his or her reactions. The helper uses an understanding of personality theory and dynamics to explain the *origins* of the anxiety. "You expected your boss to be callous the way your father was."

Interpretation enables the client to recognize pattern and meaning in behavior that seems irrational, or justified by events outside the person. "You have these nightmares about people attacking you because you're really feeling very guilty."

Interpretation can be a vital intervention when the client's inner motives, needs, conflicts, or defenses produce anxiety. The client experiences the anxiety but has no comprehension of its origins. In these situations anxiety can be particularly disabling because its origins are so mystifyingly unknown.

While interpretation can be a powerful tool, it can also be easily misused. An incorrect interpretation may add to the client's anxiety and confusion; and it may undermine confidence in the helper's abilities. Correct interpretations applied prematurely can result in intellectual understanding without real learning or assimilation by the client. Finally, too much interpretation puts the helper in the role of the all-knowing expert. This can strengthen the client's self doubts and lead to a shifting of responsibility: "You (helper) are so wise, you tell me what to do, how I should lead my life."

Behavior Modification

This is a general heading for a variety of intervention strategies for altering client behavior. They share a common *method*, which is to teach the client a different set of responses to anxiety-provoking stimuli. Space does not permit an exhaustive survey of the numerous concepts and techniques subsumed under behavior modification. The interventions are based on conditioning or extinguishing learned responses, on rewarding or punishing learned behaviors, and on providing alternative models for social learning. That behavior modification strategies work is a matter of empirical record. It is of particular importance to note that phobic anxiety has responded very well to behaviorally based approaches. Moreover, the treatment often takes effect in a short time.

Limitations on such interventions emerge from other considerations. Where the presenting problems are highly complex, as in heavy cigarette smoking, improvement based solely on behavioral intervention tends to be of short duration. A different concern is voiced by those who fear that shaping the person's behavior to reduce or avoid anxiety may also train the person to adapt to the status quo and/or avoid all anxiety, even those that generate growth.

Information and Guidance

Again, this refers to a group of intervention strategies. These have in common the helper's role as one who possesses specialized information, and/or one who is skilled in providing suggestions and knowledge to help people deal with their problems. Adolph Meyer's common sense psychiatry (1934) focused on offering practical advice to resolve anxiety arising from problems of living. The basic assumption underlying this group of interventions is that people can exercise conscious control over the conditions and events that produce anxiety in their lives. Included here as well is the correction of "faulty thinking" (Ellis, 1962). This approach finds its most effective application in short-term work with clients who are in need of highly specific structuring in their lives. People with acute, diffuse anxiety can often benefit from interventions which set limits, establish boundaries, create a sense of order in their emotional chaos: (To an elderly woman, frightened by living alone) "Many older people have the exact same worries. . . . Here is the number of a 24-hour hotline. . . . Have you talked with you children? . . ."

Many problems are the result of misinformation, mistaken ideas, or lack of knowledge. When that is the case, an instructional approach can be quick and effective. But facts often are outweighed by private beliefs, and sheer information may only be accepted intellectually. Finally, this approach depends upon the ability of the helper to be perceived as an expert authority. Carried too far, it can foster guilt or dependency in the client.

Environmental Manipulation

This form of intervention involves activating or restructuring the physical, social, or professional resources of the person's environment. It derives from a belief that the client's anxiety can best be managed by supplementing the person's own ego resources with external supports. Environmental manipulation may entail changing a child's class schedule to correspond better to a single parent's working hours; mobilizing a tenant group to protest rent increases; suggesting that a client contact Alcoholics Anonymous; requesting that a client arrange a family meeting with the counselor.

Environmental manipulation is an effective technique in crisis intervention or when working with chronically deprived, oppressed, or handicapped people. In these instances some tangible and immediate evidence is needed so that an intolerable life situation can be restructured. Often the client feels victimized and powerless. With new supports or opportunities provided the client is then able to mobilize ego resources and function more effectively, with or without counseling.

Some people tend to ascribe all their distress to external conditions and to disavow any personal responsibility to help themselves. For these people environmental manipulation, if continued as the only intervention, may result in increasing their sense of anxiety, helplessness, and anger. In other instances, exclusive insistence on environmental change may be a way of manipulating the helper to meet dependency needs which are irrational and insatiable.

Medication   This type of intervention involves the use of medicines, drugs, vitamins, herbs, or special foods. Psychosurgery and electroconsulsive therapies are also included here. The helper recommends, prescribes, or administers these, sometimes in collaboration with other colleagues. The use of medications to control anxiety is far and away the most common form of intervention. Its frequency of use is more than that of all the other procedures combined.

To a greater or lesser degree, all the medications mentioned above have proven useful in moderating or controlling various manifestations of anxiety. All medications share a reliance on an external agent to relieve the person's internal distress. They are of particular value to people who view anxiety as due to disease, body malfunction, or deficiency. Medications are also valuable for people with chronic anxiety symptoms that do not respond to other types of intervention; they are also used in conjunction with psychotherapy for people whose level of anxiety would otherwise be intolerable.

Habitual dependence upon medication can shift responsibility from the person to the helper. This risks perceiving the helper as one endowed with special powers, adding an aura of magic or mysticism to the helping process.

Relaxation

A number of techniques for managing anxiety are new to western societies. They emphasize relieving anxious distress through bodily processes of relaxation. Included here are meditation, massage, exercise, and biofeedback procedures. The several meditation and biofeedback techniques teach the client to focus attention on specific images (e.g., Barber, 1974) or physiological processes (e.g., Benson, 1975). Massage and exercise techniques work directly on muscles and tissues where anxiety has been somatized, producing physical tension.

The approaches work best with mild to moderate anxiety since they tend to be too gradual for use with severe or panic conditions. Even more hopefully, they offer the person a preventive program to forestall the accumulation of tension by regular use of the procedure. Finally, they restore control and responsibility to the person, whose own efforts are basic to effective management of anxiety. In many instances the specific techniques are but part of a broader orientation to style of living, a more holistic approach to management. At the same time, however, these techniques tend to understate the recurrent affect of personality dynamics and psychopathology in arousing anxiety. These procedures may not even aid the person to resolve the problems giving rise to anxiety.

Toward a General Theory of Anxiety Management

Pulling together all that has been covered in the preceding pages, it is clear that we are still distant from a general theory of managing anxiety. Certain principles can be identified, however, that are clinically useful.

First, anxiety is a natural, inevitable component of the life experience. However unpleasant it may be, its occurrence is not like some dread disease but more like dying—unsought but universal. To ignore the inevitability of anxiety, like ignoring death, serves only to make it more fearsome.

Anxiety has a multiplicity of causes. To be anxious is not to be on the verge of psychosis. At its most fundamental meaning anxiety like other pain, is a signal. The helper makes a real contribution by assisting clients to interpret those signals.

Anxiety can be facilitative as well as disruptive. Freud saw anxiety as a symptom of conflict. Today we also recognize that anxiety can be a challenge, heightening the senses and stimulating improved response.

Optimum management of anxiety involves tolerance and modulation, not avoidance or abolition. A general theory of anxiety management must take as its basic orientation the utilization of anxiety as naturally as one would hunger pangs. Learning to respect its value, interpret its signals, and moderate its intensity will contribute to a richer quality of life. The contemporary professional helper is more than a therapist, but functions also as counselor, educator, advocate, and consultant. To parallel this more sophisticated definition of professional role, the concept of anxiety should be freed from its one-dimensional definition. Anxiety is more than a symptom of pathology; it is a warning of danger, a challenge, a stimulant, a vital part of human experience.

Questions for Further Inquiry

1. How do you know when you are feeling anxious? What are the affective, motoric, somatic, and cognitive signs available to you?

2. What coping mechanisms do you use to manage your own anxiety? How effective are they for you?

3. Which theories of anxiety developed early in this chapter best help you account for anxiety in yourself and others? Why?

4. Even though most people do not like being in an anxious state, can you identify circumstances when anxiety might be useful?

5. Some counselors respond to client anxiety by offering support. What risks are involved with this approach?

References

Ackerman, N. W. Toward an integrative therapy of the family. *American Journal of Psychiatry* 1958 *114*, 727–33.

Albee, G. W. Models, myths, and manpower. *Mental Hygiene,* 1968 *52(2),* 168–80.

Bandura, A. *Social learning theory.* New York: Prentice-Hall, 1977.

Barber, T. *Hypnotism, imagination, and human potentialities.* New York: Pergamon, 1974.

Beck, A. T. *Cognitive therapy and the emotional disorders.* New York: International Universities Press, 1976.

Benson H. *The relaxation response.* New York: William Morrow, 1975.

Berne, E. *Transactional analysis in psychotherapy.* New York: Grove Press, 1961.

Blanck, G. & Blanck, R. *Ego psychology: theory and practice.* New York: Columbia University Press, 1974.

Carrington, P. and Ephron, H. Meditation as an adjunct to psychotherapy and psychiatry. In S. Arieti and G. Chrzanowski (Eds.), *New dimensions in psychiatry.* New York: Wiley, 1972.

Ellis, A. *Reason and emotion in psychotherapy.* New York: Lyle Stuart, 1962.

Erickson, E. H. *Childhood and society.* New York: Norton, 1950.

Fairbairn, W. R. D. Observations in defense of the object-relations theory of the personality. *British Journal of Medical Psychology* 1955 *28*, 144–56.

Feldenkrais, M. *Awareness through movement.* New York: Harper & Row, 1972.

Festinger, L. The motivating effect of cognitive dissonance. In G. Lindzey (Ed.) *Assessment of human motives.* New York: Holt, Rinehart, 1958.

Freud, S. *Civilization and its discontents.* New York: Norton, 1930.

Freud, S. *The standard edition of the complete psychological works of Sigmund Freud.* J. Strachey, et al. (Eds.). London: Hogarth Press, 1953–64.

Fromm, E. *Man for himself.* New York: Little & Ives Co., 1947.

Guntrip, H. *Personality structure and human interaction.* New York: International Universities Press, 1961.

Haan, N. Proposed model of ego functioning: Coping and defense mechanisms in relationship to I.Q. change. *Psychological Monographs* 1963, *77.*

Haan, N. *Coping and defending.* New York: Academic Press, 1977.

Hartmann, H. *Ego psychology and the problem of adaptation.* New York: International Universities Press, 1958.

Horney, K. *New ways in psychoanalysis.* New York: Norton, 1939.

Kantor, D., & Lehr, W. *Inside the family.* New York: Harper & Row, 1976.

Kernberg, O. Early ego integration and object relations. *Annals of the New York Academy of Sciences* 1972 *193,* 233–47.

Kohut, H. *The analysis of the self.* New York: International Universities Press, 1971.

Kroeber, T. C. The coping functions of the ego mechanisms. In R. White (Ed.) *The study of lives.* New York: Atherton, 1963.

Kubler-Ross, E. *On death and dying.* New York: Macmillan, 1969.

Laing, R. D. *The divided self.* Baltimore: Penguin Books, 1959.

Lowen, A. *The language of the body.* New York: Macmillan, 1958.

Mahler, M. On the first three subphases of the separation-individuation process. *International Journal of Psychoanalysis* 1972 *53,* 333–38.

Meyer, A. The psychobiological point of view. In N. Bentley and E. Cowdrey, (Eds.) *The problem of mental disorders.* New York: McGraw-Hill 1934.

Miller, N. and Dollard, J. *Social learning and imitation.* New Haven: Yale University Press, 1941.

Minuchin, S. Conflict resolution family therapy. *Psychiatry* 1965 *28,* 278–86.

Passons, W. R. *Gestalt approaches in counseling.* New York: Holt, Rinehart, 1975.

Perls, F. S. *Gestalt therapy verbatim.* Lafayette, Calif.: Real People Press, 1969.

Pierce, R. *Rolfing.* Boulder, Col.: Rolf Institute Publications, 1976.

Rogers, C. R. *Client-centered psychotherapy.* Boston: Houghton-Mifflin, 1951.

Speck, R. V. and Attneave, C. *Family networks.* New York: Pantheon Books, 1973.

Sifneos, P. *Brief psychotherapy.* New York: Grune and Stratton, 1977.

Sullivan, H. S. *The interpersonal theory of psychiatry.* New York: Norton, 1953.

Szasz, T. The myth of mental illness. *The American Psychologist* 1960 *15(2),* 113–18.

Wolpe, J. *The practice of behavior therapy, (2nd ed.).* New York: Pergamon, 1973.

Understanding and Alleviating Depression

4

EDWARD L. TREMBLEY

Overview

People of all ages and life circumstances are bringing to counselors increased numbers of complaints about being depressed. Counseling practitioners in diverse settings are well aware of this increase. The growing incidence of depression is often attributed to factors in contemporary society such as depersonalization, loss of the capacity to trust, interpersonal destructiveness in transitory but intense relationships, and a loss of control over one's destiny. The themes of depression —a sense of loss, sadness, and a pessimistic view of self, world, and future—are now commonplace in counseling dialogues.

Depression is a challenging counseling problem for at least two reasons. Depression is often such a painful experience for those who develop it that they often want a quick counseling "cure." Therapeutic change is difficult to acheive with depressed persons because they engage in rigid and irrational thinking and may be self-destructive. This chapter will review selected aspects of several theories on the development of depression and its treatment. In addition, an approach to understanding and counseling depressed persons in a systematic manner will be presented.

Understanding Depression

Candidates for Depression

There is considerable information and speculation about who gets depressed. It is not necessary to review this information here. It is important to understand that identifying candidates for depression is a function of the definition of depression that one chooses to employ. If one uses a broad-based, nondisease definition, the number of candidates for depression will be great when compared to the number of candidates if one employs a narrower, disease-based, diagnostic definition.

It would seem that candidates for depressive episodes are people who have reached their unique tolerance level for managing events that threaten their self-esteem and their needs for emotional support. Some individuals are predisposed to depressive reactions because of early childhood frustrations. The child's response to frustration forms a prototype response pattern used when later frustrations and threats to dependency needs and self-esteem occur (Laughlin, 1967). Beck (1967) reviewed evidence that suggests a genetic predisposition to depression, but concluded that "available research data does not establish conclusively whether affective disorders are genetic, environmental, both, or neither (p. 132)." At present, there does not appear to be any evidence on which the practitioner can rely that identifies factors such as social class, nationality, race, ethnic group, marital status, and personality typologies as predispositional in the development of depression.

Candidates for depression may be defined as those people who, because of past learning, character traits, or psychodynamic reasons, will find it difficult to manage one of the following common precipitants of depression: perceived threat to self-worth; actual, assumed, or predicted loss of a love object or person; fear of failure after achieving success.

The Experience of Depression

Depressions seem to run a particular, but general, course from onset to termination. Most depressions seen in counseling are reactive, i.e., they are triggered by identifiable external events of loss, threat, or disappointment. Depressions may have acute onsets, although some seem to develop gradually until the person "can't take it anymore." Acute onsets usually bring about dramatic behavior changes which are of concern to the client and to those in his or her environment. Acute onset depressions typically have a good prognosis.

Depressions tend to get worse before they get better. The client is increasingly negative, pessimistic, and helpless in outlook. There is an understandable wish to escape from the discomfort of the depression. The depressed client feels worn-out and complains of vague aches and pains. The client may have reached the sad conclusion to pull out of the search for love and meaning in life; some clients feel "thrown out" of life by others. The depressive thinks in a self-blaming manner about personal inadequacies; guilt and anger may be felt deeply. Counselors find themselves trying to relate to a person who is sad, burdened, blaming, and negative. The client's experience of depression is real, but out of proportion to the reality of life.

In its typical course, depression "bottoms-out" or reach its deepest level for a particular client when one's attention is exclusively on one's inadequacy and personal plight. The client feels worse and engages in pervasive depressive thinking at the bottom of the depression. The client feels abandoned by others and is psychologically very lonely. Depending on the depth of the depression, suicidal intentions may be acted upon as Weiss (1969) indicated: "the feeling of 'aloneness' has always been a contributing and significant factor in suicidal acts (p. 42)." The depth of depression, of course, varies greatly among clients as suggested by Figure 4–1. A gradual improvement in the depression begins after changes have occurred in the client or the client's world or both. Spontaneous remission can also occur. Some writers indicate that as a relatively deep depression begins "to lift," the risk of suicide is highest. The basic dynamics of the depression are still operative, but now the client is able to generate sufficient energy to act on the suicidal thoughts (Atwood, 1972; MacKinnon and Michels, 1971). Laughlin (1967) called this the "post-trough point of hazard" for suicide, indicating that the most

Figure 4–1 The U-Shaped Curve of Depression

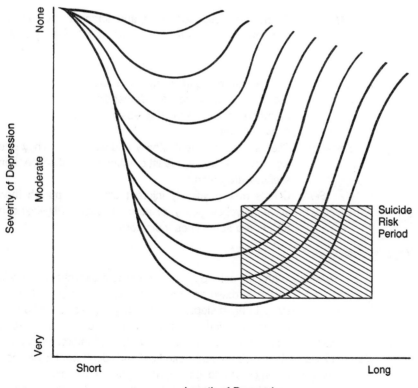

likely time for suicide is shortly after the person has started to come out of the most depressed phase. The best single indicator of suicidal risk is the expression of suicidal wishes and intentions; such expressions are to be taken seriously by counselors (Beck, 1967; Murray, 1972; Schneidman and Farberow, 1957). Laughlin (1967) described the "principle of recurrence" which states that depressions tend to recur if counseling treatment is inadequate or if there is a history of previous depressions.

Symptoms of Depression

Examination of common client statements and counselor observations about depression provides a set of indicators useful in further understanding depression. Common depression indicators are summarized below:

Appearance Indicators

Dress change: I feel like I look drab ... sad ... ugly ... I used to wear bright things.

Posture and face: Clients look worn down, worn-out, downcast, and stooped.

Action Indicators

Manner: Clients seem subdued, quiet, and humorless. Actions lack spontaneity and seem slow. There is a tendency to withdraw from others; social relations become problematic. Clients want to be cared for, but their actions are not effective in obtaining caring from others. Out of fear of rejection, clients may become too demanding, which results in greater rejection. As the depression deepens, clients withdraw into self.

Speaking: Clients seem to speak slowly and with effort. They often sigh and their voice has little volume and inflection. Long silences are common.

Self-destructiveness: Clients may physically injure themselves, punish themselves psychologically, or attempt suicide. Physical complaints are sometimes indicators.

Physical Indicators

Sleep disturbances: I can't fall asleep ... I toss and turn all night ... I'm wide awake at dawn and can't get back to sleep ... I'm tired even if I have slept ... I have nightmares ... wake up all through the night ... I can't get back to sleep if I wake up.

Eating disturbances: I don't feel like eating ... I've lost all interest in food ... Mealtimes are bad, I can't eat and I don't want to be social.

Energy disturbances: I don't want to go anywhere or do anything ... I just don't have my old steam anymore ... I'm wiped out all of the time . . . I start a job but get tired and don't finish it, or I screw it up . . . I am drained . . . I am empty.

Somatic disturbances: My bowels don't work . . . I ache a lot of the time . . . My periods are emotionally terrible . . . I'm cold much of the time . . . I don't have interest in sex anymore . . . There is something wrong with my insides . . . my guts are fouled up.

Psychological Indicators

Feelings: I am sad . . . down . . . numb . . . empty . . . bored . . . hurting . . . out of it. am afraid . . . sinful . . . rotten. I don't care about things anymore. (Clients will complain of feeling anxious, hostile, or irritable. The primary statements center on a lowering of mood. There is a lack of enjoyment with previously enjoyable events. There is a pervasive self-contempt and estrangement from self. Anger may be expressed at the perceived rejection by others. Humorless.)

Thinking: I can't do anything right anymore . . . I'm no damn good . . . what's wrong with me that they treat me so badly? I'm a loser, always will be . . . I can't concentrate . . . I'm paying the price for screwing up . . . life isn't worth it . . . I've thought about ending it all . . . of killing myself . . . I am going to kill myself, why not? I know it's bad to be this way . . . I complain all of the time . . . all I think about is my troubles . . . the world really is rotten . . . Today is bad, tomorrow will be worse, I know it. (Clients show a preoccupation with negativistic thinking about their past, present, and future. They may brood over past sins and express fears of punishment and guilt. There is a general diminution of thought processes and low initiative to consider new ideas. Harsh summary judgments are common.)

Attention: Clients are frequently so preoccupied with negativistic thinking that they become poor attenders. They miss things that people would normally notice.

Counselors witness many levels of severity of depression in their daily work, ranging from transitory episodes of "feeling down" to acute reactions that render the depressed person barely functional. Depressions are complex patterns of behavior and counselors sometimes turn to classification systems as an aid to their diagnostic thinking. Too often, however, counselors find only minimal help from systems such as the American Psychiatric Association's (1968) standard classification system. The "standard" clinical definitions may not "fit" the symptoms seen in counseling. The hard line diagnostic differentiations between neurotic and psychotic depressions seem esoteric. Many counselors would probably agree with Beck's (1967) gradualist view on differential diagnosis of depressions. He said "so far as specific depressive symptoms are concerned, the difference between the neurotic and the psychotic depressive reactions is quantitative rather than qualitative (Beck, 1967)." It is true that most counselors have been prepared to counsel "normal" persons experiencing developmental and situational social, personal, and career problems, not psychotics. On the other hand, it must be recognized that psychotic persons appear on many counselor's caseloads and remain there for reasons that may be appropriate or inappropriate. Experienced counselors understand that decisions about counseling depressed persons rest, more often than not, on definitions of acceptable behavior in a particular setting rather than on a diagnostic classification system.

Readers wishing to review detailed discussions of symptoms, case studies, and research reports relative to diagnosis of depression are referred to Beck (1967, 1976) and Becker (1977). Readers wishing to explore the biochemical nature of depression are referred to Mendels (1970) and to Stern, McClure and Costello (1970).

Highlights of Theories About Depression

Behavioral Theories

The key features of behavioral theories about depression are the focus on stimuli antecedent to the depression, the careful definition of the overt manifestations of the depression, and the specification of the consequences which follow depressive behaviors (Ferster, 1973). Depressive behaviors are seen as learned responses, the prototype of which often occur in childhood when an individual learns that passive-dependent behaviors lead to fewer negative consequences when interacting with significant others. For the adult, passive-dependent tendencies may lead to a reduced number of reinforcements, which is then construed as rejection thus deepening depression. Some persons learn to withdraw to avoid or escape aversive consequences, such as criticism; the effect of this withdrawal is positively reinforcing thereby strengthening the withdrawal pattern and increasing the likelihood of generalizing the pattern. Other depressives may learn that complaining and displaying negativistic behavior serve to keep others at a safe, non-threatening distance which is a reinforcement for and leads to an increase of the complaining behavior. At some point, of course, these "payoffs" for depressive behaviors are reduced and others tend to reject the depressive because of them.

Some behaviorists maintain that depressed persons experience a loss of effective reinforcers, not just a reduction in the number of reinforcements *per se*. The rate or schedule of reinforcement relates functionally to those behaviors they follow. The depressive's negative self-talk may lead to a significant reduction in the rate of social reinforcement, which only confirms the depressive's notion that it is not productive to assert self in search of positive social reinforcement (Lewinsohn and Shaffer, 1971). Lewinsohn and his colleagues viewed this sequence of depressive behavior as a prolonged extinction schedule in which fewer and fewer social reinforcements are available to the depressive, which paradoxically reinforces depressive symptoms (Lewinsohn and Atwood, 1969; Lewinsohn and Graf, 1973). Seligman (1973, 1975) suggested that depressives have learned helplessness from a lack of control over reinforcement contingencies in their lives.

Psychoanalytic Theories

Psychoanalytic theorists maintain that the origin of depression occurs early in life when the infant operates in a primitive and narcissistic mode (Robertiello, 1969). Inevitable need frustrations force the infant to give up its omnipotent and narcissistic orientation and assigning them to its parents. The infant comes to depend on parents for "narcissistic supplies" of love and nuturance. At this stage, loss or separation, real or imagined, of the parents constitutes a most serious threat and can result in infantile depression.

The interpersonal ambivalence of the depressive is thought to develop from the oral stage of psychosexual development in which the child loves and needs the nuturant, omnipotent parent, but also wants very much to incorporate them as part of the ego. The self-reproach of the depressive is explained by the intrapsychic struggle between the omnipotent superego and the ego which is punished for being passive-dependent and narcissistic (Fenichel, 1945; Jacobson, 1971).

Existential Theories

Existential writers see depression as a type of neurotic behavior characterized by a loss of interest in and a lack of initiative in life. Frankl (1963, 1967) wrote of life as an "existential vacuum" with no meaning, a result of the industrialization which has disrupted life's traditions and man's instinctual security. Man is pulled by the challenge of finding meaning as he confronts what he is and what he ought to be. The guilt that stems from man's inability to fulfill potentialities is considered "true" or "ontological" guilt (Kemp, 1971). Guilt is basic to depression and results from not choosing responsibly in one's life.

The depressive feels worthless, sees life and the world as meaningless. As a depression deepens, there is a reduction in general activity and a growing sense of incompleteness. Life seems "arrested." Life is lived primarily in the past, which causes further guilt since present opportunities are not attended to (Beck, 1967). The neurotically depressed person is concerned with escapism, not from guilt, but from man's knowledge that he is finite and that he will fail, suffer, and die.

Cognitive Theories

The major cognitive theory of depression has been developed by Beck (1967, 1976). Depression is considered to be a thought disorder rather then an affective or mood disorder. Depression is a series of reactions to meaningful loss. The loss diminishes the person, whether the loss is actual, imagined, or the result of deprivation over time. The depressed person experiences unpleasant and disturbing feelings which are the consequences of the person's thinking about self, world, and the future. Beck (1967) stated, "If the patient was rejected, he would experience negative affect. Similarly, if he simply thought he was rejected, he would experience the same negative affect (p. 261)."

Thus, affective disorders are secondary to and caused by cognitive disorders. The cognitive disorders are due to interpretations (thoughts) about data and events. This view has much in common with the cognitive theories espoused by Kelly (1955), Ellis (1962), and the perceptualists such as Combs and Syngg (1959). The Sequential Model of Behavior (SMB) presented later in this chapter has similarities to Beck's theory.

Beck identified a primary cognitive triad that operates in depression by progressively dominating thinking. The major characteristics of the cognitive triad are the distortion of reality and a systematic bias against self. The cognitive triad includes the elements of interpretation of experience, a negative view of self, and a negative view of the future.

Beck understood the development of depression to be the result of cognitive structures, or schema, which are based on early negative learning experiences. Through selective attention, distortions, and reinforcement patterns, these schema become entrenched in the cognitive organization of the depressive. As the schema become established and systematized, there is an increasing tendency to interpret experiences as consistent with them. Beck believed that value judgments (good-bad labels) are negative constructs or generalizations that become associated with unpleasant feelings. When an event triggers a negative construct into action, unpleasant feelings also become activated. For example, a negative construct may be, "I am not strong," which has an associated value judgment such as, "It is bad not to be strong." When an event is interpreted as indicating a lack of strength in this person, the negative value is triggered and the unpleasant feelings follow.

In summary, Beck's cognitive theory suggests that depression operates in the following sequence:

1. An event is interpreted as personally defeating or thwarting.
2. The cognitive schema regarding negative self view is triggered.
3. The person attributes perceived defeat to defects in self.
4. Person has a negative value associated with unpleasant feelings.
5. Person construes self as devalued for having defect.
6. Person sees no hope for change, views world and self pessimistically.
7. Experiences depression.

The cycle of depression deepens as it is repeated, tending to reinforce the person's cognitive triad, which maintains the depression.

Sequential Model of Behavior

The final theoretical approach to be applied to understanding depression is the Sequential Model of Behavior, or SMB. The SMB is a general theoretical framework developed from the author's counseling practice. It is designed to help counselors to be systematic in their approach to understanding any problem behavior (Trembley, 1974). Since the SMB will be new to the majority of readers, some basic definitions are necessary. The model is cognitive-perceptual, obviously related to Beck's (1967) cognitive theory, and influenced by the writing of Ford and Urban (1963), and Combs and Snygg (1959).

Four major classes of variables are used in the SMB:

1. *Situational Context or S:* The situational context is the pattern of stimuli that exist for a person at a particular time. For depressives, the counselor wonders about the external stimulus condition in which depressive responses occur or which they follow. Counselors also establish what aspects of the stimulus environment the client responds to, ignores, or misinterprets.

2. *Overt Behavior or Actions or R:* Overt behavior is defined as those actions in which one engages. Overt behavior is observable by both the behaver and other people. For the depressed client, the counselor wants to establish as accurately as possible a description of the actions (or lack of actions) in which the client engages when depressed. What are the depressed client's observable symptoms?

3. *Covert Mediating Behavior or r:* Covert behavior is defined as the internal behavior of a person, including the four major subclasses of attending, thinking, feeling, and sensing behaviors. Covert behavior is subjectively observable by the behaver, but can only be known inferentially by another person. Covert mediating behavior serves as the psychological link between a person's situational context (S) and actions (R); as such, covert behaviors are critical in understanding how behavior gets started, maintained, and changed. From the SMB perspective, the most important activity of the counselor is establishing accurate inferences about the client's covert mediating behavior patterns. How does the depressed client mediate or link up S and R?

The major point to understand about covert mediating behavior is that it is a response pattern that comes to serve as a stimulus for other responses in the chain of behavior between S and R. Dollard and Miller (1950) stated that a mediating response is "one whose main function is to produce a cue that is part of the stimulus pattern leading to another response (p. 98)." Any of the covert behaviors, i.e., attending, thinking, feeling, and sensing may serve as mediating behavior. Thus, the chaining of internal responses can be conceptualized as thoughts leading to other thoughts, feelings, attending, or sensing behaviors; each subclass of covert behavior may serve a mediating function thus stimulating other covert responses as well as overt responses. In the SMB, unconscious behavior is defined as "not attending," while conscious behavior is defined as "attending" behavior (Ford and Urban, 1963).

4. *Consequences of Behavior or PC and IC:* This classification includes the consequences which follow one's overt behavior (R). Private consequences (PC) are an especially important type of covert behavior which are self-evaluative thoughts about one's own actions. Private consequences are the most immediate and often the most important feedback one gets about one's actions. Interpersonal or social consequences (IC) are the overt reactions of others to one's

actions, i.e., social feedback. For depressed clients, the counselor wants to establish inferentially what the client says to self about his or her own actions and what others say about the client's actions. The relative importance the client assigns to IC and PC is always an important determination to make in counseling depressives.

The four basic classifications of events and behavior used in the SMB can now be shown in their *sequential* relationship in Figure 4–2. The SMB indicates that behavior occurs in a sequence and that changes in any aspect of the sequence will alter the entire sequence. Thus, the depressed client wishing to alter a feeling state may seek to change S, r, R, PC or IC. All four classifications of events and behaviors need to be explored in order to understand how a particular depression works and can be altered. The SMB, as a cognitive-perceptual model, suggests that the major therapeutic changes sought in counseling are thinking changes. If a client changes how he or she thinks about self, world, and the future, then changes in feelings, sensations, attending actions, private consequences, and interpersonal consequences will occur.

Any of the preceding theoretical views of depression can be described in SMB terminology. The SMB as conceived by the author emphasizes understanding all four classes of events and behavior as fundamental to counseling depressed clients. Like the cognitive theorists, the SMB maintains that so long as a person sees the world as rejective, the self as devalued, and the future as bleak, the person will continue to experience depression.

Counseling depressives from the SMB viewpoint involves identifying the characteristics of the SMB classes of events and behaviors for both client and counselor understanding. An understanding of the sequential relationship and the interaction of specific events and behaviors is necessary to appreciate how a depression is initiated and maintained. Time and energy are spent in counseling interviews to identify depression-related experiences of the client, especially those covert behaviors that underlie the depression. Besides requiring patience and hard work on the part of the counselor and client, the process is basically one of identifying accurate data, drawing inferences, and testing to see if the inferences about a particular client's depression fit the client's experience.

Figure 4–2 The Sequential Relationship of the SMB Classes of Variables

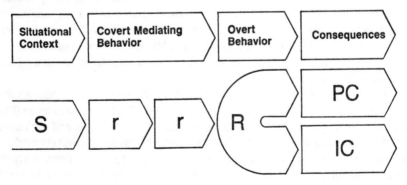

The SMB employs the concept of "therapeutic contrast" to explain therapeutic change in the depression-eliciting thinking and the depressed feelings of the client. The antecedents to depression-eliciting thoughts and of depressed feelings and their consequences are important targets for change efforts. The antecedents, S and r, are the triggers of depression-eliciting thoughts and feelings, while the consequences R, PC and IC are the outcomes of such thoughts and feelings.

The SMB shown in Figure 4–3 indicates that depressed feelings have three types of antecedents, such as S, r (attending), and r (depression-eliciting thoughts), and three types of consequences, such as actions (R), PC and IC. It follows that the treatment of depressed feelings would involve systematic attempts to modify any of the antecedents or consequences related to them. Direct treatment of the feelings *per se* can also be undertaken through catharsis, sharing of feelings, and antidepressant drugs. However, significant changes in depressed feeling states occur following alterations in depression-eliciting thoughts.

The consequences of a depressed person's behavior, especially those following overt actions (R) are important. These consequences, PC and IC, are modifiers of R. Since counseling is concerned with helping the depressed person "act healthier" as well as thinking in a more healthy manner, the consequences of overt behavior are key variables influencing the client's actions. Note also that at the covert behavior level, one type of r may be reinforced by its immediate covert consequence, another r.

In Figure 4–4, PC and IC modify r and S, respectively. When the depressed person acts in a negativistic, demanding, and inappropriately dependent manner, both the self-evaluative thoughts (PC) and the feedback from others (IC) immediately alter the covert antecedents to the depressed acts and the situation in which they occur. Figure 4–4 shows only a small part of the flow of behavior since one S → r → R → PC/IC sequence flows directly into another.

Applications of Theoretical Approaches to Counseling Depressed Clients

Throughout this section, the Sequential Model of Behavior classification labels will be used for assisting the reader in comparing other approaches to SMB.

Behavioral Counseling
The behavioral counselor is interested in modifying client problem behavior through psychological means. Counseling methods based on learning principles are central to this approach. The behavioral counselor tends to be clear and direct about the methods used, how they work, and the outcomes that can be expected for the client. Behavioral writers have a refreshingly parsimonious manner of describing their counseling which tends to demystify the process, although making counseling less glamorous for some practitioners (Bandura, 1961). London's (1972) comments, although harsh, merit attention when considering behavioral counseling approaches. He wrote that behavioral counselors "have about three

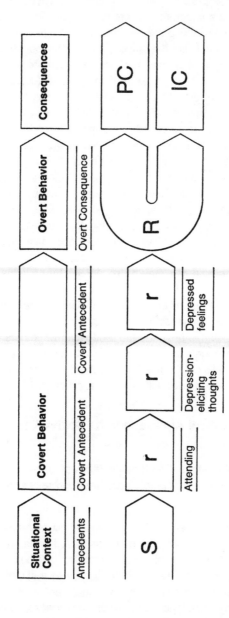

Figure 4-3 Antecedents and Consequences of Depression-Eliciting Thoughts and Feelings

principles that they ever referred to, all of which can be reduced to one or one-and-a-half principles—namely, that learning depends on the connections in time, space, and attention between what you do and what happens to you subsequently (p. 913)."

Depression is a learned pattern of unadaptive behavior which is disturbing to others and to the person having it. Strict behavioral counselors treat the client's overt actions (R), the social consequences of those actions (IC), and perhaps the situational context (S) in which the behavior occurs. Little attention, if any, is given to the modification of covert behavior (r, PC). Less strict or "soft" behavioral counselors do attend to covert behavior; fewer pay attention to unconscious levels of behavior (r) as do the "insight" counselors (London, 1964, 1969).

The functional analysis of problem behavior is an important aspect of behavioral counseling (Ferster, 1973; Krumboltz, 1966; Sheslow and Erickson, 1975). Functional analysis involves a specific delineation of the problem behavior, its antecedents, consequences, and unadaptive features.

The major behavioral counseling principles are: reinforcement, extinction, counterconditioning, discrimination learning, and punishment. It is worth noting that Becker (1977) recently commented that "the application of cognitive-behavioral treatment to depression has consistently lagged for obscure reasons (p. 107)."

Psychoanalytic Therapy

The psychoanalytic theory of depression involves disturbed responses (r, R, PC) to real (S) or imagined (r) loss of a love object. Persons become predisposed to depression because of early life traumas, particularly if they occurred in the oral-sadistic psychosexual stage of development.

Treatment of depression revolves around the reduction of guilt (r), the initiation of hope (r), and helping the client avoid self-injury (R) (MacKinnon and Michels, 1971). This is sometimes called ego support therapy (Gross, 1968). Psychoanalytic therapy also focuses on the exploration of the dynamics of the meanings and causes of depression for the purpose of promoting insight which results in the reduction of the depression and the prevention of its recurrence. This is called "insight therapy" (London, 1964) or "deep treatment" (Laughlin, 1967).

Psychoanalytic therapists who are also physicians may employ electroconvulsive shock treatment or antidepressant drugs with severely depressed patients (Costello and Belton, 1970). Antidepressant medications may have significant placebo effects and for the client may represent an unconscious magical cure. The depressed client is considered "cured" or significantly improved when the superego is done punishing the ego for its apparent weakness, defects, and failures in obtaining narcissistic supplies (Fenichel, 1945; Jacobson, 1971).

Existential Counseling

Existential counseling of depressed clients centers on the "existential encounter" or the counseling relationship. The encounter is characterized by an attitude of

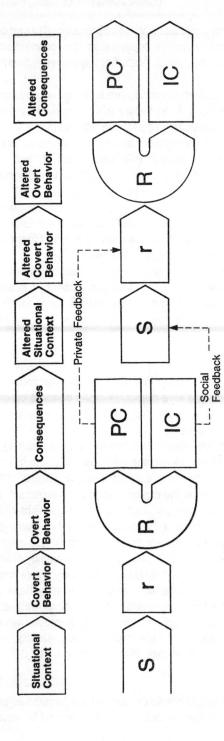

Figure 4–4 Private and Social Feedback as Modifiers of the Situation Context and Covert Behavior

openness on the part of the counselor (Van Kaam, 1970). The purpose of the encounter is to explore how the depressed person finds self and world and how one meets one's existential responsibilities (Van Kaam, 1962). The existential counselor does not have specific goals in mind at the start of counseling; indeed, the counseling outcomes desirable for a client are not known until counseling is well underway. The existential counselor does not have a set of techniques for behavior modification, or, at least, does not profess to have such techniques.

The focus of counseling is on discovering meanings that the client assigns to life (Frankl, 1963), not to locate and attend to causative factors for the depression. Clarifying statements and interpretations may be used as a way of helping clients consider meanings they have assigned to their existence. The literature on existential counseling often seems to be vague, highly philosophical, and not related to techniques, which many practitioners find esoteric (Beck, 1971).

Cognitive Counseling

The cognitive counselor helps clients identify their maladaptive ideations and automatic thinking tendencies (Beck, 1976; Ellis, 1962). Self-observation techniques are used to assist the client to identify events that are antecedent to feeling depressed, the characteristics of the depressions, and the ways in which depressions are stopped (Tharp, Watson, and Kaya, 1974). Clients are taught to observe their maladaptive thoughts objectively through repeated observation. Beck (1976) termed this technique "distancing." Clients also are taught to establish the validity of their thoughts and conclusions by checking them against reality. Clients learn to change the rules for labeling, interpreting, and evaluating self and world—a method similar to Ellis's (1962) notion of changing irrational thoughts of clients. Beck's approach to counseling depressives is a structured, problem-oriented system designed to challenge and change the client's cognitive schema. His system is fully explained in *Cognitive Therapy and the Emotional Disorders* (Beck, 1976).

Beck targets his interventions at any level and combination of components that he believes underlie depression. He seeks to interrupt the negative thinking chain with the introduction of success, positive experience, and more positive expectations. Specific techniques used may include: (1) scheduling activities to get the client increasingly active, less passive; (2) success therapy which involves assigning simple tasks that the client can successfully complete; (3) mastery and pleasure therapy in which the client keeps a record of activities mastered and activities that provided pleasure; (4) cognitive reappraisal requiring identification of the sequence (chain) between motivation and cognitions, exploration evaluation and changing depressive cognitions. These techniques are used on the target of modification such as avoidance tendencies, suicide wishes, feelings of hopelessness, self-hate, painful affect, and the tendency to exaggerate. Beck maintains that a rationally designed program of intervention activities improves self-concept, diverts the depressive from excessive self-preoccupation, and influences others to respond more positively to the client.

Sequential Model of Behavior Counseling

The Sequential Model of Behavior (SMB) offers a conceptualization of depression based on the interaction between four classes of variables having relevance to the initiation, maintenance, and modification of client behavior. The application of the SMB is contingent on counselor ability to collect accurate and relevant data about the four classes of variables: S, r, R, PC/IC.

Depressed clients usually seek counseling assistance because their feelings (r), actions (R), self-evaluations (PC), and their interpersonal feedback (IC) are disturbing. Initially a depressed client is likely to complain about depressed feelings; however, it soon becomes apparent that problems and concerns also exist in the other classes of variables in the SMB model.

The first counseling step in applying the SMB is to conduct a diagnostic inquiry. The inquiry must be sufficiently complete to provide a data base for defining the primary characteristics of the four SMB classes of variables. The inquiry rests on the self-disclosures of the client. To promote self-disclosure in a depressed person is difficult because the counselor is asking permission to know the client. As Jourard (1971) wrote, self-disclosure "is the act of making yourself manifest, showing yourself so others can perceive you (p. 19)." To self-disclose is to risk rejection, the depressive fear that the person already feels victimized by in life. Both participants in the counseling relationship are directly and immediately confronted with a dilemma in the relationship demanding attention.

The counseling inquiry for determining the nature of the SMB variables may be examined from two concurrent processes, the dynamic of self-disclosure, which provides data, and the content of the inquiry itself, which determines what data are sought from the client.

Promoting Self-Disclosure   Self-disclosure about the client's S, r, R, PC/IC variables depends on the depressed client's willingness and ability to verbalize and the counselor's skill in encouraging and guiding disclosure. A basic part of the dynamic of disclosure is the client's ambivalence toward it, i.e., the wish to disclose in order to get help and the fear of disclosing because of the risk of rejection by the counselor. For counseling to occur, the client *must* disclose.

Verbal structuring and restructuring regarding the task of disclosure is a requirement for counseling depressed clients. Counselors should plan to have their trustworthiness challenged by depressed clients. Counselors need to remain cognizant of the secondary gains that depressives obtain from the gravity of the symptoms and avoid getting trapped into providing these gains for the client.

Content of the SMB Inquiry   The SMB conceptualizes client behavior in terms of antecedents, consequences, and mediational sequences. The notion that a change in one part of a behavioral sequence will lead to change in other parts needs to be repeatedly explained to clients so that the relevance of careful inquiry is established.

The parameters of behavior and events need to be established systematically during the inquiry. Direct, well paced, and clear questions or leads stimulate the client to define the parameters for the SMB classifications:

Situation Context (S) Parameters. What brings S about? What ends S? How frequent is S? What is the relevant history of S? How long does S last? The inquiry needs to establish these if the client has experienced actual loss, rejection, failure, and a loss of control over positively reinforcing environmental events.

Covert Behavior (r) Parameters. For attending, thinking, feeling, and sensing behaviors, the central parameters to be established are the initiation, frequency, duration, intensity, history, and termination of each behavior of interest. The inquiry needs to establish the characteristics of:

a. Client-attending behavior: Depressed clients are "poor" attenders in that they miss cues present in S, r, R, PC/IC. As depression deepens, perceptions become more narrow, rigid, and defensive with a corresponding increase in the number of perceptual errors. There is often a special sensitivity to events which are perceived as confirming the basis of the depression.

b. Client-thinking behavior: The client's thoughts, interpretations, assumptions, aspirations, and predictions will be negativistic, pessimistic, and rigid. Thinking styles may be well practiced and longstanding. Cognitive themes will center around low self-esteem, pessimism, and the notion that others do not care for the client. Spinning off from these themes will be others that are negativistic, self-defeating, reality-distorting, presumptive, and demanding.

c. Client-feeling behavior: The client can be expected to experience feelings of not being loved, sadness, guilt, helplessness, detachment, and rejection. Mislabeling of feelings is common; depressives may call their anger "depression," which, if unnoticed, could lead to inappropriate treatment.

d. Client sensations: The client may experience a number of unusual (for them) sensations, such as aches, pains, "floating," and fatigue. Counselors may want medical consultation on these somatic complaints.

Overt Behavior (R) Parameters. What initiates and stops R? What is the frequency, duration, intensity, and situational context of R? What is the history of R? The depressed client may appear to be generally "slowed down" in overt behaviors. Their appearance will suggest great fatigue, a down-trodden, slumped, and haggared posture. Their speech may be slow and punctuated with sighs, tears, and "blank" interruptions. Eye contact will be minimal. Crying and deep sobbing are not unusual.

Consequences (PC/IC) Parameters. Define the initiation, frequency, duration, intensity, history, and termination of both private consequences (PC) and interpersonal consequences (IC) of R. Self-evaluations are critical consequences of client actions, but can be known by the counselor only inferentially. Interpersonal consequences can be described more objectively by the client, and the counselor can observe his or her reactions (IC) to the client. Most counselors do not have the opportunity to observe directly the IC in the client's situational context, and thus know about the social feedback the client experiences only from client reports. It is necessary to establish the sequence of events and behaviors that make up the client's depressive experience. "What leads to what?" is the primary question for establishing the sequence of behavior. Counselors must often instruct clients in careful self-observation so clients can report data on both the parameters and the sequence of depressions. The SMB assumes that covert mediating behavior can be sufficiently identified and understood through inference. The counseling inquiry permits counselors to sketch in the features of the SMB for the client. Openness to contradictory data serves as a safeguard against errors in inference. Clients are experts on their own internal experiences and serve as a criterion against which counselors can check their inferences. A useful practice is to ask clients directly to confirm or deny that a counselor inferred process is "going on" inside them.

Conceptualizing Depression in SMB Terms   Inquiry data and counselor inferences lead to a conceptualization of depression in SMB terms. The counselor establishes, with increasing certainty, the $S \rightarrow r \rightarrow R \rightarrow PC/IC$ depression sequence. If the inquiry was effective and the inferences were valid, the counselor can answer the question: How does this client's depression operate? The SMB for depressives is suggested in Figure 4–5.

Behavior Change in SMB Terms   In planning behavior change with their clients, counselors target one or more of the depressive components in SMB. The specific changes possible for a particular client vary with the unique behavior sequence S, r, R, and PC/IC operating. The amount of time and energy the client is willing to spend on the change process also is important.

Actual changes in the client's situational context may not be possible; if such changes are possible, the counselor and client define them and develop methods of obtaining them. For example, clients may learn to avoid, escape, or reduce the destructive situational context, thereby providing situational "relief" from the depression. Clients can also learn new ways of interacting with the people and events in S in order to increase the probability of social rewards.

Improved attending behavior changes can be instigated by direct counselor suggestion and instruction. Helping clients learn to discriminate between events rather than categorically responding to them is most useful to the depressed clients. New attending behaviors can first be learned by clients in the counseling interview, practiced in role playing, and then tried out as counseling homework in their situational contexts.

Changing thought patterns and sets is the *most* important part of the change process from the author's point of view. It is also the most difficult. Clients believe that they think about things correctly and to suggest that they might do so incorrectly or inappropriately is a most delicate matter to undertake. Obviously, the counselor must establish some minimal level of credibility before proceeding very far with assisting clients to learn new ways of thinking. It is useful, as a

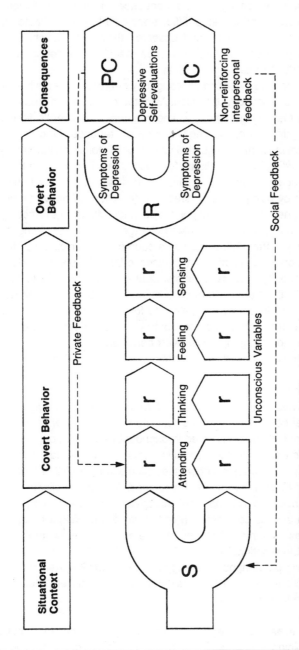

Figure 4–5 The SMB for the Depressed Client

73

preliminary step, to teach clients the sequence of their depression-eliciting thoughts. Depressives find this step difficult because they think "automatically," and it is hard for them to "stop and observe" their own thought sequences. However, this step is necessary for alternative thoughts (nondepression-eliciting ones) to be introduced later in counseling.

Feeling changes are most eagerly sought by depressed clients because they want relief from the misery of depression. As noted earlier, prescribed antidepressant medication may bring immediate improvement in a client's feeling state, thereby providing time for counseling without the interruption of distressing feelings. Improvement in client feelings also usually occur following catharsis and the initiation of counseling because clients feel less alone. Encouraging the client to marshal psychological strength and initiative to delay, reduce, or terminate unpleasant feelings by using behavior already in the client's behavior repertoire is often immediately helpful. The major point to be made with clients is that significant feeling changes *will follow from* thinking changes. Sensation changes for the depressed client will often follow the same course as modification of feelings.

Overt behaviors, once identified and assessed, can be placed under immediate cognitive control by depressed clients. Counselor suggestions to "stop that" or to do a specific thing are quite often obeyed. Overt behaviors can usually be thought of which would be more appropriate for the client than the actions engaged in before counseling. Of course, some withdrawn depressed clients need to be encouraged to engage in *more* overt behavior.

Changes in the consequences of client overt behavior will occur when modifications take place in the overt behavior. It is also the case that changes in the private consequences can occur independently of overt behavior change, i.e., clients learn to evaluate their own actions differently without altering the actions.

Interpersonal consequences constitute the main source of social feedback and reinforcement for clients. As noted throughout this chapter, depressed clients consistently distort IC to fit their cognitive sets and ambivalent feelings. The counselor can expect to learn that depressed clients routinely fail to check out their understanding of IC with the intended meanings. Depressed clients tend to assume that IC is negative. An important therapeutic phase is to engage the depressed client in serious consideration of the value and weight assigned to IC; invariably, depressed clients are not only misinterpreting the IC but are also assigning IC considerable emotional weight.

The preceding paragraphs have suggested how SMB systematically guides counselor and client attention to consideration of the current status and the changes possible in S, r, R, PC/IC.

Therapeutic Contrast   The major dynamic underlying change in client behavior in the author's opinion is therapeutic contrast. The concept of therapeutic contrast has been influenced by F. J. Shaw's (1966) work on a theory of reconciliation. Beck's (1976) cognitive therapy strategies involving challenging the cognitive assumptions of depressives and "alternative therapy" are similar to the notion of therapeutic contrast. The writer has also been attracted by Raimy's (1975) "misconception hypothesis," which he defined as follows: "If those ideas or conceptions of a client or patient which are relevant to his psychological problems can be changed in the direction of greater accuracy where his reality is concerned, his maladjustments are likely to be eliminated (p. 7)." Other writers who have influenced the notion of change as a consequence of therapeutic contrast have been Ellis (1962) and Haley (1963).

The basic process of counseling based on therapeutic contrast is relatively simple and straightforward. However, it is difficult to do in practice. The counselor's job after defining depressive sequences of behavior is to present contrast, a "different view," to the specifics of the client's behavior sequence. The presentation of contrast places the client in the *benevolent ordeal* described by Haley (1963) as follows: "All forms of psychotherapy are designed to help the unfortunates who cannot help themselves, and so the basic framework of psychotherapy is benevolence. Within that framework, the patient is placed through a punishing ordeal . . . In general, he must expose all sensitive areas of his life to a man who does not return the confidences, just as he must talk about all of his inadequacies to a man who apparently has none (p. 187)."

The counselor presents to the client a contrasting way of thinking, an alternative way of interpreting, a challenge to an automatically accepted assumption. Therapeutic contrasts are controlled by the counselor so that they are not too divergent from the client's views and thus rejected out of hand. The counselor attempts to present contrasts that are emotionally "manageable" for the client. Therapeutic contrasts are applied to those client thoughts that are inferred to underlie the depression. The contrasts are offered persistently for the specific purpose of persuading clients to alter depression-eliciting thoughts. The counselor wants to create "therapeutic doubt" about the validity of the client's thinking, assumptions, interpretations, and predictions.

As the process of change continues, the client will need to reconcile the depression-eliciting styles of thinking with the new, contrasting, nondepressing ways of thinking offered by the counselor. As the client works into the reconciliation process, the core of therapeutic change occurs. If clients persist in the reconciliation process, they begin to experience modifications in the depression. At this critical point, clients are learning that overcoming depression is possible—a sharp contrast to the original fear that there would be no end to the depression. The client begins to experience effective self-reinforcements, i.e., reduction of depression.

The treatment of the feeling states of the depressed client demands counselor patience and creativity. Feelings are automatic consequences of thoughts and to change feelings it is necessary that thoughts be altered. It is rarely productive to offer contrast to the *feelings* of the client. A depressed client feels miserable and there is nothing to be gained by a counselor suggesting that the client doesn't or ought not to feel that way. Feelings are changed by changing their antecedents and consequences, which takes time.

Counselors are more accurately attuned to the processes of interpersonal persuasion operative in counseling and psychotherapy today than even a decade ago (Frank, 1973). The counselor can often use the power of verbal and nonverbal reinforcements in the interview in helping the client first consider, then integrate the contrasts provided by counseling.

Questions for Further Inquiry

1. Think of a time when you were feeling depressed. What personal beliefs were contributing to your mood? On hindsight, can you identify some that were irrational?

2. How are family members affected by the depression experiences of one person in the family? What feelings occur and what tangible consequences result?

3. What linkages do you see between a person's views about the future and the experience of depression?

4. Describe how depression produces self-fulfilling prophesies. Think of an example of someone whom you see caught in such an exacerbation cycle.

5. How helpful is support as a counseling technique for depressed clients?

References

American Psychiatric Association. *Diagnostic and statistical manual of mental disorders, (2nd ed.)* Washington, D.C.: APA, 1968.

Atwood, G. Note on a relationship between suicidal intentions and the depressive mood. *Psychotherapy: Theory, Research and Practice* 1972 *9*, 284–85.

Bandura, A. Psychotherapy as a learning process. *Psychological Bulletin* 1961 *58*, 143–59.

Beck, A. T. *Depression: Causes and treatment.* Philadelphia: University of Pennsylvania Press, 1967.

Beck, A. T. *Cognitive therapy and the emotional disorders.* New York: International Universities Press, 1976.

Beck, C. E. Existential counseling: Some observations. *The Counseling Psychologist* 1971 *2*, 48–50.

Becker, J. *Affective disorders.* Morristown, N.J.: General Learning Press, 1977.

Combs, A. W., & Snygg, D. *Individual behavior.* New York: Harper & Row, 1959.

Costello, C. G., & Belton, G. P. Depression: Treatment. In C. G. Costello (Ed.), *Symptoms of psychopathology.* New York: Wiley, 1970, pp. 201–15.

Dollard, J., & Miller, N. E. *Personality and psychotherapy.* New York: McGraw-Hill, 1950.

Ellis, A. *Reason and emotion in psychotherapy.* New York: Lyle Stuart, 1962.

Fenichel, O. *The psychoanalytic theory of neurosis.* New York: Norton, 1945.

Ferster, C. B. A functional analysis of depression. *American Psychologist* 1973 *28*, 857-70.

Ford, D. H., & Urban, H. B. *Systems of psychotherapy.* New York: Wiley, 1963.

Frank, J. D. *Persuasion and healing.* (Rev. ed.) Baltimore: Johns Hopkins, 1973.

Frankl, V. E. *Man's search for meaning.* New York: Washington Square Press, 1963.

Frankl, V. E. *Psychotherapy and existentialism.* New York: Washington Square Press, 1967.

Gross, R. B. Supportive therapy for the depressed college student. *Psychotherapy: Theory, Research and Practice* 1968 *5*, 262-67.

Haley, J. *Strategies of psychotherapy.* New York: Grune & Stratton, 1963.

Jacobson, E. *Depression: Comparative studies of normal, neurotic, and psychotic conditions.* New York: International Universities Press, 1971.

Jourard, S. M. *The transparent self.* (Rev. ed.) New York: Van Nostrand-Reinhold Co., 1971.

Kelly, G. *The psychology of personal constructs.* New York: Norton, 1955.

Kemp, C. G. Existential counseling. *The Counseling Psychologist* 1971 *2*, 2-30.

Krumboltz, J. D. (Ed.) *Revolution in counseling.* Boston: Houghton Mifflin, 1966.

Laughlin, H. P. *The neurosis.* Washington: Butterworths, 1967.

Lewinsohn, P. M., & Atwood, G. E. Depression: A clinical-research approach. *Psychotherapy: Theory, Research and Practice* 1969 *6*, 166-71.

Lewinsohn, P. M., & Graf, M. Pleasant activities and depression. *Journal of Consulting and Clinical Psychology* 1973 *41*, 261-68.

Lewinsohn, P. M., & Shaffer, M. Use of home observations as an integral part of the treatment of depression: Preliminary report and case studies. *Journal of Consulting and Clinical Psychology* 1971 *37*, 87-94.

London, P. *The modes and morals of psychotherapy.* New York: Holt, Rinehart, 1964.

London, P. *Behavior control.* New York: Harper & Row, 1969.

London, P. The end of ideology in behavior modification. *American Psychologist,* 1972 *27*, 913-20.

MacKinnon, R. A., & Michels, R. *The psychiatric interview in clinical practice.* Philadelphia: Saunders, 1971.

Mendels, J. *Concepts of depression.* New York: Wiley, 1970.

Murray, D. C. The suicide threat: Base rates and appropriate therapeutic strategy. *Psychotherapy: Theory, Research and Practice* 1972 *9*, 176-79.

Raimy, V. *Misunderstandings of the self.* San Francisco: Jossey-Bass, 1975.

Robertiello, R. C. The role of infantile omnipotence in the dynamics of depression. *Psychotherapy: Theory, Research and Practice* 1969 *6*, 37-38.

Schneidman, E. S., & Farberow, N. L. (Eds.) *Clues to suicide.* New York: Blakiston, 1957.

Seligman, M. E. P. Fall into helplessness. *Psychology Today* June 1973, 43-48.

Seligman, M. E. P. *Helplessness.* San Francisco: Freeman, 1975.

Shaw, F. J. Collected writings. In S. M. Jourard & D. C. Overlade (Eds.), *Reconciliation: A theory of man transcending.* Princeton: Van Nostrand, 1966.

Sheslow, D. V., & Erickson, M. T. Analysis of activity preference in depressed and nondepressed college students. *Journal of Counseling Psychology* 1975 *22,* 329–32.

Stern, J. A., McClure, J. N., Jr., & Costello, C. G. Depression: Assessment and aetiology. In C. G. Costello (Ed.), *Symptoms of psychopathology.* New York: Wiley, 1970. 169–200.

Tharp, R. G., Watson, D., & Kaya, J. Self-modification of depression. *Journal of Consulting and Clinical Psychology* 1974 *42,* 624.

Trembley, E. L. A sequential model for viewing behavior and guidelines for counseling practice. In R. J. Malnati & E. L. Trembley (Eds.), *Group procedures for counselors in educational and community settings: Original and selected readings.* New York: MSS Information Corp., 1974.

Van Kaam, A. Counseling from the viewpoint of existential psychology. *Harvard Educational Review* 1962 *32,* 403–15.

Van Kaam, A. The goals of psychotherapy. In A. R. Mahrer (Ed.), *The goals of psychotherapy.* New York: Appleton-Century-Crofts, 1970. 145–61.

Weiss, S. A. Therapeutic strategy to obviate suicide. *Psychotherapy: Theory, Research and Practice* 1969 *6,* 39–42.

Understanding and Controlling Anger   5

JAMES M. SCHUERGER

Overview

More than two thousand years ago Aristotle remarked that anger is more natural to humans than is concupiscence (*Ethics*, VI). Recently, a clinical psychologist, writing in the context of a general personality test, remarked on the ubiquity of anger in human affairs (Karson and O'Dell, 1976). The common presence of anger in human life is not mysterious. Rather, each person has a need to assert his or her presence in the world—indeed, to do it willy-nilly, as do all creatures. Humans have over beasts the inner experience of choosing, the willingness to do this and to take part in that—human beings know their own assertiveness. When this assertiveness is blocked, frustrated, the inner experience of control changes and the person feels anger.

The purpose of this chapter is to place anger in the perspective briefly described above and to provide descriptions, analyses, and practical techniques for helping persons in whose lives anger is dysfunctional. Accordingly, the first part of the chapter, Toward an Understanding of Anger, begins with descriptions of the anger experience, then presents analyses of the components and functions of anger, and closes with some theoretical viewpoints on anger. The second section, Approaches for Helping People Control Anger, is an attempt to organize helpful techniques according to (1) the way anger is presented as a problem and (2) the nature of the anger. Among techniques considered are awareness, catharsis, analysis, attitude change therapy, action planning. The chapter closes with a few cautions for working with persons who experience extreme forms of anger.

Toward an Understanding of Anger

Anger as a Problem
The problem of anger usually comes to the therapist's attention in one of three ways. Either it is presented by the client as an important problem, or it is noticed by the therapist during the session, or the therapist infers its presence and importance in the client's life outside the session from something the client says or does during the session. When the client first identifies the anger as a problem, it is usually because (1) it causes trouble at home or at work, (2) the client feels uncomfortable with the anger (e.g., immoral, bad, frustrated), or (3) the anger is frightening.

When the therapist points out anger as a problem, it is often because the therapist sees the anger as a block to the solution of the client's original problem. For example, consider a first interview in which the client is slouched down in the chair, is listless and restless, mumbles, and speaks about all the problems he is having concentrating on his studies. As he talks more about his problem and what surrounds it, he speaks more and more about his wife and how he sees her as part of the study problem. His voice becomes louder, there are innuendos in his choice of words which indicate how wrongly he has been treated. Somewhere in the conversation the counselor says, "Are you mad?" Anger, while not the presenting problem, has now come center stage. In a similar way, anger is often a component of problems which clients present as depression, difficulty with parents, study problems, or problems of death and aging.

Whatever action the therapist takes with the client will be influenced by the manner in which anger becomes a part of the session. If the client mentions anger as a problem, the counselor has implicit permission to begin working with whatever techniques are available. If the client is angry during the session, the counselor does not have the same permission, but must choose whether or not to avert to the anger, to suggest it as a topic for consideration. If the client is not angry during the session but presents some clues that anger has been important in the past, the counselor must decide whether or not to follow that lead or wait for more information. In any event, it is frequently important for the counselor to be able to recognize signs of anger and to identify the nature of the anger. The next section is a kind of "taxonomy of angers" to provide some help to counselors in recognizing these signs.

The Experience of Anger
The kinds of anger presented in this section are grouped under three headings: anger not usually seen in counseling sessions; anger often seen in sessions; miscellaneous emotional states which are related to anger. The purpose of this

section is to provide a description of the angers, to help counselors identify and name what they see and hear, and to help clients become aware of what they are experiencing. Accordingly, for each of the angers that is named, this section will describe some of the feelings that clients have, ideas that frequently accompany the feelings, and how the clients look and sound while they are experiencing these feelings and ideas.

The names and descriptions of kinds of anger are not exhaustive—other names and categories are available. Categorizations of anger by other writers (see for example, Ellis and Casriel, 1971) tend to follow a particular system of thought, however, while the list of angers given below is mainly descriptive. The purpose is to provide descriptive detail about a kind of anger, then to give that phenomenon a name which conforms with accepted American usage and is not encumbered with useless connotations.

Angers not Usually Evident in Counseling   The first kind of anger rarely seen in counseling sessions is "the flash of anger," that first surge of feeling one experiences upon receiving an offense or a sharp bodily pain as from a punch in the nose or a bump on the edge of eyeglasses. The physical sensation (internal cue) is of something hot rising up from the belly into the chest and arms, into the neck and face. One often draws air into the lungs sharply, stiffens muscles, sometimes cries quickly. Often a quick shout accompanies the feeling if the source is a physical blow or pain. The sensation in the long muscles of arms and legs is of tensing. Sometimes the angered person turns to the source of irritation with widened eyes, tightened mouth, and clenched teeth. Ideation is rarely explicit, but there is a clear sense of perceiving attack and readying for action. If, following the first flash of anger as described, one verifies that some offense has been received, he or she experiences an increase of the sensations, begins to develop ways to express the anger very quickly, and either releases it by shouting or fighting, or turns away feeling very tense.

Two other forms of anger rarely seen in counseling sessions are rage and fury. Rage and fury are special forms of anger characterized by violence of emotion and sometimes of action. They resemble the flash of anger to the person experiencing them, but continue and grow. They include the feeling of heat and of something rising from the belly up through the chest. If expressed, the feelings usually are accompanied by violent action and loud shouting, and frequently leave the enraged person feeling calm and cleansed, unless the anger has been quite inappropriate. Persons who have vigorously expressed what they feel to be justified anger often report this cleansing effect, as though some terrible thing has been expelled from them. One sometimes speaks of jealous rage, the experience of wanting to smash and kill the person who has taken or defiled the mate, or the rage of the father whose daughter has been raped. Persons who have experienced the loss of a loved one, particularly an untimely death, often speak of the rage they feel, the desire to destroy wantonly. The connection of anger with death will be discussed later in the chapter, along with some of the inner dynamics of anger. Rage and fury, at any rate, are both characterized by the violence of the feelings of the person experiencing them.

It is possible to distinguish between the two by two characteristics. Fury always has in it some avenging of a real disorder, while rage has the quality of avenging a personal affront. Rage always has in it a bit of petulance and grandiosity: "How dare you do that to me!" Another difference is that fury is the passion of the powerful. We speak of frustrated rage, the terrible anger of the person who has been grossly offended and can't do anything about it, but we don't speak of frustrated fury. Fury is truly avenging.

Some persons with whom such violent angers are common also experience terror, extreme fear that they will destroy themselves or someone else in a fit of rage. They have often had intimate experiences with violence. A familiar instance is that of parents who abuse their children; frequently they have suffered physical abuse from their own parents. These persons experience themselves as destroyers, and describe the feeling of being taken over by the rage, as though by a flash flood. They fear getting angry because of what they will do, even though they may be persons who are not ordinarily characterized by feelings of impulsivity.

Angers Often Seen in Counseling   Among forms of anger which often show up in the counseling session are *resentment* and *petulance.* Resentment, unlike the flash of anger, takes place in slow motion. It doesn't usually arise in context of physical pain, nor does it have the obvious physical concomitants that the flash of anger does. In fact, the person experiencing resentment often does not notice any particular physical cues, and, if asked to describe what he or she is feeling, will talk about affronts, insults, injustices rather than feelings. On the other hand, such persons, when taught to be aware of their bodily cues, will speak of generalized tension, tension in the lower back or chest, a tight feeling in the belly. The internal feeling accompanying (or characterizing) resentment is sometimes also described as a slow burning feeling in the chest, up the back of the neck, and behind the eyes. The head is not often erect as in the flash of anger, but usually inclined forward, almost submissively. There is a beaten quality about the person described as resentful, who often appears lethargic as well as tense. The tension is easiest to notice in the face, which frequently appears drawn and thinner than usual. The ideation of persons described as resentful, as distinguished from their feelings, often concentrates on affronts or on the deprivations they have suffered at the hands of others. The tone of these insults or deprivations is often subtle and indirect. Among married couples, resentment often accompanies not a direct refusal of sexual relations, but an indirect turndown or some sign of lack of interest.

A second form of anger one often sees in counseling sessions is a petulance or "hurt." Petulance and hurt are paired because they both have a resemblance to reactions one sometimes sees in a child who has been told he or she cannot have a treat. One gets a sense of peevishness, of the child feeling punished for no good reason, of the child feeling angry and wanting affection all the same. To the observer, petulant people appear to be angry and resentful, but also wanting comfort, and body postures seem to ask for touching and holding. The person seems to shrink and retire, and sometimes speaks of wanting to withdraw or hide. If they make fists, persons who are petulant make them so that they turn inward toward their own bodies, their arms and wrists both bent so that the arms are not extended so as to fight, but as though to tighten up their already tiny selves. If they cry, the crying is not full and expressive but cramped and in short gasps. Their facial muscles are contorted sometimes, but not tensed around the mouth and eyes as in resentment; the lower lip is sometimes extended a bit. Persons experiencing this kind of anger will hardly ever describe their feelings, at least not until after the most is over. Then they will speak of feeling small, or ashamed, or wanting to hide, be covered by something. Predominant muscle tension seems to be in the back of the neck and in the forearms. Ideation seems to follow the line of "I try to be good and look how they treat me," or "Who'd want to be nice to me when I'm such a grump."

Grouchiness and Hostility   The third group of anger experiences, or emotional states often miscategorized as anger, include grouchiness and hostility. Grouchiness (irritability), while not clearly related to some provocation as other forms of anger, is most commonly seen in connection with physical discomfort, extreme tiredness, or recent wakening from sleep, and will often show in posture that is slumped, a shuffling walk, or perhaps redness about the eyes. It seems to be a defense against irritations and encroachments by people, in the sense that a person with a hangover will be grouchy, and the grouchiness serves to remind others that loud noises are painful.

Some people seem to be angry, or ready for anger, a great deal of the time, and such persons are sometimes called hostile. Since the popularity of dynamic psychology, this word is usually used to imply that the person is generally angry with the world but tries to veil the anger so that it shows in indirect attacks on those around. That is, the anger is not what one might call an honest grouchiness but has a threatening, malicious, hidden quality to it. This connotation of the word "hostile" is much overemphasized in common usage, but has a basis in the seeming randomness of the hostile person's attacks. Persons whom we call "hostile" seem to be perenially quarreling with the world without reason. They do not often exhibit the muscular tension observed in other forms of anger, nor do they speak of any of the more explicit internal cues of anger. To the observer, they seem to do quite a few things that get in the way, reduce the enthusiasm of those around them, cause great inconvenience or irritation to others. If they are talented, they sometimes poke fun at others in clever ways. In short, the usual emotional responsiveness and the physical cues to the presence of anger are not often seen, but the "hostile" person does quite a few things that seem to come from anger or "hostility."

Irritability or grouchiness may seem to be the names for the same state as "hostility" in that the person displaying "grouchiness" seems ready for a fight without any immediate provocation, just as the "hostile" person always seems to be attacking those around him or her without any immediate reason to do so. The principal difference between the two, as used here, is that hostility bespeaks a kind of masked anger, while grouchiness is evident to everybody. A hostile person often seems to be picking a fight and not admitting it, while a grouchy person will often admit his or her grouchiness, or even advertise it: "Stay away, I'm in a bad mood." A second difference between the two is that grouchiness is temporary, while hostility is usually thought of as a long-lived characteristic.

So far this section has considered anger, first as it comes to the attention of the helping professional who is hearing the client's problem, and second, as it looks, sounds, and feels to the client and observer alike. The next section moves from the purely experiential description of anger to a more functional description, to include not only what anger looks and feels like, but how it functions in human life, and what its chief components are.

The Components of Anger

The anger of a mother bear defending her cubs is legendary, and so with most of the mammals. Robert Ardrey in *The Territorial Imperative* (1966) makes a case for the power that mammals seem to get from the ownership of territory. The dog that is cowardly in the middle of the block is undisputed master in his own yard, snarling angrily and repelling intruders often by bravado, without blood. This defensive posture, sometimes called "anger" even in beasts, is in contrast to the hunting activities of a cat, wolf, or bear. None of the snarling, hair-raising, teeth-baring dramatics are seen, only well-designed, calculated efficiency. One doesn't usually speak of a hunting animal as angry.

The analogy to beasts here makes a point about much of human anger. That is, anger in itself is not well-designed to produce some gain, it is not a food-gathering or hunting procedure. It is usually a *defense*. This defensive quality of anger is apparent when a mother becomes angry and repels an intruder twice her size if he threatens her children, or when a betrayed husband shoots his rival, or when one man beats off a gang that threatens him. The anger seems obvious, justified, and powerful.

Thus, anger, as illustrated, is *defensive* and *righteous*. The other main component of anger is that it frequently accompanies the *frustration* of some desire or expectation, as in the reaction of an infant deprived of its bottle. In the rest of this section, four examples will be examined which illustrate the presence of these three components in human anger.

Example One   A father comes home from work tired at the end of the working day, and before supper his oldest son asks for help fixing a bike. The father feels a bit irritated. The small of his back tightens a little, he thinks that he would rather lie down. Nevertheless, he decides to help and goes to the basement for his tools where he sees (1) that the younger children have spilled the kitty litter around the basement, and (2) that his favorite pliers are missing. He starts shouting. He feels the heat in his chest, across his arms, the need for immediate retribution. He takes in breath, his eyes widen, he shouts some more, accusing, berating, threatening: "Where are my pliers? Who had them last? Don't you kids care what happens to my stuff? You're just a bunch of barbarians who have no consideration for anyone else! You'll see what happens when you ask me to help you again!"

The illustration shows the three main components that characterize most of human anger: (1) It is always a defense of something; (2) it occurs when one is not getting something one wants or would like (frustration); and (3) it always (after the first flash of anger) has in it the sense of righteousness—personal rights have been violated. The beginning of the example above clearly shows the *frustrated* expectation of rest and quiet. The kitty litter added to the frustration, since the tired father was going to miss more rest, either cleaning up the litter himself or getting the kids to do it. He was *defending* his ownership of the pliers, and his want to feel secure in possession of them and other tools. A skilled therapist would have questioned this client more about the pliers, since they seemed connected with more anger than they were worth, and would probably have uncovered a large amount of ego-extension in them. The third component, *violation of rights*, has to do with the father's sense of ownership of his tools and his belief that children do not have the right to make requests of tired fathers.

Example Two   Clients frequently bring problems which illustrate these three components of anger. One client, after some prior sessions in which the identified problem was career growth, began to talk about how angry he became when confronted by women who were not "sweet". He described an instance at work in which he became extremely angry at a woman who insinuated that he had not properly trained a subordinate. She was secretary to his boss, and had no real authority over him except through her boss, and he did not believe that she could or would do anything to jeopardize his job. So why all the anger? He was very busy at the time, and was not feeling rewarded at work, either from his own sense of accomplishment, from possibilities of advancement, or from praise and pay increases. He was working hard to keep up with a heavy work load, but without enthusiasm. Describing his anger, he spoke about the feeling of being unable to do or say anything to make the secretary take back the insult, even though he did yell at her until she walked away.

The three components are present in his anger. He was frustrated by what he saw as lack of payoff for his hard work and by his own lack of enthusiasm for the job. He was also frustrated by his lack of ability to make a telling comeback when he felt insulted. He was defending what he called his "honor." More psychologically sophisticated clients might have said "self-esteem" or "ego." Part of the therapy was to help him see how his way of thinking about his honor contributed largely to his anger. The belief that another person could violate his honor led him to try to defend it. He was thinking of himself as a Prussian, or as an oriental nobleman. Why not think of himself as a medieval monk, whose honor could not be assailed from without, or as a citizen of the republic, whose honor lay in cooperation and brotherhood? The third component, that his rights were being violated, he inferred from his view of himself as a Prussian—"It is wrong for anyone to question my integrity."

The suggestion of guilt feelings in this client's reaction to criticism, and the narrowing of his anger reaction to situations involving women proved to be fruitful areas of investigation. Briefly, his anger functioned as a defense against pervasive feelings of guilt which he had learned early in life. Likewise, the sensitivity to women was traced to several early frustrations associated with women, particularly with women who criticized him while not fulfilling what he believed to be their duties toward him.

Example Three   As illustrated toward the end of the last example, anger can often be seen as a defense against what would be otherwise intolerable feelings of guilt. One client spoke of blowing up at his wife when he came home late one night after spending some time with another woman. She hadn't accused him of anything, didn't seem suspicious, and in fact was mildly affectionate, but she did seem in a bad mood and did some griping about the carpeting in the apartment, which had been torn by the dog. He became angry, shouted, and said he couldn't be responsible for all her troubles. He wished she'd stop bothering him with every detail. And so on. He was defending himself against his own feelings of guilt for having been with another woman. He felt righteous because, despite the fact that he preferred to spend time with the other woman, he did after all come home to her!

Example Four   Defense against one's own guilt was central to the previous example of anger. In this example, anger comes from frustration of an expected good. A shy client with whom the therapist had been working for several sessions on social skills appeared in the office in what has been previously called a petulant mood. He was slumped down in his chair, didn't look directly at the therapist, had a dark shadow around his eyes, jutted his lower lip out a bit, spoke in a low voice. When his appearance was pointed out to him, he spoke evasively, then finally started complaining about his wife, to whom he had been married several years. She had been "pushing him around" for years. Why didn't he "stand up to her like a man;" "she had no right" to pick on him the way she did. He'd "paid his dues" and was tired of her nastiness. As he spoke, he became more animated, pounded his fist on the arm of the chair. His voice became louder and louder, his eyes widened. When queried about what he wanted from her, he eventually changed the tenor of his remarks, leaving aside the statements about her violation of his dignity and said that he wanted her to be nice to him, affectionate, loving. Having said it, and having realized that he had no direct control over her giving those gifts, he first appeared less energetic, then regained some of the vigor he had displayed while he was making his anger and desire explicit. He began to plan some actions to satisfy his desires for affection and self-respect. In this person's anger, the component of defense was present in the way he was thinking of his self-respect. He wanted to repel his wife, whom he saw as the agent of his degradation. The sense of righteousness was present in his statements about paying his dues and that she had no right to pick on him. But the chief component was his longing for affection from her and his sense of deprivation and frustration when he did not get as much as he wanted.

So far, then, anger has been considered first from the point of view of the helper: what kind of a problem does the client have, and how does anger fit into it? Second, the experience of anger has been examined: how it looks, sounds, and feels. Third, in the section just above, three components that characterize anger were presented—defense, frustration, and violation of rights. The next section is descriptive of how anger functions in human interaction. What actually happens in the client's life that is different from what would happen without the anger? Put as a direct question to the client, this section is a response to the query, "What does your anger do *for you*?"

Functions of Anger

A useful summary of the chief functions of anger in human life is presented by Novaco (1975), who lists in slightly different words the following six: (1) it energizes; (2) it disrupts ongoing behavior by agitation, interference with attention and information processing, and by inducing impulsivity; (3) it facilitates expression of negative feelings to others; (4) it defends against vulnerability to ego threat by changing anxiety to external conflict; (5) it initiates or strengthens antagonism as an internal, learned stimulus for aggression; (6) it discriminates an event as a provocation.

An example of anger as an *energizer* was seen above in example four, in which the client, becoming alerted to his anger, became more energetic even in the counseling session, and began to move toward action and utilize this energy for productive actions. This client discovered, as he thought of his several years of marriage, that he had been using his anger toward his wife for a long time as an energizer for action outside the house. Anger becomes related to loss of energy when it is turned inward, as it was with this same client in the beginning of the interview cited. He had the frustrated feelings but did not want to own up to them because he was ashamed of what he considered childish desires for affection and comforting. His anger, with no place to go, turned inward and simmered uselessly. He felt powerless and childish. When he got some experience expressing his anger in the counseling session, after being alerted to it by the counselor, he also experienced his strength and energy.

Anger as *disrupter* of behavior is illustrated in example one, as the father's anger prevented him from acting in accord with his original intention. Instead of organizing the work that he wanted done, cleaning and finding the missing pliers, he found his attention captured by the injustice that had been done to him, and was unable to focus on the task at hand or receive new information about the whereabouts of the pliers.

In the same example anger can be seen as stimulating the *expression of negative feelings* to the children who did mess up the basement and take the pliers. In examples two (the Prussian) and three (home late), negative feelings were also expressed to relevant persons, but far beyond the strength of feeling appropriate to the provocation, and in some respects, especially example two, to the wrong person. The best example of the appropriate expression of feelings stimulated by anger takes place when the expression follows closely on the incident and is not accompanied by blame of the other person.

The anger in all four of the examples above might be construed as *defense* against anxiety from ego-threat; certainly they all were defensive reactions. In example four, the ego-threat was lack of self-esteem from inappropriate timidity; "As long as I let her push me around, how can I call myself a man?" In example three, it was anxiety associated with feelings of guilt, or fear of being discovered. It is unusual to find anger functioning as a defense of some external part of the client's life, like money, position, wife; more often the defense is of the way the client views himself, or of the client's sense of control over the circumstances of his own life.

The last two functions are less directly revealed in an analysis of anger, and come from viewing anger in the context of modern learning theory. In example one, the flash of anger is only an internal experience. Almost as though to justify his experience, the father began to think of how he had been wronged by the children; he began to experience more anger, and became verbally aggressive. He had learned to associate the thoughts (that he had been wronged) with that feeling (the first flash of anger) and the combination of the two, along with the fact that he was in a position of power, served as an internal stimulus to aggression. He might have reacted otherwise, if he had viewed the flash of anger as an internal cue (a warning, a sign) that something was going on that needed attention. This function of anger, as a sign of something wrong, has important therapeutic uses.

An important function of anger not included by Novaco is that it helps clients maintain their sense of being right, superior, justified. This function is similar to the ego-defense function mentioned above, and is like the general defensive function of anger. Like the ego-defense function of anger, it serves to help maintain the person's sense of self-esteem. It differs from the ego threat function largely in the explicit tone of righteousness which it helps impart to the person's feelings or actions. A man who is working hard at his job, and thereby missing time with his family while he pursues career goals, comes home from work very late, tired, and gets greeted by his wife with complaints about the house. He receives the tone of complaint as an attack on him and his goals. He feels a surge of anger. The anger becomes a sign to him that he is right in doing what he is doing! His anger helps him maintain his sense of virtue or righteousness.

Theories about Anger
So far the descriptions of anger have not led to inferences much removed from the experience. Anger is a problem, as experienced by the angry person and the observer. There are in addition many points of view about anger which do not originate in descriptive analyses of anger itself, but in the broader perspectives on

human life, such as religion, philosophy, systematic psychology. This section presents a few of these points of view with their implications for management of anger.

The first of these is what may be called "the pressure cooker." The basic point of view is that we have energies which must flow freely, and if their release is frustrated, an explosion will occur. The relevance to anger is easily seen: "If I have desires for something and the desires are frustrated, I become angry. Unless I express the anger or get what I desire, an explosion will occur." This is actually a very old point of view, but it is ordinarily associated with psychoanalysis (see for example, Freud's letter on war in Strachey's collection, Vol. XXII) and "modern" child-rearing practices. There are times in everyone's life when the metaphor of bottled energy seems to describe quite well how he feels.

A difficulty with this point of view is that it permits the client to disown responsibility for his or her anger and consequently may actually increase the client's anger or encourage the client to seek release by means that are not in his own or society's best interests. To be more accurate, it is the incomplete application of this point of view which encourages anger, since the more complete viewpoint includes alternate ways of releasing the energies which are frustrated.

A second point of view considers anger as the expulsion, casting out, of introjections. Introjections may be described as influences which persons have over each other with which they are not comfortable, attitudes which they do not hold as their own. Standard examples are the attitudes of conscience which one gets from his parents or church group, attitudes which are indicated in therapy sessions when the client speaks of what he "should" be doing or feeling. Viewed in this way, a lot of the anger one experiences against spouses, teachers, civil officials, etc., is seen as a titanic internal struggle to win freedom from the bondage of those early influences. It is as though the true self is saying "Get out, get out!" to parents, husbands, or whatever. This point of view is also associated with psychoanalysis, and with some of the recent offshoots of psychoanalysis, including Gestalt Therapy (Perls,1974). The metaphor of struggle to cast out introjections does help some clients understand their anger and relate it to feelings of guilt. However, like the previous viewpoint, it may also reinforce anger if clients begin to believe (1) that those other persons are really in them, and (2) that anger is the only means to get rid of introjections.

A third point of view is that anger is a wicked emotion which should be neither felt nor expressed. This point of view is usually identified with Christianity. It goes far beyond the ordinary requirements of society against overt violence—the inner person must not be angry. Some historians trace the attitude to the Gospel, in which Jesus, speaking of the Old Testament stricture against murder, says that murder in the heart, anger, is also sinful. One frequently sees young people who believe that feeling any anger is terrible, homes in which the expression of any anger is intolerable. Ironically, what was originally presented as a counsel of perfection is passed on to children as a way of life requiring instantaneous acquiescence. A large part of the result is denial of real feelings, and blocking of the solution (which, incidentally, appears in the same part of the Gospel), to work out anger with one's brother. Important implications of this point of view are (1) if one experiences anger he is wicked and (2) one must never express anger.

A fourth point of view, that of modern learning theorists, is that anger and expressions of anger are responses which are learned by imitation and reinforcement. There are masses of research evidence to support the influence of imitation on the frequency of aggressive actions (see, for example, Bandura, 1973). However, unlike the earlier points of view presented, this one seems not to capture the flavor of the anger experience. The powerful neutrality and objectivity of this point of view, which extends scientific procedures first used for nonhuman phenomena into the human arena, also underlies its weaknesses. Its metaphors (moral neutrality, objectivity) are not prone to increase or energize anger as the earlier viewpoints, but neither do they provide any human motive of their own. Many clients find this lack confusing and enervating, so that the therapist must be prepared to help them clarify their own guidelines and find their own motivation.

The final point of view sees anger as a human response to ultimate mortality, unfulfilled potential, and the meaninglessness of life. One is reminded of a scene from a recent TV movie, in which one of the central characters, in the closing moments, began smashing the windshields of parked cars in response to his own terminal illness and the death of someone dear to him. Persons who have had a death in their family often experience severe anger, rage, sometimes focused on persons or situations around them, sometimes unspecific, aimless rage. This point of view is associated with existentialist philosophy, which views man's existence as fundamentally anomalous, paradoxical, and fraught with anxiety. At a less general level, it is associated with powerlessness in human society (cf. May, 1972). Implications of this point of view are (1) such anger is inevitable, (2) it is uniquely human, and (3) it is central to all other angers.

Approaches for Helping People Control Anger

Anger in Perspective

Before proceeding directly to therapeutic techniques for helping with anger, it may be useful to return to the perspective presented in the overview to this chapter. Two observations on human existence serve as introduction: (1) any individual's life is characterized in part by frustration, meaninglessness, insecurity, unfulfilled potential, awe; (2) the lives of most persons follow a similar pattern from birth to death, and at some of these periods the dangers, frustrations, and unfulfilled potentials are at peak. Viewed in the light of these statements, anger is seen as an emotion which may be expected to occur in the life of every person with some regularity, and with greater frequency and intensity at some times than others. Writers such as Erikson (1950) and Sheehy (1976) have much to say about the usual course of human life which is instructive about these critical periods of anger.

This perspective makes sense of the competition and strife in human existence, but is in danger of missing the larger necessities of the species for cooperation and communication which anthropologists point out (see, for example, Becker, *The Birth and Death of Meaning*, 1971). Anger, then, must be seen as related to the polarity between the large needs of the species for cooperation and the single person's need to be individual. This polarity does not exist in the species as such, but in each individual person existing, working his way through the world that always seems to encroach. Anger is one of the internal concomitants of the assertiveness by which one is oneself.

The question of helping persons with anger is not, therefore, a question of eliminating anger. *The useful helping process includes identification of anger and its components, deciding what part of it, if any, is useful, and developing techniques for managing and quelling the useless parts.* Most of the energy involved in anger can be best used in other forms.

This developmental, anthropological perspective on anger encompasses aspects of the theories, junctions, and components considered earlier: the defensive nature of anger, its connection with frustration, the need to keep it within bounds, its function as energizer or distracter. Furthermore, although all anger has a dysfunctional quality to some extent, some angers are clearly wildly aberrant, and this perspective gives guidelines by which to identify them.

What of these aberrant, "sick" angers one sometimes sees and reads about? How do they fit with the more common ones considered so far? Such angers are characterized by extreme social inappropriateness and displacement of the object of anger, sometimes by their chronic quality. Angers of this kind often accompany one of the minor brain dysfunctions, a chromosomal deficiency, or psychosis, particularly paranoid schizophrenia. Persons with attenuated forms of these angers may appear in counseling offices and be difficult to discriminate from those with "normal" but serious problems of anger. Apart from those with brain damage, whose anger may be appropriate but greatly exaggerated, all these persons with the aberrant angers seem to be either grossly displacing their anger from a reasonable target or projecting all their own bitterness onto the world. In the next section, as suggestions are given for helping clients with their anger, the discussion is about one of the "normal" angers unless otherwise specified.

What Therapists Can Do to Help: Introduction

In the following section, suggestions for therapists and counselors are presented under five headings: Helping Clients Become Aware of Their Anger; Helping Clients Experience Catharsis; Helping Clients Analyze their Anger; Attitude Change Therapy; Action Planning. The order in which these topics are presented might constitute a general outline of therapeutic progress, but more common would be the situation in which counselor and client would move back and forth among these techniques in the course of a series of sessions dealing with anger. Accordingly, some introduction is necessary to provide a conceptual framework and some guidelines for the time when one technique may be more appropriate than another.

In one sense it is the client's goal, stated explicitly or inferred from the conversation, which determines not only the topic for discussion but the technique as well. For example, if the client says, "I want you to help me figure out some things to do about my anger," the counselor might well proceed to analysis and action planning. From another point of view, however, it is the counselor who has control of the technique. If a client's anger, as yet unrecognized in the therapeutic context, seems related to the client's goal and becomes evident to the counselor, the counselor may take the initiative and try to help the client become aware of the anger or experience catharsis. The decision about therapeutic technique, in other words, is sometimes more or less mutual, sometimes not.

A general model for decision-making by therapist and client is presented in considerable detail by Schuerger and Watterson (1977).In the context of an on-the-spot decision about a particular course of therapy to follow, it consists mainly of (1) evaluating the evidence available that one counselor action will be more productive for the client than another, and (2) considering that evidence along with the counselor's personal valuation of the possible outcomes of the action. For example, if the counselor confronts the client, the confrontation can be productive or counterproductive, and the counselor must have some sense of whether he would rather take the risk of a certain action and fail, or not risk the action and know there was some chance that it would have succeeded.

The evidence favoring one or another counselor action is of two kinds, therefore; evidence about the client and evidence about the counselor. Evidence about the counselor includes (1) the valuation of outcomes or willingness to take risks, and (2) the kind of therapeutic action the counselor is sure he can take. Some counselors can do systematic behavioral training and some cannot; some can do Rational Emotive Therapy (see p. 96, Attitude Change Therapy) and some cannot; some can confront a client about anger or petulance and some cannot. Evidence about the client includes the information about the anger (kind of anger, circumstances, whether it is present in the session) as well as information about what the client can do and, most important, what the client wants to do.

To simplify counselor decision in the face of complex information and multiple techniques, two guidelines may be observed: first, if the client has not presented anger as a problem, or if the client shows resistence to experiencing the anger, the counselor should be cautious proceeding with either of the first two techniques, awareness or catharsis; second, if, following the analysis of anger, client and counselor are mutually engaged in planning for client action, the action to be encouraged should emerge from what the client is most interested in and what the client can best do at that stage. In short, while the techniques to be outlined below are tried and true, they do not override the central guideline of good practice—to follow the lead of the client. In addition, where appropriate in the presentation of each technique, specific hints are given about when it might be most useful.

Helping Clients Become Aware of Their Anger
Some persons coming for help know they are angry. Others come for help with problems of living and do not recognize that they are angry, or are unwilling to

admit it, even to themselves. They may be depressed, anxious, worried about how they are going to get along; they complain about how they are being treated. For them, the first problem is to get them to recognize and acknowledge their anger. To serve this end, the counselor may use the visual and verbal cues described earlier in the chapter.

A Case in Point A client is speaking to the counselor about a problem he is having with fellow employees at work. He describes some incidents, blames his co-workers for most of the difficulty. He "only wants the best" for all concerned. He seems generally listless except when he is talking about their failings. After a while, the counselor says, "You're angry." The client says, "Dr. Jones, why would I be angry?" The counselor is pretty sure the client is angry but resists knowing his own anger because of his personal values, in which anger is a wicked emotion.

Should the counselor push his insight on the client? Some counselors do this quite successfully much of the time, but it is risky. In the situation above, for example, the client seems strongly resistant to acknowledging his anger, even to feeling it. A good rule of thumb is to push only if the counselor is dead certain about the anger, and if (1) he already has a good relationship with the client, or (2) he is pretty sure the client will not be helped without some shock.

The kind of resistance described above occurs most frequently with the clients who (1) are terrified of losing control, (2) are unable to think of themselves as angry because of their beliefs, or (3) are chronically angry in a seriously inappropriate way—e.g., are projecting their own anger on others or have displaced their anger far from the source of frustration. With persons who display signs of one of the more "normal" angers in a session (e.g., petulance, resentment), gently telling them how they look or sound will often help them become aware of and begin to talk about their anger. These latter clients may then be helped to experience catharsis, the next specific suggestion.

Helping Clients Experience Catharsis
"Catharsis" can mean many things; here it refers to the feeling of release of pent-up emotion that clients experience in a session either by talking about their troubles or by crying, laughing, shouting or otherwise engaging in very active emotional release. The pent-up feeling seems to come mainly from either of two frustrations: the client is having feelings and thoughts which appear to be enormous, odd, scary, terrible, and is feeling cut off from other humans because of them; or the action which the emotions call for, such as aggression or sexual activity, is socially unacceptable. The first of these two conditions is sometimes eased merely by having a calm person hear one's story and give assurances of understanding, re-establishing a communicative bond with humanity for the troubled client. The second condition is often more quickly and directly helped by a more physical release of emotional tension, like crying. Other means of releasing the physical, "animal" portions of emotional tension are discussed under the heading Action Planning, below.

It is sometimes possible to initiate some of these release exercises in the counseling situation. Angry clients will sometimes sit sullenly, their mood shifting from anger to desperate sadness. If the counselor remarks on the change in mood just as it is reaching sadness, the client will be moved to cry and find release in that. In the course of rational-emotive disruption of a client's beliefs (see below, Attitude Change Therapy), the counselor can sometimes ridicule the client's thoughts with a mixture of irony and compassion such that the client will laugh and get release. Almost any vigorous release will do for a beginning.

In one situation the counselor had tried hard for half a session to help a client break out of his sullen, angry depression. Finally, he suggested that the client punch a pillow bunched up in a corner of the couch. The client protested some, but finally started punching, harder and harder, until he was breathing fast and deep. At this point the counselor instructed the client to sit back and breathe deeply, feeling the relaxation. The client did this for several minutes, while the counselor sat quietly, finally remarking on how much different the client's face looked—smoother, less tense, not so red under the eyes. The client countered with how clear his mind seemed, that it was the first time in several days that he really felt relaxed. The client then began to talk quietly about his father, and how badly he had treated the client's mother. After a minute or so of that conversation, the counselor asked, "How do you feel now?" The client was beginning to feel tense and angry. The object lesson for the client was (1) the need for physical release for his anger, and (2) the amount of control his thoughts exercised over his feelings (see Attitude Change Therapy, p. 96).

Helping Clients Analyze Their Anger

Catharsis is often not enough. At some point in the helping process, just as in the last example cited above, the counselor must take advantage of a pause, the completion of some part of the session, or an explicit expectation of the client to help the client move to a greater understanding of his or her anger and eventually to some new action or attitude. This help can begin with analysis.

Three aspects of the analysis of anger which have been found useful are: (1) behavioral analysis, (2) analysis into components as above, and (3) functional analysis (What is your anger doing for you?). A reason for the behavioral analysis is to introduce a tone of objectivity, to gather information about the circumstances and quality of the anger, to look for possible ways to handle it. For behavioral analysis, typical questions about the anger are: "When was your last angry incident?"; "With whom are you most often angry?"; "How many times were you angry last week?"; "At what time of day do you most frequently get angry?"; "On what day of the week do you most frequently get angry?"; "What does the anger feel like? Describe it."; or, "When you are angry, where do you feel it in your body?"

The use counselors can make of the behavioral analysis depends quite a bit on the level of familiarity they have with general behavioral techniques as developed by, for example, Rimm and Masters (1974). Minimally, what they might do is help the client look for regularities in his anger patterns and figure out some practical things to do about those regularities. For example, if a husband gets angry at his kids about every other day when he comes home from work, and his wife only on weekends, it would seem worthwhile to think about changing his "mental set" when he comes home from work, or perhaps arranging with the kids not to talk to him until after dinner. The problem with his wife more than likely has something to do with how they expect to spend their time, so how about taking some time before each weekend to work out a mutually acceptable schedule?

Counselors not so comfortable with the more explicitly behavioral techniques can still find good use for the behavioral questions as a source of material for other forms of analysis and intervention. Questions about how the anger feels can be useful as leads to examining the components, or as leads to expressing some of the anger. Some persons believe that they are angry at their children but will find, with a bit of careful analysis, that they only shout at the kids after the boss has given them extra work.

A second analysis of anger is into the three components: its defensiveness, its reactiveness to frustration or deprivation, its righteousness. Counselor questions about *defensiveness* might include: "What is your anger helping you defend? If it is your sense of your own dignity, is there some other, more fruitful way you can have self-esteem? If it is time for yourself, which you feel is threatened by the demands of those around you, can you do better than anger by careful scheduling? If it is your worth as an individual, can't you have that without being angry at your parents?"

About *frustration or deprivation*, the counselor might ask: "What are you deprived of right now, or when you were last angry? What would you like that you don't have? What do you want?" It sounds obvious, but is worth stressing, because of the way anger hides behind righteousness. For example, many persons have a problem with anger while driving, habitually blowing up if someone cuts them off, drives slowly, or does something stupid. They focus on the stupidity of other drivers or their unreasonable "hogging the road." What the angry drivers want, said simply, is to have their own way while driving. However, they don't like to say it, since it sounds so much like what a spoiled child might say. Acknowledging that part of the anger often helps.

The third area for analysis is the *function of anger*. "What does your anger do for you?" A woman speaks of her anger at her husband, who spends too much time at work, doesn't spend enough time with her, is uncommunicative. She is furious. Further conversations reveal her interest in another man. The anger is serving to justify her spending time with the other man, even though her basic attitude favors monogamous marriage. "What would you be like without your anger?"

By itself, the understanding which comes with a careful analysis of anger may be healing. The client may come to see anger in the context of internal polarity, or conflict, between desire for freedom and sense of duty, and be liberated by the understanding. Precise descriptions of the anger experience may help the client by removing excess emotional baggage. Insight is curative, but most frequently both client and counselor will find additional action useful to manage anger. For the counselor, this action is intervention, helping the client change attitudes (Attitude Change Therapy) or assisting the client in planning useful "out-of-session" actions to solve the problem (Action Planning).

Attitude Change Therapy

This approach to helping clients deal with anger has its chief modern proponent in Albert Ellis, founder of Rational Emotive Therapy (1966). His general proposition is that the way we think has a lot to do with the way we feel. Recently the same trend has been pursued by Meichenbaum (1974) and others. It has very broad applications as a total system of therapy, and is particularly useful with clients whose anger shows righteousness or defensiveness as the dominant component, and many find it by far the most useful long-term approach. About the only circumstances in which it might not be urged are (1) when the client is seriously paranoid or confused, or (2) when the client resists the approach and seems to show more interest in some action, and the counselor doesn't want to try a long, hard push.

How does it work? Ellis (1966) presents the basic paradigm to clients: (A) A stimulus takes place in your life; (B) you interpreted it in some way; and (C) you have an unpleasant emotional response (anger). The stimulus might be a husband, who comes to his wife while she is trying to study, and says, "When are you going to sew those buttons on my jacket?" The emotional response is anger. She feels a rush of blood to her face, and tells him that if he'd put it out on the chair, she'd have gotten to it. She says, further, "Can't you see I'm busy? Why do you have to bother me right now?" What interpretation of his request was she making that facilitated her angry response? She saw the question as a slightly veiled request to pay more attention to him, and felt a twinge of guilt. Then she began to think, "He has no right to disrupt my studying this way. How dare he!"

Following Ellis' paradigm, the stimulus was her husband's question. The interpretation she put on the situation was (1) "I should have done it already, and I should pay more attention to him" (ego-threat); (2) "He has no right to bother me now when I am so busy" (righteousness). The resulting emotion was anger. Ellis' Rational Emotive Therapy intervenes in the process at the second step, the interpretation, which, he says, comes from a faulty way of looking at life, a system of illogical thinking. The therapy consists of re-educating the client to think in a healthier, more appropriate way, by helping the client dispute the faulty thinking. This is the point at which many counselors balk, because to keep at a resistant client with this kind of re-education requires a lot of conviction, ingenuity, and persistence.

In the above example, the counselor might start with a frontal attack on the client's guilt. "Why *should* you have done it already? And what if you *should* have? Did you promise? If you did promise, so you blew it—so what? Are you horrible for that? Can you prove that you are worthless, horrible, sinful because you put off doing your husband's jacket? If he is irritated with you, will you die?" Another area to attack is the righteousness. "Who ever told you you had a right to privacy? If you wanted privacy so badly, might it not work better to set up a mutually agreed-upon schedule, that you both could really honor? Can you prove that you have any rights at all? Wouldn't it suit the situation better to say you wanted privacy rather than to say you had a right to it?" A third approach is to suggest what a more appropriate emotional response might have been—"You wanted some time to study and he bothered you. That sounds frustrating. Maybe if you were determined to get it, you could figure out some ways to ensure privacy when you really wanted it."

This approach to dealing with anger has the advantage of getting at the three main components (defensiveness, response to frustration, righteousness)and it is conceptually simple. It requires on the part of the helper an ideological conviction that resembles religious conversion. At its most complete, the attitudes it engenders resemble the wisdom described among the ancients—an ease with life and its limitations. At lesser levels, it can be practiced with less stubborn clients who mainly need to know what they are telling themselves and how that influences what they feel.

Action Planning

Action planning is a mutual enterprise in which both parties develop a homework assignment for the client that is most relevant to the problem. The client provides the goal, the aspect of anger most important at the time, and the counselor uses professional ingenuity to help the client decide on effective means. Here the possible actions have been limited to three kinds: physical release, expression, avoidance. Physical release, like Attitude Change Therapy, can be recommended for almost all clients with problems of anger so long as their physical condition will allow. Expression procedures are sometimes recommended to persons whose anger is connected with what seems an unreasonable deprivation, particularly those whose anger is petulant or resentful. Avoidance procedures are recommended for clients who are getting in trouble because of their anger, usually anger of one of the hotter kinds like rage.

Physical Release   The emotion of anger has physiological correlates, and some way to take care of these is required in any thorough program to manage anger. To angry clients who are working cognitively (see Attitude Change, above) to modify their anger but feel distressed right now, the counselor can say, "Do you want to feel better tomorrow? Exercise tonight." When they laugh or look askance, repeat it. It makes good sense. Human beings are animals, after all, and if they have those fight feelings and never fight, something unhealthy happens. The kinds of animal release which have been found useful with clients are: vigorous exercise, like jogging, swimming, handball, tennis; crying, shouting, throwing pottery; mock wrestling, dancing, pillow fights, tickle fights.

Another kind of release may be had from systematic relaxation training, such as takes place in biofeedback training, meditation, yoga. These procedures do not release emotional energies in the same way as the ones described above but do have a calming effect and may be used effectively with one of the other therapies just as the more violent releases. They are sometimes used in conjunction with reduction of anger by early cue recognition (see below, Avoidance).

Expression   Although anger as such is rarely useful, some clients don't seem able to make much progress with it until they have found that they can indeed express it when they want to. People characterized by this pattern represent the antithesis of those who get into trouble because they constantly express their anger aggressively. Short of actual encouragement of anger, there is something to be said for helping persons express their anger effectively, and choosing when to do so most appropriately. Five guidelines in helping clients with this aspect of their anger are the following:

(a)"Do you want to express the anger?" Many clients get wishy-washy at this point and say, "Well, I'd like to, but..." Such hesitation serves to introduce a discussion of what the client really wants. A college student, red-hot with anger, came to the counselor looking for help with a professor. Discussion went back and forth, and finally the counselor asked, "What do you want, to punish the professor and prove yourself right, or a chance at a decent grade?" After he got over the shock, the student admitted that what he really wanted most was the grade, although he'd like to "get the prof" too. Again, this situation is a reminder that anger is often best viewed as a cue or symptom of some deeper real life problem.

(b)"If you do express the anger, make it to the point." That is, express it at the appropriate person. One sometimes hears a lot of anger about "the system" when the phrase "the system" serves as a smoke screen for the person's own avoidance, for the person's general frustration in living, or for the real source of frustration whom the client is afraid to face. If an appropriate focus for the anger can be identified, that is the place for expression.

(c)"If you do express the anger, be straight, keep in touch with yourself, say it all." In other words, follow the usual skills which are taught in assertiveness training. For example, while an angry husband might say to his wife, "You're making me angry with all your nagging criticism," the more accurate statement might be, "When you say things like that, I get angry." There are two differences between the two ways of expressing the anger: first, the more accurate statement describes the angry person's feeling (I get angry) without claiming causality; second, the wording does not imply any bad motive on the part of the other person.

(d)"Don't express your anger or confront the focus of your anger unless you are willing to become more involved with the problem."

(e)"Remember, you don't have to be right to be angry."

After clients try what seems to be their first experience with adult anger, they sometimes experience a first flush of success—"I've done it!" Frequently, however, since they are inexperienced at expressing anger, they are clumsy and offend others, then are unable to follow their anger with anything constructive. With such clients, instruction in social skills, ways of saying what they mean and want, and detailed follow-up are useful. The kind of help one finds in some of the standard works on assertiveness training such as *Don't Say Yes When You Mean No* (Fensterheim and Baer, 1975), is often applicable for clients who experience such difficulties.

Avoidance   "Avoidance" here means a procedure or procedures for learning responses other than anger and aggression to frustrating stimuli. These approaches are most applicable with persons who want not to feel anger or who want not to express anger inappropriately. An alternate heading for this section might be, "How to Get Some of What You Want Without Pushing the Rest of the World Out of Shape or Feeling Miserable Yourself." These procedures all have to do with the frustration which is seen as stimulus to anger: To plan for what you want; to avoid frustrating situations; to use the experience of anger as a cue for useful action.

The two parts of "planning for what you want" that are stressed here are (1) requesting the client to say out loud what he wants, and (2) helping the client spell out in detail how he will know when he gets it. These elements were well illustrated in a session between a depressed college student and counselor. The client, a young woman, was complaining about how meaningless her life felt. She avoided looking at the counselor, spoke in a low voice. Nothing seemed to interest her. Her social life was lousy, and the few men she did meet just weren't right. She at first avoided the counselor's question about what she wanted, then began to approximate replies. "I'd like to meet . . ." or "There must be someone out there . . ." The counselor kept requesting her to say what she wanted. Finally, she looked up, slapped her arms on the chair, and said in a loud voice, "I want a really neat man to chase me!"

She hadn't wanted to admit it to herself, so her frustration and feelings of anger were turning inward, slowing her down, getting in the way of planning. Having said it, she laughed, felt better, and was ready to figure out "how she'd know when she got it." This question is useful because angry persons often miss seeing how much of what they want they already have. The rest of "planning for what you want," searching for solutions and resources, can be drawn from spelling out "how you would know . . ." It is no small part of the helper's work, but is shortened here because it would carry this chapter far beyond its scope.

The behavioral analysis of anger (above) can often yield helpful hints for another form of Avoidance Planning, that is, planning to avoid frustrating, anger-provoking situations. There are usually common circumstantial threads running across anger incidents, particularly if a client has a chronic problem with anger. For example, if a client regularly gets angry with her boss when she reads his memos, she may not be able to avoid reading the memos but might plan to read them during the most pleasant part of the day, when she is least tired, or best fed. If it is required that she read them immediately, what else about the reading might she change to counter her habitual angry reaction? Could she read them upside down, or in a mirror? Could she read them aloud, as a dramatic declamation? The key idea is to avoid totally (or to change some concrete part of) the situation that is identified as a stimulus to anger, or, if that is impossible, to change one's mental set about the situation.

A third form of avoidance planning is to help the client learn to use the anger experience as a cue, a sign within himself, that trouble is on the way, and to learn to respond to the cue in a new, more suitable way (see Functions of Anger above). The first flash of anger can become a useful warning sign instead of the beginning of real trouble. Details of this kind of learning are provided by Novaco (1975) and Rimm and Masters (1974). The new action to follow the recognition of the anger can be an attitude (see above, Attitude Change Therapy) or an action. For example, a woman client was taught to recognize the first surge of anger as a sign that she was losing her sense of her own autonomy. Through a series of imaginary scenes and role-playing mini-dramas, she learned to respond to that sign with a question to herself: "What do I want?" Anger subsided when she did so, she didn't feel overwhelmed and confused, and she often got some of what she wanted. Failing that, as she remarked, she still maintained some feeling of control over her destiny.

Do You Want To Give It Up?

There is a perversity which seems to want to keep the anger. One sees it in the client who resists the helper's efforts to teach the ways his or her thoughts of being unjustly treated serve to maintain the anger. There comes a time in many helping situations at which the question is appropriate: "Do you want to give it up?" And the question: "If you give up the anger, what else do you have to give up?" Sometimes clients will say, "Yes, I want to give it up. But I can't."

Some clients will say, "Yes, I want to. Help me figure out how." Some will say, "I want to stop being so angry, but I don't want to give it up altogether." Some will say, "No. No, I don't really want to give it up." Regardless of the answer, having the client state it explicitly usually puts the counseling at a stage to consider more accurately and profitably the realities of the client's aims. If the client asks for help, the counselor is in good position to offer the resources of his or her ingenuity. If the client wants to stop but not altogether, the counselor can point out to the client that truth and its implications: "That is your truth; are you willing to take what comes with it?" If the client does not want to give it up at all, the counselor can take that as a statement of the client's goals and ask how he can help the client work through the implications of the anger and how to minimize the ill effects of it.

Final Cautions

With clients whose anger has one of the extreme qualities described earlier (inappropriate focus, disproportionate magnitude, terror over loss of control), counselors are well-advised to be very cautious. As a general rule, the best procedure is to be gentle and honest, to acknowledge the client's anger but not encourage it, to help the client learn to discern the difference between real threats and imaginary ones. Even these extreme angers are presumably serving the client in some way, perhaps as self-reassurance that "I am someone to be reckoned with." Attempts to minimize the anger must be made in such a way as to allow the client maintenance of self-respect and honest contact with other human beings. We all have our place in the universe.

Questions For Further Inquiry

1. When you experience anger, how do you let others know it? Does your expression of anger differ under different circumstances?

2. How can you determine when your anger is appropriate and when it is not?

3. What thoughts and feelings do you experience when you are confronted by an angry client? How do you respond? What do you do with your anger when you feel it toward a client?

4. It has been said that when a person expresses anger, he or she is always defending something. How does this match with your experience?

5. Many clients deny their anger. What counseling approaches may help a client acknowledge his or her anger?

References

Ardrey, R. *The territorial imperative: A personal inquiry into animal origins of property and nations*. New York: Dell, 1966.

Aristotle. *Ethics*. London: Dutton Press, 1963

Bandura, A. *Aggression: A social learning analysis*. Englewood Cliffs, N.J.: Prentice-Hall, 1973.

Becker, E. *The birth and death of meaning: An interdisciplinary perspective on the problem of man*. New York: Free Press, 1971.

Ellis, A. *Rational-emotive psychotherapy*. New York: J. Norton, 1966.

Ellis, A., Casriel, D. Albert Ellis vs. Daniel Casriel on Anger. *Rational Living* 1971 *6(2)*, 2-21.

Erikson, E. *Childhood and society*. New York: Norton, 1950.

Fensterheim, H., & Baer, J. *Don't say yes when you want to say no: How assertiveness training can change your life*. New York: Dell, 1975.

Karson, S., & O'Dell, J. W. *A guide to the clinical use of the 16PF*. Champaign, Ill.: Institute for Personality and Ability Testing, 1976.

May, R. *Power and innocence*. New York: Dell, 1972.

Meichenbaum, D. *Cognitive behavior modification*. Morristown, N.J.: General Learning Press, 1974.

Novaco, R. *Anger control: The development and evaluation of experimental treatment*. Lexington, Mass.: Lexington Books, 1975.

Perls, F. S. *Ego, hunger and aggression: A revision of Freud's theory and method*. London: S. Allen and Unwin, Ltd, 1974.

Rimm, P. C., & Masters, J. C. *Behavior therapy: Techniques and empirical findings*. New York: Academic Press, 1974.

Schuerger, J. M., & Watterson, D. *Using tests and other information in counseling: A decision model for practitioners*. Champaign, Ill.: IPAT, 1977.

Sheehy, G. *Passages: Predictable crises of adult life*. New York: Dutton, 1976.

Strachey, J. *The complete psychological works of Sigmund Freud*. London: The Hogarth Press and the Institute of Psycho-Analysis, 1932–36.

Understanding and Alleviating Alienation   6

DAVID W. JOHNSON

Introduction

The author once spent several months conducting group psychotherapy sessions for a group home for teenage runaways who had drug-abuse problems. One of the individuals living in the home was a 13-year-old named Shirley. Shirley at that time was very young looking, attractive, intelligent, and appealing to other people. Yet she had repeatedly run away from home, from a psychiatric ward in a hospital, and from an institution for juvenile delinquents. She used drugs heavily and abusively. Shirley attempted suicide several times, slashing her wrists and trying to bleed to death. After one such attempt the author was talking with her and she reiterated several times, "I have nothing to live for! Every drug experience possible I have had! Every sexual experience possible I have had! There is nothing left for me to do or feel or experience!"

Shirley believed that there was no one she could turn to for affection and support. She was locked into her own needs and feelings, unable to view situations from anything but an egocentric point of view. She lacked any sense of purpose and direction in life. She viewed the societal responsibilities such as school and career as arbitrary attempts to destroy her individuality which must be resisted. She had no awareness of her cooperative interdependence with other people in her family, community, or society. Her identity was fragmented and diffused, resulting in dissociation from other people and a lack of any distinct impression of who or what kind of person she was.

As a psychotherapist the author sees many alienated clients like Shirley, some less dramatic and others even more tragic. There is convincing data indicating that cases such as Shirley are not isolated incidences, but that there is an increasing alienation found within the younger members of our society. In order to discuss the strategies by which alienation can be allieviated within our society, it is first necessary to define alienation and discuss its effects on the individual and on the community.

What Is Alienation?

Alienation is such a widely used concept in the social sciences that it has been used as a catch word to explain nearly every kind of aberrant behavior. *Alienation* has been defined as a feeling of estrangement from the goals and norms of the family, community, and society (Breger, 1974; Johnson, 1979; Keniston, 1965; Nettler, 1957), as feeling like an alien or foreigner in one's own native land (Breger, 1974), and as a feeling of powerlessness (Clark, 1959; Gamson, 1961; Horton and Thompson, 1962). In a more complex definition Seeman (1975) identifies six varieties of alienation: (1) powerlessness—the sense of low control versus mastery over events, (2) meaninglessness—the sense of incomprehensibility versus understanding of personal and social affairs, (3) normlessness—high expectancies for (or commitment to) socially unapproved means versus conventional means for the achievement of given goals, (4) cultural estrangement—the rejection of commonly held values in society versus commitment to societial standards, (5) self-estrangement—the engagement in activities that are not intrinsically rewarding versus involvement in a task or activity for its own sake, and (6) social isolation—the sense of exclusion or rejection versus social acceptance.

Johnson (1972a, 1975, 1979) defines *alienation* as the feeling and fact of disconnectedness from people, surroundings, and activities of the social systems (such as family, community, society, and economy) of which one is a part. The extreme example of such alienation is the city dweller who is surrounded by people he does not know, living in a residence he did not build, dependent on sources of power and transportation he poorly understands and cannot easily influence, being paid for work too minute to be meaningfully understood as part of an overall cooperative effort to produce a product or service. Technological society and large bureaucracies may especially promote such alienation. But from a psychological point of view feelings of alienation reflect a breakdown in socializing processes.

Socialization is the process of learning and internalizing the values, attitudes, roles, competencies, and ways of perceiving the world that are shared by one's family, community, and society. Later in life socialization becomes the modification of one's attitudes, expectations, and actions to coordinate with those of the people with whom one interacts within cooperative endeavors such as economic organizations and education. Much of early socialization is aimed at promoting the development of basic social competencies needed to function effectively within our society. These social competencies include a basic trust that one can rely upon the affection and support of other people, the ability to perceive situations from perspectives other than one's own, a meaningful direction and purpose in life, an awareness of one's interdependence with other people, and an integrated and coherent identity. These social competencies will be discussed further in the section on alienation and psychological health.

Processes of Socialization

Socialization and alienation are closely tied together. If socialization is effective, alienation will be a transient feeling appearing periodically in one's life. If socialization is ineffective, or if the person is socialized into a set of values and perspectives that are counter to those of the dominant society, then alienation will be a chronic and destructive feeling and state. Teenagers such as Johnny, for example, who at the age of 16 had a long record of arrests for disorderly conduct, simple battery, and aggravated assult, and who lured a motorist into an alley, drew a .22-caliber pistol and shot the motorist six times, killing him, reflect a breakdown in the processes of socialization that are necessary to inculcate a basic respect for human life and the rights of others. Socializing efforts are aimed at creating the commitment, values, and competencies necessary to continue the social system. Alienation is not only a reflection of a breakdown in socializing processes, but also a threat to the continuation of the community and society.

　　There are three important points that need to be made about socialization. First, the specific values, attitudes, roles, competencies, and perspectives a person adopts are learned. They are not genetically inherited, and they do not magically appear as the person physically matures. Second, socialization has its origin in interaction with other people. It is the members of one's family and friendship groups that provide socializing influences, and it is within such relationships that the person becomes socialized. It is parents, peers, and other people who actively confront the person with expectations as to what are appropriate values, attitudes, behavior, and social roles. Third, socialization is not a passive process. Socialization is a dynamic process in which the person seeks out and selects what he or she wants to attend to, whom he or she wants to identify with, what roles he wants to adopt voluntarily, and how he wants to respond to the demands of parents, peers, and teachers.

　　Two of the most powerful processes through which socialization is accomplished are identification and role learning. In its simplest form *identification* occurs when a person tries to incorporate the qualities and attributes of another person into himself. This process is active, ongoing, and, to a large extent, unconscious. Through actively selecting some adults, older children, adolescents, and even mythical figures to identify with, the person creatively constructs her own personality and character and transforms herself in new directions over a period of years. Identification is a continuous process whereby a person constantly is engaged in incorporating and then modifying various aspects of the people he is identifying with. Furthermore, most identification takes place without full awareness of the extent to which a person is adopting the attributes of others.

There are basically four types of identification. Identification based on love or liking and on admiration for superior competence occur more or less continually throughout a person's life, and they result in a fairly straightforward growth of the person. Identification based on anxiety or anger and on experiences of being controlled, frustrated, or mistreated in situations where there is no escape are based on feelings of helplessness and can be destructive to the person. It is the latter two types of identification that create feelings of alienation. Internalizing through identification the rejection of oneself and the desire to mistreat oneself blocks healthy psychological development and constructive socialization. The destructive aspects of identifications based on being rejected (anxiety about loss of love) and frustrated are so pervasive in alienated people that psychotherapy may be viewed as the process by which such negative identifications are replaced with positive ones. Encouraging alienated clients to identify with people they respect and who love them, while discouraging client identification with those people who reject and mistreat them is an indispensable aspect of psychotherapy.

Another powerful process through which people become socialized is by acquiring social roles. A *social role* is a set of expectations aimed at structuring interaction within a cooperative relationship. Like all aspects of socialization, acquiring social roles is an active process through which children and adolescents (1) learn to act, feel, and perceive the world in a somewhat similar manner to other people who have similar roles, (2) master the needed technical and cooperative competencies to fulfill the requirements of the role, and (3) learn what to expect from people who are in related roles. The person actively selects and modifies the social roles he wishes to adopt. Alienated people are marked by their lack of adoption of constructive social roles that provide a sense of meaningful direction to their lives and tie them into interdependent relationships with other people.

The Alienation Crisis

If children and adolescents do not have stable and healthy family relationships and friendships that promote socialization through direct learning, identification based on liking and respect, and the adoption of social roles, alienation will result. It is within interpersonal relationships that socialization occurs. If a child or adolescent is isolated, involved in destructive relationships that promote identifications based on rejection and frustration, or taught values and perspectives counter to those of the dominant society, alienation results. Is alienation widespread within our society? Is there evidence that relationships needed for healthy socialization are lacking for a large number of American children, youth, and young adults? It is to these two questions that we now turn.

There is considerable evidence that our society is in the midst of an alienation crisis promoted by the failure of healthy socialization processes to occur in the lives of many of our children and adolescents. Since 1960 juvenile crime has risen twice as fast as that of adults and more than half of all serious crimes (murder, rape, aggravated assault, robbery, burglary, larceny, and motor vehicle theft) in the U.S. are committed by youths aged 10 to 17 (*Time,* July 11, 1977). The frequency with which juveniles are involved in aggravated assault, armed robbery, forcible rape, and murder increased over 200 percent between 1964 and 1973. Bronfrenbrenner (1976) documents that the suicide rate among teenagers has risen more than 250 percent in the last 20 years, the ratio of illegitimate births per 1,000 live babies has gone up by 300 percent in the last 20 years, the divorce rate has climbed steadily, and the average verbal and math scores of senior high school students taking the scholastic aptitude examination have steadily declined over the past 10 years. These and other effective and cognitive indices of socialization indicate that alienation among children, adolescents, and young adults (as well as adults) is at crisis levels in our society. There can be no doubt that strategies on how to prevent such alienation from developing and to treat alienated clients within therapy are urgently needed.

The Roots of Alienation

Two of the more important settings for healthy socializing relationships to occur are the family and the school. There is evidence that the family is deteriorating as a socializing unit and that the excessive competition and individualism promoted by schools has detrimental effects on the socialization of American children and youth. Bronfrenbrenner (1976) has documented the radical changes taking place in the structure of the American family over the past 20 years. There have been dramatic increases in the percent of mothers working, decreases in the number of adults in the home, increases in the number of single-parent families, decreases in the amount of time parents (especially fathers) spend with young children, and increases in the number of mothers deserting their families. All of these trends indicate that children and adolescents are becoming more isolated from their parents. There is even evidence that in many cases the contact which does occur between parent and child is not constructive, as the incidence of child abuse is rising dramatically and the frequency with which parents kill their children has jumped startlingly, especially homocide involving teenage children.

A distinctive feature of modern American life seems to be segregation by age, resulting in a decrease in all spheres of interaction between parent and child. Even the increase in TV viewing and the construction of homes that separate children and adults into playrooms and dens or offices contributes to the lack of interaction between adults and children. Along with the general isolation are the trends which separate children from the careers of their parents and separate children from neighborhood and community influences. Children have fewer opportunities to observe their parents at work or to see adults in economic roles. The mobility of families reduces the impact of relationships in the neighborhood. All of these influences contribute to the alienation found among American children and youth.

Bronfrenbrenner (1976) states that over the past 30 years literally thousands of research studies have identified family disorganization as an antecedent to behavior disorders, lack of school achievement, and social pathology in children and adolescents. We are increasingly living in a society that imposes pressures and priorities that allow neither time nor place for meaningful activities and relations between children and adults, which downgrade the role of parents and the functions of parenthood, and which prevent positive relationships developing between adults and children wherein the adult is a guide, friend, and companion to the children. Current life circumstances seem to undermine relationships of trust and emotional security between family members and to make it difficult for parents to care for, socialize, and enjoy their children and vice versa.

The major socializing agency for children and youth besides the family is the school. Children are spending more time in school than ever before. Currently, however, schools are dominated by excessive competition and individualism which mitigate against the supportive and cooperative relationships necessary for identifications based on liking and respect and the adoption of reciprocal social roles to occur. Johnson and R. Johnson (1975) and Johnson (1979) review considerable evidence indicating that students view education as a competitive activity. American children are more competitive than are children from other countries, the longer students are in school the more competitive they become, and school life is so barren of cooperative experiences that students are not sensitized to the possibility that cooperation is an alternative in interacting with other students.

In an attempt to avoid many of the negative outcomes of excessive and inappropriate competition, there has been a current emphasis on individualism within schools. However, such an emphasis separates students, fosters individual learning contracts, individual materials, space, and learning goals, and provides teaching machines and computers for students to interact with—with the result that the socializing impact of schools is reduced. Bronfrenbrenner (1976), furthermore, emphasizes that because schools segregate students by age and do not provide activities for which students can take active and meaningful responsibility, schools have become one of the most potent breeding grounds of alienation in American society.

Often the students who have the most disturbed family life and therefore need to experience positive socializing relationships in other settings are ignored by schools. The Children's Defense Fund utilized a variety of government data and concluded that in the United States nearly two million school-age children between seven and seventeen are not enrolled in school. There is reason to believe that these figures underestimate the problem. Most of these children and adolescents, furthermore, are not out of school by choice; they have been kicked out. Obviously children and teenagers who are not allowed by the schools to participate in educational experiences cannot receive the socializing benefits of such experiences.

The roots of alienation are in the failure of a society to socialize its children successfully. The two major institutions given the responsibility for socializing the younger members of our society are the family and the schools. A breakdown in the effectiveness of families and schools to socialize children and youth into the basic social competencies needed to be productive citizens results in a cycle wherein alienated youth and adults are developed. These people become disconnected and estranged from other people and the normal activities of our society and in turn contribute to the further breakdown in family and community life. Such a cycle needs to be broken both at the prevention level (by restoring the effectiveness of families and schools as socializing agents) and at the treatment level (by socializing through psychotherapy youth and adults who feel alienated).

For both prevention and treatment strategies to be formulated, a clear conceptualization of healthy socialization or psychological health must be provided. Without such a conceptualization goals for socializing efforts cannot be formulated, diagnosis of current client functioning cannot be made, and hypotheses about the origins of a client's difficulties cannot be derived. An example of a conceptualization of healthy socialization is given in the next section.

Alienation and Psychological Health

The goal of socialization is to encourage the development of productive and fulfilled individuals who contribute to the survival and improvement of their families, communities, and society. It is within such cooperative social systems that psychological health and alienation are defined. The ability to build and maintain cooperative relationships is often cited as a primary manifestation of psychological health (Adler et al., 1956; Fromm-Reichmann, 1950; Jung, 1959; May, 1969; Murray, 1951; Sullivan, 1953; Johnson and Matross, 1977; Johnson and Norem-Hebeisen, 1977). Several psychologists have noted that cooperative relationships are a psychological necessity for humans (Asch, 1952; Bruner, 1966; Deutsch, 1962; Johnson and R. Johnson, 1975; Johnson, 1975; Mead, 1934). There are literally hundreds of studies comparing the effects of cooperative, competitive, and individualistic efforts toward achieving goals; for a review of these studies see Johnson and R. Johnson (1975). The overall results indicate that cooperation, compared with competition and individualization, promotes positive interpersonal relationships characterized by mutual liking, positive attitudes toward each other, mutual concern, friendliness, attentiveness, feelings of obligation to each other, and a desire to earn the respect of others.

In addition, cooperation promotes lower levels of personal anxiety; greater feelings of personal security; more mutual support, assistance, helping, and sharing; more frequent, effective, and accurate communication; higher levels of trust among people; more mutual influence; more prosocial behavior; more constructive management of conflicts; more positive self-esteem; greater task orientation, coordination of efforts, involvement in task, satisfaction from efforts, and achievements; and more empathy and ability to take the emotional perspective of others. These empirically demonstrated effects of cooperation are congruent with the proposition that cooperativeness is a central aspect of psychological health. Johnson and Norem-Hebeisen (1977), furthermore, have demonstrated a positive relationship between cooperativeness and psychological health. *Psychological health* can, therefore, be defined as the ability to be aware of and manage effectively one's cooperative interactions with other people.

Effective socialization, psychological health, and a lack of alienation all require that children and adolescents develop a set of basic attitudes and abilities (Johnson and Matross, 1977; Johnson, 1979). The first is an attitude of generalized interpersonal trust (Deutsch, 1962; Erikson, 1950; Freud, 1963; Johnson, 1975; Marwell and Schmitt, 1972; Millon, 1969). Distrustful attitudes that others are harsh and undependable have been postulated to lead to habitual affective states of depression, anxiety, fear, and apprehension, and to beliefs that others are critical, rejecting, humiliating, inconsistent, unpredictable, undependable, and exploitative. The second is the ability to understand how a situation appears to another person and how that person is reacting cognitively and affectively. This competency includes all aspects of perspective-taking and is the opposite of egocentrism. Both cognitive-developmental and social psychologists have emphasized the importance of this ability for healthy social development (Flavell, 1968; Johnson, 1975; Kohlberg, 1969; Mead, 1934; Piaget, 1950).

The third aspect of healthy psychological development is a meaningful purpose and direction in life, a sense of "where I am going." Everyone needs a purpose that is valued by others and that is similar to the goals of the significant people in one's life (Freud, 1963; Lewin, 1935; Johnson, 1975). Feelings of involvement, commitment, and meaning and beliefs that life is worthwhile, challenging, and has purpose depends on a sense of direction. People without a sense of direction flounder from one tentative activity to another, search for experiences to give their life meaning, refuse to assume responsibility for their choices, make little effort to achieve their goals, fail to use their competencies, and have low aspirations. The fourth aspect is an awareness of meaningful cooperative interdependence with other people (Johnson, 1975). There is nothing more personally rewarding and satisfying than being part of a joint effort to achieve important goals. Through cooperative interdependence with others friendships and emotional bonds are developed. In a highly technical society such as the United States high levels of interdependence are the rule, not the exception. People who are unaware of their interdependence with others usually feel alienated, lonely, isolated, worthless, inferior, and defeated. Their attitudes will reflect low self-esteem, an emphasis on short-term gratification, and the conviction that no one cares about them or their capabilities. Such people are often impulsive, have fragmented relationships, withdraw from relationships with other people, and are insensitive to own and other's needs.

Finally, every person needs a strong and integrated sense of personal identity (Erikson, 1950; Johnson, 1975; Maslow, 1954; Rogers, 1951). An *identity* is a consistent set of attitudes that define "who I am." It serves as an anchor in life. The world can change, other people can change, career and family life can change, but there is something about oneself that remains the same. During infancy, childhood, adolescence, and early adulthood, a person has several identities. Development and socialization, however, have to result in a basic unified personal identity. A diffused and ambiguous identity results in dissociation from other people and an avoidance of growth-producing experiences (Breger, 1974). People without an integrated and coherent self-identity will chronically feel anxiety, insecurity, depression, cynicism, defensiveness, unhappiness, and self-rejection. They will be unable to maintain relationships, will have transient values and interests, and will search frantically for a set of beliefs to cling to in order to superficially achieve a sense of unity.

An alarming number of children, youth, and young adults in our society feel and are disconnected and estranged from the people, surroundings, and activities of the social systems of which they are a part. Such individuals represent failures for the socializing efforts of families, schools, and other agencies who share the responsibility for socializing new members of our society. The constructive interpersonal relationships within which children develop the basic social competencies needed to be a productive and fulfilled member of our society (through such processes as identification based on love and respect and the adoption of social roles) do not occur in an increasing number of children's lives. The costs of the deterioration of the family and schools as socializing agencies to society are immeasurable. In order to alleviate alienation, strategies for preventing its development and treating it must be detailed. It is to the discussion of such strategies that we now turn.

Structuring Cooperative Learning

Alienation may be much easier to prevent than to cure. Prevention requires the formation of constructive relationships that promote positive identifications based on love and respect as well as the adoption of reciprocal social roles in cooperative activities. While schools are currently emphasizing competition among students and individualism, there is evidence indicating that if schools emphasized cooperative learning experiences, the impact on socialization and the reduction of alienation would be substantial (Johnson and R. Johnson, 1975). Consider the following example reported to the author by a teacher in the Chicago area:

John was a complete nonproducer. And he insisted on isolating himself from the rest of the class. No matter where I put his desk within the room, within three hours he would be sitting behind me and as far away from the other students as possible. Then I started using cooperative learning groups. In his spelling group he would get two or three words right out of a list of twenty from a fifth-grade speller. His group worked with him and found out that oral review would not teach him the words. He had to write the words down when he studied. By the end of the year his spelling scores in the cooperative group went up to 17 or 18 right out of 20. After the success he had in working with his classmates, and after the support he received from them, he would sit anywhere in the classroom I wanted him to. The other students were now his friends!

Cooperative learning experiences structure a positive interdependence among students so that they benefit from each other's efforts to achieve. The essence of cooperative learning is assigning a *group goal* (such as completing a set of math problems, working as a group, and ensuring that all group members understand how to solve each problem), and rewarding all members of the group on the basis of the quality of their work according to a fixed set of standards. The teacher establishes a group goal and a criteria-referenced evaluation system, and rewards group members on the basis of their group performance.

Within classrooms there may be students who are and are not alienated and who do and do not have constructive socializing relationships within their families. When teachers assign students to heterogeneous groups and assist them in learning the skills needed to work cooperatively, isolated and alienated students become integrated into constructive friendship groups. To complete assignments cooperatively, students are required to interact with each other, share ideas and materials, help each other learn, pool their information and resources, use a division of labor when appropriate, integrate each member's contribution, into a group product, and facilitate each other's learning. Communication, conflict management, leadership, and trust-building skills become a necessity for basic academic tasks, not as something to suppress until after school. And by participating in cooperatively structured learning activities the students develop the basic social competencies inherent in psychological health and social development. The basic procedures by which teachers can structure cooperative learning activities appear in Johnson and R. Johnson (1975). The interpersonal and group skills students learn as an inherent aspect of completing academic tasks cooperatively are detailed in Johnson (1972b, 1978) and Johnson and F. Johnson (1975).

If most educational experiences were structured cooperatively, the deterioration of the family would be compensated for by the socializing impact of the schools. The current competition and individualism within schools would, of course, no longer promote alienation as they would be replaced by cooperation. Such a desirable state of affairs is, however, not currently with us. There are many aliented children, youth, and young adults who need psychotherapy to increase their psychological health, social development, and integration into the social system.

Counseling with Alienated Clients

Clients who feel and are in fact disconnected and estranged from other people, their surroundings, and the activities that involve their nonalienated peers, do not usually leap into counseling with great cooperation and excitement. Runaways, drug abusers, criminals, hermits, and other types of alienated members of our society are just as estranged from the usual goals of counseling as they are from the usual goals of the work place and the community. There are clients who wish to remain institutionalized or disabled, those who do not want to give up their current destructive activities, and who are not interested in the "normal" life offered by the counselor. And they often have a great deal of anger and fear to unload on the counselor. In such cases there are fundamental conflicts between the counselor's goals for the treatment and the alienated person's goals. Counseling can be viewed as a conflict between the counselor and client in which they negotiate with each other. A negotiation approach to counseling is characterized by the following process:

1. The counselor and the client, each with personal goals for the counseling sessions, enter a relationship in which there is client ambivalence. Client ambivalence consists of the client both wishing to change to more self-enhancing patterns of attitudes and behaviors and to keep the security and protection of current but destructive patterns of attitudes and behaviors.
2. The counselor attempts to establish the conditions necessary for cooperative problem-solving. These include building and maintaining trust while decreasing client egocentrism and demoralization, and establishing the counselor as a reference person for client identification with the counselor.
3. The counselor and the client seek to define and diagnose the client's problems by: (a) identifying the current consequences of the client's functioning, including the current feelings of the client, (b) identifying current client destructive attitude and behavior patterns which are "causing" these consequences, and (c) understanding the continuity among the ways in which the client's patterns of attitudes and actions were originally learned, the ways in which they became crystallized in the client's general personality structure, and the ways in which they operate in the client's current life.
4. The counselor and the client seek to influence the client to: (a) change to more self-enhancing patterns of attitudes and behaviors that will improve the quality of the consequences of the client's functioning (including the feeling state of the client), (b) learn the basic social competencies necessary for building productive and fulfilling relationships within the context of social systems, and (c)

apply and integrate the new patterns of attitudes, behaviors, and social competencies into the client's ongoing life.

A more complete discussion of the conflict-negotiation model of helping appears in Johnson and Matross (1977). Briefly, the conditions for positive change and the negotiation of attitude and behavior change are discussed below.

While the goals for counseling are being negotiated by the counselor and the client, the counselor will be concerned with establishing the conditions necessary for cooperative problem-solving. The first such condition is building and maintaining client trust. The process involves encouraging the client to take a risk by disclosing his or her problems, feelings, behavior, and ideas, and the counselor responding with warmth, accurate understanding, cooperative intentions, and appropriately reciprocating the client's self-disclosures (Johnson, 1972a; Johnson and F. Johnson, 1975; Johnson and Noonan, 1972). Second, in order for the counselor to influence the client to change destructive and inappropriate attitudes and behavior patterns, the therapist must reduce the client's egocentrism. *Egocentrism* is the defensive adherence to one's own point of view; it is the inability or unwillingness to take the perspective of another person, and it is highly related to *closed-mindedness,* which is the withdrawal (psychologically or physically) from opportunities to explore attitudes and perspectives that are discrepant from one's own and the seeking to bolster one's attitudes and perspective by seeking out others with similar views (Rokeach, 1960). The opposite of egocentrism is *perspective-taking,* the ability to understand how a situation appears to another person and how the person is reacting cognitively and affectively. Perspective-taking is highly related to *open-mindedness,* which is the willingness to attend to, comprehend, and gain insight into attitudes and viewpoints discrepant from one's own (Rokeach, 1960). As long as the client is locked into his own egocentric point of view, the counselor will be able to exert little influence. There are three types of therapist behavior that may decrease a client's egocentrism and promote client perspective-taking: communicating that one accurately understands the client, expressions of cooperative intentions, and promoting client perspective-reversal with others (Johnson, 1966, 1967, 1968, 1971a, 1971b, 1972b, 1977; Johnson, McCarty, and Allen, 1976; Falk and Johnson, 1977).

A third condition for counseling with alienated clients is a reduction in demoralization. To be *demoralized* is to be deprived of courage, to be disheartened, bewildered, confused, and disordered. To various degrees the demoralized person feels isolated, hopeless, and helpless and is likely to plunge into drastic and rash solutions to their difficulties. The key to decreasing a client's demoralization is to interpret the client's problems in ways which attribute their cause to unstable factors that the client can influence (Levy and House, 1970; Meichenbaum and Smart, 1971). Finally, the counselor will wish to become a reference person for the client. A reference person influences the client through the process of identification. Through expressing warmth, caring, and acceptance, and through facilitating constructive client change, the client will like the counselor and see constructive similarities between self and the counselor (Johnson, 1971b, 1971c; D. Johnson and Johnson, 1972; Johnson and Noonan, 1972; S. Johnson and Johnson, 1972).

As the conditions for therapy are established, a cooperative problem-solving process is conducted which results in more self-enhancing attitudes and behavior patterns and the development of the basic social competencies needed to build and maintain cooperative relationships (Johnson and Matross, 1977).

In summary, the conflict-negotiation model of counseling consists of a set of interrelated processes involving the negotiation of the goals (based on the client's goals and the goals of promoting psychological health); definition and diagnosis of the client's problems; establishing the conditions for successful problem-solving; modifying destructive to self-enhancing patterns of attitudes and behaviors; learning the social competencies necessary for cooperative relationships with others; and integrating the new attitude and behavior patterns and social competencies into the client's ongoing life. All of these processes interact and are worked on simultaneously (they are *not* a sequence of activities), and together they define the process of therapy. Such an approach seems especially appropriate for alienated clients.

Questions for Further Inquiry

1. Can you remember a time when you and another person were alienated from each other? How did it feel for you?

2. What are the different effects of a temporary conflict as contrasted with a long-term alienation between two individuals?

3. What are some things that parents do that result in alienating their children? Themselves from each other?

4. What specific suggestions would you make to parents or teachers who wish to create growth-oriented socialization experiences for their children or students?

5. A phenomenon of our times is that many people feel alienated from the institutions of our society. What part can you plan in creating favorable change through your professional role?

References

Adler, A., Ansbacher, H., & Ansbacher, R. (Eds.). *The individual psychology of Alfred Adler.* New York: Basic Books, 1956.

Asch, S. *Social psychology.* Englewood Cliffs, N.J.: Prentice-Hall, 1952.

Breger, L. *From instinct to identity.* Englewood Cliffs, N.J.: Prentice-Hall, 1974.

Bronfenbrenner, U. Who cares for America's children? In V. Vaughan & T. Brazelton (Eds.), *The family—Can it be saved?* New York: Year Book Medical Publishers, 1976, pp. 3–32.

Bruner, J. *Toward a theory of instruction.* Cambridge: Harvard University Press, 1966.

Clark, J. Measuring alienation within a social system. *American Sociological Review*, 1959 *24*, 849–52.

Deutsch, M. Cooperation and trust: Some theoretical notes. In M. Jones (Ed.), *Nebraska symposium on motivation.* Lincoln: University of Nebraska Press, 1962, 275–319.

Erikson, E. *Childhood and society.* New York: Norton, 1950.

Falk, D., & Johnson, D. W. The effects of perspective-taking and egocentrism on problem-solving in heterogeneous and homogeneous groups. *Journal of Social Psychology,* 1977 *102,* 63–72.

Flavell, J. *The development of role-taking and communication skills in children.* New York: Wiley, 1968.

Freud, S. Introductory lectures on psychoanalysis (1916–1917). In J. Strachey (Ed.), *Standard edition of the complete psychological works of Sigmund Freud.* London: Hogarth Press, Vols. 15 and 16, 1963.

Fromm-Reichmann, F. *Principles of intensive psychotherapy.* Chicago: University of Chicago Press, 1950.

Gamson, W. The fluoridation dialogue: Is it an ideological conflict? *Public Opinion Quarterly* 1961 *35,* 526–37.

Horton, J., & Thompson, W. Powerlessness and political negativism: A study of defeated local referendums. *American Journal of Sociology* 1962, 485–93.

Johnson, D. W. The use of role reversal in intergroup competition. Unpublished doctoral dissertation, Columbia University, 1966.

Johnson, D. W. The use of role reversal in intergroup competition. *Journal of Personality and Social Psychology* 1967 *7,* 135–41.

Johnson, D. W. The effects upon cooperation of commitment to one's position and engaging in or listening to role reversal. Unpublished research report, University of Minnesota, 1968.

Johnson, D. W. The effectiveness of role reversal: The actor or the listener. *Psychological Reports* 1971 *28,* 275–82. (a)

Johnson, D. W. the effects of warmth of interaction, accuracy of understanding, and the proposal of compromises on the listener's behavior. *Journal of Counseling Psychology* 1971 *18,* 207–16. (b)

Johnson, D. W. The effects of the order of expressing warmth and anger upon the actor and the listener. *Journal of Counseling Psychology* 1971 *18,* 571–78. (c)

Johnson, D. W. *Reaching out: Interpersonal effectiveness and self-actualization.* Englewood Cliffs, N.J.: Prentice-Hall, 1972. (a)

Johnson, D. W. The effects of role reversal on seeing a conflict from the opponent's frame of reference. Unpublished research report. University of Minnesota, 1972. (b)

Johnson, D. W. Cooperative competencies and the prevention and treatment of drug abuse. *Research in Education,* 1975 (November), Eric # ED108066.

Johnson, D. W. The distribution and exchange of information in problem-solving dyads. *Communication Research* 1977 *4,* 283–98.

Johnson, D. W. *Human relations and your career: A guide to interpersonal skills.* Englewood Cliffs, N.J.: Prentice-Hall, 1978.

Johnson, D. W. *Educational psychology.* Englewood Cliffs, N.J.: Prentice-Hall, 1979.

Johnson, D. W., & Johnson, F. *Joining together: Group theory and group skills.* Englewood Cliffs, N.J.: Prentice-Hall, 1975.

Johnson, D. W., & Johnson, R. *Learning together and alone: Cooperation, competition, and individualization.* Englewood Cliffs, N.J.: Prentice-Hall, 1975.

Johnson, D. W., & Johnson, S. The effects of attitude similarity, expectation of goal facilitation, and actual goal facilitation on interpersonal attraction. *Journal of Experimental Social Psychology* 1972 *8,* 197–206.

Johnson, D. W., & Matross, R. The interpersonal influence of the psychotherapist. In A. Gurman & A. Razin (Eds.), *The effective therapist: A handbook.* Elmsford, N.Y.: Pergamon, 1977.

Johnson, D. W., McCarty, K., & Allen, T. Congruent and contradictory verbal and nonverbal communications of cooperativeness and competitiveness in negotations. *Communication Research* 1976 *3,* 275–92.

Johnson, D. W., & Noonan, M. The effects of acceptance and reciprocation of self-disclosures on the development of trust. *Journal of Counseling Psychology* 1972 *19,* 411–16.

Johnson, D. W., & Norem-Hebeisen, A. Attitudes toward interdependence among persons and psychological health. *Psychological Reports* 1977 *40,* 843–50.

Johnson, S., & Johnson, D. W. The effects of other's actions, attitude similarity, and race on attraction towards the other. *Human Relations* 1972 *25,* 121–30.

Jung, C., & DeLaszlo, V. (Eds.). *The basic writings of C. G. Jung.* New York: Random House, 1959.

Keniston, K. *The uncommitted: Alienated youth in American society.* New York: Harcourt Brace Johanovich, 1965.

Kohlberg, L. Stage and sequence: The cognitive-developmental approach to socialization. In D. Goslin (Ed.), *Handbook of socialization theory and research.* Chicago: Rand McNally, 1969, pp. 347–480.

Levy, L., & House, W. Perceived origins of beliefs as determinants of expectancy for their change. *Journal of Personality and Social Psychology* 1970 *14,* 329–34.

Lewin, K. *A dynamic theory of personality.* New York: McGraw-Hill, 1935.

Marwell, G., & Schmitt, D. Cooperation in a three-person prisioner's dilemma. *Journal of Personality and Social Psychology* 1972 *21,* 376–83.

Maslow, A. *Motivation and personality.* New York: Harper & Row, 1954.

May, R. *Love and will.* New York: Norton, 1969.

Mead, G. *Mind, self, and society.* Chicago: University of Chicago Press, 1934.

Meichenbaum, D., & Smart, I. Use of direct expectancy to modify academic performance and attitudes of college students. *Journal of Counseling Psychology* 1971 *18,* 531–35.

Millon, T. *Modern psychopathology.* Philadelphia: Saunders, 1969.

Murray, H. Thematic apperception test in various settings. In *Military clinical psychology.* Washington, D.C.: U.S. Government Printing Office, 1951, 59–71.

Nettler, G. Measure of alienation. *American Sociological Review* 1957 *22,* 670–77.

Piaget, J. *The psychology of intelligence.* New York: Harcourt Brace Johanovich, 1950.

Rogers, C. *Client-centered therapy.* Boston: Houghton Mifflin, 1951.

Rokeach, M. *The open and closed mind.* New York: Basic Books, 1960.

Seeman, M. Alienation studies. In A. Inkeles, J. Coleman, & N. Smelser (Eds.), *Annual Review of Sociology,* 1975. Palo Alto, Calif.: Annual Reviews, 1975. 91–124.

Sullivan, H. *The interpersonal theory of psychiatry.* New York: Norton, 1953.

Understanding and Managing Conflict

7

DIANE E. FREY

Understanding and Alleviating Interpersonal Conflicts

Understanding Conflict and How People Manage It

"Nightmares, Fear Haunt Rape Victim," "... Teachers Strike Gets Hearing in ... County Court," "Police Harrassment Claimed by Citizen...." "Vandals Strike Museum, Kill and Maim 20 Birds." Open any newspaper in any city any day and numerous examples of conflicts can be found. Most of these reported conflicts also model poor conflict resolutions. An inspection of most newspapers frequently indicates that violence and flight are the most commonly reported conflict resolutions. Humankind has reached some of its greatest heights and lowest depths from the influence of conflict. Yet the study of human conflict as an academic discipline is still very young.

History and Rationale

In the last thirty years, and particularly more recently, the study of conflict has become multidisciplinary. Biological concomitants of aggression have been investigated. Psychology has been turned to discover the roots of conflict in personality and the influence of motivation on conflict and its resolution. Sociological study has helped investigate institutional settings as they relate to conflict. History has lent the evidence of evolutionary trends.

Yet in spite of these efforts most people have received no formal training or objective feedback in conflict resolution. The popular idea of conflict is that it represents failure, is to be avoided, and is "bad" and "evil." Consequently, conflicts continue to be avoided or resolved inappropriately. As a result of this behavior escalation often occurs: A father beats his child because of other unresolved conflicts in his life that have escalated to a frustration point. A teacher reprimands a student for forgetting to bring a pencil to class, and the student throws a chair. An individual ridden with the accumulated effects of guilt and depression commits suicide. These are examples of the kinds of tension and misery that result when conflicts remain unresolved for periods of time intolerable to the individual.

Conflicts are an inevitable part of life. As such the goal of the study of conflict is to teach individuals how to manage and/or resolve conflicts in a way that is satisfactory to the situation. There is a need, therefore, for those in the helping professions to be models of effective conflict management and/or resolution since, for many clients, the relationship with the helper will be one of the few effective models he or she experiences. Since conflict is so inextricably related to psychopathology (Freud, 1935; Jung, 1953; Horney, 1945; Rogers, 1959) understanding it is of great value to those in the helping professions. The study of conflict also can result in personal benefits to the helper as he or she becomes more skilled at managing the conflict in his or her own life.

The remainder of this chapter includes the definition of conflict, causation, diagnosis, functional versus dysfunctional conflict, kinds of resolution styles and their evaluation, creative alternatives to conflict, preventative counseling and conflict, the role of effective education in developmental counseling about conflict, current trends and future issues in the conflict field.

Definitions

Conflict is generally viewed as a tendency to perform two or more incompatible responses at the same time, resulting in emotional, mental and/or physical stress requiring modification.

The terms "competition" and "conflict" have sometimes been used interchangeably. Although competition may elicit conflict, not all instances of conflict result in competition (Deutsch, 1973). Competition usually is viewed as opposition of goals, which can be interpersonal or intrapersonal. Conflict may occur when there is no incompatibility of goals as when two helpers, both wanting to aid a client, discuss two different treatment plans. Another example is when an individual, wanting to enhance his or her job future, cannot decide if higher education would help. Conflicts can be functional or dysfunctional. According to Deutsch (1973) this difference is important: conflict can occur in a cooperative or competitive environment. Conflict resolution choices are influenced by the context in which the conflict is perceived.

Functional (constructive) conflict has, as some of its advantages, the exposure of issues, improvement of quality of problem-solving, increased emotional involvement, increased creativity, clarification of objectives, increased cohesiveness, and establishment of group norms. (Norms characteristically aid in conflict resolution.)

Dysfunctional (destructive) conflict, characterized by a tendency to escalate, diverts energy, weakens morale, obstructs cooperative action, increases differences, and can cause psychological trauma. At its worst, dysfunctional conflict can even arrest or delay a child's social-emotional growth (Palomares, 1975).

Models for Classifying Conflicts

A variety of models for classifying conflicts have been presented in the literature. Three of these will be developed in this section.

Miller's Valence Model   Dollard and Miller (1950) identified four types of conflict: approach-approach; avoidance-avoidance; approach-avoidance; and double approach-avoidance. Each differs from the others with regard to valences or values an individual associates with either a goal object or given set of options.

In an *approach-approach conflict* an individual is confronted with two equally attractive, but mutually exclusive alternatives. For example, a football coach may have to cut one of two players, but likes the way both play. Since both options are attractive in this conflict, on the surface it may not appear stressful. However, making a decision usually requires giving up one of the alternatives and giving up something valued is usually very difficult.

In the *avoidance-avoidance conflict* two or more negative choices exist. If the choices are equally undesirable, the conflict may be very intense and frustrating. Sometimes escape is used as resolution or the person tries to avoid making a choice. A battered woman involved in severe marital conflict perceives two dissatisfying options: (1) getting a divorce with the concurrent problems of having no way to support herself and experiencing long periods of loneliness; or (2) staying in the marriage with its everyday conflicts, feelings of futility and dejection, and frequent batterings.

In *approach-avoidance conflict* an individual attaches both positive and negative values to a given future possibility. The undesirable points are not wanted, but they accompany the desirable ones. A person may want a family but yet be repelled by some of its negative elements such as less autonomy. The conflict is characterized by a lot of ambivalence. The person often feels bewildered, apprehensive, discontented, useless, and/or inadequate.

Double approach-avoidance is the same as described above except that two or more possibilities are involved, each having positive and negative value loadings. This conflict is the type most frequently found. A single person may be attracted to two individuals, each having qualities that are liked and qualities that are disliked. At times an objective third party is needed to mediate this type of conflict since the frustration and the intensified feelings resulting from it may hamper the use of cognitive processes (Dollard and Miller, 1950).

Object of the Conflict   Individuals may be in conflict with self, in conflict with a significant other, in conflict with an organization, or in conflict with humankind. The object of the conflict provides a second model for describing different types of conflict.

1. Intrapersonal—a conflict an individual experiences with self. This conflict type has been described as cognitive dissonance. An individual might be concerned about whether to resign from a job or stay with it.
2. Interpersonal—a conflict between two or more people or groups. Employer-employee conflicts are often of this type.
3. Personal-organizational—a conflict between an individual and a corporation, institution, or other type of organization. If a person does not agree with some of the policies of his or her church, such a conflict would exist.
4. Impersonal—conflict between individual and/or humankind and the environment. An individual might experience conflict as a result of decreasing resources in the environment. Research studies of spatial crowding in cities indicate changed personal reactions of individuals with increased anger generally being evident.

All of these types are interrelated. A person experiencing a lot of intrapersonal conflict could possibly escalate the conflict magnitude by in turn eliciting interpersonal conflicts and vice versa. A person involved in ecological conflicts, which would be impersonal, could generate personal organizational conflicts by forming pressure groups and/or political lobbying activity.

What classifies a conflict in any of these areas is the person's perception of the conflict the pronouns a client uses in communication help the counselor identify the object of his or her conflicts. A client who discusses a conflict using "I" terminology most of the time tends to view it intrapersonally. A client who discusses a conflict using "I," "he," or "she" terminology generally views it as interpersonal. "I," "they" usage usually means the client views the conflict as personal-organizational or impersonal.

Cognitive vs. Emotional Issues It is sometimes helpful to further subdivide either of the models mentioned into cognitive (those dealing with intellectual disagreement) or emotional (those dealing with negative feelings) issues. Cognitive issues can be (1) role invasions (imposing on someone else's work role), (2) task invasion (not acquiring service required to perform a job well, or (3) philosophical differences (believing in different concepts). Emotional issues can be (1) need deprivations (activity fails to satisfy personal needs), (2) incompatible needs (two individuals or groups want different and incompatible resolutions of a problem), or (3) personal style differences (personality factors vary). This further subdivision can aid both the helper and the client in specifying the nature of the conflict and thus lead to better management or resolution.

Causaton of Conflict Conflicts can arise from (1) *differences in information, or beliefs* (a client thinks it is better to come to the helper once a month, while the helper believes weekly appointments are better). They can be caused by (2) *difference in interests, desires, goals, or values* (the helper recommends counseling but the client would rather spend his or her time, money, and energy on a vacation trip). Conflicts may reflect (3) *scarcity of resources such as money, time, space, position* (the more time a client spends with a helper, the less time the client has for recreation). Variations in (4) *power* and (5) *status* can be causative factors in conflicts (a helper's employer indicates that a certain amount of work must be completed by a set time, while the helper knows it is impossible to finish by that time). Conflicts also may occur as a result of (6) *organizational structure* (a helper wants to deliver services to a client as quickly as possible, but four copies of the treatment plan must be completed and reviewed by other units of the organization before that can occur).

Terhune (1970) hypothesized that certain personality factors predispose a person to either cooperation or conflict:

1. People of aggressive and rigid nature are more likely to elicit conflict.
2. Conflict is more likely when the participants are defensive and withdrawal is impossible.
3. Among people who are mistrustful, one finds exploitation and retaliation.
4. Cooperativeness is likely among those who are passive and dependent.
5. When cooperation is the best resolution, those who are flexible and success-oriented will be most likely to comply.
6. Cooperation is likely among those who are generally trusting and egalitarian.
7. Such *personality factors* as insecurity and/or resistance to change can cause conflicts (the client wants to change but is afraid to take such a step because of all the uncertainty it entails). Related to this concept are incidents where a rivalry may be the cause of conflict such as when one individual tries to outdo or undo another.

Terhune indicates that personality factors should be studied as they interplay with the conflict situation, since few people exhibit behavioral constancies across all situations. For example, a person may be aggressive at his or her job and more passive in social relationships. Or an individual may feel secure in the presence of family members, but insecure and mistrustful in public.

8. *Poor communication* can also be responsible for conflicts (the helper is very evaluative in feedback to the client, rather than descriptive, thus resulting in decreasing self-esteem for the client.) Poor communication can be intrapersonal in nature also (when a client engages in negative self-talk).
9. Differing *perceptual sets* can also cause conflicts (Deutsch, 1973). The helper and/or client could perceive incompatibility where there is none (a long term alcoholic may finally lessen drinking behavior even

though past records show that this is contraindicated). Incompatibility could be seen as noncontingent by the helper and/or client, but may in fact be contingent upon changeable factors in the situation (if moved to a half-way house drinking may decrease or cease in an alcoholic client). Incompatibility may be perceived correctly but incorrect attribution is made (the alcoholic client problems are seen as being related to depression when actually they are aligned with poor support systems).

Since the causation of conflict is so varied, the existence of conflict is seldom rigidly assessed by objective data. Conflict is generally, therefore, a self-report of some negative feeling or a report from another about another. By changing his or her reaction to conflict, a person can change the direction of its effects from destructive to constructive.

Stages of Conflict Development
After recognizing types of conflicts, it is often helpful to know in what stage of the conflict process the participant is involved. Pondy (1967) identifies five stages of the conflict episode:

1. *Latent conflict.* This is used to describe a situation where there exists underlying conditions of competition for scarce resources, drives for autonomy, or divergence of goals. At this stage few emotional effects are realized since the conflict is so latent. The person(s) involved may not even recognize that a conflict exists.
2. *Perceived conflict.* Here the individual(s) recognizes the underlying conditions or points of misunderstanding but is generally unaware of concomitant feelings.
3. *Felt conflict.* Individual(s) is not only aware of the conflict but becomes tense about it. The presence of the conflict has identifiable emotional and/or physical effects. The feelings which the client experiences at this time depend a lot on the specifics of the situation but can be bitter, unloved, listless, lethargic, discontented, tired, dejected, weary, frustrated, depressed, fatigued, angry, hurt, lonely, inadequate, helpless, useless, hopeless, guilty, futile, bewildered, frightened, dismayed, furious, apprehensive, vengeful, sullen, alarmed, provoked, fearful, and uncomfortable.
4. *Manifest conflict.* Here tension is released through open aggression or covert means.
5. *Conflict aftermath.* This indicates the result of the conflict.

An example of the development of these stages might be a woman who wants to be more independent (latent conflict). She discusses this with her husband who disagrees with her goal. As she perceives the depths of the disagreement, she becomes tense, feels thwarted and discontented. As a result she has an extramarital affair (manifest conflict—covert means). This behavior results in feelings of guilt and hopelessness. When asking herself what the extramarital affair is doing for her, she assesses that it is neither hurting her husband nor helping her feel more independent. Since she values highly her marital relationship, she and her husband seek counseling (conflict aftermath). Knowing the stages of conflict aids helpers and clients to recognize conflicts as they develop and deal with them in early stages.

Conflict Management and Resolution

Approaches to dealing with conflict in a systematic manner have only recently been developed. Webb and Morgan in their 1930 book, entitled *Strategy in Handling People,* vaguely discussed conflict management and resolution by such chapter headings as, "The Secret of Making People Like You," "The Knack of Cooperation," "Winning Your Way Against Opposition," and "Putting Your Ideas Across." Some of their advice included:

> Keep in mind the various methods that can be used to win a victory. Try to choose the easiest and most certain method in the light of the man whom you face and the situation as a whole. Remember that the knock-out blow may range all the way from a bit of ridicule or a calm rebuke to a crack in the jaw. Also make it a point not to indulge in outbursts of temper, except for a specific purpose when you feel sure that this is the best way to handle a situation (Webb and Morgan, p. 252).

While they do warn against the use of violence as a general way of responding to conflict, the generality of their recommendations reflects the state of academic study of conflict at that time. They consistently viewed conflict from a winner-loser orientation, failing to recoginze that there can be creative solutions where nobody loses. Fortunately, more sensible recommendations can now be given.

Management vs. Resolution
Before styles of conflict management are discussed, it is important to differentiate between conflict management and conflict resolution. Management refers to the reduction of tension in the conflict in order to enable the person to pursue his or her goal. Resolution means that the individuals work to reduce the conflict until both parties are satisfied and/or the individual is satisfied in cases of intrapersonal conflict. Not all conflicts can be resolved, but with training, they can all be managed more effectively.

Learning Processes
Young children develop specific conflict management and resolution styles very quickly through the typical patterns of modeling and reinforcement (Bandura, Blanchard, and Ritter 1969). These early learning experiences seem to establish the more generalizable patterns used in later years. As they watch and hear

parents manage their own intrapersonal and interpersonal conflicts, children learn through imitation. Moreover, child-parent conflicts are inevitable in any household and the management methods used in these conflicts set patterns for later development. In the course of coping with these conflicts the child (as well as parent) is reinforced for certain coping styles, often on a partial reinforcement schedule. Thus some children are reinforced for compliance while others are reinforced for defiance, some for cooperation and some for the expression of hostility, some for disengagement and some for perseveration.

By the time a child reaches school age specific styles of conflict management and/or resolution have been adopted. They are open to modification but, like any other behavior, they increase in habit strength as age increases. Thus, each individual informally develops styles of dealing with conflict which may well be unknown to the person. Acquainting clients with this knowledge about self is one of the processes in working with conflict-laden individuals.

Styles of Conflict Resolution
Several models for assessing styles use people use to manage conflicts have been proposed. Three will be presented here.

Blake and Mouton (1971) proposed a model (Model A here) based on their observations concerning the methods by which conflicts are managed between people in task groups. They have developed a Managerial Grid (Figure 7-1) which takes into account the level of Concern for People and the level of Concern for Production expressed during these meetings. Thus a given conflict management approach may reflect a high concern for people and low concern for production; a high concern for production and low concern for people; or, a low concern for both or a high concern for both.

Conflict can be controlled by suppressing the others involved as in the extreme cases of police or military action. This 9, 1 category involves winning through power, manipulation, and control, rather than seeking a valid solution. Other examples are a teacher giving a student orders, a parent ordering children to obey.

The 1, 9 style is characterized by "Don't say anything if you can't say something nice." This can result in a quorum of agreement but smother creative problem-solving because of the atmosphere of not expressing differences and reinforcing sweetness and light. The use of reassurance leads by helpers most exemplifies this style. "Don't worry, time will heal all wounds."

The 1, 1 style is best characterized by "see no conflict, hear no conflict, and speak no conflict." It represents a withdrawal and/or an attempt by the individual to remain neutral. It is typified by alienation. At times clients involved in addictions appear to be using this style. Denial of conflict, for example, by clients who refuse to accompany a spouse to marital counseling because nothing is wrong with their marriage, also exemplifies this category.

Compromising one's beliefs is the underlying approach in style 5, 5. It is settling for what one can get rather than what is sound, based on available facts. A helper wants to facilitate a 24-hour marathon but the clients do not want to make

Table 7–1 The Conflict Grid

Concern for people		Concern for production results	
High 9	**1, 9** Disagreements are smoothed over or ignored so that surface harmony is maintained in a state of peaceful coexistence.		**9, 9** Valid problem-solving takes place with varying points of view objectively evaluated against facts; emotion reservation and doubts are examined and worked through.
8			
7			
6		**5, 5** Compromise bargaining and middle ground position are accepted so that no one wins and no one loses. Accomodations and adjustments lead to "workable" solutions rather than the best solutions.	
5			
4			
3	**1, 1** Neutrality is maintained at all costs. Withdrawl behind walls of insulation relieves the necessity for dealing with situations that would arise conflict.		**9, 1** Conflict is suppressed through authority-opedience approach. Win-lose power struggles fought out, decided by the highest common base or third party abitration.
2			
1			
Low	1 2 3 4 5	6 7 8 9 High	

Concern for production results

that great a time commitment, so a mini-marathon is held. A person has high priority values for honesty, yet at times compromises himself by telling "half truths" because the person also values highly emotional well being!

Disagreement is valued as inevitable in the 9, 9 approach and emotions and ideas held by various individuals are faced in a straightforward manner by frank discussion. The approach is more time-consuming immediately, but more time-conserving ultimately. Functional conflicts often fall into this category. Problem-solving and flexibility are the major approaches here. An illustrative case study will focus on this later in the chapter.

In another model (Model B) seven basic conflict management strategies are described: withdrawal, avoidance, compromise, third-party intervention, win-win, win-lose, and problem-solving. These strategies can be related to the categories in the Blake and Mouton model. Withdrawal is similar to what Blake and Mouton call style 1, 1, avoidance corresponds to style 1, 9, compromise is identical to style 5, 5, third party intervention and win-lose back fit category 9, 1, and both win-win and problem-solving strategies correspond to 9, 9. This model mainly takes on a different labeling process although the styles presented are very similar.

Palomares, (1975) has listed 17 conflict management strategies (Model C). These can be used separately or in combination:

(1) *Negotiating*—talking about one's position in the conflict and what can be done about it.

(2) *Compromise*—both individuals give up something.

(3) *Taking Turns*—one person goes first and the other second.

(4) *Active Listening*—perceiving what the other person is saying and accurately paraphrasing it.

(5) *Threat-Free Explanation*—an individual(s) communicates a position without threatening the other (person(s).

(6) *Apologizing*—an individual expresses that he or she is sorry without having to say he or she is wrong.

(7) *Soliciting Intervention*—the person(s) seeks consultation from another source(s). It can be from a book, an expert, a legal source, or a prestigious other.

(8) *Postponement*—individual(s) agrees to wait for a more appropriate time to discuss the conflict.

(9) *Distraction*—something or someone else is made the focus of attention as a way of de-fusing the conflict.

(10) *Abandoning*—the person(s) leaves the conflict situation if it cannot be dealt with and only more harm will result.

(11) *Exaggeration*—an exaggerated interpretation of the conflict is discussed to enable participant to see the real components of the conflict.

(12) *Humor*—humor that does not ridicule or insult can be used to help reduce tension in conflict and thereby ease resolution.

(13) *Chance*—a technique such as flipping a coin where the resolution is literally given to chance often helps each individual save face.

(14) *Sharing*—people use reciprocity and equality in approaching the conflict.

(Palomares states that the remaining conflict strategies are not prosocial and have numerous negative consequences. Whenever possible therefore they are to be discouraged.)

(15) *Violence*—verbal or physical abuse. Palomares states that in 99 percent of the conflict cases, violence is not an effective strategy.

(16) *Flight*—a person retreats internally or physically. The worst side effect from this approach is deterioration of self-esteem.

(17) *Tattling*—an individual attempts to enlist others to handle the conflict.

Although the Palomares material is primarily written for children, it has great applicability to adults, since most adults have had no formal training in conflict management and, consequently, are at a beginning readiness level.

Helping Clients Resolve Conflict

Obstacles to Resolution

Two serious obstacles to the resolution or management of conflict are the "conflict blindness" of the individuals involved and the impulsivity of choice. Most individuals have developed styles of dealing with conflict which have become habit over a period of time. As a conflict appears, the person tends to respond in an habitual coping style. Choices and solutions are generally not considered. A client experiencing anger toward another decides to hit the person. The client probably will not pause and think of other alternatives first. If violence is characteristically the client's resolution style, he or she will use it. Part of the helper's role therefore is to aid clients in becoming less conflict blind. Exercises and role-playing to aid in this direction will be illustrated in the case studies presented.

Process for Helping People Resolve Conflict

Increasing the client's awareness of conflict blind areas and resolution styles is usually not enough. A process of planning for conflict resolution is also an important part of a total helping process. It should be emphasized that this is a problem-solving approach and may not result in an immediate resolution. The process includes eight steps:

(1) *Trust building.* The first step involves one of establishing trust and acceptance. If there is little trust between or among individuals, ineffective communication about the conflict exists because no one is actually listening to what is being said. Instead each is trying to defend self. This acceptance of the other person must be without conditions of worth; learning how to affirm the other without blaming him or her.

(2) *Strength affirmation.* The second step involves developing within oneself a firm idea of one's personal strengths. One utilizes these strengths to build strengths in the individual(s) involved. This step greatly aids in decreasing the threat level which a conflict frequently induces. This can be done over a period of time (several months), or it can be done in a matter of a few minutes depending on the nature of the conflict and the people involved. It involves commenting on the client's strengths in a genuine manner. The strengths do not necessarily have to be related to the conflict at hand. The helper takes the time to comment to clients about progress in counseling.

(3) *Accurate message sending and receiving.* Usually this is the step where conflict management incorrectly begins, at least for those who will admit to a conflict and try to manage it. The problem is that little is accomplished when individuals try to communicate about a conflict if the prior steps have not occurred previously. The people involved usually say things they do not mean or say little at all, many times because they are very defensive. The first two steps contribute to enabling each person to feel worthy. During step three each person does active listening and asks for clarification. It involves for each person trying to see the conflict through the other person's eyes, whether the perception is correct or not. All the basics of good communication are involved here. This step is the content of the conflict.

(4) *Reality testing.* Step four involves reality testing. Each person determines if the assumptions being made are valid. Clients often comment, "No one can help me." "People just never change." "He just doesn't understand me." "She doesn't listen." In conflict resolution it is better to validate such assumptions rather than to allow them to go unexamined and possibly block movement toward resolution.

(5) *Goal setting.* Establishing goals is step five. A helper and client discuss what each wants to accomplish or, in intrapersonal conflict, the client discusses within self what his or her goals are. Several goals will become evident, some similar, some dissimilar. Individuals start there by first working together on similar goals, and often the dissimilar ones become less important later as one's worth is continuously reaffirmed. This step is not one of convincing the other person to conform to one set of goals. It involves respect for the other person's views.

(6) *Generating alternatives.* Once the goals are established step six focuses on identifying alternatives. Brainstorming is important here. Generating as many alternatives as possible without evaluating is important. The three conflict resolution models presented earlier provide a base for developing new approaches.

(7) *Selecting alternatives.* Step seven then is a process of selecting one of the alternatives previously discussed. Three questions serve as guidelines here for each alternative: (1) What is the best result of choosing this alternative? (2) What is the worst result of choosing this alternative? (3) What is the most likely result? It is also helpful for each person to review what strengths and needs he or she has for each alternative.

(8) *Planning for implementation.* Specifying the decision is step eight. Here all parties decide specifically what each person does and by when or, in intrapersonal conflict, what the time line is. Frequently conflicts begin at this step if a degree of specificity is not obtained. How many times has one family member expected another family member to accomplish some task, but this expectation was not articulated well and went undone? Consequently, another conflict was

evoked. Or perhaps the task was well specified in terms of what was to be done, but not by when, and a conflict grew out of that.

Any one of these steps which is not attended to properly can serve as the stimulus for further conflict. When reaching an impasse at one step, it is usually necessary to go to the prior step and check to see if it was accomplished properly. These steps, thus, become very much like a flow chart through which conflicts can be cycled and recycled.

Although seeming to focus more on interpersonal, personal-organizational, or impersonal conflicts, this process also has some potential for resolving intrapersonal conflicts. In these cases the first four steps involve introspection and self-talk to build client strengths, self-trust, and accurate self-communication.

Techniques

Ideally models of resolution or management should be expained when the individual is not directly involved in the middle of an intense conflict. Several different approaches have been developed to aid the client in gaining insight at these earlier stages. These can be done on an on-going basis and, in that way, should lessen the tendency toward impulsive resolution.

An initial helpful technique to use is to ask the client to list and describe, in chart form, several previously experienced conflicts, their resolutions, and the feelings experienced during and after the episodes. Through this interaction the helper can identify those individuals who feel that they do not have conflicts and those for whom everything is a conflict. (Clients usually fall on a continuum with these two situations at the extremes). The helper and the client can then identify some of the typical resolution styles the client has used and explore, if desired, how these were probably developed and strengthened into habit.

The use of simulation and games such as Prisoner's Dilemma or Kidney Machine can also serve this same purpose. In Kidney Machine, for example, seven people of varying backgrounds are described in a paragraph. Each needs a kidney machine, but only two are available. The client must choose who is to receive the use of the machine. Any game exercise or simulation depicting a conflict and asking for a resolution can be used here. Simulation is probably the best type of exercise since it can be closely aligned with the reality of everyday living, thus making the transfer of resolution styles more valid and reliable. By processing the activity and/or chart with the helper in either an individual or group setting, the client gains new insight into types of conflicts and resolution styles used in the past. For example, if the client tended to avoid or withdraw from resolving the conflict, perhaps this is done in everyday life. If the client responds in an authoritarian manner, perhaps win-lose is a style this person frequently uses. At this phase of helping the goal is identification of conflict-resolution styles.

In the next phase of helping, the client learns conflict blind areas. The client is asked to write a brief description of a unresolved conflict. This description is then given to another member of the group by the helper or, if in individual counseling, the client is asked to share it with some significant others in his or her environment. This other person discusses solutions he or she might have tried. In group counseling settings, other members may also participate. The client may begin to see numerous alternatives not thought of previously and discover that the conflict is more manageable than previously thought. In a group situation more reticent clients can learn vicariously, without feeling threatened.

After recognizing conflict blind areas, the client is then helped to use more varied alternative resolutions. This can be done through the use of role-playing, video vignettes, dramatizations, films and, for younger clients, puppetry and cartoons. All these approaches acquaint the client with viable models of conflict management and/or resolution. At this point, the eight step problem-solving model can also be utilized.

Teaching Conflict Resolution to Children

As previously discussed, people appear to develop their own conflict management patterns early in life. Consequently, helping young children learn and use effective methods of conflict resolution can be seen as an important developmental objective than can prevent ineffective conflict coping later in life. Palomares (1975) has developed *A Curriculum On Conflict Management* for children, which includes three 16-mm. films, one for helpers and two for children. The adult film describes a process of conflict management which is demonstrated in the other two films. The children in the films (one for primary-age children and the other for intermediate-age children), by using a behavioral model, discover creative alternatives for conflict. In a group setting the children discuss previous conflicts and resolutions. Other children discuss alternative behaviors and direct the other children in the group in role-playing them. A period of cognition occurs where children in the group discuss what they learned from the process.

Palomares also offers lesson guides which include topics for discussion, i.e., "A Time When Someone Wouldn't Listen to Me," "A Time When I Was Involved in a Misunderstanding," puppetry, various dramatizations, essay and role playing activities.

In the puppetry the children are given sentences describing a play. One such example is, "A child hits another child with a ball and thinks it's very funny. The second child gets mad because it hurts. They get into an argument" (Palomares, 1975). The children finish the play by using prosocial resolutions.

Another example is picture story cards with various alternatives illustrated on cards. The children pick the alternative cards they like best. In the curriculum guide are also cartoons illustrating various alternatives. Such materials are both remedial and preventative, since they aid in changing poor modes of conflict resolution and also offer new alternatives which hopefully will help children manage and minimize conflicts more effectively in their adult life.

Case Studies

The ensuing case studies illustrate both the theory and techniques described so far.

Case One

Thirty-five-year-old Ted arrived in the helper's office and stated that he thought he wanted a divorce because he and his wife argued about almost everthing. He felt hopeless and just wanted to leave his wife.

Diagnosis—The helper in analyzing this conflict decided that Ted was at the feeling stage of describing his conflict. It became the helper's task, therefore, to aid the client in developing the problem description to the manifest stage where he would have a better awareness of the difficulties.

The client had perceived the conflict as an interpersonal one and had thought of withdrawal as a resolution. The helper asked the client to explore his manner of dealing with conflict by making a conflict chart and responding to some exercises, games, and simulations. The helper found out through these that the client characteristically either avoided or withdrew from interpersonal conflicts. A conflict exchange was then completed to illustrate this to the client, utilizing the divorce conflict.

Treatment—Other alternatives such as postponement, third-party intervention, threat-free explanation compromise and negotiation were then brainstormed through the use of role-playing and video vignettes, depicting other couples in similar marital difficulties. The client decided to pursue negotiation, threat-free explanation, and third-party intervention in combination, by asking his wife to come with him to marital counseling (third-party intervention) where the other two alternatives could be explored. Negotiation finally led to a positive resolution for both parties involved.

Case Two

Twenty-five-year-old Suzanne presented to the helper a conflict dealing with a colleague. The colleague was pleasant to her when interacting face to face, but he proceeded to tell her employer all the errors she was making on the job. When asked what she had done to resolve this interpersonal conflict, she indicated that she had been avoiding the problem.

Diagnosis—The helper used the conflict chart and conflict exchange to show the client her pattern of conflict management and blind areas. In addition the client was asked to complete a helper-made questionnaire which consisted of fifteen descriptions of conflict situations and listed several multiple choice answers. The choices were representative of various conflict alternatives. Through this assessment the helper found that the client characteristically used avoidance as a technique.

Treatment—Through a third-party management strategy—talking with her employer—she discovered that her colleague did not view conflict as a part of their relationship. Consequently, instead of seeking an immediate resolution, the helper suggested the problem-solving management process discussed earlier in this chapter. The helper began with steps one and two, trust building and strength affirmation. The helper gave the client feedback about her strengths and asked her for affirmation and elaboration. It was agreed that one of her greatest strengths was her verbal fluency.

She utilized this fluency strength to build strength in her colleague. She chose qualities about him which she genuinely liked and commented about them to him. After a period of several weeks his threat level was reduced. As the strength development continued, she was guided by the helper in affirming the colleague and developing a trust relationship with him. At this time he admitted to the existence of a conflict and step three ensued.

Through active listening, perception testing, congruent responding, and clarification the two individuals discussed the conflict and found that the manifest conflict—his dislike of her and consequent discussing of her shortcomings with her employer—was not the underlying conflict. The underlying problem was his feeling of inadequacy (intrapersonal conflict for him) in working with a colleague twenty years younger than he, a female, and a more accomplished professional than he.

In step four each person checked to see if their assumptions about the conflict were valid, invalid, or of unknown validity. It was found that both people had made assumptions that were invalid and of unknown validity. The invalid assumptions—she was unconcerned about him, he was inept—were discarded. The unknown ones were clarified and validated.

In step five both people discussed what they wanted to do about the conflict. They worked on similar goals first, such as wanting to interact less competitively. Brainstorming in step six generated five alternative approaches to achieving this goal. By discussing what the best, worst, and most likely outcome of each in step seven, one alternative was chosen. In step eight it was mutually decided that he would not criticize her to another person but would come directly to her with his concerns. She asked him to work with her on a future professional project since it was a topic of mutual interest. They also decided to utilize a flow chart, displaying these steps, to aid them in any future conflicts.

Case Three

Nine-year-old Donald was referred to the helper by his teacher. It was indicated that he was constantly fighting with other children both in school and during recess (an example of the manifest conflict stage), Donald had a very low self concept with which he was trying to cope by overcompensation. He made up grandiose stories of his accomplishments to which others verbalized disbelief. This began most of the fights. Donald utilized violence as a resolution since that was the predominant strategy he saw in his home.

Diagnosis—After the counselor discussed with him several other conflicts he experienced and how he resolved them (in essence a verbal conflict chart), it became evident that what appeared to be an interpersonal conflict (fighting) at the manifest level was actually an intrapersonal conflict (poor self-esteem) at the underlying level.

Treatment—Donald was helped in raising his self-esteem through individual counseling. He was also placed in a guidance group to help him learn other conflict strategies. In the group, children shared conflicts and made cartoons illustrating all the different alternatives they had discussed. They also made an audio tape of the alternatives so that a child could borrow it and play it at home when he sometimes forgot about other alternatives. Donald borrowed the tape and also played it for his family. In the group the children also made up skits and dramatized them using different resolutions and telling how they felt. Donald started to suggest nonviolent strategies. Each child kept a log of the number of different ways they saw others manage conflict. The helper gave them unfinished stories to complete at home using several conflict resolutions. Donald's fighting behavior decreased dramatically, and he varied his strategies. He reported back to the group, which reinforced his new behavior.

Educational Applications

Other applications from the study of conflict management have been in the field of education where in-service education has helped teachers manage their own conflicts and those of the children. In many states, teachers have developed curricula in conflict management for grades K-12. In family living courses many teachers currently involve students in the concepts and application. Principals and superintendents have utilized the problem-solving process in working with central administration, in facilitating team building, and in averting strikes. Helpers have used the concepts in parent groups, in small group interaction with children and adults, and in consultation with various agencies. Conflict management applications have also been helpful for child abuse workers, counselors working with severely dependent clients, women new to the world of work, clergymen, and hospital personnel.

Trends and Issues

Future research needs to focus on investigating other constructive models of conflict management rather than the defensive destructive models which have been discussed. Interdisciplinary research programs would add considerably to these efforts. More research needs to be done in studying personality factors as they relate to various conflict situations and management strategies. For example, do authoritarian people have more difficulty in managing intrapersonal conflicts than non-authoritarian individuals? Some research studies currently have investigated how poor conflict management inhibits learning, but the data to date are not conclusive. Investigating whether there is a correlation between certain resolution styles and certain conditions would also be helpful.

Prevention of Dysfunctional Conflict

Prevention of poor conflict management is closely aligned to the field of affective education. It appears that the earlier children are exposed to effective models, the more easily they manage conflict. Conflict curricula are highly recommended for grades K-12 in an effort to prevent poor management strategies and to promote prosocial strategies. Remediation groups for adults could be conducted in a similar way to that of parenting and encounter groups now being conducted across the country. Central to the facilitation of such efforts will be those in the helping professions. Without such efforts, the same ineffective trial and error process currently effecting most of us will continue to spiral conflicts beyond their initial trust.

Questions for Further Inquiry

1. Recall a recent interpersonal conflict you have experienced. Try to picture the detail of who was involved, the time, place, and physical conditions and the content of the disagreement. Was it resolved satisfactorily? In retrospect could you have managed the conflict more effectively?

2. Have you ever been trapped by your own guilt? How did it feel for you?

3. When interpersonal conflicts develop, very often the participants become angry, their anger escalates, and then they polarize. What can a helper do to reduce the polarization and help the participants more effectively address the real issues of the conflict?

4. People often say that there are "masculine" ways and "feminine" ways of coping with conflict. What is meant by these expressions? Are these generalizations valid for you?

5. Do you believe that persons of different socioeconomic backgrounds socialize their young to cope with conflict differently?

References

Bandura, A., Blanchard, E. B., & Ritter, B. The relative efficacy of densensitization and modeling approaches for inducing behavioral, affective, and attitudinal changes. An unpublished manuscript. Stanford University 1969 13, 173–99.

Blake, R. R., & Mouton, J. S. The fifth achievement. *Journal of Applied Behavioral Science* 1970 6, 413–26.

Deutsch, M. Conflicts: Productive and·destructive. *Journal of Social Issues* 1969 25, 7–41.

Deutsch, M. *The Resolution of conflict: Constructive and destructive processes.* New Haven: Yale University Press, 1973.

Dollard, J. & Miller, N. E. *Personality and psychotherapy.* New York: McGraw-Hill, 1950

Freud, S. *General introduction to psycho-analysis.* New York: Liveright Publishing Corporation, 1935.

Horney, K. *Our inner conflicts.* New York: Norton 1945.

Jung, C. G. Collected works. In J. Jacobi (Ed.), *Psychological reflections and anthology.* New York: Pantheon Books, 1953.

Palomares, U. *A curriculum on conflict management.* La Mesa, Calif., Human Development Training Institute, 1975.

Pondy, L. Organizational conflict: concepts and models. *Administrative Science Quarterly* 1967 12, 299–306.

Rogers, C., & Dymond, R. F. *Psychotherapy and personality change.* Chicago: University of Chicago Press, 1959.

Terhune, K. R. The effects of personality in cooperation and conflict. In P. Swingle (Ed.), *The structure of conflict. New: Academic Press, 1970.*

Webb, E., & Morgan, J. B. *Strategy in handling people.* Garden City, N.Y.: Garden City Publishing Company, 1930.

Understanding and Overcoming Shyness

8

JANET C. LOXLEY

Overview

Why would "shyness" be included in a volume that covers such weighty therapeutic issues as depression, addictions, and grief? We are just beginning to realize the importance and pervasiveness of shy behavior. Zimbardo (1977) reported that 80 percent of the 2,000 Americans he surveyed labeled their behavior as "shy" during some part of their life and that 40 percent thought they acted shyly now. Shyness is a personal concern that brings many people into counseling. While it may be easy for the professional to dismiss concerns about shyness as "not important" or "they'll grow out of it," there are significant consequences for the person who behaves shyly. These might include loss of contact with others, especially intimate contact; anxiety and discomfort around others; frustration and depression over missed opportunities; and feeling disappointed and critical about oneself. For some, shyness restricts and confines their behavior but is not seen as a major problem. For others, the consequences of shy behavior can be traumatic. In either case, shyness is worth overcoming.

This chapter presents conceptualizations and examples of shyness and develops some of the different motivations or explanations for shy behavior. Treatment plans are presented for working with the different motivations. Special attention is given to the application of the cognitive-behavioral assertion model as treatment for shyness (Lange and Jakubowski, 1976).

Toward an Understanding of Shyness

Definition of Shyness

> Dr. R: "I'm sure glad I'm a writer rather than a lecturer."
> Dr. S: "Why?"
> Dr. R: "Because I'm shy."
> Dr. S: "Oh, I see!"

In everyday language "shy" is a label *and* an explanation. "I'm shy," ranks with "I have an inferiority complex" and "I have penis envy." Actually, if someone says "I'm shy" you can *guess* what that means about his or her behavior and motivations but you really don't have much information. This author assumes that "shy people" do not exist and urges that the use of the word "shy" as a trait label and explanation be discontinued. There are people who exhibit behaviors[1] that get labeled as shy by themselves or others. This distinction is important because someone who has *learned* to behave shyly can also *learn* to behave unshyly. Shyness is not a personality trait; it is a set of learned behaviors.

Basically, shy behavior deals with the quality of interaction with other people and may include acting or feeling hesitant or reticent with certain people, feeling anxious and worrying about contact with certain people, and avoidance of certain people or situations. As you think of your own experiences and those of friends, relatives, strangers, and clients, you will see that there is no one external behavior that typifies shyness. Some people think and feel they are shy, while their behavior looks assertive. They label themselves as shy, but others say, "You—you're not shy. Why you always look so confident!" Some people might be labeled as "shy" by others, but in their own thoughts and feelings are not shy.

While there are no universal shy behaviors, many behaviors commonly labeled as "shy" do come to mind:

–Feeling afraid before, during, or after talking to specific people (teachers, men, women, service people, doctors, relatives, friends, strangers, attractive people, children).
–Inability to make requests, refuse requests, agree to requests.
–Anxiety over attending public events alone (or with others).
–Difficulty expressing opinions, preferences, and feelings.
–Indirect approaches to others (limited eye contact, flirting, giggling, blushing, waiting for others to initiate).
–Anxiety about speaking in a group.

While "shy people" do not exist, the degree of shyness can be assessed by the frequency and intensity of occurrence of shy behaviors. How often does the

---

[1]"Behavior" in this chapter includes thoughts, feelings, and actions.

person behave shyly? How much does this interfere with daily life? How intense is the emotional response? The following case examples will illustrate different manifestations of shyness. Note that these people behave shyly in specific situations with certain types of people and that some had more situations and people they were uncomfortable with than others.

Jim, who was 28, said he was shy around women. His shyness manifested itself by spending hours walking around the neighborhoods of women he found attractive—hoping he might simply "run into one of them." On the rare occasion that this did happen he became so anxious about presenting himself "just right" that he would talk incessantly in a very loud tone of voice, insuring that he got a negative or neutral response, which made it even more difficult to approach the next woman.

Betsy, a popular fourth-grader, never raised her hand in class and would not respond to questions when called upon—even when she knew the answer. As a consequence, her grades were suffering and she was miserable.

A freshman woman, Joan, waited in her dormitory room hoping to be approached by others. When she was, she looked anxious—avoiding eye contact and making minimal responses. Fortunately for her there were a few very persistent women in the dormitory who kept making contact until she became less frightened and more fun to be around.

Mrs. McDonald, a homemaker, found it very difficult to converse with other adults (besides her husband) and found herself spending more and more time at home with her preschoolers. She came in for treatment when she began feeling strong resentment toward the children, worrying that she might physically abuse them. Mr. McDonald had a few "buddies at the factory" with whom he could gripe about the job and discuss sports and cars. He never saw them away from work and shared Mrs. McDonald's fears about people. He dealt with this by being critical of her since she was not meeting all of his needs. Here shy behavior was part of the larger family interaction problem, although it was difficult to convince the couple that learning to interact comfortably with other adults would help their situation. She wanted to focus on how evil she was for her anger, and he wanted to convince us how dull and boring she was.

Jerome had attended an all-black high school in Los Angeles before coming to the university and had never really talked with an Anglo his age before. Suddenly he found himself with an Anglo roommate, Dave, who had many friends dropping by. Jerome believed they were "too different" from him and that he couldn't possibly have anything to say to them. He found himself withdrawing and avoiding being in his room when Dave was there. He was feeling the strain of these new contacts and was neglecting his studies.

Motivations and Explanations for Shy Behavior

Why would people choose to behave shyly even when it is restricting or confining? What are some of the motivations or explanations for shy behavior? Given that people may be engaging in behaviors that look similar and are labeled the same, it is still likely that the motives underlying their behaviors are different. Four possible explanations for shy behavior include poor social skills, irrational thinking, previous history of reward for shy behavior, and previous history of punishment or rejection for approaching others. Each of these will be discussed.

Poor Social Skills, A Learning Deficit   The person simply has never learned the skills for interacting with others and has had minimal practice. This reason may stand alone in accounting for shy behavior in young or developmentally disabled persons, but by adolescence it is likely to combine with the irrational thinking that produces anxiety.

Irrational Thinking   At any moment in time, we are thinking, feeling, and behaving, and these processes influence each other. This thinking is often an internal dialogue where we review ourselves, others, and situations. Ellis (1962, 1974, 1975) posits that this thinking often results in excessive emotional response and dysfunctional behavior. In the situation of being at a party, people who behave shyly may think, "Parties make me so nervous I just feel like hiding," when what's really true is that their own irrational thinking about themselves, the other people at the party, and the party situation creates the anxiety. For example: "I shouldn't have come to this party. I hardly know anyone here, and I bet I'll sit alone all evening. He looks interesting, but if I approach him I'll probably blow it anyway, and then he would think I was stupid. Why can't I talk like other people? I'll bet people notice me just sitting here. They can probably see how shy I am. It's the same old story. I can't do anything right. Next time I'll just stay home. Parties make me too anxious."

All of this internal dialogue takes place in about 15 seconds and is punctuated frequently by "I couldn't stand it" and "that would be awful" either in actual words or in tonal quality. To illustrate this point, say the dialogue to yourself in a way that would lead you to be upset. It's not the party itself that makes the person anxious, it's that before, during, and after the party the person has so many opportunities to think irrational and upsetting thoughts.

Irrational thinking has catastrophic and absolutistic qualities ("It would be awful; I must; I have to . . .") and often leads to excessive anxiety, anger, or depresstion and dysfunctional behavior.

Imagine you were about to speak to a group, ask for a date, be interviewed, or travel alone, etc., and you considered yourself "shy" in this situation. Pick a situation and make yourself anxious and upset. Try it.

How did you do it? You probably *thought* something. Really upsetting thoughts usually include some "What if's . . ." and "I must's . . ." Maybe you envisioned some *terrible* consequences. Whatever you thought, it's the irrational qualities that create excessive emotional responses. In the situation you picked. what behaviors would accompany the irrational thinking and excessive upset? See the connections between thoughts, feelings, and behaviors?

The internal dialogue is formed from basic beliefs about oneself and the world. In the case of shyness these beliefs might include:

1. It is essential that all significant other people like and approve of me at all times. (And if anyone doesn't like me, it's awful and I can't stand it!)
2. The best policy is to avoid situations that I am uncomfortable in.
3. I need to do everything extremely well (or perfectly) in order to consider myself worthwhile. (And because I'm usually inadequate or not perfect, I have plenty of grounds for self-criticism.)
4. If things don't go the way I'd like, someone (myself included) deserves blame and abuse.

See Ellis (1962, 1974, 1975) for much greater ellaboration of these concepts.

These beliefs and the internal dialogue may be the underlying support system for shy behavior. In addition, people who behave shyly often have an exceptional ability to use their shy behavior as a cue to berate themselves even more, to feel even worse about themselves, and be more convinced that they'll *never change,* which would be *awful*.

Previous History of Reward for Avoiding Contact or for Indirect Contact. Think back to junior high school and remember that cute "shy" boy on the baseball team. Chances are good that many girls wished they could be the one to help him "like girls." Then there's the young girl who shows her shyness by indirect eye contact and blushing. "She's so sweet." Many people find these shy behaviors appealing, and they encourage the young person to continue the same behavior. Often, however, these behaviors are seen as less appealing (and are less functional) as the person grows older. Breaking this earlier pattern can be even more difficult for women since it is much more socially acceptable for women to remain shy (demure, naive, quiet, passive) as adults than for men to do so. Moreover, boys are less likely to be rewarded exclusively for such behaviors.

People who have achieved many goals through their shy behavior may not be motivated to change. It may take a combination of not getting what they want and feeling bad about themselves in the process to convince them to change. And for those few who are getting what they want and feel good about themselves, the counselor may point out the restrictiveness of the shy behavior but should steer away from labeling it "wrong" or "dysfunctional."

Previous History of Punishment or Rejection for Approaching Others This category may produce behaviors that look shy, but as you'll see, there are more important factors underlying the behaviors.

For example, as a child Beth was beaten by her parents for expressing strong anger or happiness and for stating her own opinions or preferences. Being bright and survival-oriented, she learned at a very young age that the best policy for her at home was, "Don't exist—don't be seen and above all don't be heard." While this made sense at home as a child, it was not functional when she was thirty, reentering the university in creative writing. Her survival instinct said "Stay bottled up. Don't let them know you're really there," and she did. Because of her limited eye contact and difficulty expressing herself in speech and writing, her professors and classmates labeled her as "shy" and basically ignored her.

Beth was not going to overcome her shy behavior through brief focus on her irrational thinking and some practice in approaching others. She needed cognitive restructuring at a much deeper level. She had some important life decisions to remake—among them that it was O.K. for her to exist and that the world did not have to be such a scary place—before much permanent change would occur. Although not a typical case, Beth provides an excellent example of why the counselor should try to understand what prompts the shy behavior before starting treatment. Just as there is no such thing as a "shy person" there is also no single method for treating shyness.

Approaches for Helping People Overcome Shy Behavior

Understanding the Shy Behavior and Setting Goals.

The cognitive-behavioral assertion training model presented here is a more general counseling model that can be applied very easily in treating shy behavior. This model is used in conjunction with basic counseling skills, the ability to listen and to conceptualize. It offers people a chance to learn how to try to get what they want in a less confining way *and* to feel better about themselves in the process.

Assuming the client has mentioned shy behavior (thoughts, feelings, actions) as a concern, step one is to identify the specific behaviors that are labeled as shy and the conditions that prompt these behaviors. In the following example a client begins by saying, "I'm shy. I just don't have anything to say." The counselor's first goal is to help the client explore and clarify the problem.

> *Client:* I guess I must be shy. I just don't seem to have anything to say.
> *Counselor:* Nothing to say.
> *Client:* Yeah, like I'll be around all these people and they're talking away and ... *(pause)*
> *Counselor:* And?
> *Client:* And I'm standing there like a big dummy.
> *Counselor:* You think you're stupid if you don't have anything to say?
> *Client:* Yeah.
> *Counselor:* When you're standing there, and they're talking, what goes through your head?
> *Client:* That I'm dumb and I wish I could disappear.
> *Counselor:* What else are you saying about yourself?

Client: That if I did talk, no one would listen and they'd think I was dumb and boring.

Counselor: And if they thought that?

Client: Well, they wouldn't like me.

Counselor: And if they didn't like you?

Client: Then I wouldn't have any friends at all, and I just couldn't stand that.

Counselor: So it's almost better to say nothing than to say something and risk sounding dumb and boring and maybe get rejected.

Client: It is better. But I wish I could say something—something really brilliant.

Counselor: Let's back up a minute. When you're standing there what are you thinking about the other people?

Client: That they all look so at ease and can say the first thing that comes to their mind. But I bet they can't talk about anything deep.

Counselor: They're great at small talk.

Client: Yeah.

Counselor: I'll bet it would be hard to join their small talk *and* say something brilliant.

Client: Well. I guess there isn't too much brilliant to say about school or rock groups or the changing sizes of candy bars.

Counselor: It's hard to be brilliant at small talk.

Client: Yeah, you know, I can really do okay when I'm alone with someone and we talk seriously.

Counselor: That's easier for you. What's different in that situation?

Client: Well, I can see right off whether the person is responding and I think more about deeper subjects and I think my opinion is really important.

Counselor: We've been talking seriously, and you've seemed relaxed and very thoughtful. So it's more the small talk with a group of people that bothers you.

Client: Actually it's small talk with anyone. I just never learned how to do it.

Counselor: Then there are really two parts. You never learned to small talk *and* you get anxious about it—worrying you'll be rejected if you talk and aren't brilliant and putting yourself down for being quiet.

Notice in this example that the counselor now has an understanding of what the person is labeling as "shyness" and of the underlying irrational thinking. Questions such as "What were you thinking about yourself? About the other people? About the situation itself?" help to clarify the irrational thinking. Anyone using this cognitive system should understand the basic beliefs, the qualities of rational, irrational, and rationalizing thoughts, and how to dispute and change belief systems. ("It would be *awful* if you didn't learn this. How could you consider yourself a worthwhile counselor if you didn't know this perfectly? You *should* read . . .")

With a clearer picture of what behaviors the person is engaging in that are labeled "shy," and the ideational supports that maintain these behaviors, the counselor is more able to develop a treatment plan. In this case the person needs to learn the social skills of making conversation and could benefit from cognitive restructuring to help reduce her anxiety and self-criticism in the situation. If she continues to hold the irrational beliefs that she must either perform perfectly or be a dummy, and that if others don't respond positively to her it's *awful,* then at minimum she will not engage in small talk *comfortably.*

If after obtaining a more specific description of the shy behavior, it appears that the client is behaving shyly due to a learning deficit or to irrational thinking or because it has worked best in the past, proceed with the next step. However, if the shy behavior seems to be related to a more serious issue, as in Beth's case, then the techniques described in this chapter will need to be supplemented with further exploration, support, clarification, and restructuring of beliefs.

Before starting the treatment plan, it is important that the client express an honest commitment to change his or her behavior. Do not assume that because the client talks about the shyness as a problem, he or she really wants to change. In most cases, simply asking "Is this something you'd like to change?" is enough. Before making this commitment, clients need to realize the consequences of not changing, the consequences of changing, and the specifics of their preferred behavior.

Below is a series of questions you can use and can teach your clients to use. Sometimes providing the client with official forms containing these questions and blank spaces for their answers is helpful.

1. Describe the behavior you are now doing that you think is not as effective as you'd like. Be specific and include feelings and actions.
2. What beliefs support your present behavior? (Be sure to include personal rights[2] and irrational ideas.)
3. What would you prefer to be doing instead? Be specific.
4. What beliefs would support this new behavior?
5. What would the consequences be of staying the same? (Think of your response, others' responses, problems created or eased for yourself and others.)
6. What would be the consequences of changing?
7. If you decided to make the change, how might you go about it? (There is no perfect answer.)

Once you understand all of this and have a commitment that the person wants to change, you can start with the treatment plan.

---

[2]See following text for explanation of personal rights.

Steps in Treating Shy Behavior

The treatment for shyness presented in the chapter is based on the cognitive-behavioral assertion training model developed by Lange and Jakubowski (1976) which includes (1) identifying personal rights, (2) distinguishing between assertive, unassertive, and aggressive behavior, (3) cognitive restructuring, and (4) behavior rehearsal. Each of the steps and their relationship to treating shy behavior will be discussed in turn.

The cognitive-behavioral treatment approach assumes behaviors (thoughts, feelings, actions) are in large part learned and can be modified through new learning. At any given moment a person's thoughts, feelings, and actions are interrelated. The cognitive-behavioral counselor helps people set behaviorally specific goals and teaches them how to change their current thought, feeling, and action patterns.

Identifying Personal Rights That Lead to Assertive Behavior   In overcoming shyness clients must come to believe that they have a right to have *and* express thoughts, feelings, opinions, and preferences and that they have a right to be treated with respect and dignity. Other personal rights include deciding what to do with one's own time, property, and body. Understanding and accepting these rights for *all* people is essential to the next step of recognizing assertive behavior.

Recognizing Assertive Behavior   Assertive behavior involves a "direct, honest, and appropriate" communication of thoughts, feelings, and behaviors that respects the rights of *both* people. Unassertive behavior is often indirect or dishonest ("Gee, I'd love to, but . . ." when you don't want to) and involves a violation of one's own personal rights. Aggressive behavior communicates thoughts, feelings, and behaviors in a way that violates the rights of others.

While many define assertion as "standing up for your rights," here assertive behavior encompasses a much wider range including the following: giving and receiving compliments; making, refusing, and accepting requests; making positive self-statements; expressing thoughts and feelings (both negative *and* positive); conversing with others; forming intimate relationships; *and* standing up for your rights.

Here are examples of assertive, unassertive, and aggressive behavior in the situation of approaching a stranger one finds attractive:

Unassertive

–Don't approach at all. Glance at the person occasionally.

–"Uh, hello. Uh, am I, uh, (*grimace*) disturbing you or anything?" (*Look away quickly*)

Aggressive

–"Hey you, come here!"

–"Let's go, baby."

–Go over and start fondling the person.

Assertive
   –"Hi, I'm Joan. I've been wanting to meet you."
   –"Hello. (*smile, eye contact*) How did you happen to come to this party?"

The judgment about each behavior is made on both verbal *and* non-verbal qualities. In teaching the client to distinguish assertive from unassertive and aggressive behavior, state the definitions and give several clarifying examples. Then describe a situation (e.g., "Your housemate is a slob and continually spills food on your property") and ask the client to act out unassertive, assertive, and aggressive responses to this situation. Discuss with the person what verbal and nonverbal qualities make the response assertive, unassertive, or aggressive. Use a range of examples including strangers, loved ones, and service people. Some situations should have the client initiating contact with others and others should involve responding to the words or actions of another. Through a variety of examples and discussions the client can develop an understanding of the terms "assertive, unassertive, and aggressive" as defined here.

Shy behavior is often labeled unassertive behavior because of its avoidant, indirect quality. Many who behave shyly have previously labeled behaviors like starting a conversation, asking to borrow something, or returning food in a restaurant as aggressive. Once they realize that they have a personal right to do these *and* that the situation can be handled without violating the rights of others, they are more likely to label the behaviors as assertive and to engage in them.

Cognitive Restructuring   This step in combination with steps 1 and 2 sets this model apart from the brand of assertion training where the client simply practices the desired behavior. In most cases, shy behavior is not simply the result of learning deficit. It generally includes irrational thinking, as mentioned previously, and the treatment includes helping the person identify the irrational thinking and substitute more rational thoughts.

In Ellis' system when a person is in a situation (A), irrational thinking (B) may lead to excessive emotional response and dysfunctional behavior (C). For example, Sarah has planned to go to a job interview (A), but has gotten so anxious that she is physically ill (C). She created the anxiety and illness through her irrational thinking (B) which included:

"What if I say too much? Or I'm too quiet? Or I sweat? What can I do? I've got to get this job, but I know I'll do terribly in the interview. I'll act stupid, and they won't like me and won't hire me. What if I don't get this job? I've gone to one interview already. I can't stand another one. If only I weren't so shy. I guess I'm just a failure. I'll never get a job. My stomach hurts."

The consequences of her irrational thinking include anxiety, illness, and probably less effective behavior in the interview itself. She may sweat excessively, go blank, stumble over words, trip over something, and present herself in a less than positive light. If Sarah does enough irrational thinking, she can manage to avoid the situation entirely by skipping the interview.

In changing her shy behavior, Sarah can change her belief system—restructure her cognitions. Assuming her preferred behavior is to have a low or moderate amount of anxiety about job interviews, you can see that dealing with the worrying is important. In Ellis' system to change irrational thinking the person can dispute the irrational thoughts (D), which will lead to a more rational belief system, a more appropriate feeling level, and less dysfunctional behavior (E).

Important questions during the disputing stage include:

–How likely or true is that? (E.g., that you will act stupid? That they won't hire you?)
–How *catastrophic* is that even if it does happen? (E.g., that you present yourself poorly? That you don't get the job?)
–What is true about the situation? (E.g., "I am going to a job interview and I'm in competition with others. I may not get the job—it's not guaranteed. It is important that I present myself well. They will be making judgments about me.")
–What is more rational to believe? (E.g., "That I want the job and I'll be disappointed if I don't get it, but I wouldn't be devastated." "That I'd be embarrassed and frustrated if I presented myself poorly, but I could live. And that wouldn't mean I was inadequate or a jerk or too shy." "That I can stand the situation and the outcome—though not perfectly since I am human." "That I want them to like me but I don't *have* to have their approval.")

Once Sarah truly believes that she doesn't have to be miserable each time someone doesn't like her or she doesn't get what she wants or she behaves imperfectly, she will be much freer to change her actions and act less shy and more outgoing. She will also begin to think more highly of herself since she will be out of a system where she labels herself "perfect/worthwhile" or "imperfect/inadequate."

Make sure that the client understands the difference between *rational thinking and rationalization.* If Sarah were rationalizing she might say: "I couldn't care less if I get that lousy job. I'm going to this interview and I'll be perfectly calm and impress them all so much they'll be dying to hire me. And if not, no big deal, no skin off my teeth." Although rationalizations may work to reduce anxiety momentarily, they are the extreme opposite of catastrophizing and do not accurately represent reality. A more honest statement for Sarah would be: "I do care what people think of me and I'd like to get that job. If I do, great; if I don't, I'll be disappointed but I can live with it. I may be calm and impress them during the interview, but I don't *have* to." Rationalizations tend to deny all feelings or preferences instead of just the excessive, self-defeating ones.

Below is an example of how the assessment form described previously was used by Marilyn, a bright 28-year-old woman who usually had little energy, partially because she spent so much time worrying. Her father was a military officer, and she had spent her childhood in countries where the prevalent belief systems supported passive, demure, soft-spoken behavior for women. Although she did not identify with these cultures, she had learned their lessons well.

1. *Describe the behavior. . . .*
   –I don't have any women for friends. Just my boyfriend. I have lots of chances to meet women—class, women's center, a women's assertion group, church—but I don't. I avoid them and I'm always anxious around them.

2. *What beliefs support . . . ?*
   –They won't like me. They'll think I'm mousy. They'll reject me and I'd hate that.
   –I wouldn't know how to approach them. What could I say? I'd whine and look away. Yech!
   –I don't want to bother them. I guess that's from thinking their time and feelings are important . . . and mine aren't. They always seem prettier and better at everything than me.

3. *Prefer to do?*
   –I'd like to start talking with some women and be friendly and maybe have them be friendly back. Then later, I'd like to ask someone to do something with me—something like a movie where we don't have to talk all the time, not like lunch.

4. *What beliefs support . . . ?*
   –That I have a right to approach people. It's O.K., and it won't ruin their day or interfere too much. That just walking up and talking casually is assertive—not aggressive. It's not as if I *trap* them.
   –That I could handle the rejection even though I'd be hurt by it (and it's not that likely to happen) and that I can learn some ways to approach others without whining and looking away—to be more open and direct.

5. *Consequences of staying the same?*
   –I'd still be lonely and envious and put myself down for avoiding (although I could stop that part). No one would be surprised. I'd be safer. Right safe seems less important than lonely.

6. *Consequences of changing?*
   –Well, I'd have friends. I'll bet some people wouldn't like me 'cause I wouldn't be the same old shy Marilyn. My parents would call me pushy —but they don't have to know. I'd like myself better.

7. *If you decide . . . ?*
   –I guess I'd start easy. Eye contact and hello—trying to keep my voice loud enough and low pitched. Then I can start saying real brief comments like "that was a good lecture." Then I can pick someone who looks safe to chat with. Maybe I can get involved in a project at the

Women's Center or church—then I'd *have* to be around other women! Both of those places sponsor events, too, and I'm sure I'll meet people who are interested in them.

This form most clearly illustrates how Marilyn is able to recognize and dispute her irrational thinking and to define her personal rights.

Behavior Rehearsal   After the person has explored any irrational thinking that supports the shy behavior and has defined the desired behavior, practice is essential. Helping clients practice is an art. It is easy to understand but difficult to do well. Several principles and procedures to help make practicing a successful experience for the client will be presented.

As noted, some people who consider themselves shy actually have excellent social skills, but have not used them because of their belief systems. Others have not done much worrying but do not know how to behave.

In addition to challenging the irrational thinking and reducing the excessive emotional responses that may precede acting shy, people can be taught some basic social skills—effective nonverbal behavior, having conversations, giving and receiving compliments, and any other skills that help in approaching people in a more confident way. They can also role-play any situation that concerns them.

While some clients are ready to start role-playing problem situations immediately, most people who behave shyly need some preparation. This skill building should be made as much of a success experience as possible. Start by asking the person to think of all the qualities of communication (other than content) that are noticed. (These include: eye contact, facial expression, hand movements, body posture, voice loudness, speech fluidity, speed of speech, voice tone.)

Then try a simple exercise like Innane Topics (Rimm and Masters, 1974; Lange and Jakubowski, 1976) with two goals—to learn to give and receive positive behavioral feedback and to realize that he or she can talk about anything, even an innane topic for a minute or longer. Behavioral feedback is an essential part of role-playing.

For the exercise you and the person write innane topics on slips of paper. (Innane topics may include lint, grease, felt-tipped pens, ear wax, pegs, shapes of syrup bottles, etc. Let your imagination go, avoiding touchy subjects.) If the client prefers you to join in the exercise, do so, but don't use this as your chance to overwhelm the person with your eloquence. The client draws a topic, monologues about it for 60 seconds (the time can be increased as the client becomes more confident) and then receives positive behavioral feedback—what you like about the *way* the client talked, not the content. "You looked right at me. Your speech was fluid and I could hear every word. You looked relaxed—I mean your face looked calm and you were leaning back." Be honest and specific about what you liked and bite your tongue about what was less effective.

Focusing on the positive aspects of the client's efforts is important. Most people have learned to be extremely self-critical and could list for you the seven ways they "blew" the exercise as well as the three (or thirteen or thirty) mistakes they have already made today. While they may not be perfectly accurate in their criticism, they are much more skilled at seeing the flaws than the good points. In order to change they need to know what they are doing *well* that they might try to retain. Besides, it feels good! Later in behavior rehearsal there will be a chance for the person (and finally you) to make suggestions for change.

At this point, in the interest of space and because there are many good resources, details about having conversations, giving and receiving compliments, dealing with requests and other exercises will not be presented.

Behavior rehearsal allows the client to practice any situation of concern. Below is a list of guidelines and principles to keep in mind.

1. Person gives *brief* description of the situation.
2. Person describes own preferred behavior—how he or she would like to handle it.
3. Person describes how the other person in the situation (stimulus person) should act so that the situation can be as real as possible.
4. Set the scene—sitting back to back if it's a phone call, side by side on a bus, standing, etc.
5. Try a short segment. (Person's first few sentences at most.) The stimulus person should be *cooperative* initially—not escalating the situation.
6. Person gives self positive behavioral feedback—what was effective about her or his behavior?
7. Counselor adds any other positive behavioral feedback.
8. Person gives self suggestions for change. Limit this to two—people have trouble concentrating on changing more than two at one time.
9. Counselor gives suggestions (up to two *total*) if person has not already made two.
10. Keep recycling steps 5–9. As the person becomes relaxed and more effective make the segments longer and/or have the stimulus person act more in a way the client worries about handling.

Role reversal may be used to give the therapist a clearer picture of the stimulus person and to have the therapist model an appropriate response. This modeling should be done only if the person is unable to come up with a response.

The following example illustrates the use of behavior rehearsal with a teenager, Chris, who has trouble asking for dates. Chris has already decided that he has a right to request (and the other person has a right to refuse) and that it would be disappointing but not awful if he was rejected.

> *Counselor:* OK, Chris, describe the situation (*Step 1*)
> *Chris:* Well, I'd be calling her on the phone to ask her to go to the movies, and it'd be in the evening.

Counselor: And how would you like to act? (*Step 2*)

Chris: Well, I wouldn't want to just blurt it out—I'd like to sound mellow.

Counselor: Mellow?

Chris: You know, calm and casual.

Counselor: And what do you want her to know?

Chris: That I'd like to go with her to the movies.

Counselor: Tell me about her. (*Step 3*)

Chris: There's no one specific girl.

Counselor: It's easier to do this if you have a real person in mind.

Chris: Well, there's Jenny. She's pretty nice and kind of shy too. She talks quiet.

Counselor: OK let's try it. We'll sit back-to-back. You say "ring ring" when you're ready. (*Step 4*)

Chris: Ring ring.

"Jenny": Hello?

Chris: Uh, hi. Is Jenny there?

"Jenny": This is Jenny.

Chris: Oh, hi. This is Chris from your math class.

"Jenny": Oh, hi, Chris.

Chris: I don't, uh, suppose you're, uh, free Friday to to go to a, uh, movie, are you?

"Jenny": Oh, yes, I am free and I'd like to go. (*Note she is initially cooperative.*)

Counselor: Stop. (*Step 5*) OK, Chris, what did you like? (*Step 6*)

Chris: She accepted!

Counselor: What did you like about how *you* acted?

Chris: Well, not much. I guess that I said it. I did get right to the point, too.

Counselor: You brought the movies up. I also like that you said who you were and that I could hear your voice clearly. (*Step 7*) Anything you want to change? (*Step 8*)

Chris: I'd like to stop sweating.

Counselor: To relax more? (*Step 9*)

Chris: Yes!

Counselor: What would be different if you relaxed more?

Chris: I wouldn't stumble on my words.

Counselor: Let's try it again, and you'll try to be more relaxed and let your words flow. (*Step 10*)

The behavior rehearsal process would continue and at some point Chris would be encouraged to be more direct in his request "Would you like to go to the movies with me Friday?" and "Jenny" would try what Chris worried about—not giving a direct yes or no:

Chris:	Would you like to go to the movies with me Friday?
"Jenny":	Oh, I don't know. I mean this weekend is kinda busy and that test is next week.
Chris:	Well, I *would* like to go out with you.
"Jenny":	Not this weekend but some other time.
Chris:	When would be good for you?
"Jenny":	Oh, I don't know exactly.
Chris:	How about if you let me know when a good time comes up? I do want to go out, but I don't want to pressure you for a time.

At this point (or before if Chris had gotten stuck) the positive behavioral feedback and suggestions (Steps 6–9) would follow. Keeping the role plays short is essential. As role plays get longer, they often avoid the essential problems, e.g., Chris and "Jenny" chat for seven minutes about math class. This may be good practice for Chris in conversations, but what he wanted to practice was requesting a date. Also it's more difficult to remember specific feedback for many of the behaviors in longer role plays.

Behavioral rehearsal is much more than simply "acting it out." Careful application of the ten principles and guidelines above can add significantly to the power of the technique to help clients act more effectively in their problem situations.

Clients can also be encouraged to practice in fantasy. Have them visualize behaving effectively and feeling good about themselves. Also have them visualize *failing* to behave the way they wanted or not getting the results they wanted *and* not getting excessively upset (Rational Emotive Imagery). By using both types of imagery they are better equipped for more of the possible outcomes.

Having brilliant insights and role-playing superbly with the counselor may be helpful (especially in not behaving shyly with counselors), but the person still should try out this new learning in the real world. Homework is essential. Several basic principles govern homework: *The client should either suggest it or agree wholeheartedly to do it; the behavior should be readily observable; there should be a high probability of success; and rewards may be built into the system.* Thus, for someone who is having trouble talking with peers, homework may start at the level of making eye contact and greeting someone and progress in small steps that the person can master until the final goal, e.g., comfortably carrying on a conversation, is accomplished. The person may choose to have a reward (e.g., ice cream cone, listening to music, or being alone) contingent on performing the homework. They get the reward for doing the behavior regardless of the other person's response.

Case Example

The following summary shows how all four steps of cognitive-behavioral assertion training plus homework (plus basic counseling skills) were used to help someone who came in saying "I'm shy."

Jim, the young man who walked around for hours hoping to "run into" women discovered that his behavior with women was either unassertive (walking around instead of approaching them directly) or tending toward aggressive. He believed this was related to two irrational ideas—wanting to be perfect in his approach and worrying that he would be rejected, which would show his true self worth. He also had poor social skills—really not understanding how to have a conversation. Since his stated goal was to have the woman immediately form a deep, caring, long-lasting relationship with him, he felt extremely pressured during the interaction. He was always able to interpret the woman's response as rejection since none ever expressed love at first sight.

After he was persuaded that he could live and still like himself if he did a less than perfect job and even if he was rejected by a woman (or hundreds of women), he practiced having conversations with the counselor that included open-ended questioning, repeating key phrases of the other person, and sharing free information of his own. He did believe he had a right to approach others and to express his thoughts and opinions. Jim was encouraged to set a hierarchy of goals for his interactions with women, ranging from "hello" with eye contact to falling in love. Next, he started doing the easier items. He discovered many "safe" places to practice his new conversational skills—before and after classes, with cashiers, clerks, waitresses, and other service people (both male and female), and in lines at the bank and the grocery store. Having a short conversation was easy in all these situations because he was there for only a limited time. With these easier goals, he found himself feeling much less pressured and more able to relax. He actually enjoyed the other person and got more positive responses. Although he still wanted to work on having more intimate, lasting relationships, he reported he no longer felt shy about approaching women.

Group Counseling

This chapter has shown how cognitive-behavioral assertion training can be used in individual counseling to treat shy behavior. Assertion training is frequently done in a group, which offers several advantages: people realize that they are not alone in their concern, the group provides a safe and structured situation to practice new behaviors with others, and group members form a support system to reinforce the individual's attempts at change. Procedures described in this chapter can be easily adapted to other counseling contexts and populations.

Summary

Through following the procedures suggested in this chapter, people can learn to change their shy behavior. This does not mean that they must never act shyly again, but means that they could behave differently if they *chose* to do so. Shy behavior can be overcome—if the person believes there will be benefit from the change, understands how his or her own irrational thinking gets in the way, accords herself or himself the same personal rights as others, and learns to use some new social skills. For the person who's been practicing shy behavior (thoughts, feelings, and actions) for many years this change is not simple; but it *is* possible.

Questions for Further Inquiry

1. Think of a time when you wanted to behave assertively but were unable to do so. What do you remember feeling and thinking?

2. Suppose a client says to a counselor, "I am shy. I have had some bad experiences as a result of my shyness, but I prefer not to change." What interpretations might the counselor make of this client's statement?

3. What may be the consequences to a marriage relationship if one partner succeeds in changing shy behavior? What responsibilities might this imply for the helper?

4. How can you integrate the cognitive-behavioral approach of this chapter with other counseling approaches, such as: transactional analysis, Gestalt, client centered, reality therapy?

5. What might be the social consequences if everyone were to learn to behave assertively?

References

Alberti, R. E., & Emmons, M. L. *Your perfect right: A guide to assertive behavior. (2nd. ed.)* San Luis Obispo, Calif.: Impact Press, 1974.

Bloom, L. Z., Coburn, K., & Perelman, J. *The new assertive woman.* New York: Delacorte Press, 1975.

Bower, S. A., & Bower, G. H. *Asserting yourself: A practical guide for positive change.* Reading, Mass.: Addison-Wesley, 1976.

Ellis, A. *Reason and emotion in psychotherapy.* New York: Lyle Stuart, 1962.

Ellis, A. *Humanistic psychotherapy: The rational-emotive approach.* New York: Julian Press, 1973 New York: McGraw-Hill Paperbacks, 1974.

Ellis, A., & Harper, R. A. *A new guide to rational living.* Englewood Cliffs, N.J.: Prentice-Hall, 1975.

Lange, A. & Jakubowski, P. *Responsible assertive behavior: Cognitive/behavioral procedures for trainers.* Champaign, Ill.: Research Press, 1976.

Liberman, R., et al. *Personal effectiveness training.* Champaign, Ill.: Research Press, 1976.

Meichenbaum, D. H. *Cognitive behavior modification.* New York: Plenum, 1977.

Osborn, S. M., & Harris, G. G. *Assertive training for women.* Springfield, Ill.: Charles C. Thomas, 1975.

Rimm, D., & Masters, J. C. *Behavior therapy: Techniques and empirical findings.* New York: Academic Press, 1974.

Zimbardo, P. G. *Shyness: What it is, what to do about it.* Reading, Mass.: Addison-Wesley, 1977.

PART II

Effective Helping With Family Issues

For better or for worse, the family is the single most powerful determinant of our personality. It is the source of our identity, the locus of our morality, the forum for most of our significant conflicts, and the primary focus of allegiance for many of us. To a very large extent we are what we have learned to be as the result of our relationships with our parents. During our childhoods we learned from them basic security or insecurity, acquired a set of scripts (healthy or unhealthy), developed certain personal scenarios for the future, and emerged with specific ways of perceiving ourselves, significant others, and the major societal institutions of our world. Some of it happened with parental intentionality and foresight; other socialization effects occurred without intention. The knowledge that one's parenting practices so powerfully influence our young represents an awesome, sometimes frightening, sometimes exciting, responsibility. For better or for worse, we are the recipients and we become the donors.

All families experience crises in the course of their evolution. Interpersonal conflicts are inevitable, financial strains create personal and interpersonal stress, the young rebel, spouses discover areas of incompatibility and combat, sickness happens, and death occurs. Some families survive and even grow through these crises; others dissolve.

The contributors for Part II of this text provide us with a wealth of material for understanding and working with families in stress. In his chapter on family counseling, Andrews integrates interpersonal systems with existential thinking to compare the effectively functioning with the dysfunctioning family units, to analyze different kinds of family interaction patterns and their developmental effects on individual family members, and to develop guidelines for providing help to dysfunctional family systems.

The experiences of divorce and loss through death have much in common. Both represent an ending to an accustomed long term, intimate relationship, and there are striking similarities in the way people cope with their loss. Both involve intense experiences of pain, grief, loneliness, inadequacy, disorientation and a sense of emptiness. Both require an intense effort to overcome dependency and discover new sources of self-reliance. Guilt regarding unfinished business and resentment related to perceived abandonment are frequent experiences. Even the stages of adjustment are similar. With the national average approaching 40 percent, divorce has become common rather than exceptional in our society. Loewenstein provides a sociological overview of contemporary divorce, examines the personal and interpersonal effects of the decision to end a relationship, provides fresh research data on the coping mechanisms of children and discusses approaches to helping those affected by the decision.

The loss of a loved one through death is inevitable for all of us. While we each have our personal mechanisms for coping, it also appears that we all go through the same sequence of stages in our adjustment and restitution efforts. Matz describes the stages he perceives through his research and clinical experiences, provides an intimate sense of what the experience is like during each stage, discusses the differences between functional and dysfunctional coping and uses case study material to provide guidelines for effective helping during each of the coping stages.

Understanding and Working with Family Units   9

ERNIE E. ANDREWS

Introduction and Orientation

Since the mid-1950s a new method of psychotherapeutic intervention into emotional and mental disorders, *conjoint psychotherapy,* has emerged and been gradually refined (Andrews, 1972). Conjoint therapy, sometimes called "family therapy" or "marriage therapy," has been the result of an interdisciplinary effort by anthropologists, communications analysts, clinical psychologists, psychiatric social workers, and psychiatrists. The conjoint approach assumes that emotional disturbances are initiated within and supported by a human system, generally a marriage or a family. These human systems are composed of interlocking, reciprocal relationship patterns which significantly influence the behavior of the individual members of the family or marriage. Persons within the family, whether parents, marital partners, or children, who manifest psychophysiological symptoms (such as recurrent headaches, colitis), or who present an awareness of significant problems in relating meaningfully to significant others—are viewed as "symptom bearers" or "identified patients" who signal disturbance in the human system in which they live.

The focal point of psychotherapeutic evaluation and intervention is, therefore, shifted from the individual person as "patient" to the individual's existing human system of marriage or family as the "patient." Conjoint psychotherapy includes all the relevant and significant members of the symptom bearer's family in the interview situation. A focal and substantive goal in this form of psychotherapy is the alteration of dysfunctional relationship patterns existing in the family which reinforce and support symptomatic behavior in a self-perpetuating, causal cycle.

The alcoholic husband and the nagging wife marriage relationship exemplifies these patterns. He claims to drink to avoid the effects of her nagging, while she claims to nag only because he drinks. Conjoint therapy assumes that for these patterns to change, both spouses must become active participants in the treatment process. Psychotherapeutic intervention would be directed toward *how* the spouses treat each other with *what* painful consequences in their joint relationship, rather than *why* they do what they do to each other. Change is attempted in the nature and structure of their reciprocal behavior which creates symptoms of emotional and mental disturbance.

The rationale for and significance of a family systems orientation with an existential focus has several basic components which are based upon both theoretical and pragmatic convictions. First, the family is considered to be the arena of both personality and relationship development. This belief is consistent with almost all the literature on human development, from the most orthodox of psychoanalytic approaches through the most current transactional and Gestalt approaches. While the basic concept of family as generating personality has remained a stable conviction, in the past two decades we have substantially added to our understandings of the interconnectedness and reciprocal effects of family systems. The exchange of psychological influence is now viewed as wholly mutual and distills itself into observable patterns of thoroughly interlocking behavior which have significant consequences for all members of the family—the adults as well as the children (Bell, 1968, 1971, and 1972; Bell and Ainsworth, 1972; Harper, 1971; Korner, 1965; Lewis and Rosenblum, 1974).

Second, because of the thoroughly interlocking and reciprocal nature of family relations, the family is seen as the sustainer as well as the destroyer of human psychological survival. It has become increasingly clear that problems within a family have dysfunctional ramifications which vary from general dissatisfaction to severe psychosis. The symptoms cover the whole range of human disability from mild arguments to outright assault and upon occasion, homicide. It is indeed a sobering reflection to note that four out of five homicides committed in the United States are committed by one family member upon another family member. It appears that the extremes of human affect which are aroused in family living make possible the ultimate of despair and hostility, as well as the ultimate in satisfaction and joy.

Third, it has become increasingly apparent that the family is also the most significant source of human aid in times of personal and relationship distress. Conjoint therapy believes that any member of the family, because of his or her emotional involvement in that relationship system, is both part of the problem and part of the solution. We have become increasingly aware that it is difficult to bring about significant and long-term personal, marital, family, and parent-child problem resolutions without involving all of the members of the family in which the problems arise.

My own early experience in child guidance clinics taught me that the failure to involve families fully and totally in the therapeutic process often becomes an experience of futility and frustration. I noted that when only individual members of the family were seen, the family was not dealt with as a total interactional unit. I also noted that when records were kept under the family name over periods of time ranging from 10 to 15 years, every child member of the family was often seen at the clinic. I furthermore noted that all the particular problems for which they were seen seemed highly interrelated. This indicated to me that problems within a family can be "infectious" and that the same problem is passed from one child to another. It was apparent that while treatment could "succeed" with one child in the family, another child would soon develop similar symptoms. This left me in the dilemma of appearing to help individuals while leaving their families still disabled. It certainly suggested adopting a perspective on human personality and its disorders which included more than an understanding of an individual's internal states. What evolved was a need to understand more fully the human systems from which individuals came, namely their families.

These observations reflect basic changes, in both thinking and practice, about human development in relationships and about the treatment of individual problems. Rather than exclusively conceptualizing both our diagnostic understanding and our therapeutic intervention in internal or individualistic terms, we now think much more in terms of the ecology of human relationship systems. While most human systems which we see in distress and in need of treatment are families, the same theories and therapy can apply to other human survival systems, even though they do not represent legal families. Examples include homosexual couples living together with long-term commitment, couples living together who are not married, and any communal living arrangement in which one's psychological survival in terms of meaning, purpose, support, and human nurturance is derived from a long-term commitment involving other people.

The existential application to this systems model is to bring the process of need satisfaction into the present where it can be dealt with directly and concretely and with immediate affective and experiential involvement. Using this focus, behavior is changed through immediate relearning rather than by insightful reminiscing or future projecting. It is an approach which makes extensive use of the experience of the interview itself as the moment of change. This theory and treatment will be described and outlined in detail in the following pages.

History of Family Counseling

Historically, therapeutic work with family units which has been called conjoint family therapy began in the early 1950 s. It is interesting to note that the basic concepts of working with the total family in the same room at the same time with the same therapist and with the expressed objective of dealing with the reciprocal interrelatedness occurred almost simultaneously in three different areas of the country: In the New York metropolitan area; in Washington, D.C.; and in Palo Alto, California. Of these three, perhaps the most influential and best known is the original group (comprised of Don Jackson, M.D., Virginia Satir, M.S.S.W., and Jules Riskin, M.D.,) which founded the Mental Research Institute in Palo Alto, California.

With close help from Jay Haley, M.A., and Gregory Bateson, Ph.D., this inter-disciplinary team began their studies with young male adult schizophrenics at the V.A. Hospital in Palo Alto. In analyzing the letters to the hospitalized schizophre-nics from their mothers, the team observed some predictable patterns: an initial expression of interest and concern followed by blame and fault-finding and con-cluding with "Love, Mother" (Bateson, *et al.,* 1958). This soon led the researchers to form the hypothesis that "double-bind communication" contributed to the devel-opment of schizophrenia. The basic belief of this early group of pioneers was that meaning in human relations and communication derives from the interpersonal context in which it occurs (Watzlawick, Beavin, and Jackson, 1967).

At about the same time, Nathan Ackerman, M.D., and his colleagues Sanford Sherman, M.S.W., and Cecelia Mitchell, M.S.W., at Jewish Family Service of New York were using the concept of "interlocking complementarity" (Ackerman, 1958, 1966) in their work with family units. They stressed the relatedness of individual mental health to the mental health of the family. Although they appeared more psychoanalytic in their orientation than the Palo Alto group, they placed great emphasis on interrelationships within the family and the consequences of that patterning in the production and maintenance of psychiatric symptoms.

Meanwhile, Murray Bowen, M.D., and Lyman Wynne, M.D., in Washington, D.C. were also engaged in long-term therapeutic work with severely disturbed families. Bowen (1960) used the concept of "undifferentiated ego mass" to de-scribe the nature of "fused" relationships in a family. In a "fused" relationship there was little differentiation among family members combined with a plea for separateness. Wynne noted that while members of these families appeared to refer to their individuality and productive relatedness to one another, at a deeper level they engaged in what he termed "pseudo-mutuality" to conceal a more basic process which devalued separateness and uniqueness (Wynne and Sanger, 1963). As Beavers (1977) was to later point out, this refers to the failure of a family "to help its offspring develop autonomous action and boundaries of self which allow a relatively clear and coherent identity formation."

Outside of the United States, but little known at that time to American mental health professionals, R.D. Laing, M.D. (1964, 1965), and John Howells, M.D. (1971), in England were also engaged in pioneering work involving family units based upon knowledge of family interrelatedness and emotional problems.

The body of information which these pioneers initially contributed has since been significantly expanded and refined and will be discussed in the following pages. Among many significant current developments has been the founding of a number of Family Institutes in most major cities in the United States. These institutes offer specific training programs in conjoint marital and family therapy for the professional mental health practitioner, as well as consultative services to individuals in clinics and hospitals. Many also have research programs and public education programs for professionals in fields related to mental health (c.f. Andrews, 1974).

A second significant current development has been the study of the healthy family which has led to a greater understanding of the family life cycle. This study has focused with particular attention on relationship processes within families that cause either functional or dysfunctional consequences for individual family members. A study done at the Timberlawn Foundation in Dallas, Texas, by Lewis, Beavers, Gosset and Phillips (1976) is a notable contribution.

Along with these two current developments there has been increasing emphasis on integrating family therapy with existing traditional therapies with individuals and groups, stimulated by Nathan Ackerman's (1967) earlier paper on "The Family Approach and Levels of Intervention."

Theoretical Overview

The approach to working with family units presented in this chapter is based on an integration of four models: a *behavior-dynamics* model that helps the counselor understand and account for the behavior patterns observed; a *model of healthy and dysfunctional interaction patterns* that helps the counselor evaluate the current level of growth and functioning of the individual family member; a *diagnostic model* that helps the counselor assess the ways in which family members affect each other; and a *model for treatment* that describes the processes by which change and improvement take place. Each model is presented in Table 9–1, and will be developed in detail in this chapter. Taken together, the four models provide the structure of the family counseling process.

Models for Understanding Family Systems

Behavior Dynamics Model: Transactional Relationship Theory

The theory of relationship which we apply to working with couples and families comes indirectly from an understanding of general systems theory which Von Bertalanffy (1969) has described. In summary, any system is comprised of component parts, which in families are people; and have a relationship to one another, which in families we call human relationships. The system produces certain predictable outcomes, which in families are any and all behavior which occurs; and boundaries that define who is in the system and that indicate its permeability of exchange with other systems. In family relationships these boundaries define the openness or closedness of a particular family in dealing with systems such as school or church. In human relationships the dyad is the most fundamental and basic unit of emotional relationship (Andrews, 1974a).

The central concept in relationship theory is that the dyad represents a reciprocal transaction which results in mutual consequences. This is schematically

Table 9-1   The Four Models for the Conjoint Family Therapy Approach

(a) *Behavior Model* ⎯⎯⎯⎯⎯⎯▶ *Transactional*

How behavior is perceived, labelled, and sequenced— includes ideas of causality, patterning, and developmental processes	Personality and relationship result from experiences between persons which are repetitive, reciprocal patterns

(b) *Dysfunction Model* ⎯⎯⎯⎯⎯▶ *Growth Inhibition*

How behavioral disturbance is recognized and labelled—in illness model is called pathology/sickness	Problem thoughts, feelings, and behavior-symptoms-result from blockage of growth energy and derive from choices reinforced by interpersonal transactions in a survival context

(c) *Diagnostic Model* ⎯⎯⎯⎯⎯▶ *Human Social System*

An understanding of structural and functional aspects of the outcome behavior of the client-family	People in an interlocking reciprocity—a transactional network of relationships with psychological survival at stake

(d) *Treatment Model* ⎯⎯⎯⎯⎯▶ *Growth by Existential Realization*

How change in structure and functioning is instigated toward satisfying joint outcomes	Learning to choose to relinquish resistance to responsible joint need meeting through experience within the interview

represented in Figure 9-1, which shows that any behavior on the part of A is reciprocally influential on the behavior of B, as in the example of the alcoholic husband and the nagging wife. Relating is completely reciprocal, self-reinforcing, and self-perpetuating; as long as she nags he will drink and as long as he drinks she will nag.

When Berne (1964) described interpersonal games, he described transactions which sometimes involved two people, but also three, four, or five. The game, in fact, is the kind of reciprocal transaction with a mutual consequence for the people involved which diminishes self-esteem and avoids intimacy. Diagnostically, it is important to keep in mind that this behavior is redundant and reflects a high degree of interlocking mutual influence.

It also becomes quite clear when we look at a relationship in this manner that any concept of blame or fault for what happens in the relationship becomes irrelevant; it is the collaboration *between* the two people that produces diminished self-esteem for both of them. It is the relationship itself that is dysfunctional.

Figure 9-1   The Dyad Relationship

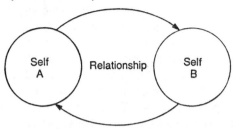

Source: *The Emotionally Disturbed Family,* Ernest Andrews. Copyright © Jason Aronson, 1974. Reprinted with permission.

Reciprocity is fundamental to the initiation and development of personality as well as to the maintenance of personality; it sustains the character of the person in a consistent manner throughout his or her life time. Reciprocal exchanges between adults either reinforce existing behavior or, if contrary to earlier learning, tend to extinguish behavior. During infancy and childhood, transactions between parent and child are incorporated by the individual into self. It is important to keep in mind that there is a considerable reciprocity in equality of influence between parents and child. This is not a one-way street. This reciprocal process has been especially clarified by the more recent child developmental work of Bell (1971), Bell and Ainsworth (1972), Harper (1971), Korner (1971), and Lewis and Rosenblum (1974).

Also important to understand is that there are two related and parallel phenomena occurring when people are involved in an intense ongoing relationship. The first is the personality or self-system of each of the individuals, often referred to as the internal state of the organism. The second is the observable behaviors by which the family members relate to each other. We selectively incorporate external experiences which then become a part of our personality and in turn are used by us in relating to another. The relationship between inner states of the person and external experience also represents the reciprocal exchange in mutual influence (c.f. Chin, 1958). In treatment it is important to work both with the personality or inner state of the person and with his relationship and external experience. They cannot be separated, but represent different and highly related aspects of life experience (Andrews, 1974a).

It is also critically important when working with human relationships to have a clear perspective on the existential and temporal frames of reference. All human beings have the capacity to recall a past, to experience a present, and to anticipate a future. But only the present is actually experienced. Its vivid reality can be dealt with directly during therapeutic interviews. When we experience in the present a recollection of the past, this often represents what we thought happened or how we selectively and distortedly remember it; the future represents a projection of how we would like things to turn out. Remember that past experiences cannot be changed, only present experience can be; the only way we realize the future is to act in the present. In dealing with a relationship system like a marriage or a family, it is not nearly so important to understand how it came to be as it is to understand how people continue to reinforce and perpetuate the way it is.

Another principle in understanding family member interrelationships is that over time formal and informal rules develop within the family structure that govern the actions of the individual family members (Jackson, 1965). For example, some couples and families may have a basic rule: all anger is destructive and therefore may not be expressed. There is, of course, no way not to ever feel anger, but it is possible not to express what is felt. This leads to an accumulation of resentment which may in turn lead to periodic violent outbursts, various somatic symptoms or neurotic phenomena, such as dissociative states. Family rules represent a kind of "delusional conviction" which people accept as truth and act upon faithfully and consistently. They are convictions about what is right or wrong, good or bad, desirable or undesirable in human relationships. Even though they follow these rules, family members are not always aware of the specific rules they follow. Often they act on the rules without being aware of what they are. In family counseling it is often the case that the established rules lead to individual problems as well as disrupted interpersonal relationship patterns.

The emotional purpose of relationship systems like marriage and the family should be to sustain psychological survival and promote growth. We have psychological needs to feel confident and capable in ourselves and with others so that we can experience meaning in life. Most basically, meaning and purpose derive from relationships which are positive; that is, they give satisfactions which enhance our self-esteem and give positive meaning to all of our existence.

Virginia Satir (1967) has most clearly described three basic survival wants which underlie our need for psychological survival. The first of these is the desire for *sense and order.* This means that we perceive relationships as having predictable outcomes and sensible exchanges. These ordered experiences provide security to our relating to another, and we emerge confident and with self-esteem enhanced. Sense and order also has to do with the whole area of communication between people; that they can relate to one another in a way that is clear and direct and congruent in the sense that what we say is consistent with our nonverbal communication. Our gestures, voice tone, and facial expression confirm the verbal messages we are giving and the other is receiving. Dysfunctional relationships are characterized by a lack of sense and order. There is little consistency or order in the relationship, and there are strong and consistent elements of incongruity and inconsistency in the communications that members of the relationship provide to each other. When the sense and order in a relationship breaks down, a basic need is not being met and all participants suffer.

The second survival want is what Satir called *productivity,* which has two components to it. Task productivity refers to who does what household maintenance activities. This can become a focal area of conflict within the family. If the necessary work is done quickly and on time, then family members have time to enjoy one another's company. If it is not, they can use the nonperformance of tasks as a basis for argument, insulting one another's self-esteem. Consequently, they will not feel very valued by one another and are unlikely to perform the tasks which are necessary in the home. The second aspect of productivity in the family is more an emotional interrelationship. It has to do with who gives support, guidance, direction, and encouragement. This includes the children and how they give to the parents, as well as how the parents give to the children. The two facets of productivity are wholly interlocking. If routine tasks do not get done people feel resentful and angry and will not give guidance and support; in the absence of guidance and support, tasks will not get done around the house. Symptoms in the productivity area frequently show up outside of the home with work failure and absenteeism, apparent deficiency in homemaking skills, and children failing in school. In essence, father will fail in the office as well as in the bedroom, mother will fail in her office as well as in the kitchen, and the children will fail in the classroom as well as the family room.

The third aspect of psychological survival has to do with the desire for *intimacy*. Intimacy is related to the awareness of *differentness* between people: to understanding the nature of the differentness between husband and wife, parent and child; and to valuing the uniqueness of the other person. If differentness is seen only as threatening, then it is something which must be rejected, which diminishes intimacy and self-esteem in relations between people. Between adults, intimacy is also related to genital sexuality but is not to be confused as identical with it. Intimacy between two people is a sharing of the self with one another; it encompasses their total persons and beings, not merely their genitals.

The family, then, is basically a social-emotional system with psychological survival significance. It either maintains and develops positive self-esteem and affirmation of self-value in its members, or leads to despair and diminished self-esteem. In the most positive sense the family can be viewed as a growth-oriented human system (Luthman and Kirschenbaum, 1974). The most vital and important product of this system is the emotional growth of its members, which is instigated by the open revealing of self combined with open nurturance in the form of concern and loving behavior.

Growth may be defined as the movement toward responsible autonomy in seeking and giving meaning to self and others by spontaneous and unique experience. Growth is choosing to be responsible for self and for self with others in meeting survival needs through honest, direct negotiation. The resulting feelings of well-being will enhance the confidence of both and support their self-esteem in the assertion of their autonomous beings. Real growth occurs when a person learns to enlarge his or her use of self. It involves the risk of self-revelation, but it has the advantage of allowing us to expand our means for dealing with differentness, with change, and with newness. People find these experiences anxiety-arousing. We have difficulty encountering them without inner self-confidence. But confidence is not something that comes from pure isolation. It stems from a relationship in which openness and nurturance are internalized by the people involved in feeling confidence about using self.

Openness in a growth-oriented relationship is to reveal what self needs to survive and what self is willing to give to other to survive. Nurturance is the manifestation of open concern and valuing of self and other (and of self with other) by direct affection and acceptance, verbal and physical. Nurturance is very supportive. It gives the conviction that somebody cares and that we are valued. It means that we see ourselves as being valuable because a meaningful other values us. There is an obvious reciprocal relationship between openness and nurturance in this formulation, both of which are needed to promote growth. The more open we are in revealing self to another, the more confident the other is in reaching out to us. Reciprocally, the more nurturant the relationship is, the more the persons in it are willing to take the risk of revealing self and of openly expressing our thoughts and feelings to each other.

In the effectively functioning family unit there is a respect and prizing for the individuality of each family member. Such families work cohesively together during times of crisis and stress. Yet each member also experiences space, permission, and encouragement for his or her personal growth. The cohesiveness of the family unit supports rather than suppresses individuality. There is at once a sense of togetherness along with space for the development of each person's unique identity.

Satir (1965) has identified five interrelated communications processes that help to describe the nature and quality of a family relationship. These processes help the counselor to observe how the family members relate to each other, to assess the quality of their relationship and to identify specific areas of dysfunctionality.

(a) *How Self is Manifest to Self and Others:*   The issue is not *whether* self is manifest, but of *how* self is manifest to other and to one's own self. If self is manifest in a way which is clear, direct, and congruent, open communication is maintained, needs are revealed, and negotiation of joint outcome is possible. Indirectness, vagueness, and incongruency are dysfunctional and prevent open communication and need-meeting negotiation. To be clear is to say precisely what is meant; to be direct is to specifically say what is meant to a particular person; and to be congruent means that what is said is confirmed and reinforced by how it is said or by the accompanying nonverbal signals. This is the basic process by which meaning is communicated from one person to another. (In transactional theory, communication is defined as any and all behavior between people, verbal and nonverbal).

(b) *How Differentness is Acknowledged to Self and Other:*   If self is clearly manifest to other, then the awareness of differentness becomes both an opportunity and a problem. If the observable difference is acknowledged as bad, sick, stupid, or crazy, defensiveness will result and self-esteem will be diminished. On the other hand, if differentness is acknowledged as uniqueness, then self-esteem is enhanced and openness is encouraged. "Differentness" is not the same as "differences," which carries a more intellectual flavor; differentness refers to basic ways in which people are dissimilar in dealing with hurt, anger, affection, and the whole range of basic affects that comprise our emotional existence. Again, it is not a matter of whether differentness is acknowledged, but of how it is acknowledged.

(c) *How Self is Separated from Other:* Once differentness is observed, the next problem becomes how the self and other can be separated. If the uniqueness of each self in the relationship is not viewed with threat and is not seen as a condition of one's own lovability and worth, then uniqueness may lead to growth. Persons may then learn new ways from each other and be aware of their differentness in timing and need in relating. However, if the perception that self is separate from other is seen as threatening to one's own lovability and worth, then separateness must be denied and a policy of fusion follows. Through fusion, or the attempt to make self and other close to identical, the threat is minimized, but at the same time uniqueness and realistic separation are denied.

(d) *How Self Makes Room for Other in His or Her Life Space:* Once differentness is acknowledged and self is separated from other, a dilemma occurs over how joint life space is to be shared in a meaningful manner. If self makes room for other on the basis of what fits who is involved, then differentness and separation may be taken into account in their joint life. If self makes room for other on the basis of who is "boss," then differentness and separation is diminished and sacrificed for the sake of a basic power tactic to control and manipulate.

(e) *How Joint Outcome Is Negotiated:* This is the culmination of the four previously described processes. Joint outcome is negotiated in a mutually satisfying manner if self is manifested to other directly, congruently, and clearly, if differentness is acknowledged as uniqueness, if self is clearly separated from other, if self and other share joint life space by deciding what fits who involved. On the other hand, joint outcome will be a manipulative effort filled with resentment and despair if self is manifest to other indirectly, vaguely, and incongruently, if differentness is acknowledged negatively, if self is not separate from other, and if joint life space is based on boss tactics.

To understand relationships in marriages and families, it is critical to be aware of these five processes, to understand their interrelatedness and particularly to see their significance in terms of the negotiation of joint outcome. This gives us a basis for the process analysis of family interaction and prevents us from being misled by content manifestations which are really the vehicle for the expression of these processes. All relevant issues in disturbed families are relationship process issues, not issues of intellectual verbalizations or symptomatic behavior.

The final component in this behavior dynamics model is an understanding of family developmental sequence. All relationship systems have an evolutionary pattern related to several kinds of naturalistic change stimuli. These are events and experiences which change the nature of the family and present a crisis for resolution or fixation upon which further family growth can evolve. Change stimuli are of three basic types: Structural change, psychological change, and traumatic change (Andrews, 1973, 1974).

Understanding structural change in the family requires an understanding of basic family structure. In its most simplified form, the family can be viewed as a human relationship system in which people enter and leave over a very long period of time. It begins with a commitment to be together by two adults, which is most typically revealed in the early marital relationship before children. It then proceeds to the parenthood and child-rearing phase of some 20 to 25 years, in which children enter the system, grow up within it, and then leave. A final marital phase comprising 20 to 30 years follows the completion of parenthood. From the perspective of the parenting dyad, the original family system ends when one of the spouses dies. Over time people make commitments and enter into a systematic relationship; some of them with maturity leave, while others, that is, the parents, remain with the system. Any time a person enters or leaves this system permanently or for any length of time, the structure of the network of the relationships within the family is significantly and noticeably altered and requires the family to realign their relatedness with each other in order to survive functionally. Structural-change crises seem to involve first-born and last-born children, especially upon school entry, adolescence, and finally adult separation.

Psychological change in the family occurs when members are faced with a choice of whether to be together or to be apart and how to deal with each state. This has much more to do with the daily being together and being apart than fundamental structural change when someone comes into the family or leaves the family permanently, although these psychological processes do occur in exaggerated form when those structural changes occur. While family members are more often apart than they are together because they either work or attend schools in different places, they are together at very key times—getting up in the morning and getting off to work or school; eating dinner and going to bed. If, when they are together, that experience is one of support and nurturing, then growth (confident esteem) is enhanced within the family. If being together is experienced defensively and with assault, then growth is diminished. If, when they are apart, they view their separation as an opportunity for autonomous realization, growth is enhanced, and being apart occurs with confidence, trust and loyalty. On the other hand, if when apart they experience loneliness and alienation, growth is diminished.

All families go through the alteration of being together and being apart and develop policies for dealing with each. These policies are accumulative and either progressively enhance growth or progressively diminish growth. They are very similar to what we understand in individual development as the ongoing dilemma and struggle for differentiation on one hand and identification and integration on the other.

The third area of change which affects the family's developmental experience is traumatic change. Accidents either by physical injury or toxic reaction, illnesses and natural disasters, defective births, are examples. All of these suddenly and expectedly alter family balance. They are not related to any typical or expected developmental patterning in the family, but they do represent an intrusion into those experiences which call for a renegotiated policy for meeting psychological needs, or the stress of the trauma will escalate into symptoms rather than satisfaction.

In summary, a behavior dynamics model has been presented which describes basic concepts and distinctions in a theory of transactional relationships. It defined the purpose of that relationship system to sustain psychological survival; explained how such systems are either growth diminishing or growth enhancing; defined five basic relationship processes by which purposeful relationship is experienced; and finally, described the components of family development and crises over time.

Dysfunctional Model

The Functional Family   To understand the concept of the functional family, one must be aware that this is not based on an absolute set of behaviors; rather it reflects a series of conclusions derived from observations of many functional characteristics. Families can be viewed as functioning on a continuum from the ideal of fully functional at one end to fully dysfunctional at the other end. This is illustrated in Figure 9-2.

The range of behavior of any family, as illustrated in the figure, is a combination of both functional and dysfunctional characteristics. Family functioning in the range illustrated by the area between points *A* and *B* would be considered more functional than dysfunctional. Both clinical experience and research have revealed that some families do function near the extreme points of this continuum. Using a similar conception Beavers (1977) distributes the functional effectiveness of families which has been incorporated into Figure 9-2. Families in the severely disturbed range of *nine* to *ten* often produce children who would be diagnosed as process schizophrenics, severe behavior disorders, and sociopaths. Those in the *seven* to *eight* range are borderline families who often produce borderline states in their children. The midrange point between *five* and *six*, which Beavers refers to as "the sane but limited," represent a very mixed collection of characteristics with significant aspects of both functional and dysfunctional behavior in relatively equal proportions. Families at the *three* to *four* range are considered adequate and usually produce children who have no severe pathologies. The *one* to *two* range, represents effectively functioning family systems, who often produce children of unusual competence. In the broad range between *one* and *four,* there are degrees of relative functionality up to the point of quite optimal.

Figure 9-2   Model of Functional and Dysfunctional Families

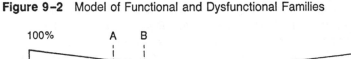
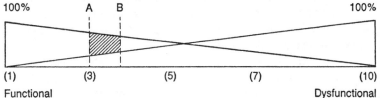

Source: *The Emotionally Disturbed Family,* Ernest Andrews. Copyright © Jason Aronson, 1974. Reprinted with permission.

In principle, the functional family is an open system which is growth oriented. The members of such families are able to express openly and directly what they hear, feel, see, and think, both about themselves and about others in the family. Family members manifest self openly and give emotional nurturance combined with loyalty and optimism. They are able to transact and negotiate with each other and with outsiders with a high degree of repreatedly productive outcome.

Lewis, Beavers, Gossett, and Phillips (1976) have described eight important characteristics of the functional family that further help to clarify the differences between functional and dysfunctional families.

1. An affiliative attitude about human encounter. Family members see attractiveness and purpose in being together and are supportive and encouraging with each other.
2. They have respect for their own and others' subjective views. This basically represents a valuing of each other's idiosyncratic ways of thinking and feeling and represents an interpersonal and personal appreciation of self and others.
3. They experience openness and communication. They feel secure about expressing their feelings about themselves and others in the family. They feel positive about revealing their thoughts and do not view these experiences as an unfair invasion of privacy.
4. There are high levels of initiative in the family. In general, family members are seekers, doers, and accomplishers rather than avoiders and procrastinators.
5. The parental coalition is complementary, affectionate, and strongly intact. There is an absence of competing parent-child dyads. Parents work closely together, both in regard to their marriage and in regard to their parenting activities. The primary satisfaction in the family comes from the marriage, with parenting satisfaction being secondary. The primacy of the marital dyad enables positive parenting without any sacrifice of one for the sake of the other.
6. They experience closeness with uniqueness and support of autonomy. There is both individuation and support with a high degree of mutual valuing of each other's personally distinctive qualities.
7. They experience spontaneous interaction. They value the experience of the moment without engaging in rigid and stereotypic behaviors more appropriate of the past. To some degree, there is a lack of expected routine, particularly in the sense of many "oughts" or "shoulds." They seem consistently open to new experiences and in fact relish and look forward to it.
8. There is an understanding of varied motivation and a willingness to negotiate rather than control in their relating. In essence, they realize that everybody has his or her unique combination of experiences, wishes, perceptions, feelings, and motivation. While there are

clear-cut lines of authority and responsibility in the family, there is an absence of over-control, domination, and authoritarianism.

Satir's (1965) description of the five basic processes of family communication discussed previously provides a similar picture of the functioning family. Self is manifest clearly, directly, and congruently; self and other are distinctly separated; differentness is acknowledged as uniqueness; room is made for other by deciding what fits who is involved; and joint outcome is negotiated from awareness and clarity.

Basically, members of the functional family experience their relatedness to one another without any threat to self-worth; they experience family relationships as nurturing, supportive, and having clearly articulated expectations. Beavers (1977) underscores what many family clinicians have noted; the presence of a strong marital coalition is the predominant dyad in the family which gives it nurturance, direction, and its most fundamental emotional viability. Children are not used as extensions of the parents or projections of their difficulties, but rather are valued for their own special qualities and seen as making a contribution to the spontaneity and creativity of experience within the family.

The Dysfunctional Family   A family is dysfunctional when it does not sustain psychological survival or promote personal growth of family members. Despair and alienation of family members are important symptoms of dysfunctioning. The dysfunctional outcome originates from choices to behave in ways which defeat self-and-other-realization of psychological survival. Five patterns characterize the dysfunctioning family. First, members of a dysfunctional family are evasive and non-self-revealing in their communication. They are often vague, indirect, and unclear. In severely dysfunctional families, observable evidence of psychosis within the family is frequently present. There is little visual or tactile contact between members. They are hard to pin down and appear to shift unpredictably in their attitudes and behavior toward one another.

Second, there is a refusal of self to nurture other, frequently accompanied by an absence of basic self-caring. The result is a mutual perception of continual victimhood in which one is constantly "done in" by someone or something outside of one's own experience. This is accompanied by a sense of helplessness and hopelessness which may vary from mild to quite severe. Third, there is a persistent denial of immediate experience. That is, family members react to each other as they would like the other to be; they are unable to experience the other's real characteristics because the other is seen not as she or he is, but as one hopes she or he could be. The result is disillusionment and disappointment because family members do not live up to the idealized version of other which each holds.

Fourth, there are strong efforts to conceal the emotional pain of dissatisfaction. This often manifests itself in psychological and somatic symptoms or antisocial acting out. People appear either as callous and tough or as withdrawn and numb, but in both cases generally as unfeeling and unresponsive. Finally, there are many attempts to disguise the despair resulting from unmet fantasies and real needs by manipulation of the other through contrived helplessness or outright power tactics. Both, of course, represent attempts to unilaterally manipulate for one's own gain at the expense of another.

The characteristics which typify the dysfunctional family increase despair and block attempts at emotional growth. Unless the real desire for need meeting is expressed directly with a request for negotiation (and it usually is not), frustration, disappointment, and hurt will be expressed deviously and indirectly in feelings and behavior which clinicians label as symptoms. Symptoms are attempts to manipulate and control others to gain assurance of caring and meaning.

At present, we break down these clusters of symptomatically expressive behavior and feelings into four categories:

a. *Anxiety states (neurosis)*   Here one's blocked attempts to manipulate or to fantasize positive outcome result in overwhelming anxiety, often with the hope that the anxiety itself will be labeled as a "sickness." The "sick" person seems helpless and often uses this state to attempt to manipulate further to bring about what she or he wishes. In other words, it is like saying: "I'm nervous about what's happening and helpless to bring about what I need. So do it for me."

b. *Nonsense states (psychosis)*   In this condition, the symptomatic person is essentially stating: "I'm crazy and therefore not responsible; you be responsible for me and take care of me so I'll feel worthwhile." This often occurs in a family where there is extreme lack of clarity, vagueness, and confusion in relationships. It also happens in situations where "madness," in the sense of anger, is confused with "madness" in the sense of insanity.

c. *Illness states (somatic complaints)*   In essence, the symptomatic person is saying: "You'll be the death of me yet unless you relieve my illness with special concern."

d. *Obnoxious states (personality disorders)*   Here the symptomatic person is basically saying: "I'm being angry or helpless, or both, about my disappointment over your lack of concern, so nuts to you. I'll go it alone without any consideration of anyone but myself."

These symptomatic patterns of behavior and feeling essentially serve as defenses to protect a person from vulnerability, pain, and hurt. They also result in a sense of being victimized, which only produces further self-defeating outcome.

When seen in terms of the Satir process categories, the joint outcome of these families is always arrived at spuriously without any positive collaboration and is therefore ungratifying. It is ungratifying because self is manifest in a vague, indirect, and incongruent manner; differentness is acknowledged only as bad, sick, stupid, or crazy and therefore threatening; self and other are fused rather than separated;

and room is made for people within the family system by power tactics and a "boss" policy. The result is a pervasive apprehensiveness and confusion; there is no support or direction in meeting the need for psychological survival through the attainment of sense and order, productivity, and intimacy in family relations.

Lewis, Beavers, Gosset, and Phillips (1976), in contrasting severely dysfunctional families with the healthy families that were the basis of their study, described eight dysfunctional characteristics which are also threads in a fabric of frustration and bewilderment. They found dysfunctional families to have an oppositional attitude in human encounter, rather than being involved in a collaboration of trusted partners, family members were engaged in warfare with adversaries. There was also a lack of respect for subjective views, manifested by the presence of ridicule and insensitivity in their relationships. Communication in the seriously disturbed family was distancing, obscuring, and confusing. The parental coalition was both weak and unaffectionate and was often superseded in dominance and authority by competitive parent-child coalitions. In fact, seeking of satisfaction in the family often breached generation lines and occurred between child and parent rather than between parents. Children were frequently used as objects of displacement in marital dissatisfaction or as objects of satisfaction in the presence of marital disillusionment. While family members revealed a substantial power and control orientation in their relatedness to each other, there was little evidence of appropriate control within the family. Situations were either very rigidly contained or else undefined with no clear guidelines for direction. Interactions within the dysfunctional family were stereotyped, highly predictable, and rigidly repetitive. Persons in these families were passive and unresponsive. There was a sense of numbness and a depreciation of assertive encounter.

Basically, the dysfunctional family is a closed system. People do not report openly and directly what they hear, feel, think about themselves and others in the family. The level of nurturance is low and there is generally an absence of physical contact or a gross inappropriateness of contact in the form of hitting or beating. Not only does the family make little use of its own contributions to one another, but its members have relatively little openness to input from outside the family from other systems like the school or the church.

As in the discussion about the functional family, the helper should keep in mind the continuum of functional and dysfunctional, optimal to severely disturbed. We are always talking about degrees of dysfunction. From the point of view of considering and planning treatment, the prognosis and early approach hinges upon our understanding of the functional aspects of even a dysfunctional system. We need to concentrate on how to expand the few functional aspects present even in a severely disturbed family if we are to help them move toward a greater degree of functionality. This process will be discussed more in detail in the following section on the therapeutic model.

Some basic comparative characteristics of functional and dysfunctional behavior in families and of helper characteristics are listed below:

Functional	Dysfunctional	Therapist
autonomous	helpless	active
spontaneous	rigid, repetitive	innovative
open	defensive	candid
assertive	hostile/withdrawn	provocative
responsible	blame/guilt	directive
changing	maintaining	instigating
caring	manipulating	supportive
nurturing	using	encouraging
direct	vague	explicit
seeking	avoiding	intrusive
confident	anxious	engaging
aware	confused	observant
revealing	concealing	clarifying
enjoyment	disillusionment	optimistic
lives now	past/future	experiential
affirming	denying	confrontive

Diagnostic Model: Evaluating Family Functioning for Intervention

In developing a diagnostic model, four basic considerations will be discussed:

a.   the idea that we are dealing with a social system in distress;
b.   the conditions of clinical evaluation of the family;
c.   the process of evaluation; and
d.   the basic skills necessary for adequate evaluation of families.

Diagnosis is essentially a data-gathering process in which the helper attempts to develop an in-depth picture of the dynamics of the total family unit. The primary questions the helper tries to answer are: What feelings, perceptions, and attitudes does each member have toward the other members of the family units? What behavior patterns does each member display to the other members and for what purposes? What influence methods does each member use with the other members? How is each affected by the others? What important role expectations does each member assign to the other members and accept for self? For the helper the diagnostic interview is an integrative experience of applying all the knowledge and experience of the systematic and reciprocal nature of human relationships and the model of family functionality-dysfunctionality.

From the very beginning it is important that we view the family as a whole, as the unit of diagnostic attention. Any consideration given to the subparts (individuals, pairs, or triads) is always in relation to the whole family system. If the helper does not have a firm commitment to this philosophy, the family rather than the helper will dictate the structure of the diagnostic evaluation. The family members will continue to hide what they have always hidden, will conceal what they have most feared and will continue to manipulate; all of these processes are, of course, part of the problem and the basis of symptomatic complaints which brought the family for help. All behaviors which occur among family members are information to be used in the diagnostic process.

We must see clearly and in a serially related way how behavior between any two or more people in the system is causally related to the concerns and symptoms which the family presents to us. The family itself is involved in blame and fault; we must be aware of what they do, unwittingly and often unconsciously, to perpetuate the problems which bring the family for counseling. It is necessary to form a picture of this transactional network of relationships which threatens, hinders, and otherwise blocks functional outcome and growth in the family (Bodin, 1968).

The understanding of what painful outcome is produced and how, are necessary ethical and professional prerequisites for any helping intervention. Howells (1971) makes this point forcefully:

> The fashionable vogue is to plunge into therapy. It is as if in surgery, at the signal of abdominal pain, we plunge in with no knowledge of the anatomy of the abdominal organs, no understanding of their function, and no systematic inquiry to discern the focus of the pain ... To help is a laudable aspiration. But to plunge into the abdomen with no prior examination ... is not to help. It is a hazardous impulse fraught with danger for the patient. In that situation, masterly inactivity and reliance on nature's own defense measures might well be more effective (p. 177).

Before proceeding to the diagnostic process, it is important to recognize that the conviction that emotional disturbance is rooted in family relations and that the family as a whole is the unit of diagnostic contention requires that the *whole family* is to be included in the *first meeting*. The possible resistance of the family to this procedure is usually based upon their stereotyped expectations of what the process is to be like, rather than on a real awareness from direct experience.

Sometimes the diagnostic process is highly structured; at other times it can be unstructured or open ended. With either approach, it is necessary beforehand to have knowledge only of the names and birthdates of all the members of the family; the date of the marriage; and who referred the family. It is generally a waste of time to ask them to state the nature of their problems since they are really only aware of the nature of their symptoms. The whole matter of the relationship between the symptoms and the real essence of their problems is the task of the diagnostic interview.

In the diagnostic interview we want to know in some depth and with some clarity how the way in which family members relate to one another is connected to the symptoms which they present to us. This requires an understanding of the five Satir processes as they relate to the three basic survival wants. We may also assess how they function in the eight areas which Beavers and his associates believe are the threads of the emotional fabric of the family. To gain an understanding of their differentness and of how they are able to utilize difference, we want to know how each family member experiences the problem. We need to know, whether they came as the result of a precipitating problem or external social pressure. We need to know what their stereotyped perceptions are of themselves, their family, the clinic, and the process of resolving their difficulties. It is helpful to know whether they are blame-oriented or change-oriented. It is also important to understand where each of the members is in his or her individual life cycle and whether that contributes to any specific family life-cycle crisis.

Some typical areas of focus in diagnostic interviews would be:

(a) *Forms of hostility expression* between family members which reveal frustration over unmet needs for sense and order, productivity and intimacy. Active hostility, such as hitting or shouting, which leads to contact of an assaultive nature, has the effect of distancing the relationship by provoking rejection. Passive hostility, varying from withdrawn sulking to virtually total alienation, also distances relatedness, as if being together is dangerous. Both forms of hostility represent defenses against expected or experienced hurt.

(b) *Specific manipulation patterns,* such as evasiveness, to conceal actual thoughts and feelings; who talks for whom and who avoids being responsible for self; the use of threats of action or withdrawal to "shape up" other to suit self; the use of martyr tactics to control other and also to make one self indispensable; and the use of somatic complaints, various "fears" and self-induced "inadequacies" to elicit need-meeting by playing an invalid role.

(c) *Hidden agendas,* such as playing "Look how hard I've tried" to justify a guilt-free divorce, separation, or placement; underlying marital concern disguised as parental concern over a "troubled child;" and using one's idea of "love" to mask a need to rehabilitate another in one's own image.

(d) *Crossed transactions in communication,* which are the result of each coming from a different view of an experience and not allowing others' views as real to them. Both parties in any transaction within a dysfunctional relationship will distort their perception of experience to fit learned preconceptions. A man who acts like his wife's father will either get excessive dependency or resentment, both of which block realization of need-meeting. Often amid much talking (frequently confused with communicating) there is little or no listening so that messages sent are not received.

(e) *Patterns of defensiveness,* such as intellectualizing to avoid experiencing (talking rather than doing); vagueness to avoid commitment of self with other; anger to disguise disappointment; rejection-provoking to avoid fears of closeness; and projecting and displacing to others to avoid responsibility for self-other consequences.

Essentially, any diagnostic observation of interview content (words and behavior) needs to be translated into relationship process (Satir's five processes) when dysfunctional outcome has blocked the attainment of psychological survival.

Symptom behavior should not be confused with underlying problems, but rather should be seen as the content manifestation of disturbed relationship processes.

The open-ended interview is a process-oriented exploration with the family about their areas of pain, concern, despair, and nurturance—that is, about their overall relatedness to one another through which they dysfunctionally realize symptoms instead of confident autonomy and nurturant relatedness. There are several possibilities for the structured interview, varying from slightly to highly structured. These include projectives (Howells and Lickorish, 1969 and Loveland, Wynne, and Singer, 1963); story telling (Kadushin, Cutler, Waxenberg, and Sager, 1969); focal tasks (Drechsler and Shapiro, 1961 and Blechman, 1974); drawing (Sherr and Hicks, 1973 and Geddes and Medway, 1977); and visual-experiential activities (Simon, 1972).

One effective technique is to give the family a very simple but concrete task to complete and then carefully observe the way in which they work on it. Whether they complete the task or not is not as important as the way in which they either negotiate or manipulate one another in order to accomplish the end. They may be asked to draw on a large piece of paper after they have each been given a crayon, either their own home or the home they would prefer to live in and then to decide upon and describe how the space in the home would be utilized. This brings out a great deal of information on the five Satir processes and will frequently replicate realistically what happens at home. The clinician may also present them with three family type games and ask them to decide which of the three games they would prefer to engage in. Again, this reveals realistic information about how they actually negotiate or manipulate toward joint outcome.

Watzlawick (1966) has described a structured family diagnostic interview developed at the Mental Research Institute in Palo Alto. This interview consists of a specific sequence of questions and tasks which provides information about (a) how family members individually, and as a family, perceive and are able to comment on their problems; (b) how they work together in various combinations dyadically and as a whole; (c) how the marriage came about and developed, and how its principal philosophy affects the children and the family as a whole; (d) their systematic alignment along the dimensions of positive and negative affect in the family; and (e) how they perceive themselves and others in the family relative to power role relationships.

In any structured procedure, it is important that the verbal directions, sequence of questions, and format be followed as described. This procedure is analogous to psychological testing in that the conditions and instructions must be kept as identical as possible with repeated use. The structured family diagnostic interview is helpful for the beginning practitioner. It helps the beginner build up a normative experience about the range of family dysfunction; it is also helpful in that the procedure itself always gives the clinician a specific next point to move to, and hence communicates security to the members of the family. At the same time, it permits the interviewer to accumulate diagnostically significant information without being unduly overwhelmed by his or her anxiety about the experience.

The basic skills necessary to perform an adequate clinical evaluation of the family are critical. Poor evaluation leads to poor planning and poor counseling. We cannot answer the question of what a counselor does in family counseling until we have analyzed what is going on within the family and of what is going on between the interviewer and the family members. Diagnostic procedures cannot be learned from reading alone; they must be learned within the context of a professional training program in which demonstration and analysis and supervised practice are involved. Five basic areas of expertise are required:

a. A thorough knowledge of the individual life cycle, as well as of the family life cycle.
b. Interviewing skills with children, adolescents, and adults.
c. A thorough knowledge of individual psychopathology and of familial pathogenic relating dynamics.
d. Prior diagnostic and therapeutic experience, under supervision, with individuals and groups.
e. Familiarity with the literature in family dynamics and disturbance, as well as an awareness of diagnostic procedures and treatment planning.

Process of Family Counseling: A Treatment Model

The helping orientation described here is both a social-growth and a remedial model which assumes three basic conditions to be present for therapy to occur. The clients must either come with these or they must emerge early within the therapeutic experience.

a. *Courage:* To be honest with self and others about what is happening, to confront the actual. (This frequently may mean giving up some cherished illusions and delusions.)
b. *Commitment to do therapeutic work:* To care enough about self and others to openly and directly reveal concern, value, and loving, and to be willing to give and take in mutual attachment.
c. *Desire for change:* This comes from choices which lead to action.

Critical Assumptions in Family Counseling

All systems of counseling represent an assumptive frame of reference as well as a methodology to instigate change from dysfunctional outcome to functional outcome. The assumptions provide the counselor with a cognitive map to provide an effective helping experience in a goal directed and consistent manner. Failure to understand and apply these basic assumptions can result in confusion, anxiety, and bewilderment for clients as well as counselor.

In existential family counseling there are two critical assumptions. One is that all behavior within the family, and especially problem behavior, results from choice

In other words, the being and feeling of all people in this relationship system derives from choices that each makes about actions and perceptions toward other family members. We accept, furthermore, the axiom "that you cannot not choose," and that only the one who chooses is responsible for that choice. Most dysfunctional outcomes in families are collaboratively self-induced and in no way represent gross limitations that prevent any choice whatever. Choice always occurs within limitation, however. To deny limitations is to deny reality; to deny choice within limitations is to deny growth. We live with the consequences of our choices, however fortunate or unfortunate they are. Growth involves choices which are responsibly made and nurtured by commitment to encounter with others.

Problem behavior which families experience represent present consequences which are the result of past choices. A dysfunctional family blocks its own growth unwittingly by avoidance, evasiveness, denial, and manipulation. These are all choices since family members could behave otherwise. A redecision may change some present consequences, although some consequences, such as suicide, are unalterable. Most dysfunctional family behavior and manipulation, however, is alterable; it does not represent a final state of being.

All "unfinished business," variously referred to as fixations, blockages, or unresolved conflicts, is viewed as a set of unmade decisions about self or self and other and exists in the present. They are a living history which results in behavior derived from deciding not to decide. Any aspect of a family's history which is significant in present behavior is still alive in behavior; it is not dead in the usual meaning of history, but lives on. Therefore, the family's history is not only observable but also usable in the present. There is no need to reminisce about how it began or how it got to where it is. It is enough to know how it affects dysfunctional outcome in the present. Existential thinking regards only the present as actual; the past and the future are mental and emotional reminisces about what we thought happened or what we want to happen. To focus on the past and/or future is to avoid living in the present, and therefore to avoid responsibility for our existential being. This is the preference of dysfunctional families who always choose to avoid present experience. It is a choice which is central to their dysfunction. Should the counselor likewise engage in this choice, she or he would then become a part of the problem rather than part of the solution.

The second assumption is that the nature of existential family therapy is an experience of choosing or rechoosing. Honesty, directness and self-responsibility are primary qualities for growth. To avoid or deny any of these three qualities results in pervasive anxiety and/or unilateral manipulation. However, being responsible and honest is worthwhile only if the experience is based on a conviction of value to self and others. The counselor must be honest, responsible and nurturant to assist the clients' relearning experience in the change encounter we call family counseling.

The awareness of choices and of the consequences of those choices must occur at the conscious level. This basic process involves an awareness of both existential despair or loneliness and of self-realization. Both require genuine and honest encounter of existential affect. In other words, the counselor must deal with behavior and with feelings about behavior which occur within the interview itself.

Symptoms are viewed as an avoidance of self-responsibility and represent an attempt on the part of family members to manipulate others to choose for them, that is, to be responsible for them. Clients hold a conviction that symptoms represent a kind of "sickness" for which they are not responsible. The counselor must be aware of this and insist that clients choose to be responsible. If clients choose to be helpless, they are denying their responsibility for present consequences, and are accepting suffering rather than seeking what they would rather have and actually need.

The experience of change results from a choice to behave differently. It is the realization of responsibility toward both self and others. It is instigated by the responsible encounter of honest affect within the framework of the interview. This means that family members must become aware of their dissatisfaction, disappointment, hurt, anger, frustration, and depressive despair, and *accept responsibility* for their contribution to the realization of this dysfunctional outcome. Frequently, family members are well aware of the negative side of their family experience, but accept no responsibility for having contributed to that very outcome. And even when they do accept responsibility, it is necessary for them to rechoose how to be together differently so that they may collaboratively effect a more functional outcome. An awareness of how vagueness and indirectness contribute to confusion and disappointment must be followed by the experience of clarity and directness, which will diminish frustration and permit an experience of reality which is gratifying to basic emotional survival.

Nature of Family Counseling

Having discussed the basic assumptions of existential family therapy, it now remains to discuss the nature of the family counseling, both in terms of its pragmatic structure and in terms of its psychological processes. The pragmatic structure has to do with who comes when and how often; with contracts and phases of treatment; seating and office arrangement; and the final decision for termination.

There is no usual spacing of interviews for family counseling. Size of the family, its particular problems, and its accessibility in terms of travel time all need to be taken into account. Most common, however, is to meet with the family one to two hours weekly. Sessions might just as profitably be held on a two-hour, every-other-week basis or as a four-hour half-day experience once a month. Intensity in family counseling is viewed as rising from the intensity of a given experience itself, rather than as from closely spaced interviews as in psychoanalysis. A larger family will require more time because of the complexity of its system.

In the initial phases of counseling, it is most preferable to have the family come on a weekly basis if possible. They often will need to come during the late afternoon or evening in order to accommodate all the children who are in school. The counselor should be aware that clients very often attempt to manipulate the structure of the counseling experience itself in order to control its outcome and thereby turn an attempt at change into part of their problem. The counselor must remember that he or she is responsible for the content, process, and structure of the sessions. It is necessary, therefore, to be very clear and explicit as to who is to come. It has proven most valuable to have all of the members of the family to come the first one to three times. If a decision is made to work with part of the family rather than with the whole family, that decision should be exclusively the counselor's, based upon his or her clinical skill and experience and upon his or her knowledge of the particular dynamics of the family.

Sufficient space must be allowed for the family. A traditional office is usually inadequate for this purpose, unless the family is small. The family interviewing room should include a number of light-weight movable chairs, as well as a sofa in an area sufficiently large that the family members may either choose to be quite close to each other or relatively distant. An area about the size of a large living room, 15 feet by 25 feet would be most appropriate. The way in which people seat themselves in relation to others in their family is diagnostically significant and may be used as a point of intervention by the therapist. Their seating represents choices and reflects the degree of affinity or alignment among family members, as well as aversion between them.

Contracts are quite helpful with two kinds of families: those who basically think, feel and behave in very explicit and concrete ways; and highly educated and intellectualized families who exhibit a tendency to drift into rambling intellectualizations and thus diminish the experiential aspects of counseling. For the counselor, contracts are valuable because they permit a continuous re-evaluation of goals and present levels of achievement (Andrews, 1974c). A basic diagnostic contract would be for one to three hours. It might represent either three interviews or a single interview. A contract for continued sessions generally will range between three and five sessions, but may include as many as ten. Again, rather than to drift aimlessly, the contract makes both family members and counselor examine what has occurred. It is important to keep in mind that the family will remain in counseling as long as its goals are being realized. The counselor will reap only frustration if he or she imposes his or her goals upon the family or engages in goal-thinking which is so cosmic and pervasive as to require fifteen years for its completion. It is also useful to keep in mind, as Holt (1974) discovered, that the majority of families in counseling are satisfied with the accomplishments of the experience, while the majority of their counselors are not. This difference may reflect a discrepancy in focal goals, with counselors being more idealistic than families. The decision to terminate may be mutually agreed upon when specific goals have been accomplished, or it may occur when the family has gone as far as it wishes to go. Families often reach an area which they do not wish to change and end the sessions at the point which represents their terminal commitment to change.

To understand the *psychological process of family counseling,* it is important to focus on the unfolding experience of the interview itself and on the use of this experience to effect change in the relationship system of the family. The initial encounter with the family sets the tone for the remainder of the contacts with them.

If the initial encounter is characterized by explanation and procedures, then the remainder of the therapy will be a procedural explanation and will not tap into the inappropriate emotionality underlying the family's dysfunction. Counselors must experience the emotional process of a family's interrelatedness, and family members must experience counseling as an emotional process in rechoosing how to relate. To be with a family is to be aware of and to experience a transactional process—a flow and exchange of reciprocal relating. Do not ask what to do until you have answered the question, "What is going on and how are the family and I involved with each other?"

In the initial meetings, the counselor meets with, experiences, reacts to an existing transactional system of the family of which they are not fully conscious and which the counselor has not previously experienced. Typically, the persons in the family will see the counselor as a way out of a painful situation. In essence, they will attempt to transfer the responsibility for the consequences of their interrelating to the counselor. As the counselor reacts to and begins to relate to the family, it will attempt to ingest the counselor into the system; or the counselor will provoke, stimulate, or initiate change in their relationship patterns through insightful or paradoxical directives (cf. Haley, 1963).

Examples of insightful directives are:

a. "Would you be willing to move closer to her to see how you experience that?"
b. "If you really want to get through to her, I suggest you take her by the hand and look her directly in the eye, and then say in ten words or less, exactly what you have on your mind."
c. "You know, I experience this family as being in warring camps. I would like the men to move over to these chairs and the women to the other side of the room to these chairs. Now when you have done this, think a moment about how this feels. Is it like it is at home, too? I know this is how I experience you here."

Examples of paradoxical directives would be:

a. "You say you are pretty good at maintaining distance, but I feel you could do that even better. Would you mind moving about four feet farther back from him?"
b. (To a child described as hyperactive by his parents, a description agreed to by the child himself). "O.K., I would like to see you do something hyperactive." (The child in fact has been sitting quietly and with obvious control.)
c. "You shout every time you talk to her. Apparently you must feel she hears better when you yell. I would suggest you yell even louder at her so she will really understand what you have to say."

Resistance in Family Counseling

Change is experienced by all people as an ordeal; resistance to change in some form is inevitable. Family members are often resistant to change for a variety of reasons: They are not consciously aware of the way in which they relate to each other; they fear that change will be for the worse rather than for the better; change requires a reworking of some basic behaviors and convictions that are deeply ingrained within us, and to change often implies some responsibility for the problem. Persons who devalue themselves cannot imagine being reacted to better or being treated better on the basis of what they contribute to the relationship; change requires painful choices that affect all parts of the family system; any change in one part will result in changes in other parts. If a father is willing to give up an overattachment to a daughter, then he may have to be prepared for a wife who is more interested in him; to change means to accept that what we have done is unproductive or that how we have been has not worked out, and we must be able to choose differently without devaluing ourselves in the process.

These are only some basic components of resistance to change which both clients and counselor experience. In this sense we share an equal humanity. The counselors differ only in their understanding of resistance to change because of their training and experience. The only way for counselors really to be aware of this resistance is to have experienced it themselves as participants in a self-awareness group. This must be a basic part of the training of the family counselor and occurs best in an experiential group. Counselors who become annoyed with their clients' problems of resistance may be projecting their own annoyance with themselves on to their clients.

There are other basic problems on the part of the beginning practitioners which will now be discussed. These represent sources of counselor resistance to awareness and change.

(a) *Counselors, not the family, are responsible for counseling* Because of their sense of responsibility for counseling, counselors sometimes misdefine the nature of the experience and the conditions under which the experience is to occur. Surgeons do not allow patients to dictate either the place or the procedure of surgery; the family counselor should not let the family dictate the place and procedures of the counseling experience. The family is free to choose to participate in the counseling or not. The counselor never needs to refuse service, but has the ethical right and responsibility to define the nature of the service in such a way that it will truly be productive. What the family does between interviews and what it does after counseling is the responsibility of the family. Family members' blatant attempts to misconstrue, misunderstand, and inappropriately utilize at home what has been learned in counseling is the responsibility of the family members. Even though they will at times blame this on the counselor, the family members make the ultimate decision of how they will live together. Counselors can help them become aware of the choices which lead to that decision, but cannot make the decision for anyone except themselves.

(b) Therapeutic process will become confused and undirected if the *counselor loses contact with the here and now.* It is not necessary to recite history, even though many family members enjoy this. The unresolved aspects of their own development will be apparent in how they relate to one another in the present. Lack of attention to nonverbal cues is often responsible for the counselor's loss of contact with the present and being seduced into verbal content. The only productive way to use the present is for what it is now and not for why it is not any better. If the family wishes to make it any better, then it may do so beginning this instant (Kempler, 1975).

(c) Some *counselors suffer from Messiah complexes.* They believe they have the power to damage, but interestingly enough, do not have the same conviction about their ability to change families. All of us to some degree would like to be omnipotent, because that seems preferable to feelings of uncertainty and inadequacy. The beginning counselor often feels inadequate because he or she is inexperienced and relatively unintegrated therapeutically. Attempts to save anybody in the interview are doomed to failure. Counselors may save themselves but only by self-understanding; they must refuse to be seduced into attempting to save others. Counselors all need to recover from the narcissistic injury which they suffer when they become aware that the job of being God has not been offered to them.

(d) It is easier than it might seem for beginning counselors to *confuse their experience with the family's experience* and regard that as a form of empathy; it really represents a projection or displacement. It is not necessary that counselors have identical life experiences with clients to be able to understand them. Many clients will insist on this, stating that counselors cannot understand them if they have not been parents themselves—or been black or been female or poor, or whatever. Their insistence is often a defense. Similarity should not be seen as the only basis for understanding in relationship. When counselors are unable to help clients with a particular aspect of their relationship, it is often because this is very similar to an aspect of relationship in their own lives of which they are unaware and which they unconsciously avoid in the same way they avoid it with their client family. The counselor may or may not be a more functional person than the members of the family which he or she is treating. He or she is usually better trained and more knowledgeable about such relationships, but not necessarily a more functional person than individual family members.

(e) The beginning counselor often prefers to use "techniques" as substitutes for basic dynamic and diagnostic understanding. These techniques often do not work because the counselors use them to restore their confidence and esteem. Some techniques are procedures with step-by-step sequences, others are behavioral "gimmicks" to elicit "material" from families. Although any procedure or behavioral simulation can yield valuable awareness when thoughtfully utilized with clear dynamic understanding and careful timing, they will not substitute for sound interviewing skills.

The greatest drawback of dependence on techniques without dynamic awareness of the family and the self of the counselor is the tendency of such techniques to give a "pompous expert" presence to the counselor. This elicits expectations of magic from family members and detaches the real self of the counselor from genuine participation in the transaction process of therapist-family in mutual therapeutic endeavor. Competent practice emanates from a thorough dynamic understanding of family transactional process and the counselor's understanding of himself or herself.

For counseling to continue with purpose and effectiveness, each family member must be willing to express clearly and openly what he or she feels, thinks, hears, and sees about self and others in the family; the counselor needs to do the same. The family members need to have a commitment to change in specific ways (I will hold her more often, speak to the point instead of beating around the bush, look him in the eyes when I want him to listen), and the counselor needs to be comfortable with his or her subjective involvement as a basis for response instead of fitting the expected stereotypes of family members who seek alliances and vindication in place of awareness and honest assertion.

Family counseling is an ordeal in which the struggle for self definition is manifested by reciprocal encounters of affect which lead to awareness, commitment, and behavior change. A new definition of relatedness can result from counseling based upon reciprocal need-meeting and satisfaction rather than upon alienation, hurt, and devious relating. Specific optimal effects of family therapy include each family member behaving in ways which are direct, clear, and congruent; separating their selves from other as a valued special person; acknowledging differentness as uniqueness; making decisions upon what best fits him or her and others; and willingness to negotiate joint relationship outcome.

The Use of Self in Family Counseling

The appropriate and thoughtful use of the self of the counselor in his or her family practice is the most productive contribution to counseling outcome. Inappropriate use of self is a basic error counselors often make. The process of the productive use of self takes considerable time to achieve. There are no short cuts to its realization, but there are effective ways of accomplishing it over a long period of time. It involves among other things, as Truax and Carkhuff (1967) have researched; the capacity of caring for other people through our humane awareness but without inflicting our own hurt child upon them; utilization of discriminatory and judgmental abilities without being punitive or rejecting in that judgment; acceptance of limitations without gullibility; empathic understanding of the client family as a spring board for intervention and support, but without confusing our life experience with their life experience; recognition of the common humanity of persons as well as their particular uniqueness; interaction with the client family with confident assertiveness devoid of needs to control others for the enhancement of our own security; avoidance of passivity which conveys evasiveness and basic uncertainity to the family; and involvement rather than avoidance. Both anxiety and confidence are contagious in the family interview. With a family which is already uncertain, it is more effective to convey confidence than to add to the anxiety already present.

Since most counselors have the potential to offer these qualities, they can be developed and integrated into the counselor's use of self by demonstration teaching, adequate supervision and his or her own personal therapeutic experience (Andrews, 1977–78). A counselor is first and foremost a person, rather than a role. To come across as being in a professional role is unauthentic, and can block the flow of authentic, honest communication.

Variations of Relationship Therapy and Combined Therapies

The focus in this chapter has been on total family units. The marital pair has not been isolated as separate from the family, but this is frequently done. It should be kept in mind that the dynamics are the same for the parental couple as for the family. With a couple we are simply dealing with the most basic dyad in the family rather than with the interlocking series of dyads which comprise the family. Sager (1966) has outlined the development of marriage counseling; and the pioneering work of Satir (1965) and Watson (1962), as well as the more recent work of Fitzgerald (1973) and Martin (1976), among others, describes this form of subunit family counseling. Often what begins as family counseling ends up a more focal and exclusive marital counseling because of the cardinal position and influence of the parents in the family system.

Other variations of relationship therapy include couples groups (Leichter, 1962; Perelman, 1960; Blinder and Kirschenbaum, 1967; and Framo, 1973) and multi-family group therapy (Leichter and Schulman, 1972; Drake, 1975). Both are complex combinations of group counseling and systems therapy which require a high degree of practitioner skill.

Most recently the concept of family counseling has been extended to its next logical step; that is, to direct work with extended family networks as originated by Speck and Attneave (1973) and further refined by Reuveni (1975). Seen as a form of intervention for specific crises rather than an ongoing form of counseling, this approach is often used in conjunction with ongoing individual and/or family counseling. The network is comprised of all persons, lay and professional, who are willing to help a specific family in crisis. The network often includes neighbors, relatives, police, physicians, social workers, and teachers. A therapeutic team works with the network with a central therapist in charge. This requires a high degree of interprofessional collaboration. The process is often quite lively and the results can be impressive.

An important consideration is whether it is appropriate for family members to have individual or group counseling experiences concurrently with their family counseling experience (Andrews, 1970). Some say that such multiple experiences can confuse and overwork the client, resulting in greater defensiveness. This writer's position is that multiple experiences are not inappropriate for some clientele, particularly adolescents who are trying to clarify their personal identities and with people who need help in developing their interpersonal skills. Each of the different counseling experiences can focus on a different facet of the client's life experiences and thus complement rather than compete with each other (Avallone, et al. 1973). The effectiveness of multiple counseling experiences depends heavily on careful coordination among the helping professionals involved, a task that is often extremely difficult to accomplish.

Summary

This chapter has presented an introduction and orientation to the rationale, basic assumptions, and cardinal concepts and processes of the human systems orientation with an existential focus to the practice of conjoint family therapy. After a brief sketch of the historical development of family theory and counseling, one focal model, existential family counseling, was presented in detail. This social-growth model is further broken down into four submodels: (a) a behavior dynamics model which described transactional relationship theory; (b) a model of the functional family and the dysfunctional family; (c) a diagnostic model to evaluate family functioning for the purposes of intervention; and (d) a counseling model which offered guidelines for treatment. Particular emphasis was placed on the understanding of process rather than content; the necessity for adequate training and supervision; and the importance of the use of self in effecting appropriate therapeutic outcome. Finally, brief comments on variations of relationship therapy and combined therapies were made.

Questions for Further Inquiry

1. What injunctions did you learn from your early family experience? How are they affecting your present-day life? Are there some you would like to change?

2. What processes in your present family structure sustain each member of the family and promote personal growth? What "games" are part of your present-day family structure?

3. All families can be understood from a systems framework. In a family you know, think of ways that moods and behavior of one member affect the moods and actions of other members.

4. What may a counselor do to help family members encounter each other directly instead of presenting bills of grievances about each other?

5. Individual family members will frequently try to make the counselor an ally against another family member. What problems does this pose for the counselor? If you find yourself siding with one member of the family is that a problem?

References

Ackerman, N. *The psychodynamics of family life.* New York: Basic Books, 1958.

Ackerman, N. *Treating the troubled family.* New York: Basic Books, 1966.

Ackerman, N. *The family approach and levels of intervention.* Paper presented at the Annual Meeting of the American Orthopsychiatric Association, Washington, D.C., March, 1967.

Andrews, E. Integrated psychotherapy in clinical practice: An introduction. Unpublished paper, 1970.

Andrews, E. Conjoint psychotherapy with couples and families. *Cincinnati Journal of Medicine* 1972, *53,* 318–19.

Andrews, E. Family therapy. In N. Brandes & M. Gardner (Eds.), *Adolescent group therapy.* New York: J. Aronson, 1973.

Andrews, E. *The emotionally disturbed family.* New York: J. Aronson, 1974.(a)

Andrews, E. Psychological and structural aspects of the family life cycle. In *Relationship dynamics and conjoint therapy with couples and families.* New York: Behavioral Science Tape Library (cassette tapes), 1974.(b)

Andrews, E. Treatment contracts in initial, middle, and terminal phases of conjoint therapy. In *Relationship dynamics and conjoint therapy with couples and families.* New York: Behavioral Science Tape Library (cassette tapes), 1974.(c)

Andrews, E. *Training program announcement.* Cincinnati: The Family Institute, 1977–78.

Avallone, S., Aron, R., Starr, P., & Beetz, S. How therapists assign families to treatment modalities. *American Journal of Orthopsychiatry* 1973 *43,* 767–73.

Bateson, G., Jackson, D. D., Haley, J., & Weakland, J. Toward a theory of schizophrenia. *Behavioral Science* 1958 *1,* 251–64.

Beavers, W. R. *Psychotherapy and growth: A family systems perspective.* New York: Brunner/Mazel, 1977.

Bell, R. A reinterpretation of the direction of effects in studies of socialization. *Psychological Review* 1968 *75,* 81–95.

Bell, R. Stimulus control of parent or caretaker behavior by offspring. *Developmental Psychology* 1971 *4,* 63–72.

Bell, R., & Ainsworth, M. Infant crying and maternal responsiveness. *Child Development* 1972 *43,* 1171–90.

Berne E. *Games people play.* New York: Grove Press, 1964.

Blechman, E. A. The family contract game. *Family Coordinator* 1974 *23,* 269–81.

Blinder, G., & Kirschenbaum, M. The technique of married couple group therapy. *Archives of General Psychiatry* 1967 *17,* 44–52.

Bodin, A. M. Conjoin family assessment. In P. McReynolds (Ed.), *Advances in psychological assessment* Vol. 1). Palo Alto, Calif.: Science and Behavior Books, 1968, pp. 233–41.

Bowen, M. A. Family concept of schizophrenia. In D. D. Jackson (Ed.), *The etiology of schizophrenia.* New York: Basic Books, 1960.

Chin, R. The utility of systems models and developmental models for practitioners. *Research reports and technical notes* #46. Human Relations Center, Boston University, 1958.

Drake, B. Psychoanalytically oriented psychodrama with multiple family groups. Paper presented at the Annual Conference of the American Orthopsychiatric Association, Washington, D.C., 1975.

Drechsler, R. J., & Shapiro, M. I. A procedure for direct observation of family interaction in a child guidance clinic. *Psychiatry* 1961 *24,* 163–70.

Fitzgerald, R. V. *Conjoint marital therapy.* New York: J. Aronson, 1973.

Framo, J. L. Marriage therapy in a couples group. *Seminars in Psychiatry* 1973 *5,* 207–17.

Geddes, M., & Medway, J. The symbolic drawing of family life space. *Family Process,* 1977, *16,* 219–36.

Haley, J. *Strategies of psychotherapy* (Chapter 7, "Family Conflicts" & Chapter 8, "Therapeutic Paradoxes"). New York: Grove & Stratton, 1963.

Harper, L. V. The young as a source of stimuli controlling caretaker behavior. *Developmental Psychology* 1971 *4,* 73–88.

Holt, S. A. A system for the analysis of goal achievement in psychotherapy. Paper presented at the Annual Conference of the American Orthopsychiatric Association, March, 1974.

Howells, J. G. *The theory and practice of family psychiatry.* New York: Brunner/Mazel, 1971.

Howells, J. G., & Lickorish, J. R. A projective technique for assessing family relationships. *Journal of Clinical Psychology* 1969 *25,* 301–07.

Jackson, D. D. The study of the family: Family rules. *Family Process* 1965 *12,* 589–94.

Kadushin, P., Cutler, C., Waxenburg, S. F., & Sager, C. J. The family story technique and intrafamily analysis. *Journal Project Technical Personality Assessment* 1969 *33,* 438–50.

Kempler, W. *Gestalt family therapy.* Costa Mesa, Calif.: The Kempler Institute, 1975.

Korner, A. F. Mother-child interaction: One- or two-way street. *Social Work* 1965 *10,* 47–51.

Laing, R. D. *Sanity, madness and the family.* New York: Basic Books, 1964.

Laing, R. D. Mystification, confusion, and conflict. In I. Boszormenyi-Nagy and J. Framo (Eds.), *Intensive family therapy.* New York: Harper & Row, 1965.

Leichter, E., & Schulman, G. L. Interplay of group and family treatment techniques in multifamily group therapy. *International Journal of Group Psychotherapy* 1972 *22,* 167–76.

Lewis, J., Beavers, W. R., Gossett, J., & Phillips, V. A. The family system and physical illness. *In no single thread: Psychological health in family systems.* New York: Brunner/Mazel, 1976.

Lewis, M., & Rosenblum L. (Eds.) *The effect of the infant on its caregiver.* New York: Wiley, 1974.

Loveland, N. T., Wynne, L. C., & Singer, M. T. The family Rorschach: A new method for studying family interaction. *Family Process,* 1963 *2,* 187–215.

Luthman, S., & Kirschenbaum, M. *The dynamic family.* Palo Alto, Calif.: Science and Behavior Books, 1974.

Martin, P. A. *A marital therapy manual.* New York: Brunner/Mazel, 1976.

Perelman, J. L. Problems encountered in psychotherapy of married couples. *International Journal of Group Psychotherapy* 1960 *10,* 136–42.

Reuveni, U. Network intervention with a family in crisis. *Family Process* 1975 *2,* 193–203.

Sager, C. J. The development of marriage therapy: An historical review. *American Journal of Orthopsychiatry,* 1966 *36,* 458–67.

Satir, V. *Conjoint family therapy.* Palo Alto, Calif.: Science and Behavior Books, 1967.

Satir, V. Conjoint marital therapy. In E. Greene (Ed.), *The psychotherapies of marital disharmony.* New York: Free Press, 1965.

Sherr, C., & Hicks, H. Family drawing as a diagnostic and therapeutic technique. *Family Process* 1973 *12,* 439–60.

Simon, R. M. Sculpting the family. *Family Process* 1972 *11,* 49–57.

Speck, R., & Attneave, C. L. *Family networks.* New York: Pantheon Books, 1973.

Truax, C. B., & Carkhuff, R. R. *Toward effective counseling and psychotherapy: Training and practice.* Chicago: Aldine, 1967.

Von Bertalanffy, L. General systems theory: An overview. In F. J. Duhl, & N. D. Rizzo (Eds.), *General systems theory and psychiatry.* Boston: Little, Brown, 1969.

Watson, A. The conjoint psychotherapy of marriage partners. *American Journal of Orthopsychiatry* 1962 *33,* 912–16.

Watzlawick, P. A structured family interview. *Family Process* 1966 *5,* 256–71.

Watzlawick, P., Beavin, J., & Jacson, D. D. *Pragmatics of human communication.* New York: Norton, 1967.

Wynne, L. C., & Sanger, M. F. Thought disorders and family relations of schizophrenics. *Archives of General Psychiatry* 1963 *9,* 191–98.

Helping Family Members Cope with Divorce   10

SOPHIE FREUD LOEWENSTEIN

Overview

Divorce and separation have become a standard feature of the American family landscape. It is currently estimated that about one-quarter to one-half of all marriages in the United States will eventually end in divorce; in addition, separations and desertions are multiplying so rapidly they are difficult to count (Anthony, 1974). Statistics indicate a 35 percent increase in the number of divorces since 1962, as well as a steady rise in the divorce rate from 2.2 per 1,000 population in 1962 to 4.6 per 1,000 population in 1974, with no evidence of a diminishing trend (Kelly and Wallerstein, 1976, p. 19). However we also learn that of the nearly one million people who get divorced in the United States every year, four out of five are remarrying (Westoff, 1975). Thus, far from signaling the death of the nuclear family, these phenomena simply indicate that our expectations of marriage have risen in the last twenty years. Women and men are no longer willing to remain in psychologically destructive or spiritually empty marriages for the sake of security and social conventions.

The women's liberation movement cannot be held responsible for breaking up families, as some writers have suggested. Reasons for divorce continue to be traditional reasons of alcoholism, incompatibility, and infidelity (Brandwein, 1977). Nevertheless, women *are* learning that emotional survival without a man might be possible for them. In addition, the increasing participation of married women in the labor market has meant somewhat greater financial independence for women, along with the psychological independence, resulting in greater choices of life styles for women; this has also relieved men of the excessive financial burden that divorces used to present.

In spite of the fact that divorce and separation have become so widespread, they remain a poignant individual drama for all participants, a drama in which the involved family members are often in desperate need of counseling help. We have learned that divorce presents a high psychological mental health risk for both parents and children and that judicious counseling in such a life crisis may make the difference between psychological deterioration or good adaptation to the changing life circumstances.

This chapter will discuss some theoretical explanations for the wrenching emotional upheaval experienced by people at the time of separation. We shall then outline some of the issues divorced people are facing in regard to overcoming the trauma of the divorce experience and in organizing their new lives. Special atten-tion will be paid to the impact of divorce on the parent/child relationship, both from the parents' and the child's viewpoint, since this is one area in which professional counselors are apt to be most in demand. A majority of divorced people remarry, and some consideration will be given to the strengths and danger points in these new relationships. The theoretical material will point to some optimal counseling techniques which will be discussed in the final section of the chapter. As a conclu-sion we shall raise some provocative, unanswered questions which bear implica-tions regarding the future of the family in our society.

Toward An Understanding of the Emotional Impact of Marital Separation on the Family Unit and Its Members

Everyone understands the pain of separation through death; widows and widowers are allowed and even expected to go through a period of grief and mourning. In divorce, however, the separation is defined as voluntary, at least by one party, and feelings of grief and emotional suffering are not always taken for granted. Such emotions come as a bewildering surprise to those who experience them (Weiss, 1975). We need to understand the paradoxical fact that people may have initiated a separation and even welcomed it on the one hand, and still suffer acutely from the loss experience on the other hand. A number of convincing explanations have been suggested by social scientists to account for this psychological paradox.

Separation as a Psycho-Social Transition
Murray Colin Parkes is an English social scientist who came to recognize the importance of life transitions through his work with the crisis of bereavement (1970). He sees life as a series of psycho-social transitions which may, but often do not, coincide with biological or developmental crises (1971). He suggests that out of such periods of upset and disequilibrium, change and psychic growth are

most likely to occur. Parkes defines psycho-social transitions as "major changes in the life space which are lasting in their effects, which take place over a relatively short period of time and which affect large areas of the assumptive world" (1971). The life space is everything and everybody that impinges on an individual's life in an immediate way. It includes: changes in one's body or mind which could be occasioned by major illnesses or operations; changes in the circle of significant others in one's life, both losses and gains; changes in one's physical surroundings, such as possessions, place of work, or home. It generally includes all-important role changes. Parkes suggests that major changes in any of the above areas for whatever reason will precipitate a sense of stress often accompanied by grief, anxiety, disorientation, insomnia, and other symptoms of depression. The more radical the change, the more severe the reaction; and in addition some people might be predisposed to suffer more from change than others.

This approach illuminates the common denominator in our reactions to such apparently disparate phenomena as giving birth, retirement, financial loss, getting the Nobel prize, or immigrating to a new country. All psycho-social transitions thus involve changes that have to be mourned as a loss of the old and familiar before new circumstances, favorable and/or unfavorable, can be integrated.

Marital separation is a particularly upsetting psycho-social transition because it usually involves multiple, drastic changes in the life space: loss of a significant other, or others if children are involved; probable economic loss; often a change in the routines of living; often a change in one's home; loss of the role of wife or husband; possibly a loss of status in the community; sometimes a change of friends. An individual's entire life style is thus undercut, and the grief and disorganization may be extreme until a reorganization slowly takes place. This theoretical formulation is compatible with the growing research regarding the stressful effect of any kind of change on human beings (Holmes and Rahe, 1967). Among all the difficult changes, it is a *loss in the human environment* that is generally experienced as most painful. Many theorists have pointed to this area as the best explanation for the intense distress of the marital separation experience.

Separation as a Breaking of Attachment Ties
Every human being in infancy becomes gradually humanized through the establishment of human bonds with the mother or a primary caretaker (Bowlby, 1973). It is through this *attachment experience* that children learn to care about others, to love and hate, grieve and laugh. The security and very survival of the child depend on the maintenance of these human bonds. When the infant experiences any disruption of this vital relationship he or she is seized with separation anxiety, typically expressed through violent crying, protest, and eventual despair and withdrawal (Bowlby, 1961). These early bonds persist in changed forms all through life since human bonds are persistent. As children grow, they establish new strong bonds to a few other individuals. So long as these bonds remain intact, people tend to feel a measure of safety and security in their interpersonal lives. However, when an established attachment experience breaks up, emotions reminiscent of the

original separation anxiety rise to the fore, flooding the person with anguish, distress, fear of loneliness, and abandonment.

Confusion arises because we equate attachment and love. However this is not even true in infancy. We know that abused children are sometimes even more strongly attached to their parents than most children because the guilt, insecurity, and unpredictability of the relationship are binding forces. For adults as well, tumultuous relationships in which there may have been alcoholism or physical abuse are particularly difficult to terminate because they involve a high degree of constant emotional arousal and intense involvement which, however painful, give focus to one's life. Discontinuance of such an unsatisfactory relationship may leave one feeling empty and purposeless; and during post-separation continuing hostile engagements with the spouse may be used to fill such a void.

Attachment is a sense of belonging together, or being familiar with someone, of a shared history, and of mutual obligations. It is different from love, affection, trust, loyalty, and respect. Attachment feelings usually persist after all these other emotions have perhaps long died or turned into their opposite.

> Jane moved out of the house after she and her husband had come to blows over one of her homosexual love affairs. She took a single room in a different part of the city while her adolescent children stayed at home with their father. Jane had felt estranged from her husband a long time and was in no way prepared for the violent pain that she was experiencing. She lost interest in her challenging job as a research project director and impulsively resigned within a few weeks, deciding that she had always wanted to be a seamstress. She started to cry uncontrollably for days and weeks, necessitating a tear-duct operation within half a year. Both her appetite and sleep were severely disturbed, and Jane lost a great deal of weight and rapidly aged in appearance in the next few months. Although Jane had had a number of good friends, she felt alienated from them and spent much of her time alone at home, reviewing the failures of her life. In spite of her anger at Harry, she took it for granted that she would wish to take care of him if he became sick. It was also puzzling to her that she could suddenly explain things to Harry about her feelings that she had not told him for years and that he was suddenly willing to listen to her. It took Jane close to one year and a half before she started to regain interest in her life and began to rebuild it step by step on a different basis.

When the marital separation is understood primarily as a loss experience, not unlike bereavement, our attention gets directed on the need to mourn and on the stages of mourning described in the literature (see Chapter 11). One must remember that it is not necessarily just the person who is mourned, but the marital relationship, with its advantages, as well as the youthful hopes and dreams and fantasies that now seem lost.

The four phases of mourning currently recognized are the following:

1. Phase of numbness that usually lasts from a few hours to a week and may be interrupted by outbursts of extremely intense distress and/or anger.

2. Phase of yearning and searching for the lost figure, lasting some months and often for years.
3. Phase of disorganization and despair.
4. Phase of greater or lesser degree of reorganization. (Bowlby and Parkes, 1974).

Some of the puzzling behavior of recently separated men and women acquires meaning in this context. Many separated persons find that they seek each other out, either in the open or secretly, and compulsively drive by each other's house or place of work. They may need to call each other on the telephone, often only to start a fight, perhaps as a protection against the continuing attraction and yearning for the other. Rage outbursts also are familiar experiences and usually-law-abiding citizens are driven to violent actions. People confess with guilt and shame to engaging in behavior that is ego-alien to them, i.e., experienced as foreign to their own character.

Here again we meet the symptoms of depression mentioned earlier—the sleeplessness, restlessness, vague apprehension, emptiness, futility, and desolation. Disorganization is often manifest in acts of poor social judgment from otherwise well functioning people, such as Jane's impulsively leaving her job at a time when both the economic and social rewards of the job would have been of survival essence. As in the mourning process, there is the risk of becoming arrested at a particular stage of mourning and not being able to move forward toward resolution.

There is some controversy regarding the similarity of divorce and bereavement. Although both experiences involve the loss of a marital relationship, it is often presumed that bereavement ends a satisfactory relationship while separation ends a state of conflict. Other major differences are thought to be the semivoluntary aspect of the separation, the more gradual and negotiable separation process, and the lack of finality in the break. Some of these differences are more real than others. We do know, for example, that the intensity of grieving in bereavement is not directly related to the quality of the marriage (Bowlby and Parkes, 1974). However the semi-voluntary and less final aspects of the marital separation do indeed differentiate it from loss through bereavement and create a particular set of emotional difficulties involving the probable presence of acute ambivalence in both parties.

The Ambivalence in the Separation Experience
Although we have referred to the original mother/child attachment experience as the most basic humanizing force in life, it is by no means a totally blissful experience. The total dependency of a helpless infant on an all-powerful mother-caretaker who has the task of socializing the child into a specific culture makes this a relationship of intense dependency, anxiety, frustration, love and hate. It is the prototype of all later ambivalent human relationships. During a conflicted marriage the negative side of the ambivalence may have been expressed for years. After the separation there may be relief from the corrosive daily mutual

provocations. They now have a new common experience, the separation. The positive side of the ambivalence is apt to emerge. Some of the qualities which had attracted the couple originally to each other may suddenly be apparent once more. There may be a new sense of friendship and willingness to communicate. In addition the couple has to cope with conflicting pulls of anger and attachment. Robert Weiss describes how couples manage their intense ambivalence: "Some suppress their positive feelings, some suppress their negative feelings, some manage by alternating the feelings they express or by compartmentalizing their discrepant feelings" (1976a, p. 143). We frequently hear that couples continue to have sexual relations in the evening while they engage in fierce court battles in the morning. *Scenes from a Marriage,* Bergman's widely acclaimed movie ode to the insoluble attachment relationship vividly shows these acute conflicts produced by ambivalence. The couple cannot live together, but they long for each other when they are apart. Due to this ambivalence, along with more practical considerations, spouses frequently attempt at least one, and often several, reconciliations before a final break is made. In view of the seriousness of the decision, the certainty that one has tried repeatedly to succeed in the relationship may be reassuring to both partners. Reconciliations are, of course, not always doomed, and experiencing the inability to live apart may well provide the motivation for finding solutions to common conflicts.

Another powerful force which holds partners together in the face of emotional and perhaps physical violence is the mechanism of *projective identification.* Neglected, split-off, disowned or even prized parts of the self are projected onto the spouse and then held onto, through identification with the partner (Pincus, 1975). Although some degree of projective identification is normal and expected in all marriages—a quasi-emotional division of labor—excessive use of this psychological process leaves the individual feeling incomplete and fragmented without his or her spouse and without a separate identity. Pincus has pointed out how this process is frequently a factor in unresolved grieving after bereavement, and it may also account for the most severe forms of grief reactions in marital separations. Such a couple would not separate unless one partner had achieved more psychological growth than the other and found her or himself eager to leave an oppressive complementary relationship.

Ambivalence, or at least a rapid alternation of conflicting emotions, is not only present in the relationship but also within each partner. Euphoria about a new sense of freedom and release may alternate with apprehension and anxiety about the future, and most of recently separated persons report rapid mood swings (Weiss, 1975).

Blame and Guilt as Two Key Emotions in the Separation Experience

Divorce often appears to be a decision by one partner forced upon a reluctant mate. This may be the perception of outsiders as well as of the separating spouses themselves. However, in the complexity of human interaction with its circular nature, appearances may be quite deceptive.

Jennifer had been married for thirty years to a perfectionistic, a nagging man who steadily undermined her self-confidence and joy in living. She did not have the strength and initiative to start a separation but eagerly promoted any relationships between her husband and other women. When her husband finally fell in love with another woman and asked for his freedom, she breathed a sigh of relief and quickly departed.

Thus it is quite ambiguous who expelled whom in the final account. It is most common that both spouses end the marriage with a sense of failure, rejection, and betrayal. A painful sense of low self-esteem is one of the most frequent aftermaths of marital separations. In order to deal with their narcissistic injury people experience an urgent need to find causes to restitute meaning in a world where old beliefs and certainties have started to crumble. Thus starts the search for ultimate causes, the nightly "obsessive reviews" (Weiss, 1975), the wondering about what actually happened and how it could have been avoided, leading eventually to guilt and blame.

Guilt is a painful emotion but it also has some useful functions. Acceptance of responsibility may avoid future repetitions of errors. It may also be easier than facing total lack of understanding which leads to a sense of helplessness and lack of control over one's life. Guilt however may also become so pervasive as to interfere with people's ability to rebuild their lives. In other situations the anger is externalized and any personal responsibility is abdicated. Such total projection of blame on the other may be useful in bolstering self-esteem, but it may also lead to rage reactions which become dysfunctional when extreme. Medea who killed both her rival and her children as an act of vengeance against her humiliation is an example from mythology of such extreme rage. More frequently, however, it is a violent husband who reacts to his extreme sense of rejection by terrorizing his family. Physical acts of violence may be commited, and attempts may be made to ruin the other person's reputation or to destroy them financially, even at one's own expense. Love and hatred are two emotions close in the emotional continuum and either of them can become an absorbing emotion that bind partners to each other. Endless legal wrangles and custody fights have the by-product of prolonging the relationship and continuing the pre-separation interaction, possibly on a very similar level. The opposite of love is not hatred but indifference.

The Threat of Loneliness
The most acutely painful emotion that men and women experience after they leave a familiar relationship and live, perhaps for the first time in their lives, without adult companionship is that of loneliness. Weiss defines this loneliness as "separation distress, but without an object ... instead of pining for a particular figure the individual pines for anyone who could love or be loved, and he or she laments the barrenness of the world" (Weiss, 1975, p. 43). He further distinguishes between the loneliness of emotional and social isolation (1973), the former being the response to living without an intimate relationship, while the latter is a response to not being part of a social network, not having any friends. Weiss feels that people have a need for different kinds of human relationships and one type of relationship

cannot substitute for another (Weiss, 1976b). Recently separated people are apt to suffer mainly from emotional isolation, but if their entire friendship network consisted of couples who withdraw after the separation, of if they move to a new neighborhood or a new town, they may be exposed to both kinds of loneliness.

Symptoms of loneliness are anxiety, tension, restlessness and sleep difficulties, similar to those of separation distress (Weiss 1975). Loneliness often drives people back into resuming hopeless destructive marriages, or into entering new unsatisfactory relationships. It drives others into alcohol or drug abuse, into overeating, compulsive working, constant TV watching, or into a frenzied pursuit of entertainments or diversions of every kind (Edwards and Hoover, 1974). Lonely people moreover, may take on a desperately needy, clinging stance which makes the establishment of new relationships increasingly difficult.

> Karen, a 51-year-old housewife had felt abandoned by her husband of twenty-four years. Her children were away at college. She described feeling totally alone as if living on an arid, deserted island. She had lost connection with the world at large and commented bitterly that no one would even notice it, if she were to die in her home. Her efforts to reach out to other women went repeatedly unreciprocated, further depleting her shaky self-esteem.

Recently separated people often describe their loneliness as an overwhelming and intolerable emotion.

Separation within Marriage

Although we have emphasized so far the great distress experienced by most people at the time of marital separation, we have omitted one group that does not fit this picture because their emotional separation had taken place within the marriage perhaps years before the actual physical separation, and the couple had merely continued to live in an empty devitalized relationship. Such situations are seldom discussed in divorce literature because these people do not present themselves for divorce counseling or create problems in divorce courts. They tend to separate amicably, and quietly go their different ways. Jennifer, described above, is a good example of a woman who lived in such an "empty shell" type of marriage. A relative lack of pain and turmoil is also true of those spouses who had established an emotionally important relationship while still married, where the physical separation only follows an already accomplished emotional separation.

Marital Separation and Children

Particular concern is often expressed about the growing divorce rate of younger couples since such divorces typically involve one or several young children. One estimate suggests that "at the present rate 18 percent of all children at some time during their growing years will live in divorced family situations" (Brandwein, 1977).

Increasing attention has recently been paid to the impact on children of different ages (Kelly and Wallerstein 1976, 1977; Wallerstein and Kelly 1974; Anthony 1974; Kalter 1977).

It is often felt that children are in special need of support at the time of separation because for the child it is a situation of acute crisis and it is also apt to be at a time when the children's most natural adult supporters, the parents, may be temporarily disabled in their parental capacities due to their own often overwhelming stresses. In addition, the marital separation is one situation in which the best interest of the child and the parents may not always coincide, thus creating the need of an objective advocate on the child's behalf.

Custody Issues and Loyalty Conflicts

Perhaps more than any other feature, the tragedy of custody fights highlights the destructive aspects of divorce. While it has been customary in legal practice since the beginning of the 20th century to accord custody to mothers, this practice is now changing. Among enlightened courts a serious effort is made to consider the best interest of the child, which includes psychological, social, and educational considerations, with mothers and fathers having equal claim to custody. Crucial decisions regarding the child often need to be made at a time of maximal distress and maximal anger and irrationality among the parents. Children may become a symbol of their former relationship and of the unresolved feelings between them (Hauser, 1977). The child is often used as a pawn between parents, to such an extent that the children involved may actually become neglected or mistreated, as happens for example if kidnapping takes place, a frequent crime that is not punishable by law if the kidnapper is one of the child's own parents.

New arrangements such as joint or split custody may facilitate the child's retaining contact with both parents, but they may also introduce more loyalty conflicts and even less stability for the children than former, more traditional one-parent custody arrangements. A recent article in the *New York Times Magazine* (Baum, 1976) describes a joint custody arrangement in which the three children spend half the week with one parent and the other half with the other parent, in two different households within walking distance of one another. The mother who wrote the article feels that the arrangement has worked out well, (it has already lasted five years) and she makes a strong case for it. One wonders, however, how many divorced parents are on sufficiently friendly terms to succeed at a task that seems to demand almost constant mutual cooperation and good will. In many situations the potentially disruptive aspects of visiting arrangements must be weighed against the danger of losing a crucial parental relationship for the child (Hauser, 1977). The continuing contact with both parents may, however, precipitate acute loyalty conflicts for the child since a child, until adolescence, is usually not accustomed to maintaining close contact with someone his custodial parent may actively dislike (Hauser, 1977). These inevitable internal conflicts become aggravated when parents give in to the all too human temptation of alienating the child against the other spouse.

The Emotional Impact of Marital Separation on Children

The impact of the separation experience on the child depends on the child's age, sex, the quality of his or her early environment, prior stresses and, above all, his or her parents' ability to handle the crisis (Anthony, 1974). Since marital separation is not a single event but a long-term process, much will depend on the child's emotional environment prior to the actual separation and the particular role the child held in the total family constellation. The custodial parent's practical and emotional adaptation to the crisis and to the new responsibilities of the single-parent role will be a crucial variable; in many situations a child's partial loss of one parent is aggravated by the custodial parent's emotional and/or physical unavailability.

The child's major emotions are apt to be intense grief, guilt, anger, and fear of abandonment. The expression of these universal emotions will vary with the age and personality of the child. All children are expected to suffer from transient situational disorders, manifest in sleeping and eating problems, overactivity, some developmental regressions and various somatic disorders (Anthony, 1974; Gardner, 1970). Sometimes, in a desperate attempt to ward off anxiety and please an adult, a child may assume inappropriate maturity or overcompliance. A preoccupation with parental reconciliation is almost always present (Gardner, 1976).

Differential Reactions and Needs of Children of Different Ages

Wallerstein and Kelly have delineated different-aged children's responses to parental separation in a series of research studies (1974, 1975, 1976a, 1976b). At all ages the child's ego capacities and cognitive maturity may shape his or her experience in particular ways. The preschool child whose cognitive thinking involves egocentric thought and confusion between wish and reality is apt to feel particular guilt, imagining that his misbehavior and his hostile oedipal wishes caused the parent's departure. This age child will also assume that his powerful mother sent father away and fears that the same fate may happen to him. These children often resort to denial and fantasy to cope with their grief. They may become tearful, irritable, aggressive, and restricted in their play.

Beginning school children, five and six years old, tend to exhibit restlessness, irritability, moodiness, separation problems, and temper tantrums. Older school children who seem to show the deepest immediate grief to the physical departure of the parent. These children are no longer able to resort to the fantasy and denial of the younger children, while the more autonomous activities of the adolescent are not yet available to them. Researchers found children of that age filled with thoughts of death, damage, loss, and emptiness and gripped by a strong sense of vulnerability. Especially boys between ages 7 and 10 missed their father acutely, regardless of their actual prior relationship with him, and they saw their mothers as angry, dangerous, and in need of appeasement. For some children school functioning was severely impaired. The intensity of the immediate response was not correlated to the child's adaptation, a year later, when some of the acute pain had disappeared for the majority of the children.

If children feel themselves to be emotionally exploited by warring parents, they will in turn fight for their own emotional survival by playing parents against each other. Such children are thus forced to develop manipulative and exploitative tendencies as adaptive mechanisms. There is also a tendency among children to split parents into good and bad figures, with the caretaking disciplining parent receiving all the anger, while the distant parent becomes loved and idealized. The visiting parent may purposefully or unawaredly play into this through a tendency to avoid discipline during his or her contact with the children.

By adolescence most children had developed enough independent resources to proceed on their own developmental course without major deviation (Anthony, 1974). This was not true for adolescents with a history of long-standing difficulties, whose problematic behavior became exacerbated by the parental turmoil. These latter adolescents were particularly vulnerable to their parents' tendencies to cross generational boundaries. Those adolescents who were able and permitted to maintain some emotional distance from the parental crisis managed best, both in terms of their own developmental needs and in terms of their eventual relationship to their parents (Anthony, 1974).

Mrs. Smith tried to involve fourteen-year-old Barbara in her separation crisis. She shared her husband's intercepted love letters to other women with her daughter and repeatedly sought out her husband at his meeting places with Barbara in order to stage a bitter quarrel. Barbara started to avoid intimate talks with her mother and decided to meet her father only secretly. Mrs. Smith accused Barbara of being heartless and insensitive, but the girl stood firm. In later years Barbara developed into an assertive, autonomous young woman who respected her mother's struggle to lead an independent life.

There is considerable controversy throughout the literature on the long-range damage of divorce on children. On the one hand, it is suggested that a grossly conflicted home environment can be more destructive than a divorce (Anthony, 1974; Nye, 1957); on the other hand, those researchers who have been most intimately involved with children take a strong position that divorce is always an emotional disaster for children (Gardner, 1976; Kelly and Wallerstein, 1977). A recent epidemiological study of children referred for out-patient psychiatric evaluation found that "children of divorce appeared at nearly twice the rate of their occurrence in the general population" (Kalter, 1977). However, no attempt was made in that study to determine the percentage of disturbed children who were living in unhappy, intact homes.

The Impact of the Marital Separation on the Parental Role

Impact on the Custodial Parent   Divorce has become the most frequent cause of single parent families in the last decade. It thus seems crucial that the single-parent family become accepted as "a viable alternative family form" (Brandwein, 1977), rather than stigmatized as a "broken" or "father-absent" family. It has been suggested that research on fatherless families has been biased and often methodologically unsound (Herzog and Sudia, 1968). Current social science literature tends to emphasize that one competent loving parent is sufficient for adequate child-rearing. Nevertheless, single parenthood imposes a serious role overload on the one parent, especially if she has to undertake full-time work (Glasser and Navarre, 1967).

After a marital separation the custodial parent, who in spite of the recent changes is still most likely to be the mother, has the burden of raising her children almost alone; but the children also give meaning, continuity, and structure to her life. They are a bulwark against loneliness, and her human loss is not as serious as that of the visiting parent. The psychoanalytic literature emphasizes the crucial importance of the father for a boy's proper gender development (Neubauer, 1960), but newer developments suggest that core gender identity is firmly established by eighteen months (Stoller, 1968) and that subsequent identification with a same gender parent merely strengthens an already established pattern.

Perhaps the greater difficulty for the single mother is to maintain proper emotional distance from her children. Generational boundaries are more difficult to maintain when there is only one representative of the adult generation. The mother might be tempted to look to her children for major companionship. She might treat her son as the man of the house and her daughter as confidante, thus inducing in her children a sense of burden, helplessness, anger, and guilt. Another danger is that a son may remind the mother of her ex-husband, either because of the latter's identification with the departed parent or because of the mother's projective needs, and scapegoating of the child might result. During adolescence sexual competition might arise with a daughter and sexual seduction might become an issue with a son.

Although we have previously emphasized parental competition for child custody, the opposite may happen as well. Children can be seen as an obstacle to the freedom and self-realization of their parent. Many children of divorce end up unwanted by either parent. It has already been suggested that children after marital separation are apt to suffer from separation anxiety, expressed through excessive dependency, obedience, or disobedience. Some children run away from home as a way of testing the parent's love and devotion.

Impact on the Visiting Parent   The father does not have the daily burden of raising his children, but his emotional loss may be acute and contribute to a sense of loneliness and lack of purpose and meaning. His relationship to his children may grow shallow and cumbersome since he may find it difficult to maintain a paternal relationship outside the daily philosophy within the family. He may feel dissatisfied with his ex-wife's philosophy of child-rearing, especially if he himself has limited authority and decision-making power. Visiting times may be problematic since it is difficult to be a 100 percent father for a certain number of hours. He often feels a sense of frustration and exploitation about paying for his children without having the full benefits of fatherhood.

Often contacts with the visiting parent become less frequent if the relationship becomes strained or if the father becomes emotionally involved with a new family.

The custodial parent may find herself in the difficult situation of comforting the child over the neglect or broken promises of the absent parent. There is some controversy about how forthright the custodial parent should be in condemning the neglectful parent (Gardner, 1970). On the other hand, in adolescence, as the child seeks to separate from his parents, he may be reluctant to spend his weekly allotted number of hours with his father.

> Bob reported with great dejection that his sixteen-year-old son had lost interest in regular visits with him. He seemed impatient during visits, tried to postpone or cancel them, and was obviously always eager to rejoin his friends. He was also reluctant to share his intimate feelings with his father.

In spite of these obstacles many fathers do find ways to maintain close and meaningful rapport with their children.

Divorce and Money

Perhaps the dissatisfaction with the part-time-father role, however, accounts for the reluctance that fathers have shown to assume continuing financial responsibility for their divorced families. It has been found "that the incomes of ex-husbands or women receiving AFDC paralleled the occupational distribution of all men" (Brandwein, 1977, p. 22). If families received support, the maximum tended to be 30 percent of the husband's income. However, a Wisconsin study found "that one year after the divorce decree only 38 percent of the husbands were in full compliance, and 42 percent were paying nothing at all; after four years from divorce decree, 67 percent were paying nothing" (Brandwein, 1977, p. 22).

Apart from men's financial hardships and understandable self-interest, men have also traditionally used the withholding of money as punitive devices against their wives. Money, property, and children, apart from their intrinsic value, have been used as symbols through which the bitterness, vengeance, and rage of the two partners against each other can be expressed. Current laws are geared toward protecting men's financial positions, and the majority of divorced women tend to face serious economic survival struggles. Statistics show unequivocally that the risk of poverty for single-parent families is very high, due to a combination of causes, such as paternal economic neglect, women's low earning power, the family's being reduced to a single income, and the difficulty of making inexpensive child care arrangements (Ross, 1975).

It is hoped that the new no-fault divorce laws will discourage the adversary aspect of divorce proceedings and therefore lead to fairer and less embittered custodial and financial settlements.

Rebuilding a New Life after the Separation

Relationship with Parents and Kin

Parents and relatives are apt to express shock, surprise, and blame, depending on the circumstances of the divorce. Here again ubiquitous guilt enters the picture with parents trying to evaluate their contributions in terms of their own child-rearing sins or current lack of support. Parental guilt in our society is life-long and stretches even into the grandchildren's generation. Although parents may be excessively reproachful and angry, they will in most cases side with their adult child and frequently be an important source of help. Conflict however may arise in turning to parents, since dependence-autonomy issues toward parents have rarely been fully resolved, and both parents and the child may be justifiably fearful of regressing back into the former parent-child relationship, especially if husband or wife return to the parental home.

If the mother is the custodial parent, *paternal grandparents* are apt to be anxious to continue their relations with their grandchildren, and they might even be supportive of the mother, perhaps realizing how difficult a person their son is. Often a sense of sisterhood can be established between ex-mother-in-law and ex-daughter-in-law, since they are no longer competing for the husband/son.

If the separating partners have positive ties to their *siblings,* they may become an important physical, social, and emotional resource. The husband might look to his sister for comfort and nurturance, while the wife may turn to her brother as an extra male model for her children, to help her with financial matters or with the upkeep of her home. Siblings may facilitate introductions to new friendships or help with work opportunities. However sibling rivalry is also a life-long process and old tensions may reappear if too much help is expected or offered.

Relationship to Friends

Friends are perhaps the most important resource during family crises and the availability of friends may well make the difference between a successful or failing adaptation. Friends tend to offer generous support during the height of a crisis, although, as with siblings, continuing one-sided support should not be expected. Often people who have not been that close before may reach out to husband or wife for different motives, some having to do with their own marital problems. Other friends become terrified of the situation and withdraw anxiously lest the separation become contagious. Such withdrawal in time of need may be experienced by the separated persons as a bitter betrayal. Friends' advice must be accepted with some caution since it might be more suitable to their own life situation. A number of "couple friends" may feel a conflict of loyalty between husband and wife. They find it difficult to maintain ties with both partners and either make a choice for one or the other, or withdraw altogether. "Individual" rather than "couple" friends tend to be more enduring; couples often find it difficult to continue a friendship with a single person since issues of jealousy often arise, as well as a gradual divergence of social interests. Colleagues from work, even if not intimate, can be a great source of support and continuity. Most separated people gradually seek and find new friends and perhaps become absorbed in new informal social networks of predominantly single persons who face similar circumstances and interests. The establishment and maintenance of new friendships is an important recuperative task.

The Establishment of Cross-Gender Relationships

Dating may be an important step toward recovery of damaged self-esteem in that it provides reassurance that one is still found desirable and attractive as a man or woman. Some people find in dating a relief for loneliness. In addition it may provide a source of excitement and adventure and new relationships may expand one's own horizon. Dating may or may not be accompanied by sexual involvement. Hunt (1966) has suggested that the world of the "formerly married" has its own subculture where sexual intimacy is achieved at a faster pace and with more frankness. However many divorced people feel uncomfortable adjusting to such new values. They may feel exploited by premature sexual expectations or they may feel anxiety and uncertainty about their sexual capacities. The dating period is thus not always unproblematic. People may re-experience the emergence of adolescent concerns about finding a partner and then measuring up to the other's expectations. A boring disappointing evening or series of evenings may leave a bitter after-taste. There may be the fear of a one-sided entanglement or the danger of a developing relationship that is based primarily on mutual loneliness and need for companionship rather than true compatibility. Weiss (1975) has outlined the steps of a gradual increasing commitment between a couple. He sees *going together* as the next step after dating, an understanding of an exclusive relationship that includes sex. Although each party preserves their own household along with considerable autonomy, there is a feeling of being connected to another person and of being able to count on one another. Men and women who do not wish to remarry often find this combination of autonomy and connectedness extremely satisfying—the best of both worlds!

> Kathy and Harry are both independent professionals in their mid-forties. Kathy lives in a suburban house with her adolescent daughter while Harry maintains an apartment in town. He joins Kathy over the weekend and one or two evenings a week while other evenings he works or spends with children from his former marriage. They often entertain together, although they have also continued their separate friendships. They have traveled together, but over Easter Kathy took her daughter on a trip to Paris while Harry visited his old parents in Florida. Kathy and Harry are deeply committed to each other, but she also values her independence. She is afraid that her relationship with Harry may break up eventually over his great desire to be married again.

The next step in commitment is *living together* which is usually a step toward marriage even when this is not formally spelled out. The purely voluntary nature of this relationship tends to contribute to its egalitarian quality. If children are present in the household, the living-in partner would take on some parental responsibilities.

Remarriage

The high remarriage rate among divorced people indicates that one or even two unhappy experiences do not necessarily lead to disillusionment and to the rejection of marriage as a valid social institution. Most of those who remarry are in their middle thirties, and marry about three years after the divorce (Westoff, 1975). Men remarry at a greater and faster rate than women because their pool of potential wives covers a broader age range; men, but not women, may marry younger mates. When a woman passes age 40 remarriage may become inaccessible to her. Data from the U.S. Census Bureau, indicates that although on the average 59 percent of second marriages dissolve, "at higher socioeconomic levels the second divorce rate is closer to the 37 percent for first divorce" (Westoff, 1975, p. 11). No doubt the fact that people have found divorce a viable solution once and might resort to it again is balanced by many people's great determination to "succeed" at marriage the second time. In addition they may be more sensitive to danger signals and confront them before it is too late.

In spite of such high redivorce rates, the literature suggests that the level of satisfaction of second marriages is often extremely high. Many men and women feel they have made their mistakes during the years of ignorance, immaturity, and inexperience of their first marriages, that they learned from these mistakes and are now ready for a truly loving, mutually enhancing relationship. "All agreed that the second marriage was the real thing at last. They had entered it with much clearer ideas about the things that really mattered to them, whether those things were love, friendship, understanding, sex or money" (Westoff, 1975, p. 12). There is little evidence in the literature that the majority of people suffer from "repetition compulsion" and make the same mistake over and over. Even if some people are inclined to repeat the same destructive marital "games," a new partner may not lend himself or herself to such repetition.

Step-Parenthood

The greater danger to second marriages seems to be the strain and drain on the couple's children. The relationship between step-parents and stepchildren is fraught with difficulties that are present even with good will on all sides. Step-parents feel uncertain about the degree of appropriate emotional closeness; about their rights and responsibilities in decision-making concerning the child; about the right amount of discipline; about their financial responsibilities. The lowering of the incest taboo frequently creates sexual tensions between step-parent and child (Fast and Cain, 1966). The children may have welcomed their custodial parent's remarriage, but once it has taken place, the step parent is considered a hostile intruder and rival for the time and affection of their parent.

If several sets of children live under one roof, the household may become divided into hostile camps. Even weekend visiting stepchildren are known to place a great burden on a new marriage since they are often delegates from an angry first spouse; they visit with the mission of driving a wedge between the new partners. The step-parent, in spite of initial good will, will grow highly resentful about the constant difficulties and chaos created by the children, while the natural parent will be hypersensitive to possible signs of the step-parent's rejection and guilty about having imposed a "package deal" on the new spouse.

Sometimes the custodial parent may be reluctant to have to share the child with a new spouse. It is therefore not surprising that children of "reconstituted" families are considered to be of particularly high psychiatric risk, more so than children of single parents. Especially vulnerable are pre-adolescent boys and girls whose stepfathers had suffered from a very high incidence of aggression, sexual acting out, drug involvement and school-related difficulties (Katler, 1977). Adolescents however seem to fare well and they, if not their parents, tend to overcome such difficulties at least in the long run.

Approaches to Helping People Who Are in the Process of Separating

Divorce Counseling as a Form of Crisis Intervention

The theory and principles of crisis intervention have been carefully formulated by Rapoport (1962, 1967) and Caplan (1960). Crisis is defined as a personal state of disequilibrium between relatively stable states at the end of which the individual may be at a higher or lower level of mental health than initially. It is a situation in which the individual's habitual patterns of problem-solving are no longer adequate. Crisis may be experienced as a threat, a loss, or optimally as a challenge. It may arouse feelings of prior similar situations, open old wounds, and reawaken only partially resolved dormant conflicts. During such a crisis individuals may find satisfactory solutions to their problems; they may redefine the problem to achieve need satisfaction, or they may avoid the problem by relinquishing former goals. If none of these coping patterns are used, people may resort to magical thinking, self-defeating regressive behavior, expressing stress through bodily symptoms or at worst, to total withdrawal from reality.

There are three major stages that many individuals are apt to experience: (1) preparation for the change or loss, accompanied by anticipatory grief; (2) acknowledgment of feelings of failure and guilt; and (3) adjustment to the new reality and its special requirements. Caplan (1960) suggests that intervention should air toward the three following steps: (1) accurate cognitive perception and acknowledgement of all aspects of the situation; (2) recognition and expression of affects which create the tension; (3) the use of available personal and institutional resources for mastering the tasks at hand.

It is generally felt that extending help during a crisis is an effective method of preserving mental health. Individuals are reached at a time when they are in special need and often in search of help and when their defenses, which may be typically quite solid or even rigid, are loosened and they are open to change. Short term intervention at such a time is apt to be more effective than prolonged intervention at other times. It can have considerable impact and move the individual along the course of crisis solution in the direction of growth and maturity, making lasting improvements in his or her life.

Parkes has also specified the function of intervention during psycho-social transitions. He feels it should be "... to facilitate change in the assumptive world and ... to make use of the relationship between patient and therapist as a 'test bed' in which old assumptions can be questioned and new ones rehearsed. Insight occurs when a person recognizes a discrepancy between his assumptive world and his life space" (Parkes, 1971, p. 110). People might need to change basic assumptions such as: marriages last throughout life; partners could be trusted; and they would always be able to depend on a spouse for basic security and even identity.

Rapoport (1967) suggests certain treatment goals for individual crisis intervention: Treatment is highly focused and segmental; the focus is on the precipitating stress, its consequences, and its meaning; stress is on cognitive mastery; help is geared toward reality adaptation; lowering of tension, guilt, and anxiety is a goal; defenses are being strengthened; links are made with past associated conflicts. Among techniques, she mentions a need to be directive, active, and advice- and information-giving; to make use of one's authority and status as an "expert"; to use the contract of time-limited contacts to structure the sessions; to enlarge a person's sense of autonomy and mastery; to provide anticipatory guidance; and to teach new social and interpersonal skills through educational techniques. She suggests that horizontal and vertical history exploration and regressive, overly dependent transference on the therapist be avoided. Termination is reached when the client begins to find solutions to his or her crisis, and follow-up appointments should be tailored to a client's particular needs.

These goals and techniques are applicable to all short-term crisis counseling and they fit the separation experience very well. Separated people suffer a great deal from their not having anticipated their turbulent emotions; explanations as to the possible reasons for their distress, giving them some cognitive mastery, is usually received with great relief. They are entering strange, new life circumstances and anticipatory guidance serves them as well as a map in a foreign country.

Trudi told of waking up in the middle of the night and planning her suicide. Then she suddenly remembered that her counselor had warned her that many people tend to do that. Reassured she was able to go back to sleep.

We have heard of the danger of excessive blame, hatred, and guilt. An important counseling goal would be to encourage people first to acknowledge these sometimes intense and extremely preoccupying feelings, express them fully and then *let go* of them, as one aspect of letting go of the relationship. Since spouses need to continue to interact around legal and financial matters and especially around their children, it is important to help husband and wife to communicate without excessive rancor. The counselor could see the couple together and function as an impartial mediator.

When links are made with the past associated conflicts, people are encouraged to review their past losses, and the anguish in the divorce experience can be related to the separation anxiety in the attachment period.

During periods of disorganization, the counselor firmly protects the client against self-destructive acts and hasty decisions. Marital separation is above all a loss experience, and much time will be spent in the mourning process, reviewing the relationship and its history and coming to terms with its ending. Since counselors are aware of the usual stages of mourning, they will be alert to clients' arrest at one stage of mourning and attempt to help move them on to the next stage. We know for example that continual denial of a loss interferes significantly with the ability to adapt to the changed life space.

Engaging in work outside the home often protects people against deep depression. Help toward assuming a working role might be an important aspect of counseling separated wives, especially the housewives.

Coping with Loneliness

We have already learned that combating loneliness too directly can become a desperate indiscriminate search for people, a process which is ultimately self-defeating. Thus several writers on loneliness redefine it as "aloneness" and advise people to embrace it as a potentially enriching experience. Moustakas (1972) explains that "Paul Tillich believed that two words were created in the English language to express the two sides of man's aloneness—'Loneliness' to express pain in being alone and 'solitude' to express the glory of being alone." He further suggests that "solitude is a return to one's own self when the world has grown cold and meaningless, when life has become filled with people and too much of a response to others."

Edwards and Hoover in their helpful book of advice to single people, *The Challenge of Being Single* similarly suggest that "we can turn loneliness into being alone and to appreciate the value of being alone and turn it to our advantage" (Edwards and Hoover, 1974, p. 79). They feel that once the fear of loneliness is overcome and it is accepted, half the battle is won. "They are the times when you can most increase your feelings of self-reliance, which is your most important asset as a single person. . . . If you can begin to look upon such moments as self-learning and growing times rather than simply dreary times to be suffered through, you will find yourself gradually breaking through any panic and self-pity into a kind of calm that may astound you" (Edwards and Hoover, 1974, p. 79).

Besides such a philosophical approach Edwards and Hoover also have a number of practical suggestions. It is helpful, they say, to discover what precipitates one's most painful episodes of loneliness and then take precautions to avoid or restructure those situations. Other helpful devices are: Talking to someone who cares and making oneself available to them in their moments or loneliness; engaging in physical exercise; doing something one has been wanting to do, either outside the home or an enjoyable home project; doing something to help someone else; becoming creative in one's own unique way. The idea is not simply to distract oneself, but to learn to enjoy the luxury of independently using one's own free time. Eventually, in the wholehearted pursuit of enjoyable activities, travels, sports, hobbies, and hopefully work, we are bound to meet kindred spirits, and perhaps these newfound friends will cut down on times of loneliness. However, once again, it is important to remember that loneliness inside a marriage or outside it, by oneself or in a crowd, is an inevitable and universal part of the human condition that we must learn to accept in order to live in peace.

Counseling Approaches Concerning Children

Providing Direct Help to Children   Kelly and Wallerstein have developed useful intervention models for children in different age groups. Their goal is "... to enable the child of divorce to affectively and cognitively integrate the impact of the family dissolution, and to minimize or prevent the consolidation of psychopathological response, and to facilitate the child's transition to new family relationships following divorce" (Kelly and Wallerstein, 1977, p. 23). Through parental interviews and observations of children, they draw up a divorce-specific diagnostic profile of each child comprising:

1.   An abbreviated developmental profile.
2.   A focus on the child's response to the parental separation.
3.   An evaluation of the child's response to the parental network.

Their intervention strategies are then based on this profile.

While Kelly and Wallerstein felt that younger children could best be reached through parent education, some of the school children and adolescents could profit from a series of counseling sessions which would be more or less extensive depending on the degree of the child's disturbance, the intensity of his or her suffering, and the emotional accessibility of the child. These counseling sessions were geared above all to reduce the child's suffering as expressed in anxiety, fearfulness, guilt, depression, anger, and longing. Other goals were reduction in cognitive confusion; increase in psychological distance between the child and the divorce situation; and the resolution of various idiosyncratic issues. With children who had difficulty expressing their feelings, they tended to use "divorce monologues," a method of universalizing the child's feelings for him or her. Older children profited most from an opportunity to receive consensual validation for their perception and to discuss their own plans with an objective adult.

Helping Children Through Parental Guidance   Even if children are not available for direct help, parents can often profit from specific guidance on how to help their children. By helping their children parents can often gain increasing mastery of themselves. Parents should be given overall understanding of the meaning of the marital separation to the child. The goal would be to arouse parental empathy while avoiding excessive guilt.

Parents should be warned gently how destructive it is for children to be used as pawns in the parental war. The negative consequences of turning a child against the other parent need to be pointed out, often resulting in the child's anger against *both* parents and in a possible identification with a bad parental image. The child needs to have the custodial parent's permission for a continuing, active, loving relationship with the visiting parent. Both parents must learn to curb their hostility not only toward the other parent, but also toward the other parent's new mate. Parents should also be warned against using their children to fill their loneliness, and other resources for adult contact might be suggested. Attention might be drawn to community organizations that have developed to meet the needs of single people. *Parents Without Partners* is one example of such a supportive transition group which organizes activities that include children.

Parents should give their children permission and even encouragement to mourn their loss. They should acknowledge their sadness and listen to their concerns. This will be a difficult task if parents have not come to terms with their guilt and their own sadness. Finally, parents should explain the reasons for the separation as clearly and truthfully as possible, keeping within the child's cognitive capacities. If parents are fair to their children in all these ways, they need not allow their children to manipulate them and exploit their guilt. Parental martyrdom in order to make up to the child for the loss of his or her parent is not useful to child or parent and should be discouraged. Many parents might find it helpful to read with their children Richard Gardner's *The Boys and Girls Book About Divorce* (1970). This imaginatively illustrated book is written for children and raises all the issues that children are concerned about. Sharing this book would be an excellent way of opening up communication about the seperation experience between parent and child.

Group Counseling for Parents

Many of the crisis intervention goals as well as the goals of parental guidance could best be reached through the medium of time-limited, problem-focused group counseling. Robert S. Weiss has developed this technique for recently separated persons and this writer has led a number of such groups with very good results. The groups may range from eight to twelve persons, all of whom are going through a recent marital separation experience. It might meet for eight sessions, which gives enough time for empathic group ties to form and yet still stops short of becoming regular group psychotherapy. Such groups might be considered a hybrid between psychotherapy and adult education. The group offers an extremely supportive setting and the leader models caring and acceptance of individual coping efforts and discourages confrontations.

Members learn that others have had similar feelings of despair, grief, or rage and learn about the universality of such taboo feelings, about reducing guilt and anomie. The group naturally becomes a problem solving place and members bring problems to the group as well as solutions, thus enhancing self-esteem through helping others. A great deal of interpersonal learning takes place. Some of the more threatening aspects of parent guidance can often be better accepted in a group setting than individually, especially if all the advice and suggestions do not emanate from the leader alone. Members often help each other let go of destructive behavior and profit from each other's objective judgments about their own situation. Members are encouraged to report weekly progress in mastery and new coping experiences to the group and receive praise and encouragement from the group. Anticipatory guidance takes place not only through didactic material but also through other group members who may be further along in a particular transition. Finally, the group provides a temporary support community. It may provide relief from intolerable loneliness and new friendships are always formed. Separation group counseling has indeed been found to be a most effective and efficient intervention method.

Conclusion

Human beings are born helpless and totally dependent for survival on the nurturance of others. During these early years strong bonds of love and hate toward other human beings, one's caretakers, are formed. It then becomes part of the human condition to attempt to reproduce such bonds all through life. The ambivalent struggle between love and hate is reproduced in later relationships, especially in marriage. When hate and/or disappointment wins out, men and women may choose to separate, but the disruption of bonds is apt to reproduce the separation anxiety of early childhood, as well as foster the emergence of formerly suppressed positive feelings, the other side of the ambivalence.

Some alarm is currently expressed about the future welfare of children who are subjected in such great numbers to the trauma of at least partial loss of one parent. Much thought is being given to protecting children to some extent against the short-term and long-term effects of family disruption. Some professionals point to the urgent need of tightening divorce laws to protect people against their own disruptive impulses. The increasing demand for divorce is seen as no more than an illusive search for ever-escaping happiness.

Others have seen divorce as a regrettable but inevitable by-product of the search for individual self-fulfillment, one that is worth its price being paid in the long run. Such professionals often emphasize the resulting poverty of wife and children as a major negative consequence and call for financial protection in this area.

Counselors who are faced with a relationship that seems to have foundered must make the difficult decision between trying to rescue the relationship at all cost, versus helping to sever those sinuous bonds and help bury the relationship. Counselors should face their own convictions on value-laden issues with honesty since they will influence the counseling process.

However, regardless of whether the decision to separate is created by false hopes and illusions or by desperation, it will evoke anxiety, disequilibrium and emotional vulnerability. Divorce often produces complete changes in people's material and emotional life space and calls for drastic revision of one's assumptive world. Men and women at this time reach out for and are open to support and understanding. It is a time when counseling intervention can be of maximum effectiveness. Counseling people in times of major life transitions is an awesome responsibility. When the process is done with sensitivity and results in the fostering and personal growth and maturation, it can be a challenging and rewarding experience.

Questions for Further Inquiry

1. What constitutes a "bad" or "empty" marriage?

2. Most people believe that "bad" or "empty" marriages are serious personal and social problems. Some see divorce as a viable solution. What is your view?

3. Some reformers battle for no-fault divorces and improved economic conditions for female-headed families, while opponents point out that such reforms might provide an unfortunate incentive to separate. Do you think no-fault divorce is a good idea? Why?

4. Adults want to have the freedom to marry, divorce, remarry, and procreate. Children, however, need stability and continuity in human relationships. What valuing conflicts does this dilemma create for the helping practitioner?

5. What factors make for minimum suffering in divorce? How may a counselor help a divorcing couple minimize suffering?

References

Anthony, J. Children at risk from divorce: A review. In J. Anthony & C. Koupernik (Eds.) *The child in his family: Children at psychiatric risk.* New York: Wiley, 1974.

Baum, C. The best of both parents. *The New York Times Magazine,* October 31, 1976.

Bowlby, J. Process of mourning. *International Journal of Psychoanalysis* 1961 *42,* 317–25.

Bowlby, J. Affectional bonds: Their nature and origin. In R. S. Weiss (Ed.), *Loneliness.* Cambridge, Ma.: M.I.T. Press, 1973.

Bowlby, J., & Parkes, C. M. Separation and loss within the family. In J. Anthony and C. Koupernik (Eds.) *The child in his family. Children at psychiatric risk.* New York: Wiley, 1974.

Brandwein, R. After divorce: A focus on single parent families. *The Urban and Social Change Review* 1977 *10,* 21–25.

Caplan, G. Patterns of parental response to the crisis of premature birth. *Psychiatry* 1960 *23,* 365–74.

Caplan, G. *Principles of preventive psychiatry.* New York: Basic Books, 1964.

Edwards, M., & Hoover, E. *The challenge of being single.* New York: Signet, 1974.

Fast, I., & Cain, A. The step-parent role: Potential for disturbances in family functioning. *American Journal of Orthopsychiatry* 1966 *36*(3), 485–91.

Gardner, R. *The boys and girls book about divorce.* New York: Richard Gardner, 1970.

Gardner, R. *Psychotherapy with children of divorce.* New York: J. Aronson, 1976.

Glasser, P., & Navarre, E. Structural problems of the one-parent family. In E. Thomas (Ed.), *Behavioral science for social workers.* New York: Free Press, 1967.

Hauser, B. Divorce and Custody. Talk delivered at the Central Middlesex Mental Health Association, Concord, Ma., February 1, 1977.

Herzog, E., & Sudia, C. E. Fatherless homes: A review of research. *Children* 1968 *15,* 177–82.

Holmes, T. H., & Rahe, R. H. The social readjustment scale. *Journal of Psychosomatic Research* 1967 *11,* 213–18.

Hunt, M. H. *The world of the formerly married.* New York: McGraw-Hill, 1966.

Kalter, N. Children of divorce in an outpatient psychiatric population. *American Journal of Orthopsychiatry* 1977 *47(1),* 40–51.

Kelly, J. B., & Wallerstein, J. S. Brief interventions with children in divorcing families. *American Journal of Orthopsychiatry* 1977 *47(1),* 23–39.

Kelly, J. B., & Wallerstein, J. S. The effects of parental divorce: Experiences of the child in early latency. *American Journal of Orhtopsychiatry* 1976 *46(1),* 20–32. (a)

Moustaskas, C. E. *Loneliness and love.* Englewood Cliffs, N.J.: Prentice-Hall, 1972.

Neubauer, P. G. The one-parent child and his oedipal development. *Psychoanalytic Study of the Child, Vol. 15.* New York: International Universities Press, 1960.

Nye, F. I. Child adjustment in broken and in unhappy unbroken homes. *Marriage and Family Living* 1957 *19,* 356–61.

Parkes, M. C. The first year of bereavement. *Psychiatry* 1970 *33(4),* 449–67.

Parkes, M. C. Psycho-social transitions: A field for study. *Journal of Social Science and Medicine* 1971 *5,* 101–15.

Pincus, L. *Death in the family.* New York: Pantheon, 1975.

Ross, H. L., & Sawhill, I. F. *Time of transition: The growth of families headed by women.* Washington, D.C.: Urban Institute, 1975.

Rapoport, L. The state of crisis: Some theoretical considerations. *Social Service Review* 1962 *36, 2.*

Rapoport, L. Crisis-oriented short-term casework. *Social Service Review* 1967 *41,* 31–43.

Stoller, R. *Sex and gender.* New York: J. Aronson, 1968.

Wallerstein, J., & Kelly, J. B. The effects of parental divorce: The adolescent experience. In J. Anthony and C. Koupernik (Eds.), *The child in his family: Children at psychiatric risk.* New York: Wiley, 1974.

Wallerstein, J., & Kelly, J. B. The effects of parental divorce: Experiences of the preschool child. *Journal of American Academy of Child Psychiatry* 1975 *14,* 600–16.

Wallerstein, J. S., & Kelly, J. B. The effects of parental divorce: Experiences of the child in later latency. *American Journal of Orthopsychiatry* 1976 *46,* 256–69. (b)

Weiss, R. S. (Ed.), *Loneliness.* Cambridge, Ma.: M.I.T. Press, 1973.

Weiss, R. S. *Marital separation.* New York: Basic Books, 1975.

Weiss, R. S. The emotional impact of marital separation. *Journal of Social Issues* 1976 *32(1)*, 135–45. (a)

Weiss, R. S. The provision of social relationships. In Z. Rubin (Ed.), *Doing unto others*. Englewood Cliffs, N.J.: Prentice-Hall, 1976. (b)

Westoff, L. Two-time winner. *The New York Times Magazine,* August 10, 1975.

Helping Families Cope with Grief   11

MILTON MATZ

Overview

Mourning is a complex process in which the bereaved separate and detach themselves from loved ones who have died and replace them with new relationships.
If the work of grieving is handled well, new ties can afford equivalent or greater
satisfaction to needs formerly satisfied by lost relationships. On the other hand,
if restitutive relationships are not established or are incapable of equivalent satisfaction, the process of mourning becomes diverted, remaining incomplete and in
danger of becoming dysfunctional.

    Mourning is a stressful process. It takes its toll psychologically as well as
physiologically. Dysfunctional grief is the root of an astonishingly high proportion
of emotional, behavioral, addictive, and psychosomatic disorders. The literature of
psychotherapy is rich with case material relating symptomatology to dysfunctional
grief. In recent years an increasing body of data has accumulated relating significant increases in the incidence of physical illness and death to populations experiencing the loss of spouse or other central family members. Parkes, in the appendix
to his book, *Bereavement: Studies of Grief in Adult Life* (1973), summarizes the
results of a number of studies. He concludes that mourning is a powerful stressor,
subjugating body and psyche to crushing pressures, which frequently cause mental and physical illness. A survey of studies on the psychological effects of childhood bereavement is found in Chapter 9 of Furman's (1974) volume on childhood

bereavement. These studies strongly suggest that childhood bereavement, even more than adult bereavement, can be a significant factor in the development of various forms of mental illness and adult maladjustment.

Counseling can shorten the period of unresolved grief, and it can increase the probability of establishing satisfactory replacement relationships. This help can be useful in preventing and minimizing the pathological outcome of bereavement. Those interested in primary prevention of mental illness see bereavement as a crucial area requiring further research and new services.

This chapter is intended to guide professionals helping the bereaved, by establishing theoretical and clinical benchmarks for assessing the individual situation. It is written from an eclectic point of view. The theoretical understanding section will help the reader understand in depth the phenomenal worlds of people experiencing grief. This section will also define the determinants that affect mourning and examine dysfunctional grief. The section on approaches to helping spotlights difficulties often encountered in counseling the bereaved and offers suggestions for management.

The purpose of this chapter is to guide helping professionals—counselors, social workers, psychiatrists, psychologists, mental health workers, clergy, physicians, and nurses—in their work with adults or near adults experiencing central bereavement—loss of a nuclear family member. It is likely that this material will also prove useful to professionals dealing with bereaved in more limited ways—lawyers, teachers, funeral directors—as well as to friends of the bereaved and to the bereaved themselves.

The bereavement counseling task is complex and emotionally draining. The novice counselor will find it difficult to translate theoretical formulations into successful clinical work without supervision. The counselor should expect to find himself or herself deeply involved, at times tearful, at times fearful, and often times feeling helpless.

Understanding Bereavement

The Phases of Mourning
Early in his clinical work with healthy and dysfunctional grief, the author concluded that a theoretical map to guide the clinician through the labyrinths of normal grief is a necessity. Without a baseline description of normal grief, it is difficult to distinguish factors which lead to pathology. The writings of Lindemann (1944), Glick, Weiss, and Parkes (1974), and Parkes (1973), in particular, extended the author's thinking about the phenomena of normal bereavement. The five stage theory of a patient's response to terminal illness, developed by Kübler-Ross (1969), made available a theoretical model for describing the bereavement process.

In contrast to the Kübler-Ross five phase model with the terminally ill, I have identified four phases to the bereavement process: (1) denial, (2) undoing efforts,

(3) depression and helplessness, and (4) re-engagement. The dynamics of each will be described in the pages that follow. There are two significant differences from the Kübler-Ross model. First, the last phase of the terminal illness model is disengagement from loved ones; the last phase of the bereavement model is re-engagement with the living so that a meaningful life can be re-established. Second, Kübler-Ross sees the terminally ill going through anger and bargaining as separate phases. In the bereavement model these processes are categorized as parts of the same phase which I have identified as undoing efforts.

Phase I: "If I Deny It, It's Not True"   A middle-aged man, recalling his initial reaction to the death of his wife after a terminal illness, describes his experience with the first phase of mourning: "I just didn't believe what the doctor told me. It was not that I didn't believe him, I believed him all right, it was more a matter of my not taking him seriously. It was almost like I didn't care, and I had to pretend to care. For a while I wondered whether I really had loved my wife. I just couldn't understand my not reacting."

The initial response to the news of a close death usually is denial. The person needs to distance the self from the pain of loss. Intuitively, the psyche fears that grief would be too much to bear and would overwhelm the individual's capacity to cope. Through denial of the emotional meaning of the loss the bereaved buys time. The denial, however, is punctuated by periods of painful emotional awareness. Denial is calculated to hold back the pain and to occasionally lift, doling out periods of painful awareness at an endurable level. The bereaved in the first phase of grief are in a state of partial emotional anesthesia, which permits them to function and attend to many of the immediate obligations which must be met.

Emotional denial is frequently seen as interferences in thinking in which it is painful to recall, talk, or think of events, names, or facts, particularly those associated with the deceased and circumstances of the death. Erich Lindemann's classic study of survivors of the Cocoanut Grove fire, in Boston, explains the somatic process which underlies denial:

> (The bereaved feels) ... sensations of somatic distress occurring in waves lasting from twenty minutes to an hour at a time, a feeling of tightness in the throat, choking with shortness of breath, need for sighing, and an empty feeling in the chest, lack of muscular power, and an intense subjective distress described as tension or mental pain. The patient soon learns these waves of discomfort can be precipitated by visits, by mentioning the deceased, and by receiving sympathy. There is a tendency to avoid the syndrome at any cost (Lindemann, 1944, p. 141).

Through the defenses of denial and avoidance the personality salvages, in a brittle way, temporary respite from pain and the capacity to continue functioning.

Phase II: "I Have the Power To Undo It"   Phase II is the most speculative of the four phases. It attempts to group together and provide a theoretical explana-

for the many seemingly unrealistic and maladaptive behaviors which at times punctuate the normal mourning process, i.e., hallucinations, undoing behavior, identification illness, search behavior, bargaining, inappropriate anger and guilt, magical substitution, and behavioral reversal. Unrealistic behaviors, to a greater or lesser degree, seem to be present in all bereavement situations. Clinical experience leads to the observation that dysfunctional grief often involves symptomatic elaboration of these unrealistic behaviors. The grief model was designed to place these behaviors into Phase II to distinguish them from the behaviors of the other phases that function more efficiently in adapting the mourner to the reality of the loss. Its positioning as the second phase is in keeping with the clinically observed tendency of unrealistic behaviors of mourning to intervene between denial (Phase I) and despair and helplessness (Phase III).

Phase II behaviors share the characteristic of opposing reality. In the face of hopelessness, they insist on hope. In the face of helplessness, they imply something can and must be done. They seem largely the product of our yearnings and wishes.

Denial and avoidance gradually give way to unrealistic feelings of potency, the major characteristic of the second phase. Overwhelming loss often elicits what clinically can best be described as childish patterns of omnipotence. The loss can be totally denied and avoided only at the price of sanity. This price is too high for most of us to pay for long. The ground is cleared for the attitude of the second phase: If you can't tolerate the loss, undo it, move the clock back, bring the deceased back to life, or at least keep alive the hope that separation is temporary and the dead can be quickened and returned.

The feelings of an adolescent girl poignantly illustrate the wish to undo, characteristic of this stage. "I kissed my father goodby on the cheek and I squeezed his hand for the last time, but the body seemed so hard that I knew then it wasn't him, not my real father. His soul had gone elsewhere and was still around and I knew that he was still alive." This young adolescent girl is expressing the central theme of the second phase—the notion that the death can be undone if the right action or attitude is taken. Second phase behavior characteristically appears to halt the process of separation and replacement of the deceased by proclaiming the battle is not yet lost—the deceased may yet be alive. Underneath the conviction seems to persist that the deceased is temporarily away and only awaits being found or enabled to return by our action.

In the above example, the grieving adolescent distorts the theological belief that the soul lives in heaven. She converts it into the notion that her father still lives on earth and, therefore, she need not grieve nor replace him with appropriate substitutes.

The simplest way to bring the dead to life is to see and hear them. Auditory and visual hallucinations are frequent during this period. These experiences often seem unbelievably real and leave the bereaved with the fear that they are losing their reason and with the strengthened notion that in some uncanny way death has been cheated.

Searching efforts frequently occur during this stage. If the dead are alive, where are they, where should I look for them? A young man, who lost his mother when he was six years old, realized, while undergoing psychotherapy, that his frequenting of bars and excessive drinking was part of his unending search for his mother, a barmaid.

A middle-aged woman, in treatment for a flying phobia, was told at the age of four that her mother "had been put into a box and flown to heaven." The woman came to associate the "box that flies" with planes. Two powerful opposing motives, uncovered in the course of therapy, developed within the woman and were the basis for her phobia: the urgent desire to be reunited with her mother represented symbolically by flying, countered by the devastating fear that flying will cause her death and tear her, like her mother, from her husband and children. Her phobia was the outcome of the conflict.

Sometimes the omnipotence is expressed in anger at people or events the bereaved regard as responsible for the death. The anger may be directed at acts of seeming disregard, irresponsiblity, or poor judgment of doctors, nurses, clergy, family members, friends, colleagues of the deceased, or the deceased themselves. The anger is expressed with an urgency which suggests that if these behaviors are immediately altered, the consequence they presumably cause, death, can be altered. Often the bereaved hold themselves responsible and change their own behaviors to undo the outcome.

Anger directed at one's own behaviors often results in dramatic alterations. A young bereaved husband exhibited this tendency. Five weeks after his wife died, he said: "I won't love any woman anymore, the women I love all die. It's better for them if I hate them." Shortly thereafter he went through a period of sharp animosity to his dead wife. Only years later, in psychotherapy, did he realize that he had hoped his altered behavior would do its magic and bring her back.

Anger at the self frequently involves an element of retribution—not only must the causative behavior be changed, the perpetrator of the behavior should also be punished to maximize forgiveness and undo the death. The alterations of behavior often involve an element of self-punishing sacrifice. The formula may be: "If I give up some satisfying behavior, the dead will return." The sacrificed behaviors may include expressions of affection, helplessness, sexual feeling, obedience, rebelliousness, ambition, independence, dependency, marriage, love, school achievement, cooperative behavior, etc.

Sometimes the drive to undo death causes the survivors to take upon themselves the final illness of the deceased and by so doing symbolically bring them back to life. By taking upon themselves the final illness, the bereaved become in the curious logic of the unconscious the deceased. The deceased again lives but now in the person of the bereaved. Many episodes of psychogenic illness, observed clinically, were based upon identification occurring during the second phase. These episodes should receive appropriate medical diagnoses though they tend to be temporary. It is easy to err in assuming psychogenicity before organic factors have been ruled out. If grief becomes dysfunctional, identification illness often contributes to the resulting symptomatology.

Although magical thinking of the second phase can assume endless forms, magical substitution is the last manifestation of magical thinking that will be described here. In magical substitution the bereaved acts as if the deceased is someone else. The father may regard his daughter as the continuation of his deceased wife. The daughter may respond to her aunt as the magical substitute for her mother. The bereaved husband may fly off into marriage with a woman he barely knows. The magical substitution is not an effective restitution, for the death has not been undone and separation and mourning are being avoided.

Behaviors and attitudes of the second phase assume the bereaved have the power to alter reality and undo death. The fact, of course, is reality has shredded the pattern of their human ties and left them helpless to stop their loss. All efforts of the second phase are destined to failure. If mourning is functional, reality crushes wishful hopes, and helplessness is eventually acknowledged. On going persistence of second phase behaviors, particularly if they appear encysted in the personality, increases the risk of dysfunctional outcome. The second phase gives way to despair and helplessness, which ushers in the third phase.

Phase III: "I Can't Do Anything About It"   The bereaved hits bottom in Phase III. The defenses of phases one and two are inoperable. The bereaved faces the loss and begins to deal with it. It is at this point the bereaved examine the ways in which the dead are missed. A husband may be missed for his fathering, financial contribution, good judgment, sense of humor, and sexual behavior. A wife is missed for her vitality, open and inquiring mind, compassion, financial contribution, and sexual behavior. Whether a spouse, child, or parent, each loss involves a unique constellation of interaction and mixture of satisfaction and dissatisfaction. As the bereaved examines these past interactions, critical questions are often raised: Can I continue on without you? How? Do I want to?

During the third phase suicidal ideation is prevalent, and the risk of suicide is greatest. Though suicidal ideation is not necessarily a sign of dysfunction, it should not be treated lightly. The appropriateness of despair does not mitigate the reality of suicidal risk.

Joseph Williams, a successful engineer in his middle fifties, was seen, as needed, for counseling by the author[1] during a period of a year and a half, beginning with the terminal illness of his wife and concluding with his marriage at the beginning of the second year of mourning. His patterns of response are characteristic of healthy resolution of grief. In the ninth week of mourning Mr. Williams describes third phase feelings:

Who is there to come home to and complain about my day? She would listen to my stories again and again. Who else could do that? The trip we had

---

[1]All case references have been carefully disguised and altered for purposes of confidentiality.

planned when the children were grown up, who will go with me? (Pause) I don't want to go on! I'm better off dead! (Pause) At least we'd be together. (Pause) But who'll take care of our daughter? (Pause, tears.) Who'll take care of *my* daughter? (Pause.) It's going to be *me!* I won't do as good a job as she did, but I won't do so bad either! (Pause.) You know there's one thing she would do that I never liked. I think I can do *that* better, or at least as well.

In the third phase the bereaved bottoms out and starts coming up. Feelings of potency, this time tentative and realistic, return. Though helpless in relation to death, the bereaved are not helpless to refashion their own lives. Piece by piece links with the past are re-examined, grieved over, given up, and partially replaced with the hope that what is lost will be replaced, with some notion of how to do it. Examining segments of the loss, helplessness and despair are experienced; yet, hope rises from the ashes. What must be relinquished is relinquished, what can be salvaged is retained—the ground is prepared for the final phase.

Phase IV: "I Am Rebuilding and Every Now and Then I Remember"   The actual work of reconstruction now begins in earnest. The bereaved turn back to pick up the threads of living. Career goals are pursued; hobbies become attractive again; social activities are resumed. Different solutions are tried to replace lost ones. Wives go to work or school to replace a missing breadwinner. A house-keeper is hired to take over responsibilities for children and household. New dating patterns are established. Many of these decisions are temporary and only partially satisfactory. Eventually they are exchanged for more satisfactory and permanent solutions.

The direction of the fourth phase is not always forward. Fresh implications of the loss and new disappointments periodically force the bereaved back to patterns of earlier phases. It is in this phase that the bereaved often becomes capable of dealing with the most painful feelings and memories of the death and funeral. These feelings usually elicit earlier phasic defenses. Though the characteristics of all the phases frequently appear side by side, the thrust of the process is forward. Tasks are tackled—probating the will, clearing out the closet, giving away clothes, selling the business, learning how to cook, going to the P.T.A. Yet, in the midst of it all there is denial—"I still can't believe it;" and magical thinking—"I woke up in the morning, and I'm sure I heard him downstairs getting ready to go to work;" and despair—"I can't go on alone." Moving backward and forward the work of reconstruction continues. With each step forward the personality strengthens its hold on the present and future, making it less vulnerable to the return of behaviors of the prior three phases.

A welcome feature of this phase is the increasing ability to remember comforting memories. Now, memories lose their sting and become gentle supporters. The middle-aged engineer, Mr. Williams, felt: "It's as if my wife were with me, encouraging me on."

In the sixteenth week of mourning Mr. Williams was well into the fourth phase.

The author's counseling notes for that session illustrate fourth phase patterns of supportive remembrance, increased ability to tolerate pain, and resurgence of earlier defenses—and life's rebuilding.

> Mr. Williams began the interview by reporting a dream which he had this morning before he woke up. In this dream he talked to his wife. She was dressed in his favorite dress and looked well. The dream made him feel marvelous all day and he wished it had lasted longer. It was the most enjoyable experience he had had in a long, long time.
>
> The dream took place in a symphony hall, at a concert attended by medical specialists. Mr. Williams was in the wings, unable to be in the main section of the room because he was dressed inappropriately. During the concert he saw his wife and asked her how she was getting along and whether she was well. She looked marvelous. He left with a marvelous feeling. The pain was gone. He described the dream as being very comforting and capable of sustaining him for a long time. The subject reported that he had been very busy with his work and had no time left for anything else.
>
> The medical specialists present in the dream all had the same specialty as the specialist who treated one of their children. The setting of the dream in a symphony hall was associated by the subject with the fact that today was the anniversary of his father's death, and his father was a great lover of symphonic music. He was comforted by the music in the dream. It was the most marvelous music, in which all the family was reunited.
>
> The subject indicates he has now begun to relive the death of his wife. He forces himself to remember in order to accept her death. Reality and unreality, however, still intermingle. He cries frequently each day. These crying periods are usually associated with feelings of depression. "It still hurts. I am still far from over it. It will take a long time."
>
> He is still aware his problems remain; his loneliness, his need to go out more and re-establish his social life. He is pleased at the support he is receiving from members of his family, who are encouraging him to rebuild his life. He still finds it hard to think of remarriage. Perhaps in five or six months he may be ready. He realizes that he has been foolish in refusing social invitations, and decides that from here on he will begin to accept them. He anticipates, however, that he will feel ill at ease with other couples and jealous of them.
>
> His depressions have become less frequent and of shorter duration. They now occur several times a day, during the first three months they lasted almost all day.
>
> Sleeping is still troublesome. Previously he would wake at seven; now he gets up at four. Asked why he gets up at four, he recalled his wife had a very bad spell at that time a week before she died. The subject, for the first time, recalled this painful event. Asked to speak of it, he described how it began during the night and interfered with sleep. Mr. Williams remembered his strong feeling of apprehension that the end was near. When the illness became more critical in the morning he realized time was very short. This morning, however, after his marvelous dream, he was able to go back to sleep and to awaken at the normal time.
>
> The subject reported he was now working efficiently. His memory is much better, though he still has difficulties with first names. The words death or dying pain him and his wife's first name especially distresses him. He indicated the first name of his wife means something special.

The client now indicated he remembers the funeral and what occurred at the cemetery. These memories don't leave him. He can't get them out of his mind. He relives them frequently.

Mr. Williams concluded the interview by reaffirming his decision to go out more often. He recalls his wife told him not to grieve too long, and he remembers her last smile. He reaffirms his resolve to rebuild his life (Matz, 1965, pp. 7–8).

Timing of the Phases   Describing the sudden death of a colleague at work, a client remarked: "I can't believe it. I can still see him working at his desk, smoking those awful cigars. There wasn't a thing I could do, he just died that quick! Well, life goes on! Tomorrow we look for a replacement."

All four phases are telescoped into a single paragraph. Grief can be very rapid when it involves a peripheral relationship. When family members are involved, particularly spouses, parents, and dependent children, the process of mourning is quite lengthy. A year or more is usual.

The phases themselves are not distinct with clear-cut beginnings and endings. Fluid relationships are always observed between the phases. Numerous issues are dealt with at different phase levels concurrently. Action often shifts back and forth in bewildering complexity across phase boundaries. The move from phase to phase is gradual and tentative rather than sudden and dramatic.

Determinants that Hinder or Further the Process of Mourning

The length, intensity, and outcome of grief can be partially predicted on the basis of specific personal, relational, and environmental determinants. When these factors are positive, healthy resolution of grief, requiring minimal professional assistance, can be anticipated. When these factors are negatively weighted, the probability of dysfunctional outcome is greatest, and the need for preventive intervention is strongest. The weights of these varying factors give clear indication of the kinds of difficulties that will arise and some notion of what will be required to deal with them.

Personal Factors

The personal resources available to the individual determine how the person will cope with the crisis. The individual's potency is influenced by age; physical and psychological health; intellectual capacity; ability to tolerate pain, sadness and helplessness; fiscal and career abilities; prior difficulties with bereavement and capacity to cope in a self-reliant way with basic life tasks. The most optimistic reading of personal factors produces the following profile: adult; male or female; physically and psychologically healthy with good intellectual capacity; capable of appropriately expressing to self and others feelings of sadness, tearfulness, and helplessness; capable of fiscal self-support or of acquiring fiscal support from others in appropriate ways; constructive resolution of past bereavement; and capable of dealing assertively with his or her needs.

Variations from the optimal profile increase risk. Age variation from the optimal adult range decreases personal resources and coping capacities. As a consequence children (Furman, 1974), adolescents, and the aged are more likely to experience intense, longer, or dysfunctional grief. Variation from the optimal in physical and psychological health, intelligence, fiscal and career abilities, and assertiveness also diminish coping abilities and increase risk. The capacity to deal with sadness and helplessness is particularly important in dealing with mourning. Turning points from despair to hopefulness are frequently preceded by tearfulness. Individuals who learned from prior separations to be rigidly defensive and fearful of sadness are likely to experience increased difficulties. Constructive earlier experiences with separation leading to the establishment of new ties, provides a measure of assurance that the present crisis will be dealt with functionally.

Environmental Factors   The social environment can help or hinder the emotional task of separation and the reconstructive task of restitution. Three environmental factors seem especially relevant:

1. The capacity of significant others to encourage and patiently listen to the bereaved's expressions of grief and helplessness.
2. The degree to which significant others spares the bereaved from overwhelming demands, which drain energy away from the task of mourning.
3. The availability of other people with whom satisfactory restitutive ties can be developed.

Cultural attitudes toward the expression of sadness and the length of time during which grief is appropriate are important aspects of the environmental response. American society generally lacks responses to grief other than avoidance of the griever or the contents of the grief. Grief, as a consequence, tends to cause embarrassment and avoidance. Americans generally see grieving as a shorter process than it is. The expectation is that two or three weeks, at most, is all that is necessary and there is a tendency to regard it as abnormal or self-indulgent when grief for family members lasts six to twenty-four months or more.

Increasing public interest in bereavement and collaboration between clergy and mental health professionals (Clemens, 1976; Matz, 1964) are partially countering prevailing attitudes and increasing realistic emotional supports. Interest of self-help groups, such as Not Alone, Inc. (Matz, 1965), is another hopeful development. The self-help group offers emotional support as well as an available pool of human resources.

Often bereavement places stressful practical demands on the survivors which interfere with mourning. A surviving spouse with young children, who must assume breadwinner and child-care roles, is especially vulnerable. Older siblings called upon to take over a deceased parent's role are also placed at increased risk. Death of a family member frequently places great practical demands on the bereaved for long periods of time. If these demands are not appropriately alleviated or redistributed, allowing the bereaved sufficient energy and time for the work of mourning, dysfunctional patterns are apt to develop.

Finally, the work of restitution can hardly occur in a human vacuum. The absence of human replacements for the deceased is likely to make restitution impossible or highly unsatisfactory. It is difficult to relinquish the past when the present is impoverished. "Why give up my memories, when there is so little in the present to take their place." This observation, made by a man in his eighties, four years after the death of his wife of fifty-six years, underscores the need for appropriate human resources.

Relational Factors   The interpersonal relationship between the bereaved and deceased, as well as the relationship between the bereaved and events of the death, provide the third set of factors to be considered in determining degree of risk faced by the bereaved.

The interpersonal relationship factor concerns the centrality (Bugen, 1977) of the deceased in the life of the bereaved and the quality of the relationship between them. Centrality refers to the degree the bereaved relied on the deceased to meet ongoing needs. The more central the deceased to the life of the bereaved the more extensive the grief.

The quantitative distribution of positive and negative feelings toward the deceased determines the quality of the relationship. Strong negative feelings are likely to evoke doubts that the deceased was treated lovingly and responsibly, particularly during the last days. Often the fear is evoked that hostile wishes in some magical fashion caused the death, or in some unwitting fashion led to inadequate care. Extensive negative feelings are likely to increase notions of the preventability of the death. These feelings are likely to exacerbate unrealistic potency feelings of the second phase and depressed feelings of the third phase.

Relationships between the bereaved and events of the death deal with the appropriateness, suddenness, and preventability of the death. Grief is likely to be minimized when death is appropriate, for example, the death of an elderly gentleman whose health had been gradually failing. The expectation of eventual death was present. The process of separation and restitution had a chance to begin in a constructive way in anticipation of death, with the support of the deceased. The death was seen as painful, but fair. The death of a child violates expectations, arouses bitterness; its unfairness provokes us to deep anger. The suddenness of death also violates expectations. It leaves no time for anticipation and dealing with the last days. Suddenness and inappropriateness increase the risk of believing we did not do all we should have done to prevent the death.

The final factor is preventability (Bugen, 1977). Although helplessness is one of the more painful feelings humans experience, it is vital that bereaved do so to allow the work of restitution to occur. As long as we believe the death is preventable and can be undone, we are unable to allow ourselves forgiveness for our failure to save the life of one we love. Only when we intensely experience our helplessness can we accept our frailty, forgive ourselves, and permit ourselves to resume life. Each bereaved is likely to carefully assess the question "Did I do all I could have and all I should have?" If the answer is yes, the drama of the second and third phases is permitted to shift to the setting of the fourth. As long as the answer is "no" the bereaved is likely to remain involved with undoing, guilt, depression, and suicidal ideation.

The issue of preventability is a cloudy one. Hindsight frequently tells us that we could and should have done differently. Yet, here too, acceptance of our present helplessness is an important ingredient in the outcome. Environmental circumstances that make it easier to conclude nothing could have been done to ease the work of mourning. Conditions which cloud the issue, or make us conclude we could have prevented the death, intensify and complicate the process of mourning.

Dysfunctional Grief

Healthy grief is resilient and forward moving. Its underlying direction is from denial, undoing, and sadness to replacement and reconstruction. Though its direction may temporarily be obscure, the overall thrust to stable reorganization is clear.

This is not true of dysfunctional grief. It involves a stopping of mourning, accompanied by an exaggeration of one or more characteristics of the first three phases. These characteristics become rigid and fixed, losing the flexible and shifting quality found in constructive mourning. Persisting over time, these features become key elements in the resulting picture. Symptomatology can include denial and avoidance of aspects of reality relating to the loss, occasionally reaching psychotic proportions; ongoing preoccupation with undoing, including search behaviors, psychogenic illness, identification with the deceased, chronic anger and guilt, hallucinations, magical substitutions, and ongoing alterations of behavior; persisting feelings of depression and suicidal preoccupation; and a prolonged inability to cope with the basic tasks of living.

Dysfunctional grief and its symptomatology are not easily diagnosed. The resulting pathology is not likely to be related to grief, particularly when powerful mechanisms of denial and avoidance are used by the mourner. Denial may make it appear as if the process of mourning has been easily completed. The onset of overt symptomatology may also be delayed, sometimes for years, further clouding the issue. Diagnostic skills are sharply tested in these situations and errors are frequent. In keeping with denial, patients often cling grimly to incorrect diagnoses further complicating matters.

It is difficult to know when exaggerated patterns of mourning first develop. Features of normal mourning may also temporarily appear rigid. Variations in the timing of phases between individuals and situations are so extensive that, at this stage of our knowledge, it is unwise to use set time spans for measuring functionality or dysfunctionality. It is more useful to assess the status of the critical determinants, evaluating how they are being managed.

Questions like the following should be asked: How central is the loss? Are ample resources available for restitution? How strong are notions of preventabilty?

Do expressions of feeling remain out of proportion to the extent of loss, indicating the persisting presence of high levels of denial? How rigid are the defenses against sadness and what forms do they take? These questions and others based on the determinants of grief shed light and are likely to explain why the process has been brought to a halt or recoiled to earlier positions. They often indicate whether the process will move forward of its own accord, or whether additional clinical and professional resources are needed.

Two dramatic and often unrecognized forms of dysfunctional grief are behavioral reversal and the anniversary hypothesis. *Behavioral reverals* are based on the tendency found in some mourners, especially young children, to seek the cause of death in their own behaviors, particularly the behaviors they used around the time of death. The client invests these behaviors with magical powers and attaches great anxiety to them. The individual tends to experience them as possessing the power to cause death to family members. By reversing these behaviors toward those they love, children experience the conviction that they keep the loved one alive. The reversed behavior tends to assume the double meaning of protecting loved ones from future harm as well as undoing the death that has occurred. When grief is dysfunctional, behavioral reversals may become exaggerated and strongly fixed.

A thirty-six-year-old career woman sought help for her ailing marriage. Her husband complained that their communication was poor. When they first met and dated she was an excellent conversationalist. Shortly after their marriage things changed radically, and she found herself tongue-tied and "without a thought in my head when I'm with him." The husband decided this probably meant she was bored with him and no longer loved him. It was at this point she decided on treatment. In interviews with the woman it was discovered that her father had died during a period of strong sibling rivalry with her brother. She felt that her father had favored her younger brother and was consumed with bitter and resentful thoughts. During this period the father became ill and died. The young girl blamed her bitter thoughts for the death of the father and she reversed them into a pattern of thought avoidance in the presence of men for whom she cared deeply. Fearing bitter thoughts as dangerous and concluding that she could not know her thoughts in advance, she established a pattern of censoring almost all thought in the presence of her husband. It was her love for him, not her lack of love, which caused her near speechlessness.

Anniversary reactions generally refer to the appropriate re-experiencing of grief at times of important anniversaries in the life of the deceased, i.e., date of death, birth, marriage. The anniversary hypothesis is a dysfunctional grief reaction which causes considerable difficulty and is hard to diagnose. Anniversary hypothesis reactions are based on rigid, extensive and persisting identifications of the bereaved with the deceased. Identification often creates an unconscious fear that the bereaved is destined to suffer the same fate as the deceased when he or she reaches the age and/or particular family constellation that existed at the time of death of the deceased. The approach of the anniversary date or the particular family constellation is often accompanied by anxiety and sometimes psychoses develop (Hilgard and Newman, 1959). Sometimes frantic attempts to cheat fate by altering family constellations.

A career woman in her middle thirties suddenly informed her husband she no longer loved him and wished a divorce. She moved out and began an active dating life. Chagrined, her husband agreed to divorce only if they first tried to get help for their marriage. Reluctantly, the wife agreed. She was the youngest of two children. Her brother, older by two years, died in an accident when he was fourteen and she twelve. The tragedy struck deeply at her family. The death of the brother followed in a year and a half by the death of the mother from heart disease, at the age of thirty-nine. The girl aborted her grief by identifying with the mother and taking on many of her characteristics. She chose the same career, married at a similar point in her life, and at the time of the reaction had two grade-school-age children. It was at this point that her unconscious fear of reliving the drama of her youth—the death of her child, followed by her own death—propelled her into action. Dramatically, she attempted to alter her family constellation through divorce. Psychotherapy succeeded in bringing the conflicting motives and fears of the anniversary reaction into awareness, permitting a relinquishing of the identificatory process and a resolution of mourning.

Approaches to Helping

The bereaved are best helped by a counselor who enables them, at their own pace, to put feelings into words, to explore the consequences of loss, and to seek satisfactory solutions. All the skills of counseling are required for this task. Four areas of special concern will be discussed: (1) physical and psychological inaccessibility of the bereaved; (2) limitations in the personal resources of the individual; (3) the issue of preventability; and (4) indicators for clinical consultation.

Inaccessibility

A number of factors conspire to make the bereaved inaccessible to counseling. Denial and avoidance, characteristic of the first phase of mourning, are obvious deterrants. Undoing activities of the second phase are concerned with helping the deceased and counseling is often perceived as a selfish waste of time which does nothing for the dead. The despair of the third phase encourages isolation and turns the bereaved away from help. Psychological avoidance is often accompanied by circumstances which make increased demands on the bereaved, decreasing accessibility. Despite these tendencies of avoidance we almost always find yearnings to talk with someone who understands and cares. In order to relate to the yearning of the bereaved for someone to talk to we must reach out to them. Three steps should be part of reaching out:

1. Informing the client that the work of grieving is hard and lengthy, lasting from a few months to two years or more.

2.   Indicating that many people find it helpful to have someone to talk with about problems that come up.

3.   Indicating the availability of yourself or appropriate others for counseling, and either setting up an initial appointment, or leaving the door open for the bereaved to be called in the near future or to call the counselor when needed.

After helping an elderly wife through day-to-day problems related to the death by cancer of her husband, a hospital social worker structured the matter shortly after the death of the husband.

"I don't have to tell you it's hard for most of us and takes a long time to get things back into perspective. It's usually helpful to have somebody to talk things over with. I think it would make sense for you and I to set up some appointments and keep on talking until things fall into place. What do you think?" The client replied, "I suppose so, but I just can't think about myself right now, I have to call so many people." The social worker replied, "I understand. Let me call you in ten days or so. We can talk then about setting up some appointments." The client answered, "I'd appreciate that."

The stage had been set for the entry of the counselor with the permission of the bereaved.

Sometimes it's best to leave matters on an as-needed basis. A woman in the eleventh week of mourning came in for an appointment and spoke constructively about difficulties with her son. The counselor suggested weekly meetings. The woman said, "It would be nice now and then, but I cannot manage it on a regular basis. Let me call you when I'm in trouble again." The counselor agreed and the woman was able to come intermittently on that basis for over a year. On this basis Mr. Williams the middle-aged engineer, was seen for a year and a half.

Psychological Inaccessibility   Once physical accessibility has been established, the problem of psychological inaccessibility must be dealt with. Bereaved are often embarrassed about the inappropriateness of their thoughts and feelings and fear the counselor will judge them childish or mad. To allay such anxieties, it can be helpful to offer information about the stages of the bereavement process and the different ways in which people react. For instance, if the presence of anxiety-provoking hallucinatory experiences are suspected during phase two, the counselor may say at an appropriate point: "Often people feel as if they are seeing, hearing, or touching the person who died, and I was wondering if that was so with you?" The bereaved often are relieved to hear it is usual and feel more free to talk about their experiences. A frequent response of the bereaved: "I'm glad to hear that. I was scared to tell you about it. I was sure if I did you'd have me committed." Reducing anxiety through education about dramatic but usual aspects of phase behavior also helps the bereaved develop reasonable notions of the intensity, direction, and purposefulness of mourning and the appropriateness of counseling.

In counseling, bereaved frequently raise themes of sadness and back away, changing the subject or altering the emphasis. It's often wise to notice these avoidances and not respond to them. At times, when we feel the bereaved can handle these feelings, it is useful to inquire about these avoidances in a low key, ready to let go of the matter if necessary.

> In a seventh week interview, a middle-aged woman grieving over the death of her 12-year-old son mentioned she would no longer be able to bug him about doing the yard. At that point her eyes became misty, and she seemed about to cry. Instead, she shook her head, put a pleasant smile on her face, and asked my opinion of the best way to get children to obey. Knowing she was able to deal with her sadness at that point, the counselor said: "Your eyes looked misty and sad when you said you would no longer be able to bug your son about the yard. It looked as if you felt like crying." The woman responded by returning to her sadness and exploring feelings relating to her loss of role as mother.

The counseling response, when appropriate, can also be taken one step further. In the last example the counselor could have added the words: "I noticed that instead of crying, you shook your head, put a pleasant smile on your face, and asked me a question about child-rearing. That sort of puzzled me." This response would be more likely to elicit attitudes toward sadness and reasons for avoidance of sadness in the presence of others. Dealing with these feelings is important when resistance to counseling is motivated by defense against sadness.

Sometimes avoidance of sadness and the counseling which elicits it is based on fear that the sadness will be overwhelming, once started it will never cease. If the counselor is confident about the person's ability to tolerate it, reassuring statements are useful. The counselor's genuineness in accepting, expressing, and valuing sadness as a constructive way of dealing with helplessness also tend to reduce inaccessibility related to sadness.

Limitations in the Personal Resources of the Individual
Healthy resolution of mourning cannot occur unless the individual has the personal resources needed for coping. Serious limitations in personal resources (i.e., health, age, intelligence) pose complex problems. All the resources and knowledge of the counselor and community should be utilized in augmenting depleted resources. The counselor needs to use considerable ingenuity, flexibility, and skill in enabling and encouraging clients with limited resources to obtain adequate compensatory supports from family, friends, peer support groups, church, professionals, social agencies, and community.

At best this is a complex task. With infants, children, adolescents, aged, mentally retarded, socially isolated, and emotionally and physically impaired individuals it is a difficult task. Each of these populations present unique difficulties, require different strategies of management, and often involve less than optimal resolutions. Our knowledge of the impact of central bereavement on each of these populations and of appropriate strategies of intervention is also painfully inadequate. These groups will not be dealt with in this chapter; each requires careful, separate examination and study.

Special Considerations with Young Children   The largest and most vulnerable population is the very young. A brief word on their management is in order, although it should be clearly understood that this matter requires more detailed exposition. The interested reader is advised to consult Furman's excellent bibliography (1974).

The centrality of the relationship with the lost parent and the particular tendency of young children to use magical thinking are key factors in childhood bereavement. Adults tend to divide their attachments among many relationships —family, friends, work, etc. The child centers virtually all his needs and feelings on his parents. The intensity and extensiveness of this tie dwarfs adult attachments and causes the tasks of relinquishment and restitution to be difficult and lengthy. The child's immediate need is for someone to physically replace the missing parent in providing daily care. Children are often unable to begin to express sorrow until a reliable relationship has been established with a caretaking adult.

Younger children are particularly given to magical thinking, assuming that thoughts, wishes, and feelings can magically alter and control reality. This pattern of thinking predisposes them to increased use of magical undoing behaviors, characteristic of the second phase of mourning. Undoing, identification illness, search behavior, inappropriate anger and guilt, magical substitution and behavioral reversal are frequently observed. Children need considerable help in exchanging magical ideas of causation for a more realistic understanding of the cause of death. As the child's intellect matures, reactions to the loss are likely to change and alter.

Children must have the help of the surviving parent (or family members) to cope with mourning. Their personal resources for realistic grieving and restitutive coping are seriously limited. Hilgard, Newman, and Fisk (1960) studied factors significant for normal development after father's death in childhood. They determined that a home kept intact by a mother, able to serve in the dual role of homemaker and breadwinner, and supported by a network of supports outside the home, were the key factors.

Major responsibility for management of the child tends to fall on the surviving parent. At minimum, clinical experience indicates they will be expected to fulfill the following psychological tasks:

1.   Provide verbal and behavioral reassurance to the child that they have assumed the caretaker role of the missing parent.
2.   Provide understandable ongoing information about the unfolding facts and consequences of the death.
3.   Tactfully encourage and accept the child's questions, observations, and expressions of sadness during the weeks, months, and years following bereavement.
4.   Answer the child's questions and correct their misperceptions sensitively, tactfully, and realistically, avoiding white lies and

ambiguous remarks—e.g., "She's away on a trip," or "You'll meet again one day"—which encourage unrealistic hopefulness and undoing symptomatology.

5. Enable the child to understand and at times to observe their own feelings of sadness and loss.

Surviving parents (and family members) often welcome counseling which helps them to manage their own feelings as well as the bereaved child. In addition to parent guidance, children can also frequently benefit from sessions with a child therapist. Management of the situation is best accomplished by a mental health professional trained in clinical work with children. When individual counseling is not available, parent support groups can be beneficial, particularly if consultation with a child therapist is available, when needed, to deal with the many complex emotional and behavioral responses associated with childhood bereavement. This course of intervention should increase the probability of healthy resolution of grief or, at the very least, increase the capability of children to deal more constructively with their loss, through personal growth or psychotherapy, when they become adults.

The Issue of Preventability

As long as the bereaved feel something can and must be done to undo the death, that the death can still be miraculously prevented, they continue to judge their efforts or lack of effort by this unrealistic standard of preventability. The longer the belief in preventability is maintained, the more numerous are their failures to undo the death. In phases two and three the bereaved are vulnerable to learning an impaired form of functioning called learned helplessness (Seligman, 1975 and Hooker, 1976). Learned helplessness, based on repeated experiences of failure to control important outcomes, is the conviction that nothing one does can affect the outcome of the event. Its emotional manifestation is reactive depression. Learned helplessness and reactive depression characterize the onset of phase three and are likely to persist and deepen as long as the notion of preventability is held.

The transition to the latter part of phase three and phase four requires a new point of view. Death must be acknowledged as nonpreventable and outside of control. Undoing efforts must be seen for what they are, a waste of time and energy diverting attention from the important arena—restitution, where events can be controlled and outcomes respond to actions. The vigorous onset of restitutive coping behaviors bring phase three to a close, and feelings of potency, validated by ongoing experience, return.

The turn from preventability to nonpreventability is a critical move. Accepting what cannot be changed, controlling what can be changed, and distinguishing between the two is the heart of the matter.

Parents grieving for children tend to experience more difficulties than other bereaved in relation to preventability. It seems likely that strong feelings of parental responsibility, appropriate and necessary for the care of the living child, tend to conflict with the emergence of appropriate and necessary feelings of helplessness after the child has died. The transition from potent caretaker to helpless mourner is particularly difficult.

Researching the illness that caused the sudden death of her two-year-old son, a mother searched for symptoms that could have led to earlier diagnosis and possible saving of his life.

> *Counselor:* (gently) I'm puzzled about the reasons for your research?
> *Client:* I have to do it for my son.
> *Counselor:* I don't know how you mean that?
> *Client:* He'd feel I failed him, if I didn't.
> *Counselor:* (gently) It's hard for me to understand a two-year-old wanting his mother to do this research and feeling you failed him if you didn't?
> *Client:* You mean maybe it's me who feels I have to do something?
> *Counselor:* Is it you?
> *Client:* I feel I *should* do something! I *should* have done something! I just stood there helpless. Why didn't I do something then?
> *Counselor:* What could you have done?
> *Client:* I don't know. That's why I'm trying to find out.
> *Counselor:* And if you find out there was nothing you could have done?
> *Client:* I'd feel very sad and yet part of me would be relieved to know that.
> *Counselor:* Relieved?
> *Client:* At least then I could rest and not feel this drive to do something and not know what it is. I'd *know* there's *nothing* I can do! Nothing! *(sobs.)* I wish I could do something, but there is nothing! *(More sobbing) (pause).* My five-year-old asked me where the baby is. I told him he went to heaven. What do you think of that answer?

The mother is beginning (repeated working through was necessary) the turn from the *impossible,* preventing the death of the baby, to the *possible,* managing the grief of her five-year-old. The counselor relied on her logical capacity to evaluate her feelings and distinguish between wishful thinking and reality.

The intricacies of preventability are endless; the possibilities for resolution are equally varied. When the turn, however, is blocked and after careful and patient exploration shows no sign of easing, clinical consultation (if the counselor is not a clinician) to assess the appropriateness of psychotherapy is advisable.

Indicators for Consultation
Consultation becomes important when the dysfunctionality of the client's grief work is beyond the helpers level of competency. The purpose of the consultation between counselor or client and another mental health professional should be to

explore appropriate ways of dealing with the current impasse, or, if that is not possible, to assess the appropriateness of psychotherapy (individual, marital, family, guidance, or group), medication, or, if there is suicidal danger or psychotic behavior, hospitalization. Of course, if clearly defined emotional or physical illness is present appropriate referral should be made.

Three key factors in addition to preventability point to the need for clinical consultation: rigid defenses against sadness, rigid defenses against restitutive coping, and suicidal danger. Because each of these factors can rigidly stop the grief process, they serve to signal more clearly than other indicators the probable onset of dysfunctional grief.

Rigid Defenses against Sadness and/or Restitutive Coping   The bereaved patient is initially avoidant of sadness and assertive coping. Time as well as careful exploration of feelings usually lead to increased ability to cope with sadness and its losses. When defenses remain rigid, particularly against restitutive coping, the mourning process cannot proceed to resolution. Careful reassessment is required. If a review of the status of the determinants of grief does not explain the situation and points out another course, it is reasonable to assume prior pathological factors are causing the impediment and to explore through consultation the appropriateness of psychotherapy.

Suicidal Danger   Thoughts questioning the value of life and expressing the wish to join the loved one in death are frequent in a bereaved population. This is especially so in the third phase of grief. Their frequency, however, should not cause us to be unconcerned about them. Suicidal ideation increases suicidal risk and should always be carefully assessed! When suicidal thoughts are followed by positive statements about living and about obligations to children and other family members, it is likely that suicidal danger is less. When suicidal ideation is not counterbalanced by positive feelings and obligations to others, or if there is a conviction that life should be given up as an act of undoing or atonement, then suicidal danger should be seen as considerable. This is especially the case if statements and behaviors of the bereaved cause us to fear for their safety. Particularly alarming would be suicide attempts or plans. Attention should also be paid to the existence of suicidal behavior in the personal or family background of the bereaved. A history of suicide or suicidal behavior increases risk. When suicidal danger is present, it is vital to refer the bereaved or consultation to determine appropriate treatment.

Summary

Healthy grief work enables mourners to mobilize their inner resources and those of the environment to create new patterns of satisfying ties and relationships. If the work has gone well, the person stands at a new beginning: enriched by fresh ties, strengthened by hard-earned knowledge of inner resilience, and encouraged by memories from the past that support steps into the future. The purpose of counseling the bereaved is to help more individuals work toward this goal.

Questions for Further Inquiry

1. Do the stages of grief work discussed in this chapter fit your personal experience with grieving?

2. From your personal experiences how well do our funeral and mourning customs help with grief resolution? What changes would be meaningful to you?

3. How may a helper decide when and if a person has spent too much time grieving?

4. Some people believe that there is an important degree of selfishness in the grief process. Do you agree or disagree?

5. What does the research literature suggest about children's ways of coping with grief? How might this information affect the way counselors work with children?

References

Bugen, L. A. Human grief: A model for prediction and intervention. *American Journal of Orthopsychiatry* 1977 *47(2)*, 196–206.

Clemens, N. A. An intensive course for clergy on death, dying and loss. *Journal of Religion and Health* 1976 *15*, 223–29.

Furman, Erna. *A child's parent dies: Studies in childhood bereavement.* New Haven and London: Yale University Press, 1974.

Glick, I. O., Weiss, R. S., & Parkes, C. *The first year of bereavement.* New York: Wiley, 1974.

Hilgard, Jr. R., & Newman, M. F. Anniversaries in mental illness *Psychiatry* 1959 *22*, 113–21.

Hilgard, Jr. R., Newman, F. F., & Fish, F. Strength of adult ego following childhood bereavement. *American Journal of Orthopsychiatry* 1960 *30*, 788–98.

Hooker, C. E. Learned helplessness. *Social Work* 1976 (May), pp. 194–98.

Kübler-Ross, Elisabeth. *On death and dying.* New York: Macmillan, 1969.

Lindemann, E. Symptomatology and management of acute grief. *American Journal of Psychiatry* 1944 *101*, 141–48.

Matz, M. Judaism and bereavement. *Journal of Religion and Health* 1964 *3(4)*, 345–52.

Matz, M. An anatomy of normal grief. Unpublished manuscript, Case Western Reserve University School of Medicine, 1965.

Matz, M. Not alone, Inc.: A proposal to establish peer support groups for the bereaved. Unpublished manuscript. Case Western Reserve University School of Medicine, 1976.

Parkes, C. M. *Bereavement: Studies of grief in adult life.* New York: International Universities Press, 1973.

Seligman, E. P. *Helplessness: On depression, development, and death.* San Francisco: Freeman, 1975.

PART III

Effective Helping With Special Client Populations

In previous sections of this text we have presented chapters dealing with common concerns that clients of any background may present to the counselor, and chapters dealing with family concerns. In this final section chapters are presented that provide specific information about working with clients whose concerns can be understood and resolved more easily by knowing more about the *groups* of which they are a part (e.g., adults, women, young children). Each group has certain characteristics that distinguish it from each of the others. While each person seeking help is unique and must be understood in terms of his or her own particular circumstances, it is helpful to know the characteristics of the reference group of which the client is a member.

Developmental themes run through much of Part III. Patterson presents a detailed description of the developmental issues, tasks, and crises that are a part of modern day adulthood. Similarly Schlossberg and Kent use a developmental framework to describe the particular problems of women in a society where women's (and men's) roles are ambiguous and in the process of change. Until recently adults have been regarded as capable of managing their own affairs; adulthood has been regarded as a time of stability and maintenance rather than a period of growth and change. In these two chapters, the authors present a picture of adulthood as a time of dynamic and potentially fulfilling change. Each chapter presents useful perspectives on counseling with adult clients which have emerged from their practice.

By contrast, the developmental issues of childhood have been abundantly described in the literature of counseling, psychology, and education for many years. But the helping process itself has received less attention. Nelson and Keat have been among the leading voices in literature on child counseling, and Hatch provides a special perspective from his experience with learning-disabled children. It is not by accident, then, that the two chapters on working with children, normal and learning-disabled, focus heavily on diagnostic and treatment procedures. Both also emphasize the importance of being able to enter the child's world as a prerequisite to effective helping. It is easy to forget what was important to us as children, and the authors of these two chapters help with that recall. Then they provide systematic approaches to understanding and helping children—approaches that recognize the child's special need for guidance in finding new ways of satisfying needs and desires.

The final two chapters of the book describe the etiology and helping strategies for two of the most pervasive and difficult to help client problems— delinquencies and abuse of alcohol and drugs. These are problems largely associated with adolescence and adulthood and they seem to be related to inadequate accomplishment of the developmental tasks of adolescence. Blum and Zalba present a model for helping delinquents that integrates multiple causative factors and prescribes interventions based on specific causes. Burnett provides useful guidelines for understanding the developmental deficits that lead to chemical abuse. Since physiological responses to various drugs differ greatly, she describes some general helping principles for all cases of abuse, then devotes considerable emphasis to the particular problem of alcoholism. Counselors working in virtually every setting will encounter clients with problems of delinquency and chemical abuse. These chapters present the insights of practitioners who specialize in working with these difficult problems.

Effective Helping with Adult Clients

12

LEWIS E. PATTERSON

Overview

For many years counseling with the adult client received little attention from the counseling profession. Adulthood was seen as a period of stability that followed the tumult of growing up. Senility was understood to occur for some later in the period of adulthood, but senility was treated mostly as an undesirable occurrence to be endured rather than to be understood and ameliorated. Adults, it was assumed, had made their choices about career and their arrangements for living their domestic lives. They were expected to be able to manage their affairs independently, and seeking help was often considered a sign of weakness.

The early efforts in the guidance field focused mostly on initial vocational choice, which was assumed to occur at the point of leaving formal education. While later career development theorists talked of the need for life-span understanding of the career process, they too focused heavily on the adolescent period in their studies.

Influences of Freudian thought also operated against widespread application of the helping process to adults. The treatment focused on the pathology of the more seriously impaired rather than on the coping problems of the many. And, since the early formative years held so much importance, the further one moved from childhood the less one was seen as a viable candidate for helping. According to Lawton (1973), "Freud himself rejected the elderly as a class, leading to the unfortunate neglect of the psychodynamic process of later life by the practicing analyst" (p. 339).

The two streams from which the counseling profession developed did not focus on the full range of the adult years. The result was an incomplete picture of adult development and the absence of any substantial work on the counseling process with adult clients.

The potential of counseling with adults is now receiving widespread attention. Professionals and laymen alike are beginning to recognize that change, not stability, is the pervasive quality of adult life. Rapidly changing technology renders occupational stability less certain than it once was. Changing roles of women and men in the work world and in the family present adults with an endless series of decisions about how they will live their lives. Choices about whether to marry, whether to stay married, and whether to have children are recognized as a right and responsibility of adults. As a by-product of the human potential movement, there is a new perspective that adults have a right to fulfillment, not simply stability at any price. Gail Sheehy's (1974) best seller, *Passages,* appealed to millions because it helped adults facing change to realize that they were not alone in their experiencing.

Counselors who choose to work with an adult clientele will, of course, apply many of the principles of good counseling that apply with any clientele. There must be a foundation in the relationship and listening skills, goal setting, decision-making, and planning. There must also be counselor awareness of the salient issues of adulthood (Schlossberg, 1976) to provide a structure for diagnostic understanding of adult concerns. There must be an awareness of the responsibilities adults bear in their daily experience and the relationship of these responsibilities to motivation for counseling. In a youth-oriented world the counselor (usually comparatively young) must work toward elimination of age bias in his or her work (Troll and Nowak, 1976; Bocknek, 1976).

Following the format of other chapters in this volume, the first section will focus on understanding the salient issues, and the second section will develop implications for the helping process. Many of the ideas presented in the following pages have emerged from a rather recent but intensive interest on the part of professional helpers in developing a body of knowledge about working with adults. While many of the concepts seem well substantiated, there is much more to learn.

Understanding the Salient Issues of Adulthood

Stages of Adulthood
It is not surprising that the first efforts at understanding adulthood were patterned after stage theory which had served well to provide a structure for understanding childhood and adolescence. However, it was soon learned that adults lead much more varied lives than children (longer time span permits more variations on the theme), and that both the nature of experiences and the time frames are less

predictable for adults than for children and adolescents. Sex differences in experience and sequence are also greater for adults than for children and adolescents. Neugarten (1976a) has even questioned whether an understanding of adulthood is strictly a "developmental" issue, since a part of the adult experience is actually decline. Nevertheless, general trends or directions in development based on common experiences of adults can be identified and are useful to the counselor who is trying to understand the meaning of a client's life and life concerns.

In *Childhood and Society,* Erikson (1950) made a significant early attempt at describing life-span development. The last three of the developmental stages he described referred to young adulthood, adulthood, and maturity. In young adulthood the person, emerging from a search for identity, is ready for *intimacy*. The person is ready to make commitments to other people even if they involve sacrifices and compromises. The avoidance of such experiences may lead to a sense of isolation and the inhibition of further development. Thus, the counselor in working with the young adult should focus on indications that the client is able to affiliate with others without fear that he or she will lose his or her own sense of identity and integrity in the process. Lacking such evidence, one would conclude that ego strength is limited and that the client may not yet have become secure in his own identity.

The task of adulthood, according to Erikson, is *generativity*, the concern in establishing and guiding the next generation. Those who do not have their own offspring may "generate" in other creative directions, but unless productivity occurs, Erikson said that a return to "pseudo-intimacy" will occur. Such individuals never become the mentors of the young and instead continue to act as if they themselves *were* the young. Fulfillment eludes them, for others are no longer willing to treat them as the young. Erikson referred to this condition as "stagnation."

Maturity for Erikson is described by the term *ego integrity*. He describes this condition rather than defining it, in part by stating that it includes "an acceptance of one's own and only life cycle as something that had to be" (p. 268). This level of ego-integrity includes some sense of a world order and of historical perspective. As an alternative to achieving ego integrity, there is despair and fear of death. If one does not have a sense that life has been a part of the world order and has had value, then there is no readiness for death. The work of the counselor includes the process of helping the mature adult come to a high level of acceptance of self, in spite of disappointments that life may have rendered.

Erikson's formulations have the advantage of being sufficiently broad to encompass persons of different sexes and different cultures. Longitudinal research (Lowenthal and Weiss, 1976; Britton and Britton, 1972) suggests that the developmental periods and related tasks are not so discreet and sequential as Erikson suggested—that more than one agenda is salient at any given point in an adult's life. One need not complete one level of development fully to begin encountering the next level in some sector of his or her life. The breadth and consequent universality of Erikson's formulations are, of course, a limitation when a counselor works toward specificity with a given client. Much is left unsaid about the more concrete manifestations of the developmental process.

Levison, Darrow, Klein, Levinson, and McKee (1976) have proposed a sequence of developmental periods for men ages 18–45. They sought to identify the "various developmental periods, tasks, structures, and processes" (p. 21) associated with early adulthood and the mid-life transition. Through biographical study they identified the following periods and associated issues or tasks:

1. Getting into the adult world (early 20s through 27–29). Developmental task is "to explore the adult world, to arrive at an initial definition of oneself as an adult, and *to fashion an initial life structure* that provides a viable link between the valued self and the wider adult world" (p. 22). Included are occupational, sexual, and friendship dimensions.
2. Age 30 transition (28–32). Involves an assessment of the initial life structure in anticipation of the greater commitment of the next stage. Levison *et al.* state that unless a man begins to make significant progress toward order and stability by age 34, he has little chance of achieving a satisfying life structure.
3. Settling down (early 30s to early 40s). "The man establishes a niche in society, digs in, builds a nest, and pursues his interests with the defined pattern" (p. 23). "Making it" is important.
4. Becoming one's own man (middle to late 30s). Thrust is toward independence from supervisors and mentors.
5. Mid-life transition (early to mid 40s). The task is to reconcile the goodness of fit between the life structure and the self. In building an initial life structure, certain aspects of the self were rejected, repressed, or left dormant. Now these seek expression. Issues that are often crucial are those of bodily decline and mortality, the sense of aging, and the acceptance of feminine aspects of the self which were repressed in the settling down period.
6. Restabilization (around age 45). A reintegrated life structure that is carried into middle adulthood is built.

This study ends with the beginning of middle adulthood, so the rest of the life pattern is not described.

The description of the life stages of male development by Levinson *et al.* (1976) seems to organize and make sense of the progress of the "normal" male through this period of his life and provide some clues to what might be considered pathological departure from a usual pattern. In many respects these conclusions coincide with Erikson's broader outline. Clearly, however, the age designations for the various stages should be used broadly, and the periods of restructuring of life patterns will be dramatic for some persons, almost invisible for others. Other authors (Brim, 1976; Schlossberg, 1976) are less inclined to describe such an orderly sequence of tasks and to relate that sequence so specifically to chronological age.

To describe the adult woman's life in terms of stages is even more difficult than describing the adult man's life. Life tasks vary dramatically according to the several patterns of career and domestic orientation that a woman may choose (Patterson, 1973). It is probable that many women experience some of the sequence just described for men, but to describe a single set of stages that applies in any consistent way for most women is not as tenable. It is increasingly true that women are spending major portions of their lives in employed work, usually in the early adult and middle years with a child-bearing period interrupting their employment for a time. The end of the child-bearing period and related physiological changes are more clearly apparent for women than men and are important events in the lives of many women. And finally, most married women can anticipate a period of widowhood or perhaps a single state related to divorce earlier than widowhood would occur. Later sections of this chapter, as well as parts of Chapter 13 have been developed to provide more insight into issues of importance to adult women using structures other than stage theory to accomplish that aim.

Role Transformations and Transitions

As adults move through the life cycle, their roles change with respect to five main dimensions: vocation, intimacy, family life, community, and inner life (Schlossberg, 1976). Over time, most people move from entry level jobs to more responsible jobs that usually involve the supervision of others who are often younger. We establish intimate relationships that often lead to marriage or other close associations. We experience change with respect to parental and extended family and usually procreate our own children. We assume a community role, sometimes committing considerable energy to the community and sometimes not. And we change over time in the ways we think about ourselves and our lives.

It is useful to keep these dimensions of change in mind as one considers the role of the passage of time in the life cycle. Neugarten (1976b) said, "Adults carry in their heads, whether they can easily verbalize it or not, a set of anticipations of the normal, expectable life cycle" (p. 18). She stated that it is not until adulthood that one creates a sense of the life cycle and that the ability to create a sense of a personal life cycle differentiates the healthy adult personality from the unhealthy.

Combining these thoughts about the dimensions of the life cycle and time perspective leads to a view that each adult has a loosely formulated idea about what roles he or she might reasonably be fulfilling at various periods in the life cycle. It is important to recognize that the sense of expected life cycle is not the same for all persons, but rather is influenced heavily by experience (socioeconomic factors, sex, ethnic heritage, etc.). The expected life cycle of a factory worker differs in some ways from the expected life cycle of a retailer. Role expectations of the Jewish professor and the WASP professor are subtly different. A woman has sex-related expectations for herself that differ from those of a man, even as occupational equity becomes more possible.

Role transformations, then, must be regarded as inevitable occurrences over the life cycle. Transitions may be said to occur at certain significant points where one moves from one manifestation of role to another, for example, when the last child leaves home returning the parents to the state of sharing lives as a couple once more.

While it is possible to generalize to some degree about role transformations and transitions for adults in a given culture, it is especially important for the counselor to remember that each individual's sense of the life cycle will be highly personalized. Therefore while a stage theory of adult development serves to identify broad patterns of development, individual clients may skip stages entirely or experience stages in a different sequence or at different times. The same can be said, of course, for the importance of individual differences in working with children and adolescents, but the impact of longer experience leads to even more diversity in the expectations and the capacities of adults.

When Transition Becomes Crisis

Since we began to recognize that adulthood was not a stable and placid period for most people, it has become common to refer to a number of the transitions of adulthood as crises. Thus we read of the mid-life crisis, the crisis of menopause, the crisis of the empty nest, the crisis of retirement, and the crisis of death, to name a few. There is strong evidence to suggest, however, that these transition points in life do not become crises for most people.

Building on the concept that each individual develops a view of what is a normal and expected sequence of events in his or her own life, it has been found that a transition does not become a crisis if it is an anticipated, "normal" event in the personal life cycle. Neugarten, Wood, Kraines, and Loomis (1963) studied menopause as a possible time of crisis in the lives of 100 women. They found that there was no evidence to support the view that women experience menopause as a crisis. For most women it is an expected event that is not unusually stressful, even though there are certain transitions in a physical and psychological sense. The study team then proceeded to study the "empty nest" as a possible crisis and learned that the postparental period was associated with a higher level of life satisfaction than other life periods. It is, of course, true that some women experience both of these periods of transition as crisis, but according to Neugarten's hypothesis, such a clinical problem occurs when the individual has developed an incomplete or inaccurate personal sense of the life cycle. Thus it is important for the helper to realize that crises may occur at transition points but to exercise care not to assume crises where none exist. Neugarten (1976b) summarized her work by saying:

> it is the unanticipated life event, not the anticipated—divorce, not widowhood in old age; death of a child, not death of a parent—which is likely to represent a traumatic event (p. 20).

Following is an overview of the causes and content of the male mid-life transition according to Brim (1976):

1. *Endocrine changes.* From about age 30 on there is a gradual decline in the secretion of male hormones. It is not known to what degree this may relate to other physiological or psychological changes.
2. *Aspirations and achievements.* There is a reckoning with what one has accomplished (occupationally) in life as compared with one's aspirations, and a recognition that there is a limited period of time within which to close any aspiration-achievement gap.
3. *Resurgence of "the Dream."* Brim adopted Levinson's view (referred to earlier in this chapter) that in mid-life one may focus on previously unrecognized or suppressed parts of self. Thus, in the context of the achievement-aspiration gap, it is conceivable that one could accomplish what one set out to accomplish and still mourn the loss of "the Dream" that had remained dormant till now.
4. *Stagnation vs. generativity.* This correlates with the Eriksonian concept of shifting one's life interest and concerns to the development of the next generation.
5. *Confrontation with death.* This is described most vividly as the change in mid-life when one ceases counting time since birth and begins reckoning with the life cycle according to time left till death.
6. *Relationships with family.* There are several ways that relationships within family change at mid-life, but one of particular interest is a confrontation of the achievement-aspiration gap in the success of one's parenting. Included is the recognition that one lacks the power to mold his children into ideal beings.
7. *Social status and role changes.* Changes in work and health and family are usual.

Considering all these variables and the question of whether they constitute the basis for a crisis, Brim said:

> a "male mid-life crisis" will occur for some men if there are multiple simultaneous demands for personality change; for instance, during the same month or year the man throws off his last illusions about great success; accepts his children for what they are; buries his father and his mother and yields to the truth of his mortality; recognizes that his sexual vigor and, indeed, interest, are declining, and even finds relief in the fact (p. 8).

The salient issues for mid-life males are very important for the professional helper. There is reason to believe that most males, at least those with any tendency toward introspection, are encountering issues of identity that are for their time in life just as important as the identity issues of adolescence are at that period in life. For many they will seem a natural and expected occurrence rather than a crisis. Even so, Brim concludes with the statement that ". . . the growing pains of mid-life, like those of youth and of old age, are transitions from one comparatively steady state to another, and these changes, even when they occur in crisis dimensions, bring for many men more happiness than they had found in younger days" (p. 8).

Lowenthal and Weiss (1976) related the crises of adulthood to intimacy and concluded that there are two "high risk" adult populations; middle- and lower-class women in the early post-parental stage and middle-aged men. In each instance the crisis seems related to a lack of intimacy in their lives. For the women, the intimate relationships with their children are gone and they long for better communication with their husbands. The "overwhelmed" men rate themselves "low in their capacity for intimacy and mutuality" (p. 14). The authors conclude that "close interpersonal relationships serve as a resource against life's crises" (p. 16).

In summary, it appears that for men and women alike, transitions can and usually do occur without crisis. The potential for crisis is higher at some times during adult life than at others, but it is by no means predictable that all persons of a given age and sex will be experiencing the same thing at the same time. Some transitions are pleasant, some may be neutral, others moderately stressful, and some reach crisis proportions. The helper must learn to distinguish crisis from other responses to transition. Improvement of interpersonal relationships may serve to help a client in crisis over the difficult period.

Mentoring and Adult Development

Imbedded in Erikson's concept of generativity is the view that adults reach a point in their lives where fulfillment is at least partially dependent on their involvement with bringing on the new generation. By the same token, the new generation seeks identification with successful older persons in the process of affiliating self with the adult world. It seems appropriate then to say that in young adulthood, people need mentors and as they age they need to be mentors.

Levinson et al. (1976) report that the presence of mentors is an important component of life during the 20s and 30s. Levinson says that the mentor "takes the younger man under his wing, invites him into a new occupational world, shows him around, imparts his wisdom, cares, sponsors, criticizes, and bestows his blessing" (p. 23). The mentor is usually 8–15 years older and functions more as a peer and older brother than as a wise old man or father. In time, the younger man must become his own man. Thus rarely do we find a man over 40 who has a mentor. Levinson comments that the absence of mentors for women in responsible employed positions continues to serve as a limiting factor in women's career development.

While it is probably not a universal experience for all persons to have mentors, mentoring relationships are clearly important to both the giver and the recipient of the guidance that is involved. The teaching function is important, but the mutual ego fulfillment is probably even more vital to effective occupational and personal functioning. Super and Overstreet (1960) has referred to the failure to identify with the adult world as a major cause of vocational immaturity, and the absence of available and credible mentors may well be a causative factor.

The Process of Disengagement

Just as the young adult must find a place for himself or herself in the adult world and the middle-aged adult shifts to a focus on "generativity," the older adult usually begins at some point to decathect from the younger production-oriented society. Since the early 1960s gerentologists have been engaged in a great debate about how this process occurs. Cummings and Henry (1961) introduced a theory of "disengagement" which stated that as people grow old, there is a mutual withdrawing of the individual from others, and others from the individual. Each in a sense loses interest in the other and by mutual consent, there is an increasing isolation of the older person. Through this decathecting process, the older person comes to accept his role in old age as more private and less active. The disengagement theory was proposed as an alternative to the hypothesis of "loneliness" as a condition of old age. In a sense, one can relate successful disengagement to Erikson's concept of "ego integrity" where one gains satisfaction from reflecting on the quality of the life lived rather than on the immediate productivity of the here and now.

It appears, however, that other people do, indeed, continue to measure their self-worth in terms of their ability to do what they did when they were younger. For them, successful aging is aging as little as possible.

Neugarten, Havighurst, and Tobin (1968) have found that successful aging may take different courses for different people, depending upon their personality type. Thus, the "disengaged" may experience high levels of life satisfaction just as may those who remain heavily involved in the social roles of middle age. A consistent finding, nevertheless, is the fact that introversion increases with age (Neugarten, 1976a).

Sex-Role and Aging

In early adulthood when women and men are trying to establish themselves in the adult world, they tend toward exaggerated expressions of that which defines them as feminine or masculine. As adults grow older they seem to be more accepting of impulses that are often socially associated with the opposite sex. In Neugarten's (1976a) research (with David Gutmann) on sex-role changes with age, men have been described as moving from active mastery to passive mastery to magical mastery over the period of their lives. In early roles as breadwinner, they are very active in mastering the environment in search of a place for themselves. With greater maturity, they become more established and adopt a more passive approach. With old age, when in fact mastery facility may be diminished, they resort to pretense in order to feel still in control. By contrast, women, who tend to be more passive in younger adulthood, frequently move to an active mastery stance when children grow and become less dependent. Gutmann has studied this phenomenon in several cultures and has tentatively concluded that this shift in personal mastery style is a "species phenomenon" which can be found in humans regardless of the culture in which they are socialized.

Synopsis of Salient Issues of Adulthood

A basis for understanding the adult client can be found in the literature of the psychology of adult development. While simple sequential developmental stages are not universally applicable, there are some predictable issues of adulthood that the counselor should have in mind as a context for understanding clients:

1. Change is perhaps the one certain condition of adult existence.
2. Well functioning adults seem to go through a process that involves making a place for themselves in the adult world, establishing themselves as productive in the sense of creating and/or mentoring, and finally reflecting on the value that life has held.
3. Some authors have tried to be more explicit about the developmental stages, but as the number and specificity of stages increases, their universality decreases.
4. Transition points in adulthood frequently are created by role transformations of maturing (e.g., the end of the parenting period). While transitions are points where difficulty is more likely than during stable periods, all transitions do not become crises.
5. Crises occur at transition points when multiple changes occur simultaneously or when a particular role transformation is not anticipated. Mid-life tends to be a time when both women and men experience a number of simultaneous transitions and is thus a likely crisis period.
6. Many older adults begin disengaging from social roles and this is a satisfactory aging process for many.
7. Men typically become more accepting of nurturing and compassionate impulses and may become more passive (less aggressive) with age. Women usually become more comfortable with competitive achievement roles as they age.

Understanding the Presenting Problem

Since most adults are able to manage many of their life concerns without the aid of a professional helper, it is important to be aware of those conditions that create stress levels that lead to the seeking of outside help. These conditions are best understood in terms of the concepts of adult development presented in the preceding pages.

Very frequently the client presents an initial concern about feeling "stuck" and fearing that he or she will not lead as fulfilling a life as had been hoped for. This relates to the concept that we all have inner clocks which describe appropriate times by which certain things should be accomplished. It is also an expression of a fundamental value that life should ultimately be meaningful. People feel stuck when they can't find work which they consider appropriate to their abilities and their time in life. They feel stuck when they fear they will not accomplish their life goals or live out a dream. They feel stuck when significant relationships with others have lost meaning and they don't know what to do about it.

Many other clients will find it difficult to adjust to a role transformation. They find themselves bewildered by the experience of a new life condition—a new job, a change of marital status, the end of the parenting period, the death of a spouse, retirement. In counseling they seek to redefine aspects of their identity and worth and to learn new ways of coping with their new situations.

The capacity for intimacy sustains people across many life difficulties. People with a strong capacity for intimacy tend to find help among family, friends, and acquaintances. Therefore many of the people who seek professional help may be those for whom intimacy has been difficult.

Finally, it is wise to be aware that an adult client seeking help is likely to have a store of concerns which will be interrelated and cumulative. A "final straw" often motivates the initial visit to the counselor.

The Process of Helping Adult Clients

Purposes of Helping

Most adult clients are self-referred, that is, they arrive at the helper's office with the hope that they may somehow improve their lives through involving themselves in counseling. More often than not, they have tried to sort out why they do not feel satisfied with their lives, but they have found themselves unable to control those things which create distress for them. Schlossberg (1976) stated succinctly that the purpose of counseling with adults is to return to them the locus of control over their own lives.

It is true, of course, that many clients arrive at the counselor's office convinced that their lives will be improved only if significant others or specific sets of circumstances are changed. It is important to remember that it is the client himself or herself who must change if counseling is to succeed. External circumstances may indeed be difficult, but if they are to change, it is most often the client who is in the best position to engender those changes. The adult who does not like his or her job can decide how to improve it or how to seek a different job. The adult who is burdened with the care of an aging parent can seek help in bearing that burden. An adult who is angry at his or her children can learn to understand this anger and find more productive ways of accomplishing his or her goals with the children. A part of being in control involves knowing what one wants and needs and being able to be satisfied with what one can reasonably attain. Being in control is being motivated by what is meaningful, not being driven toward undefined goals.

Counselor Readiness: Age Bias as an Issue in Counseling Adults

One of the very sensitive concerns that adult clients bring to the counseling office is the belief that a particular problem they have is one that they should have mastered "at their age." Further, there is a concern that in a youth-oriented society they may be discriminated against because of age. Unfortunately many counselors have indeed assumed a position that is less than tolerant of older clients. Troll and Nowak (1976, p. 14) suggest three kinds of age bias:

1. Age restrictiveness: setting of arbitrary or inappropriate age limits for behavior.
2. Age distortion: misperception of the behavior or characteristics of any age group.
3. "Age-ism" or negative attitudes toward any age group.

Counselors of adults should examine their attitudes about the relationship of age to the ability of a client to make good use of counseling. As in any other instance of counselor bias, age bias can limit the counselor's effectiveness with the clientele against which the bias is felt. It is essential that the counselor eliminate age bias, while at the same time maintaining an understanding of age-related issues of his or her clients. It is a serious error to assume that a 55-year-old client cannot develop new components of his or her life; it is an equally serious error to assume that the client will not experience some bias in the outside world if those new developments include seeking employment in a new location or seeking a new personal life style. The unbiased counselor is able to work with a client seeking to cope with the issue of age bias in the culture at large.

Client Readiness

When considering the readiness of adult clients for the helping process, there are two opposing trends that must be considered. The first is the familiar old adage that "you can't teach an old dog new tricks." Taken in perspective this can mean that habits that have been practiced over long years, attitudes that are well ingrained, conceptions of reality long held are more difficult to change than those held for a shorter duration. It can be assumed that adult clients are likely to be more set in their patterns of thought and behavior than younger clients.

Counterbalancing this quality of habituation is the adult's greater experience with the process of living and of making self-determining choices. Bocknek (1976) described the adult client as being able to give voice to expectations, to make objectives explicit, and to take responsibility in a goal-oriented working relationship. Schuttenberg (1975) characterized the adult as seeking increased self-direction, capable of using experience as a learning resource, ready to learn what is perceived essential, and oriented toward problem solving as an approach to learning.

Taken together, these readiness qualities in the adult client suggest that the starting point for counseling may well be different from the starting point for the younger client. Since the adult client is likely to have a more thoroughly developed sense of who he or she is and what he or she wants to work on, it is especially important for the counselor to use this information in the process of structuring the counseling relationship and setting goals for counseling. Counseling will frequently focus on understanding the client and helping the client cope with a fairly specific set of concerns by mobilizing already present coping strategies.

Diagnostic Process

In the initial session with any client, the counselor focuses on what brought the client to counseling, how the client seems to be coping with his or her life, what sort of help the client is seeking, what sort of help the client may need, and the counselor's ability to participate in the helping process with the particular client given the client's needs. The first session should focus on understanding enough about the client to begin the planning of the helping process.

Diagnosis and diagnostic labels are a controversial subject in the literature of counseling. Objections to diagnosis, however, are usually aimed at systems with large numbers of diagnostic categories. Because such classification systems become increasingly arbitrary, many helpers think that the diagnostic process becomes a cognitive experience that depersonalizes the "being with" aspects of counseling. Yet, a concrete understanding of the nature of the client's issues is essential to growth-oriented counseling. A language that helps the counselor develop those concrete understandings will include some diagnostic categories.

In working with adult clients, there are three general diagnostic categories that are useful in developing initial plans for the helping process:

1. Clients facing situational problems that have temporarily overtaxed coping skills.
2. Clients facing developmental problems that are characterized by ineffective or uncomfortable responses to their changing maturity.
3. Clients with potentially debilitating levels of psychopathology.

As one proceeds from the first to the third category, the helping process required becomes more complex. Clients in the later categories frequently exhibit the problems identified in the earlier categories as well. Some brief descriptions of case material will illustrate the point.

Case of Eleanor (Situational Problem—A Role Transformation)   Eleanor was a 55-year-old unmarried insurance executive who was responsible for supervising the work of 22 automobile insurance adjustors. Her presenting problem was that she was very unhappy with her job and was considering leaving the company where she had been employed for the past 30 years. She came to counseling seeking some testing that would help her plan a change of careers, possibly to a completely different field or maybe to another company. She seemed quite distressed.

As her story unfolded, the counselor learned that Eleanor had worked in the claims department of the insurance company for many years, first as a clerical worker, then as an adjustor. During all that time she had been happy in her work, had a number of friends, maintained close ties with family, and led what she recalled as a very happy life. She had particularly enjoyed the role of adjustor because she was not confined to an office and she had the opportunity to meet and work with a lot of people. Even though she was the only female adjustor in the department, she enjoyed a casually pleasant relationship with co-workers and on occasion talked with other adjustors about their work. There appeared to be no work related difficulty and the client's personal life was satisfactory to her.

When the counselor asked Eleanor to try to pinpoint when it was that she first began to feel dissatisfied in her work, she concluded that the difficulty had been confined mostly to the last 10 months. Eleanor had not associated her dissatisfaction with the fact that she had been promoted to a supervisory role 15 months previously. As she and the counselor discussed the matter further, most of her stress seemed to come from that part of her work where she had to evaluate the work of other employees. Not only did she experience stress while on the job, but she spent her evenings and nights worrying about whether she was being fair to those she evaluated and rehearsing how she would handle upcoming situations. Her whole life had become so focused on this problem that she no longer saw family or friends regularly and her life had become a sequence of working and preparing for work.

At this point it was clear to both counselor and client that a move to a parallel position in another company, even if it were available, would probably not be a success. After some work with psychometrics and some further discussion, Eleanor decided to request a return to her position as adjustor. She decided that she did not have the prerequisite personality for the supervisory position and that she saw no way that she could change or would want to change a lifetime of habit in her interpersonal style.

In this instance, the problem was primarily a *situational* one. The role of the counselor was that of helping the client understand how the onset of her unhappiness coincided with her change of situation. From there it was a matter of deciding how to best use the coping skills she possessed, which had served her well for many years. While it could be argued that the client could have changed in some ways that might have allowed her to maintain her supervisory position, she chose not to go in that direction. The counseling agenda focused on "How can I use what I am and be more fulfilled?"

Case of David (Developmental Problem)   David was a 27-year-old married furniture finisher. When he came to the counselor, he described himself as feeling "stuck" in his present job. It was not an unpleasant job in some ways—he enjoyed making good looking things. But he had been with the company since he dropped out of college seven years ago. College had been difficult because he was not sure what he wanted to do, shifting from engineering to anthropology to art. By contrast, the job had been stable, provided for his physical needs, and allowed him the independence from his family to marry his high school sweetheart. David, married and with no children, had married at the time of leaving college.

David told the counselor it seemed to him that he was not making enough of himself. He should be able to hold a professional job that he would feel proud of, he should be more sociable, and he should not be so crabby with his wife. Through further conversation it became clearer that he had never regarded his present job as the start of a career and that in an Eriksonian sense he had never really psychologically affiliated himself with the adult world. His present job was much like his summer jobs during high school and college.

His wife had been working for a local department store when they were married and over the years she had been promoted several times and now was manager of the women's clothing department of the main store. She felt well established in her career and made no secret of her comparisons between herself and David. He found it particularly difficult to socialize with her business associates and thought himself unsociable because he did not enjoy their company. Increasing conflict with his wife had contributed to his decision to seek counseling (though it was not stated as the presenting problem).

In this instance, David had mistaken the outward signs of maturing—full time job and marriage—for the real thing. Only after living for some time with his misconception did he begin to realize its emptiness. When he came to the counselor, he was ready to do some highly motivated work on defining who he was and what he wanted to do. He quickly reaffirmed feelings of worth that he was beginning to lose. He developed a career plan that satisfied both his interests and his need to be a professional person. He reembarked on a college program with new resolve.

Unfortunately, the relationship between David and his wife had become too encumbered by hurt to be restored. They separated, and David (who initially had stated that only his wife could make him happy) had begun dating other women by the time counseling concluded. At age 27 David had actively taken up the pursuit of his own development which had been in moratorium for seven years. The counselor working with David first had to develop some diagnostic conclusions. While two negative situations (job dissatisfaction and marital conflict) existed, counseling in a narrowly sectored way about those situations would have missed the essence of David's real malaise. Therefore, the counselor led David to work broadly on those aspects of his life which related to developing an adult identity which would allow him to recapture his self-esteem. The counseling agenda focused on the question, "How can I develop from where I am to become the person I want to be?"

Jeffrey (Debilitating Pathology)   Jeffrey was a 43-year-old single "manager" of a book store. Manager is placed in quotes since the presenting problem was that he carried the title of manager, but in fact no one would listen to him. The store was one of several owned by the family, and Jeffrey had been given his own store to manage upon completion of his Master of Business Administration degree at a prestigious university. However, his father retained control of most of the important business decisions, including the purchasing, pricing, and advertising. An accountant kept the books. This left mainly the day-to-day supervision of employees in the store as Jeffrey's most significant duty. Over time, the employees began to realize that Jeffrey could not make decisions when problems would arise, and they increasingly began calling his father at another store for decisions about routine matters. Jeffrey was motivated to seek counseling when he came to the realization that no one employed in the store paid any attention at all to what he said and that the store ran as well or better in his absence as when he was there.

Further exploration of Jeffrey's life revealed that he had always lived at home and still lived much as a child might. His mother chose all his clothing for him, cooked all his meals, and even supervised his bedtime and woke him in the mornings. He had never had close friends of either sex, had never dated. He described himself as uncomfortable in the presence of other people because he never knew what to say. He was bright and reasonably well read. In the structured situation of school, college, and graduate school he had been able to respond well enough to academic assignments to develop a reasonably good record. He was experiencing extreme distress about his job, because he knew he was really doing nothing useful and he felt degraded when employees ignored him.

While it was clear to the counselor that the client was both bright and educated, Jeffrey's style of presenting his problem approximated that of a ten-year-old boy. When the counselor probed the client's feelings about his living situation, it became clear that he had no real sense of the inappropriateness of what was occurring. Further, he seemed to have no anger at his father for "helping out" with managing the store. He seemed only to feel hurt that the employees ignored him.

In working with Jeffrey, the counselor concluded that he was far enough out of touch with the usual role of a man at mid-life that the helping process would be extensive. He was seriously distorting the real meanings of his failure. While he was experiencing a "situational" problem with his employees and while his present circumstances resulted from "developmental" deficits, his present state was dysfunctional in coping with the smallest details of looking after himself. His living environment continued to support his childlike approach to life. He was afraid to behave as an adult because he lacked the skills to do so.

Counseling in this instance included environmental manipulation, skills training, assertiveness training, and identity definition. The counseling questions were "Who am I, what can I become, how can I begin?" The client required supervision at every step as he began to try to learn the role of a man because he had suppressed most of the messages from the world outside his family which suggested the need for self-definition, valuing, and autonomous living. In many agencies a client such as Jeffrey would be referred for rehabilitative services in addition to therapy.

Two common themes in the cases recur in much of the counseling with adult clients. First, in all three cases the client's distress encompassed his or her work life and her or his personal life. Freud talked about disturbances of work and love as sources of human suffering, and if one interprets both terms broadly the statement seems profoundly true of most adult clients who seek counseling. They report disappointment in their ability to fulfill their expectations in creative work and/or they report an inability to relate satisfactorily to significant others. Frequently dysfunction in one arena impinges upon the other; improvement in one arena leads to improvement in the other. These generalizations seem to hold true whether the issues are situational, developmental, or pathological, even though progress is quickest with situational problems and slowest with pathological patterns of behavior.

A second theme common to each case is that of the client's ability to deal with authority issues. Eleanor shrank from the authority role of supervising others, even though she was able to function quite adequately in her role as adjustor where her decisions could be based on clearly stated regulations. David and Jeffrey, while very different, shared a tendency to relate dependently with significant others long past the time when it is typical for adults to establish independence and develop a new readiness for interdependence.

Still another response to authority, not illustrated in these cases, is the hostile response. This response is found in persons who become so angered by authority that they are unable to accept the most rudimentary structuring or supervision from family, friends, or employer. Such persons frequently experience repeated dismissals from their employment, as well as stormy personal lives. Whether dependent or hostile, inappropriate responses to authority frequently create for a client situations where he or she is not in control. Causation is usually found in the relationships to significant others during the formative years. The finishing of unfinished business is an important part of freeing the client to begin to behave differently.

It is important for the counselor to understand the factors that are contributing to the client's distress. The distress may be related to an impending role transition, to vocational dysfunction, to interpersonal conflict, etc. It is equally important that the counselor make some choices with the client about which issues to work on. Bochnek (1976) makes the point that there are times when underlying psychopathology may be ignored or minimized in developmental counseling. Counseling can focus on changing particular situations or behaviors which will help the client gain more life satisfaction without addressing all psychopathology. Thus in the case of Eleanor, no attempt was made to help her assume a supervisory role more comfortably. In the case of Jeffrey, it was not possible to compensate for all past deprivation. In both cases, decisions were made or skills were developed that helped the client live a more satisfying life, while leaving certain stones unturned. It is not possible to decide which stones to turn unless one is aware of the stones. Along with an understanding of adult development, a structure for diagnostic assessment helps the counselor get beyond the surface material presented by the client and to underlying motivations and aspirations upon which future planning can be built.

Interactive Process

Counseling with any individual will involve an interactive process based on certain fundamental principles of counseling. The precepts outlined in chapter one serve to describe important attributes of the counseling process. The content of counseling with adults will differ in certain respects from the content of counseling with children or adolescents. The adult client has more experience and typically is in a life position where there is greater pressure to assume responsibility for decisions, actions, and interpersonal behavior.

The interactive process with adults can be based on a generic model of helping such as that of Egan (1975). His model for counseling includes three stages wherein the client is expected to begin with self-exploration, move to deeper levels of self-understanding, and finally to develop a plan for action.

During Stage I of the counseling, the counselor encourages self-exploration by offering a helping relationship characterized by empathic understanding, genuineness, and respect (Rogers, 1965). These are "receiving" skills and they are undergirded by concreteness—a focus on real happenings and their consequences. While offering these conditions the counselor of the adult client begins to look diagnostically for the salient issues of adult development that relate to the client's presenting concerns.

During this exploration process the client will inevitably describe past life experiences. The counselor should help her or him differentiate conditions of the past from conditions of the present so that a clearer understanding of attitudes, goals, and behaviors may emerge. In the case of Jeffrey, it became clear that his goal of being treated as a responsible adult was negated by his present behaviors originally designed to meet the conditions of childhood. Frequently problems involving adults in relationship to their parents result from an inability on the part of one party or the other to separate the past with its dependency relationship from the present where a dependency relationship is dysfunctional.

Clients with unresolved authority issues may try to manipulate the counselor into parental kinds of behavior, displaying either hostility (toward "the system" or the counselor) or dependency (seeking solutions from the counselor.) During the first stage of counseling it is important to build trust, but at the same time to help the client focus on concrete concerns about which she or he personally must make decisions.

Egan describes Stage II of counseling as the time when the counselor begins to use the trust that has been built to get involved more potently in helping the client understand himself or herself. The counselor now responds not just to what the client says but also to what he or she implies. Confrontation is used to help the client see parts of his or her story that are in conflict with one another (e. g., "I want my adult children to move out, but as a good mother I cannot ask them to leave.")

The counselor might at this stage help a client to "reclaim" a part of himself or herself that had been left behind at an earlier period in life (Passons, 1975.) Such reclaimed qualities can lead to changes in careers, addition of fulfilling leisure activities, and even new decisions about marriage and lifestyle.

Many clients at this stage discover that they have "unfinished business" that continues to sap their energies from new pursuits. David, for example, was unable to become comfortable with his goal of becoming an artist in part because he continued to respond to parental tapes that urged him to develop a more pragmatic career. He defined success in his father's terms and yet was unwilling to spend his life achieving that kind of success. He had to finish that business before he could develop his own new standard of success.

Learning from the past is another element of self-understanding that becomes an important part of the counseling process. Eleanor rediscovered her happiness by contrasting the recent past with an earlier period and coming to an understanding that she needed to move from the supervisory role to resolve her problem.

During Stage II of counseling, the counselor becomes more active in talking about the immediate relationship between himself or herself and the client. This talk may include active discussion of any hostility or dependency that may be impeding the client's progress.

In the process of developing increased self-understanding, the client at this stage should also be able to formulate any goals which would lead to more satisfactory living (e.g., "I want to get my adult children to move out and still feel okay about myself as a mother."). Some clients may be finished with counseling at the conclusion of Stage II. Having experienced both catharsis and clarification of their issues, they may well have discovered latent strength and skills to cope more effectively with their lives.

Stage III is a planning stage, a time when the counselor provides support for the client to begin actions on his or her own behalf. A decision-making scheme should undergird this work and many appear in the literature of counseling. A particularly useful decision-making format designed for use by adult women is *How to Decide* (Scholtz, Prince, and Miller, 1975), an adaptation of the format used in decision-making materials developed earlier for adolescents. Fundamentally, however, all the decision-making models are an adaptation of the scientific method:

1. State the problem clearly.
2. Collect relevant information.
3. Generate a set of alternatives.
4. Test the alternatives for possible consequences.
5. Conclude which of the alternatives will be helpful.

It is important to restate that the process of planning with adults is not different from the process of planning with adolescent clients. However, the issues are related to the time in life of the client and often have to do with either work or marital concerns.

At the information step of the planning process, the counselor of adults needs a good knowledge of career search and career change literature. A new perspective on career search (Huldane, 1975; Bolles, 1975) that has recently emerged is particularly relevant for adults. It is a strategy that urges the client to decide exactly what he or she wants to do and where. Then the client is helped to develop a self-marketing strategy to increase the likelihood of gaining the attention of a particular set of employers. This is in contrast to the older practice of going from place to place to determine whether an opening exists that one might fill. The proponents cite a high success rate in helping clients find meaningful career-oriented positions.

Egan's Stage III in the counseling process looks very much like Frank Parson's turn-of-the-century model: That durability, instead of indicating outdatedness, seems to indicate a nearly universal need for people to receive planning help at certain times in their lives. However, the modern perspective on helping devotes much more energy to the processes of problem-definition and self-understanding as readiness steps for planning.

Emphasis in the helping process will be related to the client issues identified and classified in the diagnostic process. A client who is experiencing a concern that is primarily situational will move fairly rapidly through Stages I and II and will devote the majority of counseling time to considering the workability of various alternative ways of coping with the situation. Counseling is usually short term. The client whose coping skills are adequate for normal living may still experience a stagnation in his or her development. In that instance counseling will focus very heavily on Stage II, so that reachable new goals may be identified, and Stages I and III serve their usual functions of getting the problem defined and the development of strategies for implementing the new goals. Counseling will usually conclude after 10 to 15 sessions. With a client who is so confused that he or she cannot even communicate the essence of his or her concern, then extensive work at all three stages of counseling will be necessary. Distortion of reality and dysfunctional behavior is usually very evident with clients in this category. Counseling is usually long-term.

Helping the Adult Client: Synopsis

The adult client is frequently well motivated for counseling. He or she is often self-referred and enters counseling with the desire to make changes in his or her life. Life experiences usually have been cumulative and provide a breadth of potential strength, as well as the potential for debilitating beliefs and attitudes. It is important that the counselor meet the adult client with a readiness to consider any alternative, taking the client's age into account without allowing age bias to interfere with the work.

The helping process involves effective diagnostic work to determine the nature and extent of the client's concerns. Based on his or her knowledge of the salient issues of adulthood, the counselor is able to assess whether the client's concern is primarily situational, primarily developmental, or primarily pathological. Treatment plans are developed accordingly, so that with some clients the work is primarily planning, with others developing a deeper level of self-understanding and goal directedness, and with still others reordering fundamental beliefs about themselves and their world.

Questions for Further Inquiry

1. Taking as an example some transition that you have experienced in the past, analyze that transition and your adaptation to it.

2. Identify an adult you know whom you regard as "immature." What is the basis for your impressions? How do your impressions relate to the principles of adult development in this chapter?

3. How can a counselor assess whether a client is experiencing a transition as a crisis?

4. Describe the qualities that constitute the good "life" for a 25-year-old person you know. For a 45-year-old person you know.

5. What are the emotional effects of "unfinished business"? How may a counselor help a client work through "unfinished business"?

References

Bocknek, G. A developmental approach to counseling adults. *The Counseling Psychologist* 1976 *6*(1), 37–40.

Bolles, R. N. *What color is your parachute?* Berkely: Tenn Speed Press, 1975.

Brim, O. G. Jr. Theories of male mid-life crisis. *The Counseling Psychologist* 1976 *6*(1), 2–9.

Britton, J. H., & Britton, J. O. *Personality changes in aging*. New York: Springer, 1972.

Cummings, E., & Henry, W. E. *Growing old*. New York: Basic Books, 1961.

Egan, G. *The skilled helper*. Monterey, Calif.: Brooks-Cole, 1975.

Erikson, E. H. *Childhood and society*. New York: Norton, 1963.

Huldane, B. *How to make a habit of success*. Washington: Acropolis Books, 1975.

Lawton, M. Powell. Clinical psychology? In C. Eisdorfer, and M. P. Lawton (Eds.), *The psychology of adult development and aging.* Washington: APA, 1973.

Levinson, D. J., Darrow, C. M., Klein, E. B., Levinson, M. H. & McKee, B. Period in the adult development of men: Ages 18 to 45. *The Counseling Psychologist* 1976 *6*(1), 21–25.

Lowenthal, M. F., & Weiss, L. Intimacy and crisis in adulthood. *The Counseling Psychologist* 1976 *6*(1), 10–15.

Neugarten, B. L. The psychology of the aging: An overview. *Master Lectures on Developmental Psychology*. Washington, D.C.: Journal Abstract Supplement Service, American Psychological Association 1976.(a)

Neugarten, B. L. Adaptation and the life cycle. *The Counseling Psychologist* 1976 *6*(1), 16–20.(b)

Neugarten, B. L., Havighurst, R. J., & Tobin, S. S.. Personality and patterns of aging. In B. L. Neugarten (Ed.), *Middle age and aging*. Chicago: University of Chicago Press, 1968.

Neugarten, B. L., Wood, V., Kraines, R. J., and Loomis, B. Women's attitudes toward the menopause, *Vita Humana* 1963 *6,* 140–51.

Passons, W. R. *Gestalt approaches in counseling*. New York: Holt, Rinehart, 1975.

Patterson, L. E. Girls' careers: Expression of identify. *Vocational Guidance Quarterly 1973 21*(4), 269–75.

Rogers, C. R. The interpersonal relationship: Core of guidance. In Mosher et al. (Eds.), *Guidance: An examination*. New York: Harcourt, Brace & World, 1965.

Schlossberg, N. K. The case for counseling adults. *The Counseling Psychologist* 1976 *6*(1), 33–36.

Scholz, N. T., Prince, J. S., & Miller, G. P. *How to decide: A guide for women*. New York: CEEB, 1975.

Schuttenberg, E. M. Androgyny: New focus for graduate professional education. In *Improving college and university teaching yearbook*. Oregon State University, 1975.

Sheehy, G. *Passages*. New York: E. P. Dutton, 1974.

Super, D. E., & Overstreet, P. L. *The vocational maturity of ninth grade boys*. New York: Teachers College Bureau of Publications, 1960.

Troll, L. E., & Nowak, C. How old are you?—The question of age bias in the counseling of adults. *The Counseling Psychologist* 1976 *6*(1), 41–44.

Effective Helping with Women   13

NANCY K. SCHLOSSBERG
LAURA KENT

Introduction

> The women's revolution ... is a social convulsion of a magnitude hitherto
> unknown in human history. It both reflects and portends cataclysmic changes
> in basic structures and processes of society and in the psyches of individual
> men and women. ... [But] changed or changing perceptions of the self and
> society generate new sources of conflict and ambivalence and of guilt and
> shame as well as new sources of motivation and new patterns of aspiration.
> (Westervelt, 1973, pp. 3–4)

"You've come a long way, baby," runs the familiar advertising slogan. It is undenia-
ble that in recent years women have made sizable advances in many areas, while
treading water in others. Whatever progress they have made can be attributed to
a variety of factors: general demographic trends; broad social upheavals such as
the Civil Rights Movement (which awakened public awareness to the injustices
inflicted on racial minorities and made inevitable the analogy between the condition of blacks and that of women); and the student unrest of the 1960s (which gave
young women some experience with and taste for political action, even as it
revealed the sexism of their male compatriots); the pioneering efforts of individual
women; and a mass of federal legislation, including the Equal Pay Act of 1963, Title
VII of the Civil Rights Act of 1964, the Equal Employment Opportunity Act of 1972,

and Title IX of the Education Amendments of 1972, all intended to assure greater equity for women, both educationally and occupationally.

Government and private enterprise have undertaken action to eliminate, or at least lower, many *structural* or *institutional barriers,* defined as those "organizational patterns and practices ... which hinder or halt" the development and achievement of women (Roby, 1972). Examples of such action are the extension of better credit terms to women, the abolition of antinepotism regulations, and the treatment of pregnancy as a disability to be covered by health insurance and sick-leave policies. As structural barriers are being changed, however, the question remains: Are the internal barriers that previously prevented women from developing to their full potential breaking down? On this, the evidence is only indirect.

For instance, over the years the proportion of entering freshmen agreeing with the statement "the activities of married women are best confined to the home and family" has declined steadily from 66.5 percent of the men and 44.3 of the women in 1967 to 36.8 percent of the men and 19.5 percent of the women in 1976; whereas the proportion agreeing that "women should receive the same salary and opportunities for advancement as men in comparable positions" has gradually climbed from 76.5 percent of the men and 87.1 percent of the women in 1970 to 88.2 percent of the men and 96.1 of the women in 1976 (Astin, Panos, and Creager, 1967; American Council on Education, 1971; Astin, King, and Richardson, 1976). Similarly, considerable evidence exists to indicate that young women are less restricted in their occupational aspirations and their choice of life styles than their mothers were. On another front, among entering freshmen 57 percent of the men but only 8 percent of the women had taken four years of mathematics in high school; thus, over 9 in 10 entering female freshmen were disqualified from taking the calculus sequence in college which excludes them from 15 out of 20 possible majors (Tobias and Donady, 1977). Thus, few women end up working as architects, accountants, business managers, research scientists, and bankers.

In short, as indicated in the quotation from Westervelt, major changes seem to be occurring at both the social and the individual level, while at the same time remnants of past sex stereotyping remain. To define the current status of women as a group, a more detailed but still necessarily brief review of areas in which change has occurred, as well as areas in which no change has taken place, is in order. After this overview, some of the special problems and concerns that may bring women to a counselor for help are identified. The next section presents a model that should be useful for the counselor in helping women. Some of the implications for counseling are summarized in the concluding section.

Between Two Worlds

The major demographic changes that are currently affecting the lives of women are summarized in the following statement by Jean Lipman-Blumen:

Women are living longer, marrying later and less often, remarrying less frequently, having and expecting to have fewer children and more often planning
to have no children. . . . The divorce rate has continued to climb steeply. . . .
More often than in the past, both young and older women are living alone. . . .
(Women) are heading families more often . . . more women are remaining
childless, . . . but postponement, rather than a permanent rejection, of child-
bearing (seems to be the rule) (Lipman-Blumen, 1977, pp. 11–13).

Thus, many of our sex stereotypes are clearly a distortion of the real world. Women
are no longer confined to the roles of wife, mother, and homemaker; and even
those who adopt these roles do so for shorter periods of their lives. Less than a
century ago, a marriage was usually terminated by the death of one of the partners
about two years before the youngest child had left the parental home; today, the
parents are often still relatively young when the last child leaves the nest, and they
face a "postparental period" lasting as long as twenty years, during which they are
alone together again. Some couples apparently find this period to be a "second
honeymoon" that allows for the reawakening of an intimacy lost when adolescent
children were present in the house, whereas other couples find the postparental
period traumatic, especially after the husband retires and is home "under foot" all
day.

Since the life expectancy of women is greater than that of men, and since
most men marry women a few years younger than themselves, the death of a
spouse is more frequently an experience of women than of men. Because of
differential treatment of the sexes in most pension and retirement plans, the widow
is more likely than the widower to face financial deprivation in the later years of
life. Susan Ross, an attorney for a group of women filing a complaint against
Columbia University, made the following point:

If a man and a woman, each making $20,000 a year, both enroll in the
university's pension plan at age 30, and $250 a month is paid into the plan
for each person until retirement at age 65, the man will receive $2,750 more
per year in retirement benefits than his female colleague. (AAC, March, 1977,
p. 3)

In other words, a woman is penalized because some women live longer and some
men die earlier, though over four in five men and women who live past age 85 have
common death ages.

What is not generally recognized is that half of all widows in the United States,
not counting those who have remarried, are under age 60 (Lopata, 1973). In
addition, many women find themselves facing life as divorcees—one estimate
holds that, in 1971, two in five marriages ended in divorce (Weiss, 1975)—and
though the divorce rate continues to climb, the remarriage rate has leveled off and
even declined somewhat. Partly as a consequence of these trends, the number
of families headed by women has risen; in 1972 families with female heads constituted 14 percent of all families with children, an increase of 40 percent over the
1960 figure. Many of these female-headed families live much closer to poverty

than average, with a median annual income of only $4,000 in 1972, as compared with a median annual income of $11,600 for all families with children under age 18 (Lipman-Blumen, 1977).

Another trend to be noted is that more young people are delaying marriage and choosing to live alone, a pattern that is having serious effects on housing construction, rental rates, and retail sales; since 1970, the number of young adults living by themselves has increased 145 percent for men and 119 percent for women (Reinhold, 1977).

The point of all these statistics is the common image of women as being always protected and cared for by men-the-breadwinners is outmoded. Many women of all ages are on their own and must provide for themselves. Many others are married but find they have to work to supplement the family income or choose to work because they have fewer or no children to occupy them.

Occupational Status

And just how are women faring in the world of work? Again, some statistics are in order. Nine out of every ten females will work at some time in their lives (U.S. Department of Labor, June 1975). Today, women constitute about 40 percent of American workers, and their labor force participation has risen steadily over the last several decades. In 1975, 45.6 percent of all women age 16 and over were in the labor force. More women are entering and remaining in the labor force after they get married and have children; and many women in the 45–64 age group are remaining in the labor force, and in some cases even entering it for the first time or re-entering after a long absence (Lipman-Blumen, 1977).

But despite this "flood of women into jobs," which Eli Ginsberg has labeled "the single most outstanding phenomenon of our century" and one with "long-term implications that are absolutely unchartable" (Bird, 1976), women as a group tend to be confined to low-paying, low-status jobs. According to one recent report, "the median yearly salary for full-time employment for women is $6772 compared with $11,835 for men" (Swift, 1977, p. 14). Women constitute only 2.3 percent of the workers who make over $25,000 a year. They continue to predominate in the traditionally female-typed occupations of clerical work, nursing, and teaching. Many are confined to what one author has termed "pink-collar ghettos"—beauty shops, restaurants, department stores, offices—where they often work for minimum wages, typically taking orders rather than giving them (Howe, 1977). Those in blue-collar jobs generally work as factory operatives, where again the pay is low. The higher-level professions and the managerial positions continue to be dominated by men. Thus, in 1970, women constituted only 4.9 percent of lawyers and judges and only 1.5 percent of engineers (Lipman-Blumen, 1977).

In the 1975–76 academic year about one in four full-time instructional faculty members in the nation's academic institutions was a woman, but only one in ten holding the rank of full professor was female, compared with two in five at the instructor level, the lowest step on the academic ladder (American Council on Education, 1976). Women are also poorly represented at the administrative levels in the educational system: In 1974 women accounted for about two in three elementary and secondary school teachers, but only 15 percent of school principals were women (Niedermeyer and Kramer, 1974). The vast majority of people in top administrative positions at the college level are male; women constitute only about 16 percent of the total group, tend to be concentrated in positions relating to student affairs and external affairs or to be deans of nursing and home economics and head librarians, and earn only about 80 percent as much as men with the same job title at the same type of institutions (Van Alstyne et al., 1977). Of people who have doctorates in science, unemployment rates are higher among women than among men, and those women who are employed are less likely than their male counterparts to work in prestigious colleges and in private industry and tend to advance less rapidly (Vetter, 1976).

In short, the world of work is still a man's world in that men are less likely than women to suffer unemployment, are most likely to occupy top positions, and are paid higher salaries whatever their position. Women, now as in the past, are concentrated in "helping" fields and tend to be subordinates and assistants.

Nonetheless, signs of change are everywhere; women are making breakthroughs in the world of work (although the recent economic recession in this country and the consequent freeze on new hiring in many fields has undoubtedly slowed their progress) and are gradually beginning to enter the male domain. For instance, between 1960 and 1970, the numbers of women increased by more than 5,000 in each of the following male-dominated occupations in the skilled trades: auto mechanic, carpenter, compositor and typesetter, dental laboratory technician, electrician, heavy equipment mechanic, machinist, painter, printing press operator, telephone installer and repairer (Hedges and Bemis, 1974). In 1940, only 9 percent of real estate agents and brokers were women; by 1973 the figure had risen to 36 percent. The proportion of bartenders who are female went from 2.5 percent in 1940 to 30 percent in 1973 (Waldman and McEaddy, 1974).

Moreover, more women are becoming self-employed, usually in retail trade and in businesses providing personal services (beauty shops, child care services, laundries), though some run professional services such as nursing homes. In 1940 women constituted only 17 percent of all self-employed people; in 1973 that figure had risen to 26 percent; the increase in absolute numbers was about 75 percent (Waldman and McEaddy, 1974).

Conversely, more men are entering fields traditionally reserved for women. Thus, in 1974, United Air Lines employed about 450 male flight attendants out of approximately 7,200. In the first ten months of 1973 nearly 75 percent of the new clerical personnel hired at AT&T were men; and the number of male telephone operators tripled during the same period ("Now 'Men's Lib' Is the Trend," 1974). The number of entering male freshmen who plan to go into nursing increased 246 percent between 1966 and 1974, compared with an increase of only 115 percent in the number of entering female freshmen with these career plans (Holmstrom, Knepper, and Kent, 1976).

Educational Status

Educational patterns are changing as well, and since education is still the principal means whereby a person gains entry to higher-status jobs, these changes are hopeful. Now as in the past, females are successively "cooled out" at each higher level of the educational system. Thus, boys and girls enter the school system in approximately equal numbers, and the sex distribution remains about the same up until age 17. In 1974 high-school dropout rates were higher among black girls than among black boys, whereas the dropout rate among whites was about the same for both sexes (U.S. Department of Health, Education, and Welfare, 1976, Table 60). In 1973–74 slightly more girls than boys graduated from high school, though in the past female graduates more heavily outnumbered male graduates; this shift is attributable to generally lower attrition rates at the high school level (DHEW, 1976, Table 59). Of 1973–74 high school seniors who planned to work full-time rather than go on to college, 48 percent of the girls but only 28 percent of the boys gave marriage plans as their reason (DHEW, 1976, Table 62).

Scholastically, girls do better than boys until puberty. Most authorities agree that any drop in girls' achievement at that point is attributable to the effects of sex-role socialization rather than to a diminution in ability. Though women are less likely to go on to college than are men, those who do enter post-secondary education usually have better academic records than their male counterparts. For instance, among first-time, full-time freshmen entering the nation's colleges and universities in 1976, close to half of the women, but only one in three men, had high-school grade averages of B+ or better. Moreover, for this same group, women were just as likely as men to rate themselves as above average in academic ability and drive to achieve, though substantially less likely to rate themselves high on mathematical ability, mechanical ability, and intellectual self-confidence (Astin, King, and Richardson, 1976).

Women are much less likely than men to go on to graduate and professional schools, and those who do enroll are more likely to fail to complete the degree. Nonetheless, looking at long-range trends, one finds grounds for optimism. At the freshmen level, the gap between the sexes with respect to degree aspirations has narrowed: In 1966, 55.3 percent of the men but only 39.8 percent of the women planned to get a master's, doctoral, or professional degree, a difference of 15.5 percentage points; in 1976, 52.7 percent of the men and 46.5 percent of the women planned to get these advanced degrees, a difference of only 6.2 percentage points. Moreover, women among entering college freshmen are more likely to plan on careers in nontraditional fields such as law, medicine, engineering, and business: 19.4 percent in 1976, compared with 5.9 percent in 1966. Women have also become more likely to value such "male" goals as becoming an authority in their field, obtaining recognition from colleagues, having administrative responsibility over others, and being very well-off financially; and they are slightly less likely to give high priority to the "female" goal of raising a family: A goal endorsed by 56.8 percent of the women and 57.5 percent of the men in 1976 (Astin, Panos, and Creager, 1966; Astin, King, and Richardson, 1976).

In 1964–65 women were awarded 42.4 percent of the bachelor's degrees, 33.8 percent of the master's degrees, 10.8 percent of the doctorates, and 3.5 percent of the first-professional degrees; in 1974–75, the comparative figures were 45.3 percent, 44.8 percent, 21.3 percent, and 12.4 percent, respectively (Eiden, 1976). Between 1970–71 and 1974–75 the absolute number of women earning doctorates increased by 59 percent, compared with a decrease of 2.6 percent among men; and the number of women earning first-professional degrees rose by 180 percent, compared with a modest 37.4 percent increase for men (DHEW, 1977).

The Total Picture

Another encouraging indication of the breakdown of sex-typing in education, in employment, in life styles generally is the considerable attention given by the media to women and men who have vaulted the barriers. Women employed as jockeys, firefighters, zoo keepers, construction workers, police officers, and stock-brokers are featured in special reports on TV news programs and in mass-audience magazines such as the Sunday supplement *Parade.* Men who have elected to drop out of the world of work in order to become homemakers and to spend more time with their children are equally regarded as newsworthy. Part of this attention is no doubt attributable to the media's continuing search for novelty, but it can also be taken as both the cause and the result of greater public acceptance of "deviation" from conventional sex roles.

In looking at the total picture, then, one must conclude that, at this point, women as a group are in a transitional stage. The norms that operated in the past have lost much of their potency. But it is equally clear that our society has not yet reached a point where women have achieved equality or where individuals of both sexes can freely develop their full human potential. We are betwixt-and-between, at the moment, or to use Matthew Arnold's more poetic phrasing, we are "Wandering between two worlds, one dead,/The other powerless to be born" (Arnold, 1855).

Special Problems of Women

The transition which women as a group—and indeed society as a whole—are experiencing is a painful one, though it holds promise of a future condition that will be both more satisfying and more just. It is painful, even shattering, to find that the old norms and standards no longer hold, that one has to find new values to replace them, that one even has to redefine one's own self and roles. Obviously, individuals vary considerably not only in the degree to which they fear and resist change, clinging defiantly to the old myths—or, conversely, the degree to which they welcome and accept change, becoming its advocates and champions, pioneering the "brave new world"—but even in the degree to which they recognize that change is taking place and that traditional notions of what constitutes "femininity" and appropriate roles for women conflict with new ideologies. The situation is by no means a well-defined, clear-cut choice between alternatives. Even those who declare themselves firmly to belong to one camp or the other may experience problems in working out the details of their lives. The special problems that confront women as a group at this point can be summed up in three key terms: ambiguity, overloading, and sense of powerlessness.

Ambiguity

The problem of ambiguity and the feelings of ambivalence that it breeds goes deeper than the overt conflict between traditional and feminist ideas and values, though it has its beginnings there. Most of us have been socialized to accept traditional values and norms. This is as true of younger as of older women since the traditional view received particularly heavy emphasis in the two decades following World War II (Westervelt, 1973) when the vast majority of American middle-class white women lived the lives described so vividly by Betty Friedan in *The Feminine Mystique* (1963)—submerged in suburban domesticity, functioning chiefly as consumers of goods and producers of children. Even women who did not challenge the existing sex-role stratification system, according to which women always occupy the lower-valued positions, were nonetheless subjected to some degree of status inconsistency in their multiple roles as wives, homemakers, and mothers. Indeed, these traditional roles are themselves inherently ambiguous, ostensibly calling for passivity, dependence, weakness, and softness, but actually requiring initiative, leadership, strength, and toughness.

As some women openly rebelled against this existence and gathered followers to their cause, and as a greater number of "ordinary" women entered the world of work, the situation changed. Now it is generally regarded as "okay" for women to have careers, to compete (to some extent) with men, to develop as human beings. When Gary Trudeau's character Joanie Caucus (who, after twenty stultifying years of marriage, became a liberated woman and went out on her own) finally graduated from law school, her fictional achievement sufficiently captured the imagination that her name was included on the list of law school graduates read out at the University of California's Boalt Law School commencement services, and this event was duly noted by the *Washington Post.*

But what other messages are women getting from the media? As was mentioned previously, both television and the press give a fair amount of coverage to "newsworthy" women. Moreover, the film industry is finally turning its attention to female characters. Jane Wilson remarks: "Credible female life has hardly been a noticeable feature of American movies in recent years, . . . but now, all of a sudden, there is a rush of movies in varying states of preparation in which women are presented as real people involved in a gamut of relationships" (Wilson, 1977, p. 1).

But these apparent triumphs for the women's movement are only part of the picture. Various critics—for instance, Leslie Fiedler and Kate Millett—have commented on the sexist bias in much of Western art and culture. In English and American literature, for instance, women are usually minor characters and are depicted according to polarities: the Saint or the Witch, the Madonna or the Whore, the Earth Mother or the Castrator. In those instances where they are given heroic dimensions, their suffering or resistance to fate is passive; in those instances where they have power, that power tends to be malign (Stimpson, 1976). The quest for identity differs according to the sex of the character:

> Male characters defy authority in order to become just, humane authorities themselves. . . . The narrative of the growth of self is one of justified resistance, rebellion, and self-creation. Anger is proof of strength sufficient for necessary independence. Female characters, on the other hand, evade evil authority in order to submit to and to support righteous authority. . . . The narrative of growth of self is one of adolescent pride and resistance, but eventual submission. Anger is, at best, proof of stubbornness (Stimpson, 1976, p. 224).

The more popular contemporary media—films and television—have not done much better by their female characters. Consider, for example, two recent movie characters that won Academy Awards for the actresses portraying them: Big Nurse in *One Flew Over the Cuckoo's Nest* and Diana Christensen in *Network.* The former is the stereotype of the castrating female, the malign black witch. As the head nurse in the psychiatric ward, she holds a position of power which she gravely abuses, driving Billy Babbit to suicide, provoking McMurphy's attack on her, thereby bringing about his total dehumanization through prefrontal lobotomy. The only other female characters in the film are the subordinate nurses, who are presented as aspiring Big Nurses, and several amiable but mindless prostitutes. The character Diane Christensen has been called a "grotesque parody of a liberated career woman" (Wilson, 1977), a "psychopath in skirts" (Feldman, 1977). She is more cold-blooded in her pursuit of success than any of the male characters in the film, more totally absorbed in the manipulative world of big-business television, more emotionally sterile in her relations with other people. She even talks dirtier than anyone else. What kind of message does the movie audience get from seeing such characters on the silver screen? At the very least, they learn that women are unsuited to positions of power, that authority makes them unfeminine and destructive, that the pursuit of achievement warps and sours them. Even the much more sympathetic portrayal of a woman's quest for identity and independence in *Alice Doesn't Live Here Any More,* which won Ellen Burstyn an Academy Award the previous year, leaves the viewer with a feeling that Alice can only be a full and satisfied person if she attaches herself to a man.

And what of television, which has a so-far-unmeasured but indubitably heavy impact on most American lives? The latest figures indicate that the television set is turned on for an average of six hours a day, that the adult male watches it three hours a day, the adult female about four, and the children about five hours (with viewing time peaking at about age 12) (Lipman-Blumen, 1977). Again, the messages are ambiguous.

Maude is clearly a liberated woman, but few women in the audience would choose to emulate her stridency and abrasiveness. Edith Bunker, of *All in the Family,* has her rare moments of assertiveness for which she is usually cheered by the audience, but only because she has reassured them by her otherwise steadfastly dependent and subordinate status. *Laverne and Shirley* are similar throwbacks to an earlier brand of comedy. *Rhoda* is both appealing and assertive; but apparently the writers and producers of that show felt that the options open to them for writing around a character who was both married and pursuing a career were too limiting and so have forced a separation.

The long-time success and much-mourned demise of the *Mary Tyler Moore* show may awaken hope in feminist hearts: Here was a woman, sexually attractive but wholesome, in her mid-thirties, moderately successful in her career as TV-news producer, and apparently quite happy with her singlehood. But, as Wilson points out, Mary Richards was at heart a "denmother," playing a nurturant and supportive role to the other characters in the show: "the perfect, undemanding, all-give-and-no-take combination of old and new womanhood" (Wilson, 1977, p. 24).

Television commercials arouse equally ambivalent feelings. Though more effort is being spent to show women engaged in other than household duties— e.g., riding motorcycles, working outside the home (though usually in offices or as Avon representatives)—the majority of commericals still rely on the stereotypes: women as sex objects, whose protein-enriched hair, mint-fresh breath, and smudge-proof eyeshadow causes men to lust after them; or women as domestic drudges, who spend their time comparing laundry detergents, squeezing toilet paper, and worrying about their family's intake of fiber.

Overloading

The ambiguity of the messages that women are now receiving from the society around them leads to a second major problem: that of overloading. Uncertain about whether to play the old roles of supportive wife, understanding mother, and competent homemaker or the new roles of career woman (or simply wage-earner) and independent human being, many women find themselves trying to take on *all* these roles.

Popular checkout-counter magazines such as *Women's Day* and *Family Circle* urge their readers to perform miracles: to prepare low-budget, nutritious, yet exciting meals; to become informed consumers of everything from cars through packaged foods to health services; to keep themselves attractive through diet, exercise, easy-to-care-for hairstyles, and clothes that "say something important about *you*"; to keep abreast of current events; to be active in community affairs; and to demonstrate their skills through macramé, flower arrangement, vegetable gardening, bread baking, crepe making, and minor repair work on household appliances. Indeed, it seems ironic that, just at the point when modern technology has relieved women of much of the burden of keeping house and when they are urged to expand their interests beyond the kitchen, bedroom, and family room, the do-it-yourself craze has come into being, creating yet more busywork for the conscientious woman.

Striving to fulfill these various mandates, many women are unable to to arrange their priorities. Trying to be all things to all people, they can satisfy no one, particularly not themselves. Experiencing failure at everything they undertake, some may even suffer breakdowns.

Sense of Powerlessness

It is no wonder, then, that—

> Neurasthenic neurosis has been called "the young housewife's syndrome," and by far the majority of people in this category are women. The neurasthenic is "tired all the time." Even small chores require a major effort. Mental concentration is difficult. . . . Frequently, [the neurasthenic] is overdependent on others, and also hostile to them, for she regards them as being the source of her problems (McCormick and Carter, 1977, p. 139).

Of course, only some women respond to the inner conflicts resulting from ambiguity and overloading by becoming neurotic. Nonetheless, evidence indicates that women are more frequently treated for mental illness than men are and, in addition, are more vulnerable to certain kinds of mental disorder. Specifically, findings show that:

1. Married women "suffer far greater mental-health hazards and present a far worse clinical picture" than do married men (Bernard, 1972, p. 28).
2. "Comparing single men and women, . . . it is the women who show up well and men poorly" with respect to mental health (Bernard, 1972, pp. 30–31).
3. "Women are more depressed than men. Young, poor women who head single-parent families and young married mothers who work in low-level jobs show the greatest rise in the national rate of depressive symptoms" (Guttentag and Salasin, 1976, p. 153).

The most plausible explanation for the greater incidence of depression among women—and especially among married women, women with children, and low-income women—is not that women differ biologically from men nor that women are more willing to admit distress and to seek treatment. Rather, the explanation is psychosocial. According to Dohrenwend (1973) and others, life-event stresses, whether positive or negative, have an additive effect; if the individual experiences too many such stresses within a given period, her or his physical and mental health may be impaired. Seligman (1974) uses the term "learned helplessness," a feeling that he believes triggers depression. Discussing Seligman's theory, Guttentag and Salasin (1976) state:

> The etiology of a particular depression . . . includes a past history of learned helplessness which creates susceptibility in the individual. In addition, there are some current situations of helplessness which are the immediate environmental agents for depression (p. 172).

Combining these two theories, one gets some insight into why women—and especially certain groups of women—are more prone to depressive symptoms. Not only are they buffeted by heavy stresses in their lives, but also they have been taught to be helpless. From their earliest years, girls are socialized to be dependent and affiliative, boys to be independent and initiative. Boys are taught to achieve directly, through mastery of the environment; girls are taught to achieve vicariously.

> A vicarious achievement orientation involves finding personal fulfillment through a relationship with another, through the activities and qualities of another individual with whom the vicarious achiever, to some degree, identifies (Lipman-Blumen and Leavitt, 1977, p. 61).

Women are traditionally taught to identify with the dominant man in their lives: at first, their fathers, later their husbands. Indeed a married woman's very identity is defined by her husband; she takes his name and she is characteristically described in terms of his occupation and socioeconomic class. The married woman is "helpless" in that one condition of a traditional marriage is her acknowledgement that she is dependent on the man; the married woman who finds herself divorced or widowed is even more helpless in that she has never learned how to function independently. Though these rigid patterns of sex-role socialization are changing, remnants still cling, as the earlier part of this paper has emphasized.

Given this background, it is easy to see why married women are more likely to suffer depression than never-married women (who must perforce function independently); why low-income women are more susceptible than those at higher income levels (the low-income woman is more likely to have been raised in a traditional home and to have adopted its values and is also more likely to undergo severe stresses—caused by financial strain—in her life); and why women with children still living at home are more likely to be depressed than women who are childless or whose children have grown and left the family nest.

· To elaborate on this last point: Despite its many qualifications and joys, parenthood has been called a "period of chronic emergency" (Gutmann, 1975), intensifying when children reach adolescence (Lowenthal et al., 1975). In our society women still have the primary responsibility for raising children, as is reflected by the semantic fact that, as commonly used, the verb *to mother* means "to care for tenderly, to nurture," whereas the verb *to father* means simply "to beget." Yet, for many parents, raising children seems to be something of a no-win situation. People are not given training in raising children, indeed, there is no general agreement about what constitute appropriate child-rearing practices, and the fashion changes from one generation to the next. Moreover, whatever practices are adopted, the mother gets no very immediate feedback as to the success of her methods. It takes a long time to determine whether a child has turned out "well," and even then exact criteria are difficult to specify. Thus, the mother is confronted with day-to-day uncertainty and often with a feeling of helplessness.

It should be emphasized that men are equally subject to the feeling of being powerless, though that feeling has different roots than in the case for women.

Conditioned to believe that they are the masters of their fate, men are victimized by the impersonality of a technological society where, in most cases, they are no more than cogs in a huge machine. Evidence indicates that most men—even those who have been successful in their careers—reach a point when they become disenchanted with their lives, when they come to feel that they have betrayed their youthful dreams, and when they long to develop other aspects of their personalities that have been submerged in the interests of getting ahead. But they too are "locked in" to the lives they have built (Levinson et al., 1977). One of the paradoxes of the traditional pattern of sex-role socialization is that, in mid-life, the sexes seem to undergo a crossover and a reshuffling of roles: Men develop a greater need for affiliation, and women a greater need for assertiveness and achievement (Gutmann, 1970). But at that point, many adults of both sexes may feel it is simply too late to change their lives.

The sense of powerlessness, then, is not sex-specific. It afflicts both men and women, though for somewhat different reasons. It is at this point that the counselor can play a role: by enabling clients to take control over their lives and to develop their full humanity.

A Transition Model for Counseling Women

The model for counseling women that is presented in this section is not dependent on one's ideology; rather, it is premised on the notion that women as a group are in a state of transition; that sex roles are changing, but at a confusing and uneven pace; and that individual women are at different points in the transition and encounter different problems with it. The model makes no assumptions about what specific stance the client should be encouraged to take or what decisions she should make; it offers instead a way for the client to look at and understand her particular situation and to take responsibility for it.[1]

The counselor does not, of course, deal with women-as-a-group; the counselor deals with individual clients who come with specific problems. Most of these problems can be analyzed within the context of the transition model. Throughout their lives, women make transitions continuously: They get married, have children, get divorced, are widowed, change jobs, retire, move, have operations or illnesses, and so forth. The model for studying adults in transitions has three major components (Figure 13-1). First, to help the client going through a transition, the counselor must have an understanding of *transitions in general.* Second, the counselor must to able to analyze the three kinds of *factors that influence an individual's adaptation to transition:* (1) the characteristics of the transition itself, (2) the characteristics of the pre- and post-transition environments, and (3) the characteristics of the individual experiencing the transition. Fi-

---

[1]We will not review here the extensive literature on the biases of counselors and others in helping professions. For a fuller discussion of this question, see the two issues of *The Counseling Psychologist* that deal with women: Vol. IV, No. 1 (1973) and Vol. VI, No. 2 (1976).

Table 13-1 A Framework for Studying Adults in Transition

Transition	Factors Influencing Adaptation to Transition	Adaptation
1. Events such as: birth of a child job change marriage moving retirement major illness widowhood	1. *Characteristics of Particular Transition* event itself source: internal, external timing: on-time, off-time affect: positive, negative duration: permanent, temporary degree to stress	1. *Level of Current Functioning* overall mental health level of life satisfaction adequacy of role and social functioning
2. Degree of difference in environments, pre- and post-transition, which affects —assumptions about self and world —relationships in family, work, and community	2. *Characteristics of Environments, Pre- and Post-Transition* interpersonal support systems —intimate relationships —network of friends —family cohesiveness and adaptability institutional supports environmental context	2. *Movement through Phases Following Transition* pervasiveness to reorganization
3. Opportunity for growth or deterioration	3. *Characteristics of the Individual* sex-role identification psychosocial competence —self attitudes and introspection —outlook: optimism vs. pessimism —coping orientation previous experience with transition	

276

nally, the counselor should be able to assess the individual's *adaptation* to the new environment.

Transition

The term *transition* can be used to cover a variety of events and thus is difficult to define precisely.[2] Perhaps the best general definition is that of Parkes, who regards a *transition* as any major change requiring the "individual to restructure . . . ways of looking at the world and . . . plans for living in it" (Parkes, 1971, p. 102). The crucial element is that the change necessitates "the abandonment of one set of assumptions and the development of a fresh set to enable the individual to cope with the new altered life space" (Parkes, 1971, p. 103).

One way of examining a transition is to assess the degree of difference between the pre-transition and the post-transition environments, which may have a profound effect both on one's assumptions about the self and the world and on one's relationships in the family, work, and community. To illustrate: The pre- and post-transition environments may differ very little if one moves from one apartment to another in the same neighborhood (unless the move is part of a more profound transition, as that when one separates from one's spouse or leaves the parental home); whereas when one moves to a foreign country, the differences may be great enough to precipitate "culture shock." One example of a transition that may involve vastly altered assumptions about self and world is the birth of the first child; this is also an example of a *role increment* (Lowenthal et al., 1975), whereby one adds the role of parent to one's repertoire of roles; other examples of role increments are getting married, taking a job, being promoted to a position of greater responsibility. Retirement from the world of work is another kind of change that has considerable impact on one's assumptions about self and one's relationships. This is an example of a *role deficit,* since one is losing the role of worker. Other examples are getting divorced, being widowed, seeing one's children leave home.

Any transition can be an opportunity for either growth or deterioration (Moos and Tsu, 1976). Thus, the transition represented by the women's movement may be for the individual woman a chance to develop her potentiality—by going back to school, for instance, in order to upgrade her job skills or by defining her relation with her husband more satisfyingly. Or, because of the threat it represents, the individual woman may retreat into depression or into the excesses of the "total woman" syndrome ("The New Housewife Blues," 1977). The transition of job retirement becomes for some people a stimulus to develop new interests and take up new activities and for others a dead-end marked by inactivity, boredom, and feelings of worthlessness.

Factors Influencing Adaptation

What determines whether a person grows or deteriorates as the result of a transition? Why do some people adapt with relative ease while others seem unable to

---

[2]Some writers use the term *crisis* almost interchangeably with *transition;* but we have avoided that term here because of its somewhat dramatic conotations. Many of the concepts, however, come from crisis theory.

do so and may suffer such severe strain that they seek outside help? To answer these questions, and to intervene in ways that will be helpful to the client, the counselor must examine three kinds of mediating factors: the characteristics of the particular transition, environmental characteristics, and individual characteristics.

Characteristics of Transitions   As already indicated, many kinds of life events can be classified as transitions, but most transitions can be described using a common set of variables: source, timing, affect, duration, degree of stress. Let us take the example of residential move, a kind of transition that has become a fact of life for many Americans. One recent study indicates that, over a three-year period, some 100 million persons "changed their addresses. The average person ... will move 13 times" during a lifetime (Allied Van Lines, 1974).

One dimension of a transition that helps to determine its impact is the *source: internality versus externality* (Lipman-Blumen, 1976). Is the transition a matter of choice on the part of the individual, or was it forced on the individual by some other person or some external agency? Typically, married couples change residences because of the husband's job requirements. The husband himself may decide that he has a better chance of getting a good job in his field by moving to another area or that a move to a home in suburbia would improve his occupational status; in such cases, the source of the transition is internal insofar as the husband is concerned but is external for the wife. She moves because her husband wants to move, and in the traditional marriage, the wife's needs and desires are subordinated to the husband's. Or the couple may move because the husband's company transfers him, in which case the source of the transition is external to both husband and wife. Generally speaking, the more internal the source of the transition, the easier the transition will be and the more likely the individual is to adapt easily. To have control over the changes in one's life is obviously to be desired, though not always possible.

The second characteristic of a transition is its *timing: on-time* or *off-time.* According to Neugarten (1977), "There exists a socially prescribed timetable for the ordering of major life events," and most adults have built-in "social clocks" by which they judge whether they are "on-time" or "off-time." To be "off-time," whether early or late, carries with it social penalties. Moving at the time one enters the senior year in high school is "off-time" moving away from family when newly married is "on-time." Although residential moves are not a kind of transition that is socially prescribed, many other kinds of transitions—such as getting married, going to school, taking a job, retiring—are linked very definitely with age. Generally speaking, it is easier to adapt to an on-time transition than to an off-time one. According to Neugarten, the woman who finds herself widowed at age 60 generally has less difficulty adjusting to her widowhood than the woman who is widowed at age 30; the older woman, though deeply grieved, has "rehearsed" for this possibility.

The third characteristic of a transition is its *affect: positive or negative.* Some kinds of change are welcomed by the individual: getting married, getting a desired job, having a child, these transitions usually generate feelings of excitement and pleasure. Other changes are feared and dreaded: losing a job, getting divorced, being forced to retire. Most changes probably have elements of both positive and negative affect. Thus, one may anticipate a residential change with pleasure, as a chance to live in a larger and more comfortable house or in a more pleasant neighborhood or city, but at the same time feel pain over leaving one's neighbors and friends and fear over facing the unknown. Similarly, becoming a parent may be a source of joy and satisfaction but will also contain elements of discomfort and irritation. Developing and implementing career goals may be exciting personally but produce role strain, especially regarding children.

Duration—whether a change is regarded as *permanent or temporary*—is a fourth characteristic that helps to determine how an individual perceives and adapts to a transition. Thus, the family that regards graduate study for the wife-mother as temporary will react differently than the family who regards the study as a more or less permanent thing, one which will lead to changed family roles. A transition that is painful and unpleasant may be more easily borne if the individual is assured that it is of limited duration—as when one enters the hospital for surgery that one knows will be minor and will have no lasting effects.

Finally, a transition can be characterized by the *degree of stress involved.* Holmes and Rahe define stresses as "those life events which require adjustment on the part of the individual" (Holmes and Rahe, 1967, p. 213). By this definition, any transition, whether positive or negative in affect, involves some degree of stress. The Social Adjustment Rating Scale (Holmes and Rahe, 1967) is an instrument which assigns numerical values to different kinds of life events. "Death of a spouse" ranks at the top of the scale, whereas such items as "vacation," "Christmas," and "minor violations of the law" are at the bottom of the scale. Generally speaking, the smaller the amount of stress involved, the easier it will be for the individual to adjust to it. One must bear in mind, however, what was said earlier in the discussion of "learned helplessness" about the additive nature of stress. To experience a number of changes within a given time period, whatever the nature of the changes, may be detrimental to one's physical and mental health. For instance, an individual will probably adapt more easily to a residential change that occurs in isolation, so to speak, than to a residential move precipitated by marital separation or divorce, the death of spouse, or other life events that are themselves major stresses.

Characteristics of Environments, Pre- and Post-Transition   As mentioned earlier, it is possible to assess the impact of a transition by looking at the degree of difference between the pre- and post-transition environments. The three most salient characteristics are (1) interpersonal support systems, (2) institutional supports, and (3) the physical setting.

Interpersonal support systems include (a) intimate relationships, (b) network of friends, and (c) family cohesiveness and adaptability. *Interpersonal intimacy*— a relationship characterized by similarity, reciprocity, and compatibility—has been found to "serve as a resource against life's crises" (Fiske and Weiss, 1977). For instance, data show that to be widowed is more traumatic for men than for women because men are less likely to share their inner world with others (Fiske and Weiss, 1977); when they lose their wives, they literally lose their best friends. Men's inability to form close relationships with other people may also be a factor in their shorter life expectancy. Women are more likely than men to have close interpersonal relationships with someone other than the spouse; with a "best friend," for instance. A residential move may mean a break in that tie, with subsequent ill effects and difficulties in adaptation. On the other hand, because of their greater capacity for mutuality, women may be better able than men to replace that friend.

Network of friends obviously encompasses a much broader range of people, all the way from fairly casual acquaintances to people that one sees frequently on social occasions. Women tend to have more friends, to be more deeply involved with them, and to have more complex perceptions of them than men do (Weiss and Lowenthal, 1975). Typically, married couples have two sets of friends: individuals of the same sex and similar interests whom they may have met before marriage, and "family friends" with whom they form ties on the basis of the husband's work. Weiss (1975) has pointed out that, when couples separate or divorce, the network of family friends is often lost to the wife, who thus suffers greater social isolation than the husband. A residential move clearly involves a break with the network of friends, thus adding to the sense of loss and distress.

Family cohesiveness and adaptability is, according to Lipman-Blumen (1976), of crucial importance during a period of transition. A person will cope differently with that transition depending on whether that person is part of a family or not; and, if so, how close-knit and flexible that family is. The degree of support that a woman receives from her family is all-important when she makes such transitions as returning to school or beginning a job.

The second kind of environmental characteristic that influences adaptation is the kind of *institutional support* an environment offers. Institutional supports may take the form of outside agencies to which a person can turn for help and support —e.g., community services, mental health facilities, schools and libraries, volunteer organizations—or they may take the form of rituals that help to define and legitimize a transition. A funeral is an example of such a ritual. Beyond a possible visit from the welcome wagon, or the housewarming ceremony, residential moves have few rituals connected with them. The other kinds of agencies and services offered by the new environment may make a considerable difference to the individual's adaptation.

Physical Setting. Included in this category are such features as climate, urban or rural location, neighborhood, living arrrangements, and work setting, each of which may make a considerable difference in ease of transition. In general, this aspect of the environment has been studied more extensively by architects and city planners than by social scientists. Thus, C. A. Doxiadis's science of ekistics rests on the assumption that one's "environment affects . . . biological, social, and behavioral growth and development" (Spierer, 1977, p. 26). Three important dimensions with respect to physical setting are comfort, privacy, and aesthetics.

Characteristics of the Individual   No matter how a transition is defined on some objective scale, an individual's adaptation to it will depend on the characteristics of that individual, most notably (1) sex-role identification, (2) psychosocial competence, and (3) previous experience with the transition.

With respect to *sex-role identification,* as was pointed out earlier, males and females are socialized to different attitudes and behaviors; the extent to which the individual has internalized these norms may play an important role in his or her ability to adapt. Thus, the woman who conforms to the "feminine" stereotype—dependent, passive, conforming—will find herself at a disadvantage in adapting to transitions that require her to be independent, assertive, and self-reliant: divorce or widowhood, for instance. Conversely, the woman who has defied the stereotype and led an independent life may find the transition of marriage difficult, particularly if she is called upon to sacrifice her own desires and needs to her husband's— as is often the case with a residential move. Counselors must be able to assess the degree to which the individual woman identifies with the prescribed sex-role. This is not to suggest that the goal of counseling is to move women from a vicarious to a direct-achievement orientation but simply that the counselor must take this orientation into account. A woman who has always functioned vicariously and suddenly finds herself the sole support of her family is forced by circumstances themselves to make this switch; for other kinds of transition, it is unnecessary.

Several recent studies have attempted to define and measure *psychosocial competence* (also referred to as "autonomy" or "maturity"). For instance, Tyler and Gatz at the University of Maryland, using an instrument called the "Psychosocial Behavioral Attributes Scale," identified as major components of competency (a) attitudes toward the self, including a favorable self-evaluation, a sense of responsibility, and the ability to introspect (Lieberman, 1975); (b) attitudes toward the world, including a moderate optimism in one's ability to interact with the world and thus to influence events; and (c) such behavioral attributes as having an "active coping orientation; high initiative; realistic goal-setting; substantial planning; forebearance and effort in the service of attaining goals; and capacity for enjoying success, suffering failure, and building from both" (Tyler, n.d.).

Ability to cope may be closely related to another characteristic of the individual: *previous experience with a transition of a similar nature.* Thus, a person who has in the past successfully adapted to a residential change may have developed strategies for coping with another such change in the present; she may have learned the necessary steps to take in order to rebuild the supports that were lost through the move. Though past experience may not lessen the stress of the present transition, it can facilitate the individual's more rapid progress through the adaptive process.

Adaptation

What constitutes effective adaptation to a transition? Like transition, the term *adaptation* has a variety of meanings. Some writers use it to mean personal growth and development, others to mean homeostasis. Adaptation can be measured in two ways: as level of current functioning, and as movement through the phases following the transition. Specifically, *level of current functioning* refers to "overall mental health, ... level of life satisfaction and self-esteem, adequacy of social functioning, maintenance of integrated, consistent self-concept, adequacy of meeting central inner task" (Lieberman, 1975, p. 144).

A more dynamic approach to measuring adaptation involves assessing the individual's movement through the various stages following a transition; that movement is typically along a continuum from *pervasiveness,* during which the change permeates every part of one's existence and consciousness, to *"boundedness,"* at which point the change has been contained and integrated into the self (Lipman-Blumen, 1976). For example, Kübler-Ross (1969) describes five stages experienced by people who realize they are dying: denial and isolation, anger, bargaining, preparatory depression for impending loss, and acceptance. Bereavement over the death of a close friend or relative similarly moves from "almost global denial or 'numbness,' ... bitter pining and frustrated searching, ... succeeded by depression and apathy ... with a final phase of reorganization when new plans and assumptions about the world and the self are built up" (Parkes, 1971, p. 106).

Each different kind of transition probably has its own typical pattern or sequence of stages moving probably from an "acute stage in which energy is directed at minimizing the impact of the stress, to a reorganization phase in which the new reality is faced and accepted" (Moos and Tsu, 1976, p. 14). One function of the counselor is to help the client understand the typical sequence of phases associated with various kinds of transitions, to identify the phase that the client has reached, and to suggest strategies for progressing smoothly to the stage of boundedness and integration.

Conclusion

In applying this model to the problems of women who seek help, the counselor must first of all bear in mind that women as a group are in a state of transition. A revolution is taking place: Old social values and norms that buttressed the sex-role stratification system are being replaced by a new vision of human life and potentiality, though so far the details of the coming post-transition environment have not crystallized. Individual women are at different stages in this transition, but virtually everyone is in some way affected by it. To some degree, this generalized transition state exacerbates many of the problems that people face in adapting to the more commonplace transitions of life. For instance, a woman who might in the past have accepted a residential move required by her husband's job may now find such acceptance difficult because the women's movement has made her more conscious of her own desires and rights as a human being. Just as plausibly, the women's movement may have provided her with a rationale for feelings of bitterness and helplessness that otherwise would have remained inarticulate, hidden, and destructive. The point is that the women's movement must be recognized as an important element in the lives of individual clients, as a milieu in which other problems and difficulties are played out.

Specifically, the counselor can utilize the model in three principal ways:

First, the transition model can help a client gain insight into an understanding of her problems. Very often, adults who experience difficulties in coping with transitions are doubly disadvantaged because they feel that, as adults, they should not have such difficulties: They believe that they should be "mature," "competent," able to make whatever adjustments are required of them. The transition model can give assurance that such difficulties are, if not universal, at least widespread; that the problem is susceptible to analysis; that virtually all transitions have similar patterns. For instance, it may be helpful for a client to realize that virtually any change is ambivalent in its affect: that it has negative as well as positive aspects.

Second, the transition model emphasizes the importance of support systems as a factor in adapting to transition. With that knowledge, the client can be encourage to seek out support groups, to form what Weiss (1975) calls "supplementary relationships" during the transition. Moreover, the counselor can draw on his or her expertise in suggesting the kinds of institutional supports available.

Third, the model can be useful in helping clients to plan and prepare for transitions. Parkes says that "adequate advance planning and preparatory training can transform what is potentially a major change in the assumptive world into a quite minor transition" (Parkes, 1971, p. 113). Levine points out that the single most effective strategy for coping with crisis is "seeking and utilizing information about a threatening situation" (Levine, 1976, p. 76).

To restate: Women are betwixt-and-between, and counselors of women must intervene with delicate balance. The goal is to help women adapt to transitions and resolve ambiguities in their own individual ways and according to their own values while also helping them move beyond where they are in order to become independent, autonomous human beings.

Questions for Further Inquiry

1. What stress has the changing roles of women caused in your life? How have you attempted to deal with this stress?

2. Are there any occupations which you think are inappropriate for women? For men? Why?

3. In the section on Occupational Status, Eli Ginzberg was quoted as saying that the "flood of women into jobs" is "the single most outstanding phenomenon in our century" and one with "long-term implications that are absolutely unchartable." Speculate on what some of these long-term implications might be.

4. The traditional female roles of wife, homemaker, and mother have been described as ambiguous, ostensibly calling for passivity, dependence,

weakness, and softness, but actually requiring initiative, leadership, strength, and toughness. In what ways is this statement valid? To what extent are traditional male roles ambiguous?

5. Would you agree with the statement in the section on Sense of Powerlessness that women are more prone to depressive symptoms than are men? Draw from your own experience to support your conclusion.

References

Allied Van Lines. *The mobile American male.* Ill.: P. O. Box 4403, 1974.
American Council on Education. *A factbook on higher education. Third issue/1976: Institutions, faculty and staff, students.* Washington: ACE, 1976.

American Council on Education, Staff of the Office of Research. *The American Freshman: National norms for fall 1971.* ACE Research Reports *6(6),* 1971.

Arnold, M. Stanzas from the Grande Chartreuse (1855). In W. H. Marshall (Ed.), *The major Victorian poets: An anthology.* New York: Washington Square Press, 1966.

Association of American Colleges. Project on the status and education of women. Pension issue is long-lived: A review. *On campus with women* 1977 *3(16).*

Astin, A. W., King, M. R., & Richardson, G. T. *The American freshman: National norms for fall 1976.* Los Angeles: American Council on Education and University of California at Los Angeles, 1976.

Astin, A. W., Panos, R. J., & Creager, J. A. *National norms for entering college freshmen, fall 1966.* ACE Research Reports 1967 *2(1).*

Bernard, J. *The future of marriage.* New York: World Publishing, 1972.

Bird, C. Interview with Eli Ginsberg. *Working Woman,* December, 1976.

Dohrenwend, B. S. Life events as stressors: A methodological inquiry. *Journal of Health and Social Behavior,* June, 1973.

Eiden, L. J. Trends in female degree recipients. *American Education* 1976 *12* (9).

Feldman, S. Picture shows: Network. *Human Behavior* 1977 *6* (*2*) 76.

Fiske, M., & Weiss, L. Intimacy and crises in adulthood. In N. K. Schlossberg & A. D. Entine (Eds.), *Counseling adults.* Monterey, Calif.: Brooks/Cole, 1977.

Friedan, B. *The feminine mystique.* New York: Norton, 1963.

Gutmann, D. Female ego styles and generational conflict. In J. Bardwick, E. Douvan, M. Horner, & D. Gutmann (Eds.), *Feminine personality and conflict.* Belmont, Calif.: Brooks/Cole, 1970, pp. 77–96.

Gutmann, D. Parenthood; A key to the comparative study of the life cycle. In N. Datan & L. H. Ginsberg (Eds.), *Life-span developmental psychology: Normative life crises.* New York: Academic Press, 1975, pp. 167–84.

Guttentag, M. & Salasin, S. Women, men, and mental health. In L. A. Cater, A. F. Scott, & W Martyna (Eds.), *Women and men: Changing roles, relationships, and perceptions.* New York: Aspen Institute for Humanistic Studies, 1976

Hedges, J. N., & Bemis, S. E. Sex stereotyping: Its decline in the skilled trades. *Monthly Labor Review* 1974 (May), 14–22.

Holmes, T. H., & Rahe, R. H. The social readjustment rating scale. *Journal of Psychosomatic Research* 1967 *11,* 213–18.

Holmstrom, E. I., Knepper, P. R., & Kent, L. *Women and minorities in health fields: A trend analysis of college freshmen. Vol. II: Freshmen interested in nursing and allied health professions.* Report submitted to the Bureau of Health Manpower, Health Resources Administration, Department of Health, Education, and Welfare. Washington: American Council on Education, 1976.

Howe, L. K. *Pink collar workers: Inside the world of women's work.* New York: Putnam, 1977.

Kübler-Ross, E. *On death and dying.* New York: Macmillan, 1969.

Levine, M. Residential change and school adjustment. In R. H. Moos (Ed.), *Human adaptation: Coping with life crises.* Lexington, Mass.: Heath, 1976.

Levinson, D. J., Darrow, C. M., Klein, E. B., Levinson, M. H., & McKee, B. Periods in the adult development of men: Ages 18 to 45. In N. K. Schlossberg & A. D. Entine (Eds.), *Counseling adults.* Belmont, Calif.: Brooks/Cole, 1977.

Lieberman, M. A. Adaptive processes in late life. In N. Datan & L. H. Ginsberg (Eds.), *Life-span developmental psychology: Normative life crises.* New York: Academic Press, 1975, pp. 135–59.

Lipman-Blumen, J. A crisis perspective on divorce and role change. In J. R. Chapman & M. Gates (Eds.), *Women into wives: The legal and economic impact of marriage.* Sage Yearbook in Women's Policies Studies, Vol. 2. Beverly Hills, Calif.: Sage 1976, pp. 233–58.

Lipman-Blumen, J. Overview: Demographic trends and issues in women's health. In V. Olesen (Ed.), *Women and their health: Implications for a new era.* Washington: National Center for Health Services Research; Health Resources Administration; U.S. Department of Health, Education, and Welfare, 1977, 11–21.

Lipman-Blumen, J., & Leavitt, H. S. Vicarious and direct achievement patterns in adulthood. In N. K. Schlossberg & A. D. Entine (Eds.), *Counseling adults.* Monterey, Calif.: Brooks/Cole, 1977.

Lopata, H. Z. *Widowhood in an American city.* Cambridge, Mass.: Schenkman, 1973.

Lowenthal, M. F., Thurnher, M., Chiriboga, D., & Associates. *Four stages of life: A comparative study of women and men facing transitions.* San Francisco: Jossey-Bass, 1975.

McCormick, A. G., & Carter, S. Do you feel a little neurotic? Here's what it means. *Vogue,* March 1977, 139–140, 143.

Moos, R. H., & Tsu, V. D. Human competence and coping: An overview. In R. H. Moos (Ed.), *Human adaptation: Coping with life crises.* Lexington, Mass.: Heath, 1976, pp. 3–16.

The new housewife blues. *Time,* March 16, 1977, 62–70.

Neugarten, B. L. Adaptation and the life cycle. In N. K. Schlossberg & A. D. Entine (Eds.), *Counseling adults.* Belmont, Calif.: Brooks/Cole, 1977.

Niedermeyer, G., & Kramer, V. W. *Women in education administrative positions in public education: A position paper.* Philadelphia: Recruitment Leadership and Training Institute, 1974.

Now "men's lib" is the trend. *U.S. News and World Report,* March 18, 1974, 40–43.

Parkes, C. M. Psycho-social transitions: A field for study. *Social science and medicine* (Vol. 5). London, G.B.: Pergamon, 1971, 105–15.

Reinhold, R. Trend to living alone brings economic and social change. *New York Times,* March 20, 1977, 59.

Roby, P. Structural and internalized barriers to women in higher education. In C. Safilios-Rothschild (Ed.), *Toward a sociology of women.* Lexington, Mass.: Xerox College Publishing, 1972, pp. 121–40.

Seligman, M. E. P. Depression and learned helplessness. In Friedman and Katz (Eds.), *The psychology of depression: Contemporary theory and research.* Washington, D.C.: V. H. Winston & Sons, 1974.

Stimpson, C. R. Sex, gender, and American culture. In L. A. Cater, A. F. Scott, & W. Martyna (Eds.), *Women and men: Changing roles, relationships, and perceptions.* New York: Aspen Institute for Humanistic Studies, 1976, pp. 201–44.

Swift, P. Idle children: Keeping up with youth. *Parade,* June 19, 1977, (14).

Tobias, S., & Donady, B. Counseling the math anxious. *Journal of the National Association for Women Deans. Administrators, and Counselors* 1977 *14,* 13–16.

Tyler, F. Individual psychosocial competence: A social configuration. Unpublished manuscript. College Park, Md.: Department of Psychology, University of Maryland, n.d.

U.S. Department of Health, Education, and Welfare; Education Division; National Center for Education Statistics. *Digest of education statistics,* 1975 edition. Washington: U.S. Government Printing Office, 1976.

U.S. Department of Health, Education, and Welfare; Education Division; National Center for Education Statistics. *Women's representation among recipients of doctor's and first-professional degrees, 1970–71 through 1974–75. Washington: U.S. Government Printing Office, 1977.*

U.S. Department of Labor, Employment Standards Administration, Women's Bureau. *Twenty facts about women.* Washington: USDL, 1975.

Van Alstyne, C., Mensel, R. G., Withers, J. S., & Malott, F. S. *Women and minorities in administration of higher education institutions: Employment patterns and salary comparisons. Special supplement: 1975–76 Administrative compensation survey.* Washington: College and University Personnel Administration, 1977.

Vetter, B. Women in the natural sciences. *Signs* 1976 *1* (3), 713–20.

Waldman, E., & McEaddy, B. J. Where women work: An analysis by industry and occupation. *Monthly Labor Review* 1974 (May), 3–13.

Weiss, L., & Lowenthal, M. F. Life-course perspectives on friendship. In M. F. Lowenthal et al., *Four stages of life: A comparative study of women and men facing transitions.* San Francisco: Jossey-Bass, 1975, pp. 48–61.

Weiss, R. *Marital separation.* New York: Basic Books, 1975.

Westervelt, E. M. A tide in the affairs of women: The psychological impact of feminism on educated women. *Counseling Psychologist* 1973 *4,* 3–26.

Wilson, J. Hollywood flirts with the new woman. *New York Times,* May 29, 1977, (11), 19.

Effective Helping with Young Children

14

RICHARD C. NELSON

Introduction

Counseling services are available to most segments of our society. Due to accreditation requirements, the ratio of counselors to clients may be greatest in secondary schools, and colleges and universities may be next in line in providing services. Adults, both in and out of the work force, have access to numerous services, including mental health clinics, family service agencies, psychologists, and psychiatrists. Special counseling services are available to returning service personnel, the unemployed, the aging, and the hospitalized.

Children may be counted among the segments of our society for whom helping services are not readily available. Professionals who focus on children exist in relatively small numbers within family service agencies and in welfare and protective services. Child guidance clinics and child psychiatric services are in short supply.

Signs of growth in child services seem to be most encouraging within the elementary school structure, where counseling services are in a crucial period of development. Myrick and Moni (1976) noted that approximately 700 elementary school counselors were employed in the nation in 1954, nearly 4,000 in 1967, and over 10,000 in 1975. In an era of economic stagnation this continuous growth is appreciable.

Efforts made to the present provide an effective experience-base for future growth in helping services for children. However, the kinds of developmental and remedial services that children require cannot be effective unless they are available. For the promise of effective help for young children to be realized, there will need to be a greater commitment in priorities and in dollars allotted.

Attention is given here to clarifying some special needs of young children and how those needs may be met through counseling. Topics considered are the following: (1) the special concerns of children that require counseling, (2) concepts and principles needed to understand children, and (3) special approaches to counseling with young children.

Toward an Understanding of the Special Concerns of Children

The Rosy View

There is a kind of nostalgia about youth, a rosy glow that colors the thinking of many adults. We can look from a distance at a group of children playing and decide that they have no cares in the world, that their lives are filled with enjoyment and pleasure. We smile and walk on, a bit regretful that the pressures of the day, of work, and of adult responsibilities do not allow us to pause and really soak up the joy and excitement of the scene. Let us take a few moments and zero in on a particular group of children and, as we watch their behavior and explore their thoughts, come to an understanding of some of the special concerns of young children.

The Reality

The children we are watching are eight-year-olds; they are playing kickball during recess. Among them, Pat knows that she is the best kicker on the team. She approaches the rolling ball and kicks at it viciously. Her kick goes awry, the umpire calls it a foul ball, and the muscles in Pat's neck tighten as she comes back to take her place. The runners on second and third yell toward Pat "You can do it," one says. "Come on, hurry up, recess is almost over!" yells the other. Pat's second kick is solid and high, it soars over the second baseman, catches a bit of wind and is held up briefly. The runners ignore the fact that the ball may be caught and are tearing around the bases. The centerfielder gets under the ball, but it slithers through his fingers.

"I knew you couldn't catch it," says Pat, as she strides into second.

The bell rings.

"Why'd'ya pitch it so easy?" Jimmy challenges the pitcher.

"When are you going to learn to catch?" Marie says to the fielder.

"Whew," says Susie, the on-deck batter, thankful that the bell rang.

Two girls clasp hands, walk toward the building, and one whispers to the other, "Do you see what Dale is wearing today?" and she throws back her head and laughs.

Stan, the last child to depart the playground kicks a rock or two from his path and internally screams because neither team wanted him to play. "You stink," said one of the captains, and the words still reverberate in his ears. Stan remembers a comment his father made yesterday, and many times before: "Why are you always sitting around sulking? This is the best time of your life!"

"If this is the best, then it really *can* get worse," Stan says to himself.

"You're the last one in again," his teacher scolds. Humor is intended, but none is perceived.

Idyllic, isn't it.

How Pat and Stan and the others feel about themselves can tell us a great deal about the special concerns of children. Assuming that Pat is a well-liked, athletic, active girl, even assuming that she is intellectually capable, the anecdote above may signal two areas of concern. Pat may hear from a girl friend that she has not been included in a slumber party because she is "too much of a tomboy," and she may also have a deep sense of the pressure on her to kick in the tying and winning run. Moments of achievement may be exciting and rewarding, but even for an eight year old, moments of failure may seem crushing.

Stan, judged by the yardstick of athletic prowess, is a failure, and he knows it. But not being chosen says more than that. Children do not reject a potential team member on ability alone. Those who are well-liked, but nonathletic, may be selected late, but they are chosen. Stan can read his failure as a matter of *his* being rejected, not just his athletic ability.

There are a great many ways in which young children are incapable and feel that incapability. There are things they cannot reach, words they cannot read, tasks they cannot perform, and their appetites, behaviors, and feelings are regulated somewhat by others. There is little or nothing that affects the lives of adults —divorce, infidelity, sexual activity, boredom, the aging process, business failures, or international maneuvers—that does not affect the lives of children either directly or indirectly. Often they *are* powerless, far more often they feel powerless, to effect events in their world.

Children see themselves, and are seen even in law, as "owned" by the adults around them. There is a great deal of responsibility-taking by adults, a reality that has its advantages and disadvantages. On the one hand it helps children in the main to be hopeful and optimistic, since they can assume, "Adults will provide." On the other hand it stands in the way of children taking action and developing a sense of responsibility for themselves. At any rate, Pat and Stan and others among those eight-year-olds experience a reality that may bear little resemblance to the nostalgic view many adults have when they recall a distant childhood or pass a group of children at play.

The Developing Self Concept

If we look beyond nostalgia to the reality, we may remember such concerns as being the smallest kid on the block, being left out of activities, name calling, the issue of best friends, not doing as well academically as we might have liked, difficulties with brothers or sisters, or kids our own ages, the pressures of ball games, boredom, nightmares, or not feeling good about ourselves in general or in some particular way. Adults who cannot remember any of those things can count themselves among the very fortunate; those who cannot recall those concerns affecting others around them—classmates, neighbors or a brother or sister—can count themselves among the oblivious.

For many children self concept is a fragile, tentative thing. They have neither learned to give reinforcement to themselves, nor learned to reject as unimportant the arenas in which they cannot perform well. Although in reality a good deal of adult counseling is directed toward building positive views of self, adults who are nonathletic or nonmusical, for example, may discount the importance of that shortcoming and focus on the things they *can* do. Young children can ignore some shortcomings also, but their self concepts are more readily damaged by inabilities in arenas others value.

Harris (1967) tells us that the position, "I'm Not OK—You're OK," is "the universal position of early childhood" due to limits on abilities and the extent to which children feel they are dependent on others. This idea combined with the notion that children are groping for identity and may even find security in a negative self-view, makes it somewhat easier to understand that a child might do a great deal to reinforce a negative self concept. "When others say I'm bad I at least know who I am, so I'll prove to others that I *am* bad." Lecky's (1945) notion that self-consistency, not positive self-development, is the cornerstone of self concept, supports that understanding.

Children need to be taught that they are OK. And many need this in the face of their rejection of the information. Parents who are caught up in their life problems or who are dealing with their own inadequacies often are unable to teach their children to feel OK about themselves. Teachers who are pressed by their own concerns often are unable to do more than support those children who already feel good about themselves. For children who hold negative self views this may act as an unintentional reinforcement. Children need significant others who feel good about themselves and who can help them learn to feel that they are OK. The adults in their lives, likewise, need support in order to reinforce children.

In the grand issues of life children generally are unable to choose with whom they will live, what relationships they will end, whether or not they will attend school, whether teacher A or teacher B will serve their needs better, ad infinitum. Blinded by a self-view and by the limits placed upon them in these major choices, children cannot see, and are not helped to see, the hundreds of little ways they daily can and do choose for themselves.

Children and adults need assistance in understanding their power to choose in everyday events. What is this power to choose? Did you ever have a little child look up into your eyes and say, "I love you"? There is power in that statement. Did you ever watch a child make his or her way across a classroom tapping a pencil on the head of one classmate, waving to another, pointedly ignoring three or four others, and touching or speaking to five others? That child would probably have no concept of having made eight or ten choices along the way—or of having the power to do so.

In later portions of this chapter some attention will be given to the "how" of building a broader selection of choices. Suffice it to say at this point that the development of skills in choice-making is considered essential if children are to have a sense of power in their own lives. Children need to be helped to see that they act—and are not merely acted upon, that they are agents in their own lives —and are not merely instruments of the wills of others. Children who come to hold such views are in a position to contribute to their self concepts, thus they are not limited by the views others hold of them.

I view positive self concept as a matter of making the kinds of choices that help one feel good about oneself. There is a place in the world of children for many people who can help them make such choices and attain a positive view. There is also a place for specialists who can concentrate upon building positive choices and self concepts.

Counseling Needs—Beyond Self Concept.

In my elementary school guidance text (Nelson 1972) I specified four types of guidance needs; I continue to see each of these needs as important.

Remedial Needs   "Jimmy is an out-and-out bully who demands money from other children, threatening to beat them, yet he verges on tears when his school work is poorly done. Disciplinary actions may be needed; but beyond that, here is a child who seems to be crying out for help in relating to other children in positive ways.

Susie sits, pained by her own shyness, hoping no one will notice her, putting all but her entire fist in her mouth, and lowering her eyes whenever another's meet them. There is a nonverbal expression of eagerness to be involved in the classroom, a fleeting, vicarious smile when an amusing thing is said or an especially good response is given. Everyone in her environment, even those who have helped her become so painfully shy, has attempted to push and prod her into volunteering answers, saying hello to others, and sharing her special interests" (Nelson 1972, p. 59).

Children like Jimmy and Susie who have adopted self-defeating life styles are the focus of the remedial efforts of helping professionals. Every collection of young people includes those who exhibit poor mental health through behavior patterns which have evolved over their life spans. These include the children who need the best efforts of our most highly trained professionals so that their problems are alleviated, rather than carried forward into adolescence and adulthood.

Immediate Needs   "Johnny's best friend may have moved away yesterday. If he is understood, if he is helped to verbalize or express through play his sense of loss, frustration, and anguish, he may well say later to a chum who is highly angered over a home conflict, "Why don't you see the counselor? He helped me when I felt bad" (Nelson 1972, p. 60).

All children experience events which they wish to share, and immediate circumstances bring grief or joy or a mixture of feelings. One child may be happy upon the birth of a younger sister or brother and fearful of the competition, another may be glad to have orthodontic work done yet fear the dentist and dread the braces, and a third may be excited about summer camp yet be worried about leaving home and anxious about poor swimming skills.

A flexible guidance program staffed by professionals can help children encounter the immediate events that press in so hard upon them at times. An important outcome of contacts at such times may be awareness that mixed feelings are perfectly normal when the objective is both feared and desired. Children need to know that people in and out of the school setting can take time to show concern for them when they have some kind of immediate need.

Exploratory Needs   There are times when children "just want to talk." Such times are often undervalued and counselors and teachers alike may show little tolerance of these exploratory needs. Perhaps if these needs are cast in another light, adults would see them as desirable growth-producing experiences. Children are assigned the adults they encounter by virtue of the family into which they are born, the neighborhood in which they live, and the school which they attend. In their exposure to a counselor children may be given an opportunity to choose either to relate or not to relate to an adult. When seen in the light of an opportunity for children to reach out, to explore interests, to discuss social relationships, and to clarify attitudes, the chance to explore in a safe environment can be indicative of growth toward maturity.

It may not seem to be very productive for the counselor to spend time viewing Val's picture or listening to Gerry tell an anecdote about an uncle, but the communication established at such times may be an important developmental step as the child learns to communicate with adults. Most children are action-oriented beings who exist in a world which tends to be sedentary. A place to let off steam, to have one-on-one attention, and to move about freely may be an essential haven from settings which may demand more control than they possess.

When we defer the opportunity for young children to seek counseling until adolescence or adulthood we do not provide this outlet or the place for them to sort out their ideas when the occasion demands. Further, the delay in introducing such opportunities conflicts with the time when young people develop a strong urge to solve problems on their own or with the help of peers. I greatly value these exploratory conversations between young children and adults; certainly they can become too much of a drain on the time of the counselor, but avoidance of "just talking" may tell children that they will have to develop a "real problem" before we will be inclined to listen to them.

Developmental Needs   In the processes of growing and learning, children encounter interdependent steps on the road to maturation. Havighurst (1952) postulated nine tasks that occur in middle childhood: learning physical skills for ordinary games; building wholesome attitudes toward oneself as a growing organism; learning to get along with agemates; learning an appropriate sex role; developing fundamental skills in reading, writing, and arithmetic; developing concepts necessary for everyday living; developing conscience, morality, and a scale of values; developing responsibility for an independent self; and developing attitudes toward social groups and institutions. The degree to which children successfully complete each task influences the prospect for successful completion of the next related task in the series, and depends on successful completion of earlier, related tasks. Children who need assistance tend to be those who have difficulty with one or more of these tasks at a level which troubles them or draws the notice of other children or adults.

Erikson (1963) explored the matter of development from a different vantage point. He conceptualized eight stages of development. The sense of trust, sense of autonomy, and sense of initiative for most children develops prior to the usual age of school entry; the sense of duty and accomplishment develops within early school years; and the later sequence includes a sense of identity, a sense of intimacy, a parental sense, and a sense of integrity. As with Havighurst's formulation, Erikson's stages suggest regions that create difficulty for children. Those children who have developed little sense of trust, of autonomy, of initiative, or of duty and accomplishment perceive themselves or are perceived to be in need of assistance.

Hill and Luckey (1969) proposed eight essential guidance learnings which they suggested human beings need to acquire as children, as adolescents, or as adults. They include the following areas in which maturing must occur: understanding of self, responsibility for self, the ability to make decisions, the ability to solve one's own problems, understanding of human behavior, an ability to adjust to the demands of life, and developing a sense of values. These essential learnings specify areas which we should give attention to if we wish to provide effective services to children.

Whether we view children's concerns from the vantage point of developmental tasks, developmental stages, or essential guidance learnings, it is clear that developmental matters should be considered by those who work with children. Toward one end of the continuum, effective helping can include anticipatory classroom and small group guidance efforts of teachers and counselors that are directed toward helping children deal with those matters before they become problems for remediation. Educating for self-awareness, exploring values, encountering classroom problems, exploring choices and decisions involving those matters, and sex education, are examples of educative processes that can be designed to contribute to the growth and development of children. Toward the other end of the continuum, effective assistance can include depth therapeutic efforts of child psychiatrists and clinic staff members for children in groups, within the family, or individually. These efforts are directed toward remediation of long-term or severe difficulties that block reasonable individual development. Inordinate fears, destructiveness, debilitating withdrawal behaviors, and severe compulsiveness are examples of concerns which may be dealt with by highly trained professionals.

Guidance with young children can be proactive rather than reactive more easily than with any other group. There is no point in children having to pass beyond immediate, exploratory, or normal developmental needs in order to receive attention. Both the everyday needs and the special needs of children merit our attention.

A Brief Excursion into Psychological Concepts and Principles

Carl Rogers (1942) pointed out quite some years ago that there appears to be a need in individuals to grow, and that counseling is a matter of removing obstacles in the way of growth. Most children evidence the will to growth through everyday behavior in their imitations of adults, in their trying-on of roles, and in the energies they expend in the development of skills. The behavior of children is directed toward personal growth, even though it may be channeled down self-defeating avenues, and guidance is best when it frees children for normal growth.

Self-referral, when offered to young children, results in a high proportion of children taking advantage of the opportunity. In a local summer school program, for example, counselor-trainees on their first visits to classrooms offered individual or small group counseling to over 200 elementary school students; 85 per cent of the children sought individual counseling, group counseling, or both. Children come to counseling out of curiosity and for all manner of other reasons; often they are as refreshingly direct as the child who plopped himself down and said, "I don't got no friends." Those who are involved in guidance experiences (including counseling) because they want to be involved are in a much better position to take advantage of the gains which might accrue.

Referral by others as a sole or primary route for young children to get to a counselor risks what Barclay (1967) calls "the mysterious stranger" phenomenon. The stranger appears and plucks from the midst of other children a child who is already perceived as different. The "differentness" of that individual has been accentuated and he or she may be less accepted by classmates even if progress is made through counseling. Furthermore, the counselor is being typed as an individual who works with these "different" children. By contrast, if the counselor meets a throng of waving hands and a chorus of, "When are you going to see me?" on a visit to the classroom, children who are selected are viewed as lucky and special, whether they volunteered for counseling or not. It is much easier for children to accept the teacher's suggestion, "I'd like to have you talk about this with the counselor," when that individual is seen as a sought-after person.

Accessibility of services is essential to the self-referral model which is suggested here. Counselors can ill afford to offer that kind of opportunity if they have a large counselor-pupil ratio or serve a number of buildings. Further, remedial needs tend to be the focus of counselor efforts when ratios are high; then, in essence, the counselor serves the kind of function which has traditionally been associated with school psychologists. This functioning is important, but it warps the accepted professional image of the counselor, and results in these individuals taking on counselees who may need specialized assistance which they are unable to provide. Children's needs can be better met when they have ready access to the services of an in-building counselor, and when child guidance clinics, family service agencies, and child psychiatrists are available to meet the special needs of the few.

One related point is that of immediacy. Children live in a here-and-now world, and the hurts they experience often need prompt attention. Too many of their concerns are overlooked and they work through the situation by themselves, but with a residue of damage to their self concepts and a too early awareness that adults cannot take time to help them. The moment passed may mean that the crisis is passed—or that the moment is lost.

Myrick and Moni (1976) recently reported that Florida had a ratio of 1 elementary school counselor to every 1.7 schools. Next, 12 states had ratios ranging from 1 counselor for every 5 schools to 1 counselor for every 3 schools (or slightly better). At the other end of the scale, 13 states reported one counselor *or fewer* for each of 13 schools; this included Alaska with a ratio of 1 counselor to every 50 schools and West Virginia with 1 counselor to every 30 or more schools. Other professional services tend to be even more thinly spread. Certainly in most states the kind of accessibility and immediacy called for in this article is not the current reality, even if we agree that it should be.

Training for responsibility through choice is another principle toward which counseling efforts can be directed. Young children are often able to accept more responsibility for their choices than they are encouraged to do. We are raising children in a rather schizophrenic world which suggests that they are responsible for very little as children, then, as adults, they are fully responsible for everything (unless they plead insanity or the public is touched by the deprivation of their circumstances). Teaching children about their choices and then expecting them to act in responsible ways is an alternative to this split logic.

Is it reasonable (meaning is it consistent with good learning theory) to engage in explorations in the realm of choice with young children? Children encounter situations constantly in which they must choose. Someone says hello, a child new to the classroom walks by, an assignment is given, food is placed on the table, someone asks what went on in school today—the day demands many behaviors, and however programmed the responses appear to be, most of them are choices. "Knowing behavior," says Galloway (1976), "means having the capability of responding appropriately to stimuli." Choice-broadening experiences, if well-designed, increase the likelihood that appropriate responses can be given by children. The reality is that there are *many* appropriate responses in most situations and this is a reality that children need to understand.

Learning experiences designed to build choice-making skills can be related to the developmental and remedial needs of individual children or of children in groups. These experiences can and should be based upon an analysis of the skill in terms of learner abilities, should demonstrate effective choices, should be designed to guide initial responses into effective channels, should be organized to provide for appropriate practice, should provide immediate and ongoing feedback, and should encourage independent future action (Klausmeier and Goodwin 1966). If learning experiences about choice are designed to meet these criteria, they are likely to result in cognitive and affective gain in those children who most need to develop effective coping skills.

Special Approaches to Counseling with Young Children

Entering the Child's World
For counseling to achieve maximum effectiveness, counselors must enter the child's world. Self-referral has been suggested as one way in which that can be done; the child's world is entered since he or she seeks the contact and the counselor may assume that the child has some focus in mind. Through the resulting child-directed discussion the counselor learns what is important and of concern to the child. Listening and encouraging children to talk seem like obvious means of entering the world of children; however, too few children have available to them the kind of listening they need, when they need it.

As a part of this kind of listening, it seems desirable for children to experience reflection of their feelings. More even than adults, children need to hear what feelings their words suggest, without skepticism, without disapproval. They can then own those feelings and, ultimately, take action that may result in different feelings. Children need to know that they are heard, and reflection of feelings tells them that we have entered their world.

Play media in counseling offers a special vehicle for getting close to children. Focus in this presentation doesn't permit a lengthy discussion of that topic. However, it is perfectly sound behavior for the counselor to sit with children at play; to provide clay, drawing materials and other media for expression and communication; and to respond to the actions of children almost as if those actions were words. Many children are perfectly capable of conducting a rather mature discussion of a concern while simultaneously making use of various materials, and the use of those materials may or may not relate to the dialogue. Children generally are active beings who play through the adventures and concerns they encounter in everyday life. We, as adults, permit children to present ideas on their terms when we make play materials available to them.

Conceptually adults enter the world of children when they consider the child's yardstick for success. One counselor viewed an interview as a failure, and told the teacher so, saying, "In forty minutes I only got two sentences out of Susie voluntarily." The teacher put the matter in perspective nicely by observing, "That's two more sentences than I have ever heard voluntarily." While no one asked Susie her view, she may well have felt very good about the volunteering she did. Certainly adults need to make the best guesses they can, or determine from them directly, whether children's expectations are being met. Our sense of impatience— because we use *our* yardstick for success—does little to facilitate the potential for growth of the child. Using the child's yardstick can turn our attitudes around.

Broadening the Child's View

Children tend to view the world simplistically. When they are helped to see the choices they have available to them, their view can be broadened. Timmy complained that his mother always "got out of the wrong side of the bed," and that his day was often spoiled before it started by his mother's "bad mood." After clarifying the situation, the counselor suggested that Timmy use a spare alarm clock the family had on hand. Timmy was amazed that his own action changed the situation dramatically. His power to "make" his mother furious, thereby unleashing a chain of negative events, never occurred to him. Timmy had not observed that he had any choice in the matter.

Even when a choice is observed, however, it may be seen too simplistically. Billy, a boy who was involved in an average of eight fights per week, saw only an either-or option. He could fight or walk away. When he fought he got into trouble, but when he walked away he was violating norms he had learned at home and risking his own self-respect. The counselor helped Billy build a list, ultimately containing fourteen items, showing things Billy could do when he began to feel like fighting. "Fight" topped the list so that Billy realized he could still use the option that had proven most viable for him. Other options included: climb on the monkey bars, get involved in a game, try to talk it out, ignore the situation, etc. Billy reported in the next counseling contact that he hadn't gotten to try any of the ideas because he just hadn't felt like fighting. Closer examination suggested that Billy had used many of the alternatives *before* he had gotten to the fist-fighting stage. Counselors use graphic representations, felt pens, and lists to great advantage in helping children to sort through alternatives.

In a recent article (Nelson, 1976), I explored the system I call Choice Awareness and described Laura, a sixth-grader promoted to seventh, who had developed a terrible relationship with her dad. Laura felt helpless in producing change in the interaction until we helped her see that she needed to start the action. She asked for a game of checkers on the first day, and commented on her dad's "sharp" appearance on the second, before he could start "hassling" her. Encouraged by her successes, and despite the fact that she had said, "I'll never, never, never, never, never be able to do that," on the third day she did much to change the pattern of interaction by saying, "Hey, Dad, I want a better relationship with you."

Besides helping Laura become an initiator in her relationship with her dad, we concentrated on helping her find "OK" choices that she might try. Choice Awareness (Nelson and Bloom, 1975) as a system provided a base for this exploration. As we saw it, Laura was mired in what we call sorrowing choices, and the solution to her dilemma seemed to be in changing to enjoying choices with her father. Choice Awareness can provide fundamental clues as to what choices children and adults are habitually making, and what others might serve as constructive alternatives. Counselors can aid children in this search, pinpointing, as for example with Laura, the alternatives which relate to their needs.

Choice Awareness assumes that we are making choices all the time, that each choice can be made in a great variety of ways, and that although our long-term goals in our relationships tend to be positive or neutral, we may be making many choices which run counter to these goals. In the case of Laura as we have suggested, exploration centered on two of the five kinds of choices postulated in the Choice Awareness system, sorrowing and enjoying. The full complement of choices in the system are included in the acronym *CREST,* which stands for Caring, Ruling, Enjoying, Sorrowing, and Thinking/Working. *Caring* involves any action which responds to need and is designed to be helpful. *Ruling* includes any leadership action such as suggesting we go to a ball game or other desirable event, as well as the Don't's and Must's of leadership behavior. *Enjoying* comprises compliments and brief interactions which convey warmth and affection, as well as actions that take more time—going bowling, for example. *Sorrowing* includes any response to hurts or worries, ranging from speaking of them, to becoming miserable about them, to taking out one's frustrations on another. Finally, *Thinking/Working* comprises the hundreds of choices daily in which we are asking, answering, planning, informing, and doing.

Any of these choices may be initiations or responses, self-or other-actions, habits or new behaviors, and, of particular importance, "OK" or "OD." The latter in this case stands for an overdose, overdone, or an overdraft on the interpersonal account we have with one another. Laura was making sorrowing choices, primarily being miserable, and these choices did not feel OK to her; furthermore, they were experienced as OD by her father. Our efforts were directed at helping her find OK enjoying choices with which she could initiate interactions.

Children's views may be broadened in another way which uses the Choice Awareness system. Few children or adults are aware of the multiple feelings they have in stress situations, yet it is not particularly difficult to broaden their perceptions concerning this. Stress often stems directly from the many approach-avoidance aspects of a situation. Stan, whose classmates did not want him to play, felt many things: left out, angry because he was excluded, confused because he did not know what in him turned others away, guilty because he sensed that he shared some part of the blame, and relieved because his athletic inadequacies would not be on display. From among his feelings Stan had to choose the one(s) to act upon. Children who act out of anger can be helped to see that their left out feelings, for example, could be dealt with instead of their angry feelings. When relief is part of the mixture, even as an underlying feeling, children can be helped to see what they can do with this feeling. The either-or view children have of their choices blocks out the fuller range of options from which they might select; a broader view can often serve them better.

This exploration of children's choices has of necessity been sketchy. For a fuller examination of these ideas the reader is encouraged to consult the sources mentioned (Nelson and Bloom, 1975; Nelson, 1976). Another book (Nelson 1978) details choices for adults in a personalized way which has much to offer those who work with children.

Peck and Jackson (1976) described a Florida study involving 25 guidance units and reported that those students who were seen five times or more during the previous year made average school grades and showed significant improvement in those grades over the previous year; further, those counseled children gained significantly in self-concept. Counseling services, then, may broaden the child's view academically, and thereby aid in positive self-concept development. Direct work with children on self-concept, and indirect effort which helps children feel successful, thus improving self-concept, are important aspects of effective helping.

Helping the Child Take Action

Helping children take action requires that teachers, counselors and other helping professionals believe in children. The bully, sissy, tomboy, and shrinking violet are harmed by our stereotyping and fulfill the prophecies those labels suggest. Teaching children that they are OK begins with believing that they are and that they can and want to grow toward personal maturity. When we believe in children, the varieties of helping approaches have a much greater chance of succeeding. I have met a number of college students who were spurred on by someone's statement, "You'll never amount to anything!" My guess is that those who rise to the top in the face of such statements are at the tip of the iceberg; the bulk of others, feeling bad about themselves already, form the much larger base of the iceberg which never surfaces in the college setting. Children need more from us than our challenges.

In the past many helping professionals have been very hesitant to share with children their honest perceptions of them—positive or negative. I believe that it helps children immensely to have a caring adult with whom they have a trusting relationship *ultimately* share with them his or her honest feelings. "I think what I'm going to say will hurt, Stan, but I care about you and I want to share something with you that turns me off. I get bothered by your really grubby hands and neck (body odor, runny nose, etc.) and I'd like your permission to talk about it and to try to work with you on it." Certainly such statements made too early in counseling can destroy the relationship; on the other hand, facing concerns honestly, sooner or later, is what counseling is all about. Few children would be hearing of the concern for the first time. Other children are much too honest not to have said, "You're filthy!" or "You stink!" However, it may be the first time that an adult has tried to explore the matter without nagging or expressing anger with the child. What I am saying here is that there needs to be existential integrity in counseling with children. What I feel as a human being for that other person is uppermost in my mind; it is a valuable part of me and of what I can give another person. It may be the foundation upon which children can be helped to take action.

An essential aspect of counseling involves helping children to understand the counseling relationship—to become counselees. Children need reinforcement when they focus on matters involving feelings and concerns; few need reinforcement for lengthy disgressions into stories of Aunt Lou's travel adventures or detailed reports about a television show or movie. Children need to be encouraged directly to take action and to use the time between counseling contacts to think, act, plan, try out, or tally particular behaviors or events. Counselors need to make time for some children to "just talk" because that is a deep need; for many other children the contacts should soon become productive in a visible way, or be discontinued. We need to "teach" many children how to use counseling time, however, since they do not have clear perceptions of its possibilities.

Behavior modification, which I believe can and should be applied humanistically, offers many ways of helping the child to take action. When children are reinforced for their positive actions and when their negative actions are ignored, much that is helpful can happen. Too many children are given all the attention they ever get when they misbehave; behaviorists rightly suggest that the attention is very often the reinforcer. Behavior modification processes which let the child in on the changes that are being made can contribute much; I believe that the child can and should be enlisted as an agent in his or her own change.

There are times when I wish we could get a computer rather than a person to relate to a child when behavior change is targeted. The computer could be programmed to reinforce endlessly or on a regular schedule. Too many teachers and parents forget to encourage and become angry; too many teachers and parents forget to ignore harmless behaviors and set up intermittent reinforcement. Rather than resort to computers, however, children need human beings who discipline themselves to maintain a reinforcement schedule and to ignore nonconstructive behaviors until they are extinguished.

Children can enter actively into the reinforcement process, as Bowersock (1975, p. 25–26) suggests in the following bit of dialogue:

> *Counselor:* Tommy, did you know that you have been teaching your parents to do some things that you don't like?
>
> *Tommy:* What kinds of things?
>
> *Counselor:* Well, for example, what do your parents do that you don't like?
>
> *Tommy:* They yell at me too much.
>
> *Counselor:* Yes, they do yell a lot, but you are teaching them to yell. . . . Suppose Dad tells you to turn down the TV and you don't do it. What happens?
>
> *Tommy:* Sometimes he tells me again, but pretty soon he yells at me.
>
> *Counselor:* Right. And then what do you do?
>
> *Tommy:* When he yells, I turn it down.

> *Counselor:*   The problem here, Tommy, is that when you do this you are rewarding Dad for yelling.

Bowersock goes on to suggest to the counselor that children can, by modifying their own behavior first, modify the behavior of adults around them. Children often can actively and advantageously participate in the behavior modification process.

Role-play offers counselors and children unique opportunities. Through role play counselors gain insight into ways children experience their problems as well as into blocks which might exist in the way of possible solutions. Children gain through behavioral rehearsal and are helped to take action constructively.

The Choice Awareness system enables children to take action through providing a cognitive–affective structure for making choices. The system is cognitive in that it helps children and adults comprehend the meaning of their own and others' behaviors. It is affective as well in that it considers choices through which children and adults express their joys and sadnesses.

Two basic approaches for the use of this system seem complementary to each other, and therefore both are desirable. First, in classroom (or smaller) groups children can explore, implement, practice, and gain through feedback on making broader choices. This can help them to acquire a cognitive structure and a vocabulary for understanding their behavior and that of others, and also provide them clues for more effective interaction. Second, in individual counseling contact, armed with the vocabulary and concepts, both the child and counselor are enabled to explore more effectively the nature of the concern and to consider alternative behaviors (choices) the child might use in confronting problems. Knowing what actions he or she might take is fundamental to the selection of effective actions.

Meeting Developmental Needs

Direct as well as indirect methods can be used effectively to meet the developmental needs of children. One of Hill and Luckey's (1969) essential guidance learnings, understanding of self, can be used to provide an example.

Jimmy's understanding of self omits awareness of his effects on others; he doesn't see how hurtful his abuse of others is since he sees other children as objects. Exploration within a group or classroom setting may help Jimmy see that he is both affected by others and has an effect on others. In a warm, accepting setting, Jimmy may hear about the hurtfulness of children to others and may relate it to himself; or he may be directly and caringly confronted about his own behaviors, and elect to make different choices. If in Jimmy's case he has been exposed for so long to adults and other children who are unaware of their effects that he does not acquire this learning readily, individual or small group counseling may be directed toward helping him see how he does affect others. He may be enabled to understand and experience these effects through discussion or through the use of role play or play media. It may be that neither group nor individual counseling efforts contribute sufficiently to Jimmy's understanding of self, yet the level of the problem may suggest that further effort is needed. Remediation may require the special assistance of any of a variety of professionals outside the individual school setting. Thus, the degree to which the developmental need is experienced, and the degree of difficulty experienced in meeting the need influence the amount, kind, and frequency of assistance that may be applied.

Each of the developmental tasks, stages of development, or essential guidance learnings has implications for effective helping with young children. Ultimately choices made by children, their parents, their teachers, or others in their lives will need to be modified if the way is to be cleared for children's developmental needs to be met. Where these needs are not met in reasonable sequential fashion, primary tasks of the helper include assisting children and others to clarify the choices that are being made, and those that need to be made for progress to occur, to encourage the development of environments in which new choices are valued, to promote the tryout of new choice patterns, and to offer feedback and assistance if further changes are warranted.

Using Multidimensional Approaches

Effective helping for children often requires that counselors use multidimensional approaches. In order to meet the special needs of individual children, creative counselors draw from various counseling theories and utilize a variety of human resources.

From phychoanalytic constructs counselors borrow such notions as looking for cause, considering possible unconscious determinants of behavior, and acknowledging the formative nature of early experiences. Counselors may utilize transactional analytical concepts to explore the communication patterns of children. Reality therapy suggests that counselors examine children's values and behaviors and confront discrepancies. From Adlerian theory counselors learn to consider purposes of children's actions, their mistaken goals, and their self-defeating behaviors. From behaviorists counselors take the concept that behavior is learned and new learning can substitute for old. Counselors utilize self-theory when they stress an accepting relationship as a major route to attitudinal development and behavioral change. Finally, counselors who think of counseling as a search for meaning in life and in the moment are expressing an existential attitude.

Eclecticism, borrowing freely from a variety of theoretical approaches, can be criticized especially when it is experienced as "tricks of the trade." However, when diverse approaches are utilized in direct reference to the individual needs of children, eclecticism is defensible—even commendable.

In addition to making use of several counseling theories, counselors incorporate multidimensional approaches when they call on various human resources to meet the needs of children. Elementary school guidance programs have led the counseling field in developing teacher-counselor consulting relationships. Most teachers affect the lives of many children yearly and a *great* many over a career. Seeing the potential for creating a positive atmosphere for large numbers of children, counselors have accomplished much through effective consultation. Acknowledging that "two heads are better than one," and assuming that the counselor is a less threatening person from whom to seek assistance, many teachers have been willing to use counselor services directed at helping them cope with individual children with the classroom group. Brown and Kameen (1975), for example, demonstrated in their work that teachers were willing to review videotapes with counselors, and gained from the experience, even though they were not willing to let their colleagues see the same tapes. The consulting relationship with teachers is an important dimension in making counseling effective for young children. When consulting opportunities are offered they are generally well-received by elementary school teachers; these teachers work so many hours a day with the same children that they often become acutely aware of children's needs and their own limitations.

Parent consulting, too, which acknowledges the tremendous importance these adults have in the lives of their children, is another foundation upon which successful counseling programs are built. Parents of young children are often both hopeful and concerned, and time may be very well spent in consulting with them. Teacher and parent consulting alike can be individualized, can occur in small groups focused on particular problems, or can occur in forums which offer such benefits as mutual sharing of concerns and group assistance in dealing with those concerns. It seems rather unsatisfactory to deal with teacher and parent consulting in just a paragraph or two, but these approaches clearly undergird the ideas explored thus far.

Small group procedures offer particularly powerful means for assisting children. Children need to see that others have concerns which trouble them, that they are not alone in experiencing difficulty in getting along in their world, and that they can be helped by talking through their troubles and by enlisting the assistance of others. Children are often cruel to one another, as witness the comments of the eight-year-olds on the playground; adults who can help mobilize the reservoir of care and concern which also exists beneath their surface negativism, contribute significantly to interpersonal relationships.

Children need to be helped to express their feelings and concerns directly to those involved instead of casting adults in the role of arbiter. It may take many interventions, but they are worthwhile when a child finally says, "Pat, when you don't let me play on the team, I really feel hurt." Children need to learn to talk straight with one another. Further, group members can help individuals find ways to change the labels they wear: shy, bully, sissy, etc. In the group and in the classroom children can be helped to see and to change their behaviors and their effects on others.

Many concerns can be dealt with as developmental learning processes, and resources are available to help counselors and teachers assist children to explore how they get along with others. The DUSO Kits (Developing Understanding of Self and Others) and the Focus on Self Development Kits are among attempts to create guided opportunities for children. My own work in Choice Awareness, I believe, will take its place in the future along with those resources, since it is designed to help children and adults look at ways in which they now choose in their minute-to-minute interactions, and consider ways in which they can choose in the future. Assisting children in groups to learn to interact successfully with one another is an important dimension of effective helping with young children.

Currently, in a great many ways, peers are being used as facilitators with one another, helping as co-counselors, being trained to give direct counseling assistance, and working with peers and younger children who have specific learning problems. Children in difficulty often rise beautifully to the challenge and become more productive members of the school society when they are asked to give assistance to those who need their help.

Counselors of young children are establishing themselves as adaptable and creative in encountering various concerns of children for two major reasons: first, because those children seem so eager for their support and assistance; and second, because, in contrast to their secondary school counterparts, these counselors do not carry the burdens of pre-college and pre-vocational testing, record keeping, and information-giving. The eagerness of children for assistance with their concerns and the lack of schedule restrictions upon counselors make possible the strides that have been made to the present in helping young children within school settings. Continued growth and development in counseling and referral services for young children require expanded financing. These are ideas whose time has come.

Questions for Further Inquiry

1. How did the world look and feel to you when you were a child? What factors in your life influenced these perceptions? Which of these recollections were typical of other young children? Which do you regard as unique?

2. Many chapters of this book focus on working with adolescent or adult clients. What different assumptions might a helper make about young children that would affect his or her counseling with them?

3. It has been said that play is children's work. How may a helper use this principle to create counseling activities for children?

4. How may the process of helping children become aware of the choices in their lives contribute to their preparation for adulthood?

5. How might the ideas in the chapter on self concept apply to understanding Pat and Stan described early in the chapter?

References

Barclay, J. R. Effecting behavioral change in the elementary classroom: An exploratory study. *Journal of Counseling Psychology* 1967 *14*, 240–47.

Bowersock, R. B. Helping children modify adult behavior. *Elementary School Guidance and Counseling* 1975 *10*, 24–30.

Brown, J. A., & Kameen, M. C. Focused videotape feedback: A consultation approach with teachers. *Elementary School Guidance and Counseling* 1975 *10*, 4–12.

Erikson, E. H. *Childhood and society.* New York: Norton, 1950.

Galloway, C. *Psychology for teaching and learning.* New York: McGraw-Hill, 1976.

Harris, T. A. *I'm OK, you're OK.* New York: Harper & Row, 1967.

Havighurst, R. *Human development and education.* New York: McKay, 1952.

Hill, G. E. & Luckey, E. B. *Guidance for children in elementary schools.* New York: Appleton-Century-Crofts, 1969.

Klausmeier, H. J. & Goodwin, W. *Learning and human abilities.* New York: Harper & Row, 1966.

Lecky, P. *Self-consistency: A theory of personality.* New York: Island Press, 1945.

Myrick, R. D. & Moni, L. A status report of elementary school counseling. *Elementary School Guidance and Counseling* 1976 *10,* 156–64.

Nelson, R. C. *Guidance and counseling in the elementary school.* New York: Holt, Rinehart, 1972.

Nelson, R. C. Choice awareness: An unlimited horizon. *Personnel and Guidance Journal* 1976, 462–67.

Nelson, R. C. *Choosing: A better way to live.* North Palm Beach: Guide Lines Press, 1978.

Nelson, R. C. & Bloom, J. W. *Choice awareness: An innovative guidance process.* New York: Houghton Mifflin, 1975.

Peck, H. I. & Jackson, B. P. Do we make a difference? A state evaluation. *Elementary School Guidance and Counseling* 1976 *10,* 171–76.

Rogers, C. R. *Counseling and phychotherapy.* Boston: Houghton Mifflin, 1942.

Effective Helping with Learning Disabled Children   15

DONALD B. KEAT II
ERIC J. HATCH

Overview

In recent years the provision of supportive helping services for learning disabled children has become an important area of research and investigation. The primary purposes of this chapter are to provide an understanding of learning disabled children and their problems and to present a multimodal model (called HELPING) that counselors can use to help such children. Topics such as labeling, identifying and evaluating learning disabled children are discussed. A case study is presented to demonstrate the application of the HELPING model and to show how its use can be generalized to a variety of children with learning disabilities.

Terminology

Estimates of school-age children who experience a learning disability range from 2 percent to 40 percent. These data suggest that educators have not been able to totally agree on either causes or definitions.

One widely accepted definition comes from the language of public law 91–230 as written by the Department of Health, Education, and Welfare:

> The term "children with specific learning disabilities" means those children who have a disorder in one or more of the basic psychological processes

involved in understanding or in using language, spoken or written, which disorder may manifest itself in imperfect ability to listen, think, speak, read, write, spell, or do mathematical calculations. Such disorders include conditions such as perceptual handicaps, brain injury, minimal brain dysfunction, dyslexia, and developmental aphasia. Such terms do not include children who have learning problems which are primarily the result of visual, hearing, or motor handicaps of mental retardation, of emotional disturbance, or of environmental disadvantage.

While this and other definitions imply that some sort of central nervous system impairment exists medical proof is not required of such impairment for a child to receive special services in the school. The medical and clinical proof for such impairment is not strong. Many children with known and independently verified brain damage do not exhibit the patterns which are presumably thought to exist in a child having learning disabilities. Nevertheless, children are often referred to a physician as one of the procedural steps for inclusion in the learning disabilities classroom. This procedure enables many helpers to allay the fears of parents who believe that their children may be suffering anything from mental retardation to some incurable brain disease. Despite the frightening connotations which the term "learning disabilities" has to some parents, the term is not nearly as frightening as "brain injury," "brain damage," or "minimal cerebral dysfunction," all terms which have been used and were in vogue at one time or another.

A whole glossary of technical language exists to describe the educational and behavioral manifestations of the learning disabled child. All of the characteristics to be mentioned are most likely to occur among learning disabled children but may also occur among nondisabled children. For this reason estimates of learning disabled children often are too high. It is also convenient for some to label a child as learning disabled so that he or she can receive help in a classroom with a smaller student/teacher ratio. This decision can sometimes help the child educationally, but the underlying manifestations of the behavior may never be totally addressed. Learning disabled children are often described as hyperactive, uncoordinated, inattentive, and as having a poor visual and/or auditory discrimination. They often manifest a left to right confusion and may reverse letters or symbols when doing written work.

Identification

Discrepancy between a child's intellectual capabilities and achievement in school is an identifying factor which seems to hold more universal acceptance than others. Many programs define a two-year discrepancy as significant while others resort to formulae which vary from simple to relatively complex. It is also generally accepted that for a child rightfully to be called learning disabled, he or she must exhibit an IQ which is near average, average, or above average. Some debate exists about this since it is possible that a child who is mentally retarded or a child with some sort of sensory impairment may also exhibit strengths and weaknesses within his or her own learning profile. This train of thought, however, seems to be more involved than legislators and professionals are generally willing to accept at the present time, and therefore it is more a theoretical debate than a basis for educational placement.

While it is beyond the scope of this chapter to give an involved medical explanation of brain damage or organicity in children, the helper should have an understanding of some of the theoretical bases upon which the field of learning disabilities has been predicted. As mentioned earlier, some sort of minimal cerebral dysfunction is thought to exist in children who are manifesting educational and behavioral signs of a disability. The manifestations of the problem will depend on the locus of the hypothesized brain dysfunction, the extent of the damage, and perhaps also the age and developmental period in which the damage occurred. It is generally hypothesized that cerebral dysfunction is associated with events occurring during pregnancy, at birth, or in the early weeks after birth. Prenatal influences are thought to include noxious agents affecting the development of the fetus and the chemical or mechanical factors which may damage the neural tissue of a newborn child. An unusual delivery and/or anoxia are common causes for birth difficulties. Verifiable neurological impairments such as cerebral palsy, conditions such as prematurity, RH compatibility and Rubella can be causes of cerebral dysfunction. Recently biochemical and nutritional factors within either mother or child have been hypothesized to be possible causes of cerebral dysfunction (Feingold, 1975; Stevens, Stevens, and Stoner, 1977). Some practitioners do not eliminate the possibility that early, severe, and prolonged sensory deprivation in infants and young children will also lead to subtle alterations in neurological structure.

The Psychological Examination
Very often the classroom teacher is the first person to suspect that a child has a learning disability. In many schools the teacher works through the school counselor who in turn has contact with the school psychologist. At other times this procedure may be reversed, or the child may be identified via some other screening procedures (e.g., preschool or kindergarten testing). One of the first things to be determined is whether the behavior exhibited in the classroom is the result of a learning disability or the result of a social or an emotional disorder. It may also be that the teacher's classroom management techniques are not suited for a particular child. Here the school counselor can often serve an important screening function, making a judgment of the likelihood of a true learning disability. Once a child is referred, the school psychologist may administer an intelligence test, a test of visual perception, a test of auditory perception, some achievement tests, and occasionally, some sort of projective technique. A thorough examination of the child will also include some classroom observation of behavior as well as a lengthy conversation with the child's teacher. Skillful school counselors or psychologists will take the time to train teachers to observe some of the behavioral manifestations of a potential learning disability.

Very often children with learning disabilities show wide discrepancies between performance on tasks requiring language use and tasks for which language use is not crucial. The Weschler Intelligence Scale for Children-Revised (WISC-R) is the most frequently used assessment instrument for such diagnosis. This test divides intelligence into a Verbal and a Performance section and yields a profile of scores for each part, as well as a Full Scale IQ. It is not uncommon for learning disabled children to exhibit anywhere from a 15 to a 30 point discrepancy between their Verbal and Performance IQs. Since scores on these subscales for the learning disabled child usually vary greatly, the overall score has very little validity. The total IQ becomes, crudely speaking, an average of all their abilities; such a number is not very descriptive of a child's learning strengths and deficits. Analysis of the eleven subscale scores is much more useful in assessing a child's individualized strenghts and weaknesses.

The Use of Labels

Despite all the literature that analyzes the disadvantages of labeling, at some point the school psychologist must make a determination as to whether the child fits the criteria for inclusion into a learning disabled class. Once this is done, conferring with parents becomes an important function. In the first session, diagnostic findings should be explained, and questions that the parents may have about the diagnosis should be answered. Although parents will often nod their heads in agreement and seemingly understand what is being reported, it is not unusual for them later to distort what was originally communicated and to become very disturbed about the results of the diagnosis. Their reaction may depend on the community's perceptions of what the term "learning disabilities" means. By and large, the term is still somewhat stigmatizing and is often initially confused with the notion of mental retardation. Professionals often unthinkingly increase the chances for this notion to flourish when they mention that they would like to put Mr. and Mrs. Smith's child in a special class. "Special" to many parents connotes special education, which to them is synonymous with mental retardation.

There has been much research on expectancies and self-fulfilling prophecies (Rosenthal and Jacobson, 1968). One of the hallmarks of a learning disabled child is his or her self concept which, depending upon several factors, is often in the process of deteriorating. These children can see that they are having difficulty learning things that their peers learn with ease. Then, depending upon how significant adults react to them, they will either come to accept some of their deficiencies or will feel more and more worthless. On a system-wide level some of this negative cycle can be eliminated simply by avoiding the use of the term, "learning disabilities." Therefore, it is probably much wiser for a school district to call such a classroom a resource room or some other nondescript term as opposed to calling it the learning disabilities classroom.

The World as Experienced by the LD Child

Relatively little has been written on the learning disabled (LD) child's perceptions of the world. In general, it is believed that the physiological and psychological boundaries of such children are more permeable than those of most children. That is, their "filtering" system often has difficulty in sorting out stimuli and feelings in an appropriate way.

On a physiological basis, audio and/or visual perceptions are the modalities most often affected. Many LD children have an extremely difficult time "screening out" the essential from the nonessential with regard to figure-ground differentiation. To understand the concept of figure-ground (and as a means of demonstrating these concepts to parents and teachers of such children) stop as you are reading this sentence and take note of all the noises in the room which you were not aware of until they were called to your attention. Some of these noises, such as the buzz of an overhead fluorescent light, may be barely noticeable. However, some LD children hear the buzz of that light to an intense degree or hear it "over" the teacher's voice.

Another example involves using as an analogy an experience that most adults have at one time or another—turning down a blaring radio which is interfering with other communication in the room. Some LD children may constantly be experiencing an interfering auditory blare, such as a buzzing light, a loud radio, a rattling radiator, or playground noise. Not only may this make the words of the teacher indiscernible, but it can also frighten the child to have so little control over which stimuli are penetrating and taking precedence.

It is also, then, easy to see that if the wrong stimuli are being received, wrong (and possibly bizarre) responses are being made by the child in communicating with others. Those working with such a child find it hard to know how to respond in turn. It should be remembered that every LD child is impaired to a different degree, and, therefore, the severity of what has just been described varies.

In the visual realm, a good example of the learning disabled child's experience pertains to the figures used in many introductory psychology texts. If perceived the first time, they appear to be one thing, and if the eye is blinked, they become something else. This is an example of the concept of visual figure-ground differentiation. What is an interesting diversion for adults can be a nightmare for learning disabled children! But the ability to walk in the LD child's shoes is important to understanding and empathizing with them (see parent exercises under the Personal Relationships mode, later in this chapter).

This permeable boundary difficulty of the LD child creates a loss of a sense of control, accompanied by anxiety, fear, and general sense of feeling lost. It can become more and more difficult for such a child to know any realities or consistencies in his or her world. Another effect is a loss of a sense of personal mastery. The sense of mastery is basic to the continuing development of pride, adequacy, and self-esteem.

In sum, the learning disabled child may be operating with varying degrees of deficiency in terms of seeing, hearing, and emotionally experiencing the world as others do. It takes a great deal of adult nurturance and structuring to help such a child psychologically survive and grow.

Roles of the Helper

A learning disabled child is the concern of an entire educational team. The school counselor often coordinates such a team which might include the teacher, the psychologist, the nurse, the reading specialist, the speech therapist, the learning disabilities specialist, the social worker, and administrators. One of the weaknesses of our educational system with regard to such a child is the amount of paperwork and red tape involved. Even if it could be demonstrated that some of this paperwork is unnecessary, there are many other facets of dealing with a learning disabled child for which paperwork and information exchange is necessary. It is very frustrating for professionals to deal with this type of child and not have at their disposal all the previous information which has been gathered regarding the case. Toward this end, it cannot be stressed too strongly that any contact that any professional has with a learning disabled child should be put in writing so that all that has been said in regard to coordination can be facilitated.

It is important for the helper to perceive self as an advocate of both the parent and the child. As such, he or she should be knowledgeable about placement procedures and about parents' rights in the matter of placement. The due process laws that now exist guarantee that a child will not be placed in any classroom other than the regular class without the knowledge and informed consent of the parent.

Professionals working in this field must also be very knowledgeable about both developmental and educational expectancies. The work of professional helpers is often based on the principle that parents and others expect either too much or too little of their children. This principle applies particularly to the relationship between a learning disabled child and his or her parents.

Helping parents deal with their anxieties about their learning disabled child is a primary helper function. Guilt may also be a prevalent parental feeling. Many parents believe that somehow they could have prevented their child from becoming learning disabled if only they had done something differently. In some geographic and socioeconomic settings a child who is different in any way is thought to be a punishment by God for sins committed. If these kinds of notions prevail, even at a minimal level, the learning disabled child will have a very difficult time being accepted by significant others. Therefore one of the main roles of the helper is to help parents work through feelings of nonacceptance and to help them learn ways to show acceptance. Acceptance is much easier for a parent if that parent believes that the child is not a "lost cause." Everyone can cite examples of someone with little or no formal schooling who has become a success in life. Although examples of this sort can be overstated, it helps to continually stress to parents that everyone has a unique combination of strengths and weaknesses. Therefore, a working philosophy for parents to understand and for the school to employ is that the weaknesses will be remediated to the extent possible, but that the strengths should not be forgotten and in fact stressed.

Parents are often reluctant to consent to any kind of special placement because they believe that their child will languish there forever. Two things that the helper can do in that regard are to take parents for a tour of such a classroom before a placement is made and to stress the fact that he or she will continue to be an advocate for the child. Parents may, through the helper's facilitation, request a yearly re-evaluation of the child to see what progress is being made.

The "HELPING" Model: A Case Presentation

One of the authors (Keat, 1976a, pp. 116–23) has previously presented a multimodal case of a learning disabled child (Scott). The multimodal approach which was used in that case was based upon the "BASIC ID" acronym (Lazarus, 1976). Since that time another acronym has been developed (Keat, 1978) which uses the same seven modes but rearranges them (*H*ealth, *E*motions, *L*earning, *P*ersonal Relationships, */*magination, *N*eed to Know, *G*uidance of A, B, C's), i.e., "HELPING".

The Case of Chuck

The HELPING approach will be discussed for Chuck, an 11-year-old boy who was in sixth grade at the time of contact. The family was intact; father worked as a computer scientist and mother was a schoolteacher. Older sister (aged 15) was the "star" of the family and got good marks in school. At the time of initial contact the reasons for referral were poor work in school (below expectancy in science and language arts, but a good reader), excessive sibling rivalry, lack of responsibility, and tension caused by overt marital conflict. Chuck had a long history of difficulty and had been seen by several evaluation clinics. Although he had just spent two years in the learning disabled classroom, he was now in a regular sixth-grade classroom.

Although the multimodal approach indicates that the helper starts where the primary concerns are (in this case they were learning and personal relationships), for purposes of clarity of presentation we will cover the modes in sequence (HELPING). The multimodal helper can start with any mode, shift gears to another mode, and then go back to the same mode or on to other zones in effecting this comprehensive treatment approach.

Problems and Treatment Strategies

Health   The biochemical balance of the child's body is an extremely important consideration for treatment. If there are any physical manifestations which might lend themselves to some dietary or drug forms of treatment, then these approaches should be considered.

An important part of the total helping program is to control the child's diet. "Removal of offending foods from the diet of disturbed or learning disabled children can result in dramatic improvement of behavior, attention span, and concentration. Cane sugar and rapidly absorbed carbohydrate foods should be eliminated from their diets" (Cott, 1975). Proper diet is best controlled if "junk foods" (e.g., candy, sodas) are not allowed in the house. Chuck consumed an excessive amount of sugar and its related products. Therefore, we used a dual approach. During our sessions we talked about diet and read passages from nutrition books

Table 15-1 Multimodality Profile for Chuck

Modality	Problem	Proposed Treatment
Health	Excessive ingestion of sugar	Diet therapy
	Hyperactivity	Drug therapy
Emotions– Feelings	Tense–Anxious	Relaxation exercises, TM
	Anger expression	Directed muscular activity
Learning– School	Not getting homework done	Restructure home environment
	Poor handwriting	Perceptual-motor training
	Low in science	Tutoring
	Good reader	Reward
Personal Relationships	Sibling rivalry	Instant replay
	Family troubles	Family meetings
	Lack of father involvement	Buddy program
	Marital conflict	Communication training, Fight training Child coping skills
Imagination– Interests	Low self-esteem	Enhancement program
	Wide range of interests	Focused skills
Need to Know– Think	Irrational self-talk	Reprogramming self-sentences
	Sex education	Bibliotherapy
Guidance of A, B, C's	Assignments not done	Contracting
	Lack of responsibility	Natural and logical consequences

(e.g., Yudkin, 1972), which pointed out the danger of sugar. In addition, parents (seen once a month) were given a suggested menu of foods to avoid (Keat and Guerney, 1978). They also read other sources on nutrition (Fredericks, 1964; Feingold, 1975; Smith, 1976).

In some other cases (Keat, 1976b), we have noted improved behavioral characteristics after instituting "orthomolecular" treatment. "There is rapidly accumulating evidence that a child's ability to learn can be improved by the use of large doses of certain vitamins, of mineral supplements, and by improvement of his general nutritional status through removal of 'junk foods' from his daily diet (Cott, 1975)." If one is interested in this approach, a self-taught regimen can be developed (e.g., Rimland, 1968; Cott, 1975; Keat and Guerney, 1978), or one can refer to someone who practices this orthomolecular approach and conducts urine, blood, and hair tests to determine body needs.

If neither of the above approaches seems to be effective or the child is too hyperactive, then referral for some medication may be indicated. Much controversy exists regarding the use of drugs with learning disabled children. Since one of the manifestations in many cases is very hyperactive behavior, it seems at first glance that the administration of a drug which will reduce this hyperactivity would have a beneficial effect, and indeed in some cases this is so. However, before such a step is undertaken, it must first be determined whether the hyperactivity is more of a problem to the child or to the adults who must work and live with him. That is to say, drugs should never be used as a substitute controlling technique for those adults who may not have effective child management skills. Some children are so hyperactive and so distractible that even given the best of child management techniques they are unable to attend to a task for any length of time, and for such children drugs may be beneficial.

Several factors should be considered in any drug treatment, and a school counselor should be very knowledgeable about them since he or she is probably the one who on a regular basis will have more involvement with the child's educational progress and the monitoring of behavioral reactions to medication than the school psychologist or the family physician. Some drugs have "paradoxical effects." That is, drugs that would make the average person very drowsy have the effect of making some learning disabled children more hyperactive.

A second factor is that it is very difficult to prescribe an exact level for any given child without continued monitoring of the drugs' effects. Therefore, it is very important to stress to parents that they stick with one physician and see that physician until the appropriate dosage is determined. Even then it becomes important to periodically monitor dosage because as the child grows in age, height, and weight dosages will have to be adjusted.

A third problem is that many parents forget to administer the drug to the child before the child comes to school. In addition some parents prefer not to give children drugs during certain periods, such as during holidays and summer vacations. This may be very justified but makes things more difficult from the educator's point of view when the child resumes school. It may well be the role of the helper to at times make friendly reminders and phone calls as well as to help parents develop a procedure whereby forgetting to administer the drugs is kept to a minimum.

Counselors should also recognize that a child who takes drugs is aware that he is somehow different from other children because of this ritual. Therefore, parents and others who work with the child must explain to him or her the necessity for drug use and deal with possible feelings of differentness. Often children perceive themselves as sickly because they take drugs, and this often leads to other types of somatic complaints. Parents must also understand that drugs are only an adjunct to treatment; they are not a cure for learning disabilities. Many times it will take hours of counseling to help parents understand this.

With Chuck, Ritalin had been used during most of the previous year in the LD classroom. It seemed to be helpful in increasing his attention–concentration. We phased this out in the sixth grade and concentrated on dietary regulation. This approach, combined with a maturing neurological system, seemed to maintain and even increase his periods of focused behavior.

Emotions-Feelings   Two important emotions which counselors are often called upon to work with are tension and anger. Chuck evidenced high levels of anxiety.

Therefore, he was trained in relaxation procedures. This approach involves teaching appropriate breathing, tensing-relaxing of 12 muscle groups in the body, conjuring-up pleasant scenes and images, and repeating calming sentences to oneself. In addition to instructions learned in these sessions, Chuck utilized taped relaxation instructions (Keat, 1977). Another approach which can be useful to combat tenseness is Transcendental Meditation (TM). For this a student can either enroll in a local TM class (Hemingway, 1973) or rely on self-teaching (Akins and Nurnberg, 1976). Chuck chose to attend the introductory TM lectures and enrolled in a TM class. He stayed with the two twenty-minute daily sessions for a few weeks but then dropped this from his regimen.

Chuck's anger was also a concern. Helping here consisted of teaching Chuck how to preprogram himself for the constructive release of "mad" feelings. Such anger-release training involved conjuring-up anger stimulating scenes, then figuring out how he could preprogram himself to react effectively. For example, when someone would name-call, what could he do? First, on a physical level there is directed muscular activity in which Chuck was trained to do isometric squeezes (Wittenberg, 1964) with his hands when angered, or to pound pillows if available. Secondly, at a verbal level, he was trained to say socially appropriate things. Finally, he was trained in imagery in which he realized that he could do anything he wanted to the antagonizer, in his "mind's-eye." But he could not, of course, act on these images behaviorally.

Learning-School   Helping learning disabled children learn from their school experience is a central focus of treatment and usually the one of greatest concern. One of Chuck's main problems was not getting his homework done. He was often in trouble with his teachers because assignment responsibilities were not being met. It is important to remember, nevertheless, that learning disabled children, due to the nature of their hyperactivity, need as do all children and perhaps more than most children, the opportunity for play and recreation, particularly right after school. It is very difficult for any child (but particularly a learning disabled one) to immediately sit down and begin more work at a time when he or she is looking forward to some play. After the bus ride home and about an hour of play time, an arrangement was negotiated with Chuck's parents in which mother would initially check his assignments at 5:00 P.M. in order to determine what needed to be done. If it was in the English or social studies area, she would monitor it. In case it was science or math, father would be the consultant. Then the time needed was determined. Five to six was one potential work hour (6:00–7:00 meal, 7:00–8:00 TV), and 8:00–9:00 was the other potential hour. In addition, cooperation of the school was enlisted by having each major area teacher sign his contract and note any special assignments (see more about contracting under the final mode). This was an elementary school where the child was exposed to four main teachers, although sometimes one teacher would have two areas.

Another concern was poor handwriting. As in most deficiencies, a two-pronged approach (i.e., school, home interventions) can be used. Some special school program can usually be set up with the consultation of the counselor and/or learning disabilities specialist with the classroom teacher. And many communities also have special perceptual-motor training programs which are ongoing during the year on weekends and over the summer (the one in our community is run by a group called Junior Museum).

The second major prong involves collaboration between parents and teachers. Some parents may just want to support the teacher's program. More adventuresome parents may want to actively involve themselves in a program and set aside 15–30 minutes a day to work on the problematic area (e.g., Rosner, 1975, pp. 258–67). Chuck's parents went along with the prescriptions from the learning disabilities specialist and worked with him on handwriting for three 15-minute periods each week (Monday, Wednesday, and Thursday). In working with such a child it is important to keep in mind the child's frustration tolerance and try to keep conflicts to a minimum. When a child becomes involved in "extra" schooling, the effect is similar to asking an adult to work overtime. Therefore, some additional rewards may be considered to be relevant as compensation for these efforts.

Science was another area in which Chuck was experiencing difficulty. This was an area for which the father could be of some periodic help. But this became a battleground and was undermining the father-son relationship. Therefore, we sought out a therapeutic tutor who could not only teach Chuck in the deficient area, but could also form a positive relationship. (We've found that a good source of therapeutic tutors are master's degree counselors-in-training who have had classroom experience and have a special interest in certain subject matter areas.)

It is important to offer support and encouragement for a child's strong points. In the heat of difficulties, this can easily be forgotten. For Chuck this meant rewarding his reading efforts. He was a good reader and everyone made a point of emphasizing this as well as giving him special recognition for his skills. Arrangements were also made for him to tutor a peer.

Personal Relationships   All of the problems in Table 15–1 arise within the family context. It is very difficult for a family to coexist with a learning disabled child who exhibits high levels of hyperactivity and inattentiveness. The family's life style will often determine the degree to which these patterns will create stress for the total family unit. Some households by nature are much calmer and more structured than others. Both of these attributes are desirable for the environment best suited to a learning disabled child. Often families have difficulty creating these supportive conditions. Mother and father may disagree about the areas in which a learning disabled child is or is not capable. In the experience of most helpers the fathers seem to have greater difficulties in accepting the child's inability to perform at a peak rate in certain areas, particularly if coordination difficulties are involved. A helper can do much to facilitate communication between husband and wife. It is particularly useful to have all the family members actively recognize the strengths that the learning disabled child has.

One of the most difficult things for the parents of a learning disabled child to understand is that he or she may not be capable of the progress they would like to see in a given educational area. Parents often think that given enough practice the child will begin to show improvement. This can be a very damaging attitude. A child simply may not be capable of the achievement levels the parents expect and, therefore, will feel more and more unsuccessful the more he or she is pushed. That in turn will lead to anger, resentment, and disrupted relationships between parents and child.

Some educators believe that the prime difficulty with many learning disabled children is not the learning disability per se, but rather the concomitant emotional difficulties that so many of them experience because others do not understand their condition. It is very difficult for many learning disabled children to concentrate for long periods of time. Yet that is exactly what parents are asking them to do by giving them more and more of the same work. Parents are often better able to understand this when an analogy is drawn from their own working lives. For example, if the father works at a gas station, it might be helpful to ask him how he would feel, if after a day of changing tires, he came home and were asked by his wife to change a flat she had incurred that day. Even then the analogy is not complete because, at least the father has the capability to change the flat. If you can help the parent actually experience some of the child's frustration, they will often be more empathic. Some exercises we have used are:

1. The helper and one parent simultaneously read passages from different books out loud and then ask the other parent to report back about what they heard (to give them some sensitivity as to auditory perception troubles).
2. Present a picture of a five-cornered star with double lines on a 8 ½ X 11 sheet of paper. Give the parents a mirror and ask them to trace around the path of the star. This provides some sensitivity to perceptual-motor difficulties (Try it yourself. Most people cannot accurately complete even one of the ten paths without error and usually perseverate at the first corner. A very frustrating experience!).
3. Another task is to have the parents learn a new set of symbols for letters (these can also be different colors for increased complexity). For example, $C = 1; E = V; P = \phi; R = \backslash; T = \Lambda; A = <$ and then ask them to spell simple words like CAT or PET (visual association memory skills related to reading).

Just a few of these activities should allow the parents to walk in their child's shoes and experience some of their child's difficulties. Acceptance of the disability on the parents' part is an extremely important facet of the overall treatment.

Sibling resentment is another difficulty in the family of a learning disabled child. In some families, the learning disabled child receives so much special attention and consideration that other children within the family become very resentful. In other families the learning disabled child can feel that the star in the family

(Chuck's older sister) is the one who gets everything. When sibling rivalry is intense and fights often break out, the instant replay procedure (Bedford, 1974) can be useful. In this approach the parents are taught (by reading and discussing Bedford's little pamphlet with them) to handle flare-ups by having the child replay the situation after it has happened (i.e., setting, time, persons, preliminaries, end result); to identify feelings involved (both types and intensity); to talk about how they were upsetting themselves about the situation (self-sentences); and finally to generate alternative options or plans for when a similar situation comes up again.

Some of the same types of problems can be discussed during family meetings. This is a Dreikurian (Dreikurs, Gould, and Corsini, 1974) concept in which the family meets at a particular time and place (e.g., Sunday evening, 6:00–7:00 P.M.: around the table), rules are established (e.g., one person speaks at a time), and there is an order of business (e.g., old business involving psychological homework tasks; new topics such as chores around the house, and so forth). In Chuck's family one of the core topics was equitable allowance and the distribution of chores. The "job jar" (Dinkmeyer and McKay, 1973) procedure was a useful one for this problem. For this the household jobs were generated, written on slips of paper, folded up, placed in a jar, and everyone took a turn drawing their responsibilities. (When an assignment is drawn by a lottery, it's hard to be upset at one's parents because the adult could draw the same job next week!)

When a father is relatively uninvolved with a child, an attempt can be made to have him set aside a "quality time-alone" (Keat and Guerney, 1978) period on a recurring, hopefully daily, basis. If this is not possible (e.g., the father's job requires that he be out of town for extended periods), then the helper may need to establish a "big brother" or "buddy" relationship. In most communities there are volunteers that staff such programs. For Chuck it was a matter of arranging a Buddy through the university placement program.

Marital conflicts are frequent in the families of learning disabled children. Some helpers feel secure in offering help at this level; others do not. We shall outline three procedures used with Chuck's parents. *Communication skill training* was useful. This involved reflectve (or active) listening, I-messages, and problem-solving (Keat and Guerney, 1978). *Fight training* (Bach, 1968) also helped because their conflicts often became open and heated. We structured a 20-minute period, twice weekly, when each would have 10 minutes to talk. Some of the rules for the session were to keep a normal conversational tone, to cover one subject at a time, and to avoid "museum pieces" (or dirty laundry accumulated over time and carried around "bottled-up" until the "blow-up"). Daily schedules and organizing things around the home were examples of topics covered.

The final procedure had more to do with the child counseling sessions. The goal for this procedure was to train Chuck in ways of coping with his parents. We generated this list together to help him tolerate parental fighting. This included ignoring (in own head); getting out of house (do own thing); taping the arguments; playback; developing a "good child behavior expectation list" (Gnagey, 1975); refereeing; distracting them (e.g., to TV); and going to one of the friendly neighbors for help. Indeed, sometimes we feel more optimistic about helping children learn to cope with upset adults than we do about changing the adults.

Imagination-Interests   How a child views self is crucial to his or her development. When the counselor attempts to build a positive self-image, he or she needs to investigate what the child does well and then encourage, support, reinforce these behaviors. By receiving appropriate positive "warm fuzzies," (Freed, 1973) the child can learn to realistically evaluate what he can do well. Chuck recently reported that "I'm really good in building things" (an accurate statement based on a realistic self-image).

A wide range of interests can have both positive and negative features. On the positive side, the child has a wide-open world to explore which is constantly changing. However, the negative aspect for Chuck was that he was sometimes like a child exploring a smorgasboard and not taking the time to really enjoy one activity or putting forth the effort to complete an event. One of the helper's tasks was to attempt to focus his efforts on one project and to see it to completion. Once he enjoyed the closure of the task and its rewards, he would go on to something else.

Need to Know–Think   People often learn and therefore tell themselves irrational self-sentences (Ellis and Harper, 1975; Hauck, 1972). The first step to correct these mistaken ideas (Lazarus and Fay, 1975) is to identify them. Chuck had heard from some peers and teachers that he was dumb and belonged in a special class. This was the "crapola" (Keat and Guerney, 1978) which they were feeding him and which he learned. The second step is to figure out more positive self-sentences to combat these previously learned statements. Chuck learned to say "I'm a very good reader" and "I'm really quite smart in certain things." Then, the final step for the child is to work and practice saying the new sentences to self until they replace the old ones. Recently Chuck told the counselor that "I guess I'm an average student, and maybe even a little above average in certain things."

Helping Chuck learn appropriate information and healthy attitudes about sex was also a concern. Sometimes this is covered in classrooms, or parents may discuss it with their children. But in many cases the helper can be the most effective teacher for the child. With Chuck we read parts of Pomeroy (1968) as well as all of Mayle, Robins, and Walter (1975). As questions were raised, they were clarified and discussed. The use of books usually places some distance between the subject matter and the child, and therefore makes the topic less threatening. Bibliotherapy, of course, can be used in many other problem areas such as divorce (Gardner, 1971) and minimal brain dysfunction (Gardner, 1973).

Guidance of Acts, Behaviors, and Consequences   Chuck had difficulty in completing assignments. Behavioral contracting was used for this difficulty. We delineated what he had to *do* (complete homework) in order to *get* certain things (e.g., points accumulated in order to allow attendance at a particular and desirable club meeting). The key is usually to identify what is going to get the child turned-on (something he likes) to do the less desirable task. *A reinforcement survey schedule for children* (Keat, 1974, Appendix D) or *A reward survey for children* (Keat, 1978) can help with this procedure. This menu provides a rather complete catalogue of rewards for clients. Although a counselor can use part of a session to complete it, the child usually takes it home and returns it the next week. After Chuck worked for the points and a club meeting attendance, he began receiving money rewards (five cents per point attained. Points were based on the teachers' daily verification that he had completed the assignment by their signing his contract). It is generally better to have a written contract because then there can be little debate about what the child has agreed to *do* and what he will *get* for accomplishing this task.

Chuck also had difficulty taking responsibility. A good procedure for this objective was to let him experience the effects of the consequences of his behavior. Since one of Chuck's problems was keeping his possessions in order, prior to a camping trip we developed a list of things he would need to take on the trip. He took this list home, checked each item off as he prepared it for the trip, and then forgot to put the things in the car! He experienced the consequences of his behavior by not having the things along which he needed. Next time he will probably not forget. Or, we can place "put things in the car" last on the list!

Summary

This chapter has presented an overview of counseling concerns with the learning disabled child. Topics included: terminology, identification, the psychological examination, labels, child's perceptions, and the roles of the helper. Using the HELPING acronym, the reader was presented both case-specific as well as generalizable procedures which can be useful with the learning disabled child and his or her family. The case in illustration has been quite successful and Chuck has experienced a relatively good year in school. The helper's role in the treatment program is gradually being phased out as the child, parents, and school carry on with the outlined program.

Questions for Further Inquiry

1. What attitudes toward learning disabled children do you detect in your professional setting? Which of these attitudes would you like to change and why?

2. Recall someone you know who has a learning disability. What irrational beliefs about self may be causing that person difficulty? Identify some more rational alternatives you would like to use to help the person learn to say to self.

3. Try any one of the three sensitizing activities on page 317. Be aware of the emotions you experience as you do the activity.

4. What special considerations should a counselor be aware of when working with parents of a learning disabled child? How do the ideas about the family as a system (Chapter 9) apply?

5. The authors take the position that the professional helper should be a child advocate. What special stresses might this create for the counselor?

References

Akins, W. R., & Nurnberg, H. G. *How to meditate without attending a TM class.* New York: Crown, 1976.

Bach, G. R., & Wyden, P. *The intimate enemy.* New York: William Morrow, 1968.

Bedford, S. *Instant replay.* New York: Institute for Rational Living, 1974.

Cott, A. Treatment of learning disabilities. *The Journal of Orthomolecular Psychiatry* 1975 *3,* 343–55.

Dinkmeyer, D., & McKay, B. *Raising a responsible child.* New York: Simon & Schuster, 1973.

Dreikurs, R., Gould, S., & Corsini, R. *Family council.* Chicago: Henry Regnery Co., 1974.

Ellis, A., & Harper, R. *A new guide to rational living.* Englewood Cliffs, N.J.: Prentice-Hall, 1975.

Feingold, B. *Why your child is hyperactive.* New York: Random House, 1975.

Fredericks, C. *Nutrition: Your key to good health.* North Hollywood, Calif.: London Press, 1964.

Freed, A. *TA for tots (and other prinzes).* Sacramento, Calif.: Jalmer Press, 1973.

Gardner, R. *The boys and girls book about divorce.* New York: Bantam Books, 1971.

Gardner, R. *MBD: The family book about minimal brain dysfunction.* New York: J. Aronson, 1973.

Gnagey, T. D. *How to put up with parents: A guide for teenagers.* Champaign, Ill.: Research Press, 1975.

Hauck, P. A. *The rational management of children.* New York: Libra Publishers, 1972.

Hemingway, P. D. *The transcendental meditation primer.* New York: Dell, 1975.

Keat, D. *Fundamentals of child counseling.* Boston: Houghton Mifflin, 1974.

Keat, D. B. Multimodal therapy with children: Two case histories. In A. A. Lazarus (Ed.), *Multimodal behavior therapy.* New York: Springer, 1976. 116–32. (a)

Keat, D. B. Multimodal counseling with children: Treating the basic id. *Pennsylvania Personnel and Guidance Association Journal* 1976 *4,* 21–25. (b)

Keat, D. B. *Self-relaxation program for children* (tape). Harrisburg, Pa.: Professional Associates, 1977.

Keat, D. B. *Multimodal therapy with children.* New York: Pergamon, 1978.

Keat, D. B., & Guerney, L. *What every parent needs to know about raising children.* On press, 1978.

Lazarus, A. (Ed.) *Multimodal behavior therapy.* New York: Springer, 1976.

Lazarus, A., & Fay, A. *I can if I want to.* New York: William Morrow, 1975.

Mayle, P., Robins, A., & Walter, P. *What's happening to me?* Secaucus, N.J.: Lyle Stuart, 1975.

Pomeroy, W. *Boys and sex.* New York: Delacorte, 1968.

Rimland, B. *High dosage levels of certain vitamins in the treatment of children with severe mental disorders.* San Diego, Calif.: Institute for Child Behavior Research, 1968.

Rosenthal, R., & Jacobson, D. *Pygmalion in the classroom.* New York: Holt, Rinehart, 1968.

Rosner, J. *Helping children overcome learning difficulties.* New York: Walker and Company, 1975.

Smith, L. *Improving your child's health, biochemically.* Englewood Cliffs, N.J.: Prentice-Hall, 1976.

Stevens, L. J., Stevens, C. E., & Stoner, R. B. *How to feed your hyperactive child.* New York: Doubleday, 1977.

Wittenberg, H. *Isometrics.* New York: Universal Publishing and Distributing Company, 1964.

Yudkin, J. *Sweet and dangerous.* New York: Bantam Books, 1972.

Understanding and Overcoming Delinquency

16

ARTHUR BLUM
SERAPIO R. ZALBA

Overview

Consideration of how to counsel with delinquent youth requires highlighting some basic issues that counselors should face regardless of the problems shown by the youthful clients they are trying to serve. The issues which need to be considered include: (1) the normal developmental tasks of youth at the particular age involved; (2) the developmental areas in which the problem behaviors occur, reflecting an aberration, or deviance, from socially acceptable norms; (3) the absence, or inadequacy, of the societal resources typically available to support youth in successfully mastering age-related developmental tasks; and (4) the substitute or alternative resources—e.g., individual counselors, peer groups foster parents, institutions, etc.—most likely to help the youth move away from the problem behavior toward a more socially desirable way of growing into responsible, productive, and satisfying adulthood.

Delinquency as a Social Problem

While juvenile delinquency is again in the public limelight, it is, of course, an age-old problem. As a standard textbook of over a quarter of a century ago stated, "Wild children, wayward youth, and headstrong progeny are terms we meet in medieval literature. The problem of lawless youth is not new." (Teeters and Reinemann, 1950). And most people are familiar with the graphic picture of widespread delinquency by organized gangs of thieves in Victorian England as portrayed in Dickens' novel, *Oliver Twist*.

In 1950 Teeters and Reinemann estimated that "... about six in every one thousand children under eighteen years of age in the country are involved in juvenile court delinquency cases." Not included were youth who were neither apprehended nor taken to juvenile courts.

There is a definitional problem in estimating the incidence of juvenile delinquency in the U.S. today—namely, what is to be included in the category of delinquency. Is *delinquency* simply delinquent behavior at any time in one's life, without regard to the seriousness of the behavior, the number of repetitions, or the duration of a series of single episodes? Which specific behaviors should be counted as delinquent?

We want to define delinquency in such a way that we can identify those youth who are engaged in a *pattern* of behavior that already has led them to, or is justifiable cause for taking them to a juvenile or criminal court. Most adults will admit having broken the law before reaching adulthood. It is not the one-time or infrequent minor trespass that is of primary concern to society or to the counselor. It is the repetition of such behavior over time that concerns us and/or the extreme and serious nature of any one particular episode—an armed robbery, a forced rape, a knifing or shooting.

Juvenile courts have jurisdiction in dealing with two kind of delinquent behaviors: (1) offenses against our criminal codes; and (2) so-called "status" offenses. In contrast to criminal offenses—behaviors considered crimes if perpetrated by adults—status offenses are not illegal behaviors for adults. These offenses include truancy, runaway, out of parental control, curfew violations, drinking alcoholic beverages, promiscuity, and the like. It is the *status* of being a juvenile that makes such behavior delinquent. The overriding concern that links the two kinds of delinquency is our society's demand that youth conform to norms of social behavior and that they accept the authority of the family and the state to regulate and limit their behavior.

As was indicated earlier, any estimates of the incidence of juvenile delinquency in the United States today must be strongly qualified. A significant amount of delinquent behavior is unidentified or unreported. Even delinquency cases brought to the attention of law enforcement and judicial agencies may be handled unofficially rather than officially. And statistical reporting of official proceedings is less than accurate or complete.

The most recent accepted national statistics come from the F.B.I. Uniform Crime Reports. They indicate that in 1975 a total of 1,675,711 youth were taken into custody by police: 41.6 percent were released without official action; 1.4 percent were referred to welfare agencies; 1.9 percent were released to other police departments; 52.7 percent were referred to the juvenile court; and 2.3 percent were referred to adult criminal courts.

It is well established that delinquency rates generally vary according to sex (approximately five times as many boys as girls—Teeters and Reinemann, 1950) and social status (a higher rate for lower than for higher socioeconomic-status boys—Gold, 1966). In addition, it is clear that youth from lower socioeconomic-status homes are more likely to be taken to court by police for a given offense than are youth from higher status homes (Gold, 1966).

Some studies also indicate that in communities of under 40,000–50,000 population the dominant social class grouping of the community tends to influence the delinquency rate of youth from the other social classes. In a small, predominantly middle-class town the delinquency rate for lower-class youth will tend to approximate that of middle-class youth rather than that of their counterparts in large cities. In addition to having higher delinquency rates, the large city lower-class youth are more likely to commit more serious offenses (Clark and Wenninger, 1962).

Success of Correctional Services

In his comprehensive review of the literature on the outcome of correctional services to both adults and juveniles, Martinson (1974) reached the conclusion that the research done "... gives us little reason to hope that we have in fact found a sure way of reducing recidivism through rehabilitation." There are, however, some indications of some treatment success with certain interventive (treatment) methods, as they are specifically linked with certain types of offender, types of treatment settings, and types of workers or change agents. As Palmer (1975) has suggested, we must increasingly address such questions as which methods work best for which kinds of clients; and what conditions are linked with successful outcomes? At the very least, Martinson advises, research indicates that "... if we can't do more for (and to) offenders, at least we can safely do less." In effect, he makes a case for less incarceration and more treatment of offenders while they are living in the community.

While the literature does not make clear the specific linkages between treatment methods and client types, there are some findings that suggest that such linkages can and should be made. For example, among boys classified as *amenable* to treatment (presumably the more "neurotic" rather than "psychopathic" boys) those *receiving* individual counseling did *better* (lower recidivism) than did those not receiving counseling. And, of the boys classified as *non-amenable* to treatment, those *receiving* counseling did *worse,* than did those not receiving counseling (Adams, 1961). Another study found that with "psychopaths" those *receiving* self-government group psychotherapy did *worse* (twice as many new offenses) than did those not receiving such treatment (Craft et al., 1964).

Adolescence and Its Problems

Adolescence is a period of change, transition, and upheaval on the part of adolescents themselves, and it is shared by or inflicted upon the significant others around
them. The turmoil is related to the crucial nature of the developmental life tasks
and circumstances that face youth during this period of their lives. The tasks are
numerous and varied, and the solutions reached affect the adolescents the rest
of their lives, even though there is constant reassessment and modification of
them. Some of the more salient tasks are listed below in four groupings: (1) Values,
Beliefs, and Goals Tasks; (2) Personal Identity and Image Tasks; (3) Interpersonal
Skills and Relationships Tasks; and (4) Social Roles Tasks. Some of the tasks cut
across two or three of the groupings, but since our purpose is solely to identify
them rather than to theorize about them, they will be presented only under one
heading. It is also clear that some of issues dealt with by adolescents are also
faced at earlier and/or later stages in life. They are included here, however, as they
have a strong influence on adolescent behavior and adjustment.

1. *Values, Beliefs, and Goals Tasks*
   –Development of personal values and ethics.
   –Development of beliefs in the social, societal, political, and religious
   realms.
   –Development of personal goals.
2. *Personal Identity and Image Tasks*
   –Dealing with changes in body size and shape; physical coordination;
   grace/awkwardness; beauty/ugliness; health/illness/physical disabil-
   ity.
   –Dealing with a high need for excitement and action.
   –Development of personal perceptions of one's own powers/weak-
   nesses; of competences and mastery in social, physical and material
   tasks.
3. *Interpersonal Skills and Relationships Tasks*
   –Clarification of one's peer group memberships.
   –Development of interpersonal skills for purposes of joining, resisting,
   and capturing others; peer group roles.
   –Development of dating behavior and skills.
   –Dealing with separation from family dependency and roles, including
   such issues as aggression/submission, independence/dependence,
   love/hate, inclusion/aloneness.
   –Dealing with nonparent adults in such realms as school/employment/
   neighborhood/family/elsewhere; with equals/superiors/inferiors in
   power or status.
4. *Social Roles Tasks*
   –Development of occupational goals and skills.
   –Development of preliminary life style attitudes and practices.

–Development of sex, marriage, and family roles.
–Choosing reference groups.

Theories of Delinquency Causation

A number of theories have been proposed for explaining juvenile delinquency. Each of them adds to our understanding, but *none* provides us with definite answers or a single, usable "grand" theory. Most theoreticians challenge the utility of lumping all delinquents into a single diagnostic category, and they agree that there is need for a series of differentiated diagnostic categories based on a variety of variables. Nevertheless, they typically proceed to present *their* theory in such a way as to imply its applicability to a wide spectrum of the delinquent population. By doing this, they disregard other types of delinquents whose deviance is unexplained by *their* theory. Thus, while each of the theories has added some insights, few have addressed the issue of multiple causes and multiple types of delinquency. Fewer still have attempted to provide a *process* for systematically reviewing the many factors that should be taken into consideration in arriving at an explanation for the behavior of an *individual,* or of a *subgroup of delinquents.*

Many of the delinquency theories *imply* that they deal with specific target populations, and they carry additional implications about the treatment of choice. Given that each of the theories offers some insights into a subgroup of delinquent youth, a counselor, in order to make good use of the range of theories available to him or her must undertake an assessment process that allows him or her to place the individual client within the appropriate theoretical subgroup(s). He or she can then utilize the intervention insights and techniques that are linked to the appropriate theories. It is our assumption that too often the choice of intervention is made before there is an adequate assessment, and that counselors tend to utilize a single counseling technique with which they are familiar, without considering its relevance for the wide *variety* of delinquent subtypes.

In this chapter we present a *typology* of delinquents' problems based on existing theories, taking advantage of their implications for setting counseling goals and choosing the focus of treatment. We have not attempted to review *all* of the existing theories of delinquency, nor to specify *all* of their treatment implications. Rather, we have tried to present *groupings* of the major theories for use by practitioners in client assessment and treatment planning. In the last section of this chapter sample case studies are used to illustrate the application of the classification scheme.

Theory Groupings

We believe that delinquency theories can be grouped into the following six categories: I. socialization or value development theories; II. institutional provision and opportunity theories; III. peer group and gang theories; IV. family theories; V. personality and self-image theories; and VI. physiological theories.

I. Socialization or Value Development Theories

Explanations of the relationship between value development and delinquent behavior have been offered from a variety of perspectives, including the differences in value orientation in delinquency areas (Kobrin, 1951), the importance of differential associations (Sutherland, 1947), the effects of lower-class culture (Kvaraceus and Miller, 1959) and of neighborhood values (Shaw and McKay, 1942), the importance of the concept of anomie (Merton, 1949), and the theory of neutralization (Sykes and Matza, 1957).

Emerging from this range of theoretical approaches, there are three subgroups of delinquent youth: (1) socialized youth whose delinquent behavior must be explained by other factors; (2) unsocialized youth whose behavior is a result of the lack of internalization of values and who, therefore, are susceptible to situational stimuli and stress; and (3) negatively socialized youth who have a clear set of values but whose values are in conflict with those of the larger society. These subgroups are indeed different—any counseling approaches must be adapted to those differences.

Value development is seldom addressed directly as the focus of treatment; instead, it is usually incorporated into such concepts as self-image. The critical point in the theoretical approaches cited above is that one's social environment is the source of one's value orientation; consequently, efforts to affect the youth's values or socialization process must be directed at the environmental source as well as at the individual. Each of these sources identifies a different environmental factor, thus interventions should relate to the *particular* environmental factor which is influencing the specified subgroup of delinquents.

II. Institutional Provision and Opportunity Theory

A second group of theories explains delinquency on the basis of the blockage of legitimate opportunities for success and the resulting use of illegitimate means for achieving legitimate ends (Cloward and Ohlin, 1961; Cressey, 1970), the failure of schools to provide adequate education (Polk and Schafer, 1972; General Accounting Office, 1976), the negative effects of labeling by institutions (Becker, 1963; Thorsell and Klemke, 1972) and the consistently high unemployment rates of youth. Although these theories can be grouped for classification purposes, each implies a specific but different target for intervention.

These theories call attention to the importance of institutional arrangements in the society which can make it nearly impossible for some youth to either acquire needed skills or to have effective access to employment opportunities. Existing drop-out rates in the schools, the failure of school systems to provide basic educational preparation or adequate vocational programs, and the persistent inability of the economic system to absorb youth into the labor market—unemployment rates for youth often are over 40 percent—are frequently subjects of newspaper articles. More recently they have become the basis of law suits. We must engage in efforts to bring about institutional changes that will result in more adequate educational preparation for youth, and an expansion of employment opportunities for them.

However, we cannot *wait* for these basic institutional changes to occur in planning treatment programs for *today's* delinquents. Counselors must find ways to make optimal use of available opportunities and act as advocates for their clients with existing institutions. Effective treatment planning requires that major attention be given to these obstacles to opportunity for youth, and that counselors have knowledge about and access to such existing resources as special education and job-training programs. They must assume an advocacy posture in attempting to get school systems to develop needed educational programs that meet the specific needs of their clients. The theories in this grouping emphasize the need for treatment planning to relate specifically to the educational and employment needs of youth.

III. Peer Group and Gang Theories

A number of theories have been based upon the observation that a significant amount of delinquent behavior in our society takes place in the context of peer groups and gangs. Beginning with the classic studies of Thrasher (1936) and Whyte (1943) there has been elaboration of this school of thought with such concepts as peer subculture (Cohen, 1955; Miller, 1958; Scott and Vaz, 1963; Bloch and Neiderhoffer, 1958) and counter-culture (Yinger, 1960), and with some in depth studies of particular types of groups (Yablonsky, 1963; Short and Strodtbeck, 1965).

The writings indicate that peer groups exert two types of influences that result in delinquent behavior. First, peer groups can effectively set normative standards for the behavior of their members—they may demand conformity with group norms of delinquent behavior. Second, groups can create the stimulus, contagion, or support for occasional delinquent behaviors which are neither consistent with the values of individual members of the group nor represent ongoing group norms.

The importance of peer groups as a contributing factor to delinquency has led to the development of approaches that emphasize working with the peer group as a whole to prevent and treat delinquency. It is important, however, to recognize that as each theory specifies the particular type of influence the group exerts, assessment must identify, and group interventions relate to different types of group influence. As indicated earlier, for one group member the group may provide a normative influence, while for another, the same group may provide contagion. An intervention thus must be analyzed and planned both in relation to the group and to the individual member involved. These matters must be taken into consideration when forming therapy groups, where one must be clear as to the *goal* of the group, the *appropriate intervention* to achieve the goal, and the *differential selection of members* in light of the group goal.

IV. Family Theories

A number of theories have been proposed which associate family variables with delinquent behavior. Glueck and Glueck (1962, 1974) and Nye (1958) have each reviewed the most relevant of these theories. The variables which have been studied from a number of different perspectives include broken homes, single-parent families, deviant behaviors of the parents, role confusion in the family, family inconsistencies in discipline and limit setting, the lack of parental affection and provision, and deficient communication. While each of these variables has been found to be associated with delinquency behavior in particular studies, they apply to only a small percentage of the total delinquent population; they offer no explanation for the large number of youth who experience similar family situations but do not become involved in delinquent acts. Perhaps it is because of the established importance of the family in child development and the accessibility of some families to treatment, counselors have tended to attribute greater importance to the explanatory value of family theories than existing evidence warrants.

Again, interventions must be designed that rectify or compensate for the specific deficiency involved. In addition to individual and family counseling approaches, consideration must be given to the use of homemakers, Big Brothers and Big Sisters, jobs for youth, and income provision programs for independent living arrangements. Removal from the family may be indicated in the most extreme cases. Older delinquents often cannot wait until their family is rehabilitated. The family pattern may be so fixed or may contribute so greatly to their needs to rebel that other alternatives must be sought. In all cases an assessment should be made as to how well the family provides for the needs of the youth; any interventions in a youth's family life should be made on the basis of very specific treatment goals.

V. Personality and Self-Image Theories

Since counselors most often interact with individual delinquents, it is understandable that a great deal of emphasis has been placed on individually oriented personality and self-image theories to explain delinquent behavior. Psychoanalytic theory (Aichhorn, 1936; Friedlander, 1947; Redl and Wineman, 1956; Schoenfield, 1971) identity development (Erikson, 1950), learning theory (Ullmann and Krasmer, 1969), labeling theory (Lemert, 1967), and self-image concepts (Reckless, Dinitz, and Murray, 1956; Reiss, 1951) represent only a small sample of the delinquency theories based on personal psychology.

Still, we have not answered the basic question: To what extent is delinquent behavior the result of internalized, self-perpetuating dynamics, as compared with external factors? Given that a youth may be responding to environmental influences, at what point do these influences, and the gratifications he receives from his delinquent behavior, affect his personality development to the point where the initial stimulus is no longer needed and the behavior itself is self-regenerating? At the same time we must ask whether therapy can be effective if the self-regenerating aspects of the behavior are neutralized, but the initial environmental stimuli remain unchanged. We often expect that changes in an individual will prove powerful enough to equip him to withstand the pressure of the environmental forces with which he must contend. For many delinquents, however, staying "straight," in view of the daily situational stresses they face, requires that they have individual strengths far beyond those of the average person.

Individual counseling approaches vary greatly, depending upon the theories of behavior from which they are derived. These variations may be less critical than the question of whether the other variables involved in the case, discussed earlier in this paper, contribute significantly to the delinquent behavior. It has been our experience that much of the failure in treating delinquents happens because intervention has been limited to individual counseling. Counseling can be very helpful, but in many cases it must be combined with work directed toward other contributing factors.

VI. Physiological Theories

The debate as to the differential effects of heredity and environment rage on, and although not resolved, cannot be ignored. Although the earlier work on physical characteristics by Lombroso (1918) has been invalidated, later studies on body type (Sheldon, 1949), on inherited aggressive tendencies (Lambo, 1971), and the more recent work on sensory-motor development and learning disabilities (General Accounting Office, 1976), on biochemical and nutritional imbalance and minimal brain dysfunction, and on perceptual motor deficiencies, cannot so easily be discounted. Consideration must be given to special approaches to those cases which also show evidence of physiological and biological dysfunction, as well as other problems more amenable to environmental and psychodynamic explanation.

The theories cited above are representative of the *range* of theories developed to explain the phenomenon (or more correctly, *phenomena*) of juvenile delinquency. For the most part the study samples from which these theories are drawn include male delinquents only; little attention has been paid to whether they are applicable to females. And the theoretical groupings tend to cut across traditional academic disciplines. The practitioner thus must be prepared to select the appropriate knowledge from more than one discipline to help him understand the acts of the particular individual with whom he must deal. Let us now proceed to see how these theories can be put to practical use in the assessment and treatment of juvenile delinquents.

Approaches for Controlling or Overcoming Delinquency

The six classes of theories indicated above can be translated into six focal points for treatment. For some delinquents the treatment plan must address value development or change in values. For others, affecting societal institutions and lack of

Table 16–1   Client Assessment Profile

Area	Assessment (+/–)	Treatment Plan
I. Value Development		
II. Institutional Provision and Opportunity		
III. Peer Group		
IV. Family		
V. Personality and Self-Image		
VI. Physiological Factors		

opportunities become crucial. And in still other cases, peer groups, family influences, or intrapsychic conflicts should become the counselor's main concern. In cases in which there are physiological factors at play, special programs and approaches must be developed that will at least neutralize their negative effects.

In order to avoid reductionism—the use of only a limited number of explanatory theories or therapeutic approaches—the assessment process must provide a systematic means of insuring that consideration is given to a good range of alternative explanations. The diagnostic statement should fully reflect each delinquent's situation. In cases in which there are multiple causative factors at work, the treatment plan should explicitly indicate the specific approaches which will be used to modify or compensate for each of the relevant factors. Then we will be in a better position to assess whether what we can offer is powerful enough to offset the pressures toward delinquency. We might also then be better able to evaluate the reasons for our successes and failures.

We are proposing an assessment scheme for delinquent clients based on the six groupings of delinquency theories described above. Rather than classifying a client according to one model, we propose that a profile be developed wherein the client is assessed in all of the areas. If the client has no problem in a given area, we would record a plus (+). Conversely, inadequate development or provision would be recorded as a minus (–). Treatment might then focus directly on the problem areas (–), or on the nonproblematic areas (+) as a means of compensating for or offering alternatives to the problematic behaviors. The Client Assessment Profile is depicted in Table 16–1.

Four sample cases will be used to illustrate how the Client Assessment Profile can be applied to assess and treat clients.

John

John is a 16-year-old boy, living in a middle-class suburban community, who was apprehended for shoplifting in the auto parts department of a discount store. Investigation indicates this was his first offense. He is doing well in school, is a popular member of the basketball team, the family is close-knit, and he expresses real concern over his behavior. The delinquent act resulted

Table 16–2   Client Assessment Profile of John

Area	Assessment	Treatment Plan
I. Value Development	+	Individual counseling
II. Institutional Provision and Opportunity	+	Career counseling
III. Peer Group	+	None
IV. Family	+	Family therapy
V. Personality and Self-Image	+	None
VI. Physiological Factors	+	None

[1]Joy-riding is the street term for stealing a car for a short period of time in order to ride around town—usually in the company of friends. The car is then abandoned, rather than sold in its entirety or in parts.

from his wanting a special auto ornament for the family car, but he had run out of allowance money to purchase it and did not want to ask his parents for additional money.

The assessment indicates that John is functioning well and that in none of the six assessment areas is there evidence of serious problems. His act of shoplifting was the result of an adolescent interest in cars and a desire to be "sharp." His unwillingness to ask his parents for funds was reflective of a wish for independence.

Charges were dropped on the condition that John would have two individual counseling sessions, and that he and his family would have two family counseling sessions. The focus of individual counseling with John was on reinforcing his positive adjustment and helping him see clearly the potential negative consequences of his behavior (I, V). The sessions with the family were directed at relieving any strain in relationship caused by John's shoplifting, and reviewing the normal problems of adolescence in such a way as to encourage a continuation of freedom of communication and mutual problem-solving within the family (IV). There was some discussion of part-time employment for John in both individual and family counseling sessions. In view of John's desire to continue playing basketball and his plans to go on to college, he came to the conclusion that he preferred not to work during the school year (II).

Bill

Bill is a 17-year-old boy, the youngest of three children of working class parents. He was apprehended for curfew violation and auto joy-riding.[1] Although presently not working up to capacity in school, his grades are average. He has friends who are not prone to difficulty; he dates only occasionally. He is aware of the seriousness of his behavior and expresses some guilt about taking the car. This is a second marriage for his mother and for the second time she has married an abusive alcoholic. Bill has been beaten by both his father and step-father when he has tried to protect his mother during fights. Bill had run away on three occasions when he was younger, and these episodes were followed by periods of depression and unpredictable expressions of anger and violence by Bill in the home. Bill's mother is talking about divorcing her second husband.

The assessment profile for this case indicates that the problem centers in the family, in Bill's reaction to the marital conflict, and in his anger toward his passive mother and toward abusive males. His reactions have been internalized, as demonstrated by his periods of depression. The car theft followed a fight at home. It reflected Bill's tendency for flight and escape from difficult situations and also from his feelings. The family is at the point of disintegration.

Individual counseling goals in this case would include: (1) support in the areas of value development, school work which is shaky, and peer group associations (I, II, III); (2) stabilization of his living arrangements (IV); (3) compensation for the lack of family support (IV); and (4) better management of his angry feelings (V). Efforts at family therapy seem to hold little promise given the tenous nature of the family and the mother's repeated choice of abusive, alcoholic mates. Suggestions that the mother may seek help for herself are appropriate, but even if this occurred, it is doubtful there would be positive results quickly enough to help Bill. Rather, exploration should be undertaken with Bill's siblings to determine whether they can provide him with an alternative living arrangement (IV). Individual counseling is a possibility. It should come from a male counselor, focusing on how Bill handles his angry feelings, with an awareness that Bill needs a strong but accepting male figure whom he can imitate, and from whom he can experience the concern and guidance never provided by his father or step-father (V).

Peer group therapy should also be considered since it might be possible to build on Bill's ability to relate to peers, especially if he is unable to trust adult males (III). The group may provide a means of help to Bill in managing his anger, understanding that his family situation and his reactions are not unique, providing a place

Table 16-3 Client Assessment Profile of Bill

Area	Assessment	Treatment Plan
I. Value Development	+	Individual counseling
II. Institutional Provision and Opportunity	+	Individual counseling
III. Peer Group	+	Individual counseling
IV. Family	–	Move out of home Group counseling
V. Personality and Self-Image	–	Individual counseling Group counseling
VI. Physiological Factors	+	None

to release his feelings, and affording a context for mutual support from his peers in *managing* his life rather than fleeing (V).

If an alternative living arrangement cannot be found, Bill will need help in managing his time at home and developing alternative plans of how he will resist becoming enmeshed in the problems of his parents (IV). At seventeen, he needs real help toward independence and may also need help in group therapy in learning how to relate to females (III). The assessment profile focuses on the problem areas, but alternative treatment approaches for dealing with the problem through compensation or substitution must be considered when a specific problem area, as in this case the family, cannot be addressed or corrected easily.

Chip

Chip, a 16-year-old boy, is the eldest of four children of a mother receiving public welfare assistance, whose husband deserted the family when Chip was 7-years-old. Chip was recently apprehended along with three other boys, for purse snatching and assault of a woman at a downtown store. Chip had been expelled from school for fighting and incorrigibility. He is a member of a delinquent gang. The family resides in a deteriorated section of the inner city. Since his school expulsion, Chip has been employed as a lookout for a "numbers dealer."[2] He functions comfortably within this environment and has been given responsibility and earned recognition from the criminal element in the neighborhood. His mother says she has lost control over Chip; for the good of the other children she has just stopped being concerned about him. Upon arrest he was belligerent and stated that the woman whose purse he snatched could afford to lose the money and was stupid to resist, thus *she* caused the assault.

Although there was every likelihood that Chip had taken part in previous delinquencies, this was his first arrest and the court referred him for probation services. Chip presents the type of assessment profile which requires a range of interventions which go far beyond individual counseling, and for whom the prognosis of ultimate success is questionable. In relation to his value development, Chip can be classified as negatively socialized. He has come to accept his delinquent behavior as an acceptable pattern, and this acceptance is reinforced by his peer group and the neighborhood environment. Within this value system and in his environment Chip is able to function appropriately, obtaining recognition and showing an ability to plan and follow through on his plans. He is "street-wise."

There is little evidence of internal conflict and Chip is comfortable with his present behavior and functioning. Although society does not approve of his behavior, Chip's self-image is one of adequacy and his ability to fulfill the responsibilities given to him indicates adequate ego functioning. The problem is one of negative socialization and anti-social values rather than a poor self-image. The goal is to exploit his strengths and direct them into socially acceptable channels. His mother

---

[2] "Playing the Numbers"—an illegal form of lottery—is a widespread form of organized gambling in inner city neighborhoods.

Table 16–4 Client Assessment Profile of Chip

Area	Assessment	Treatment Plan
I. Value Development	−	Male employment supervision Peer group counseling Group home
II. Institutional Provision and Opportunity	−	Employment
III. Peer Group	−	Peer group counseling Group home
IV. Family	−	Male employment supervision Peer group counseling Case management and coordination Group home and returns
V. Personality and Self-Image	+	Peer group counseling Group home and returns
VI. Physiological Factors	+	None

is too overwhelmed with her own survival and the younger children to be of much assistance.

Legitimate opportunities are not readily available to Chip; those that are available are incongruent with his values. The school has been unable to devise a program to remedy his poor school work and behavior. His school failure also leaves him unprepared for socially-acceptable employment.

The treatment focus in this case must relate to Chip's resocialization. For this to occur there has to be some "payoff" to Chip for changing his way of life. Change has to be further reinforced by peer support and recognition. Any plan for this youth must begin with adequate employment. Ideally, a job needs to be located which pays above minimum wage or at least provides obvious opportunities for advancement (II). In addition, the work situation should include male adults who have succeeded, are from the type of environment in which Chip finds himself, and who can be enlisted into the process of socializing Chip (I). These adult figures will need to be street-wise themselves, and demanding, yet understanding, and accepting of the problems Chip will face in taking on a new value orientation. Both in the roles they play and in their communications with Chip, they will need to provide role figures worth emulating, demonstrating the potential payoff that could result from changing (IV).

Peer group therapy will also be needed in order to decrease, and hopefully eliminate the influence of his present peer group (III). The focus in the group would be on values and peer norms, utilizing approaches akin to Highfields (Weeks, 1963) or Positive Peer Culture development (Vorrath and Brendtro, 1974) to maximize the peer influence and to compensate for the lack of family control (I, III, IV). The peer group sessions would also need to focus on the work situation and provide support and controls for appropriate work behaviors (V).

Plans would need to be made with Chip for his use of leisure time. It is unlikely that he will just give up his existing friendships and group affiliations unless there are meaningful alternatives (III). The therapy group should provide some help with this effort. But it will be adequate only if the members of the group are from the same neighborhood and the group extends its relationship beyond the group session. Effort should be made with group service agencies to discover possible alternative recreational and group outlets.

Although an individual counselor might be assigned to this case, his role would be that of facilitator and coordinator rather than therapist. The mother should be kept informed of these efforts and her support enlisted, but it is unlikely that much more than passive support can be expected (IV). This mother is not rejecting, but she has limited resources that can be mobilized. If Chip responds to these efforts, future educational planning may be appropriate.

We approached this case initially from a probation perspective as a means of exploring the variations in type of interventions which are necessary, as compared to the first two cases. Not only the format for help—individual counseling, group work—but also the focus within these formats was varied.

Chip's assessment profile, however, would probably make him a better candidate for a community group home than for outpatient services. An intense experience of six months in a group home in which the focus is on value development and peer group pressure might be needed to break the pattern of negative socialization (I, III, IV). The work experience could then be initiated from a supportive environment, with restrictions on the negative neighborhood pressures and peer group influence (III). Following this "moratorium," the plan would remain relatively the same as has been proposed. With six-months relief, the mother may be able to mobilize her strengths to provide additional help (IV).

It would not be surprising or considered a treatment failure if, after the first six months in the group home, Chip gets into trouble again and needs to return to the group home for a second "moratorium" (III, IV). We do know that in the process of resocialization youth must test their new values. They may need continued reinforcement in that process. Just as we plan continuing in-service training for staff, group homes may also need to provide four-/or six-week refresher courses to their graduates. Thus, to respond appropriately to assessment profiles of boys like Chip, we may need to plan community group residence programs that actually recall the youth periodically for short periods of reinforcement. In view of the high "relapse" rate of such boys, it seems preferable to take such preventive measures than to subject them to the high risk of additional societal failure and its negatively reinforcing consequences.

Joe

Joe is a 15-year-old boy, youngest of five children, whose mother has had repeated hospitalization for depression and whose father, a trucker, spends much of his time away from home, often by choice. Joe was apprehended for car theft with a group of boys and has a past record at the court. All of Joe's siblings have been involved with the court and all have been in state correctional institutions during their adolescence. Joe has periods of depression and is also known for his fighting and defiance of authority. He is four years behind in school and was identified at age 9 as having a learning disability.

Joe's profile is one which would call for institutionalization. There are almost no areas of strength to build upon. It will take a total environment to affect his behavior. But planning should go beyond the simple solution of sending him away. Thought needs to be given to the problem areas that the institution can realistically be expected to help with. And, plans must be developed for post-institutional help.

There are a number of problem areas that might be addressed in the institution during Joe's stay there. Indeed, the choice of institution for Joe should be made on the basis of the fit between Joe's needs and the institution's programming.

The most pertinent programming needs, in this case, would include some kind of positive peer culture, in a very structured environment, with peer group meetings that deal with asocial behaviors and the harm they cause to Joe, to his peers, and

Table 16-5 Client Assessment Profile of Joe

Area	Assessment	Treatment Plan
I. Value Development	–	Institutional structural environment Peer group counseling
II. Institutional Provision and Opportunity	–	Institutional placement Vocational training/ employment Post-institutional planning
III. Peer Group	–	Institutional placement Peer group counseling Post-institutional activity groups
IV. Family	–	Institutional placement Post-institutional living arrangement Family counseling re separation
V. Personality and Self-Image	–	Peer group counseling Educational work on learning disabilities
VI. Physiological Factors	–	Educational work on learning disabilities

to others (I). Value would be placed on Joe's responsibility to help others—especially his peers (III, V). In peer group meetings there would be opportunities for Joe to express anger, frustrations, fears, and aspirations (V), and there would be peer and institutional pressure to change behavior (I). Another desirable institutional program element would be special education services to deal with Joe's learning disabilities. While the probability of success in such work with Joe might be relatively low, any success would provide a payoff in such problem areas as Joe's self-image, his relationship with peers, and his employability, as well as attacking directly an area of "physical" disability (II, III, V, VI).

Given the family situation, it is not likely that Joe will be able to return home. Thus, while he is gone, alternative living arrangements must be developed, whether with a sibling or in a group residence (IV). Even if special help is offered in education, Joe will probably need either vocational training or a job on his return to the community (II). Some thought and effort needs to be given to developing a post-institutional vocational or work program while Joe is away since these arrangements generally take more time than will be available if we wait until his discharge to start planning. Even if the family members cannot maintain Joe they will need encouragement to support Joe's institutional experience, and preparation concerning the likelihood that he will not return to them (IV).

Thought will need to be given to developing alternative peer group experiences and leisure time activities in the community if he does indeed go to live with a sibling or if he is placed in a community group home (III).

Much of the failure of institutional treatment can be accounted for by poor or nonexistent post-discharge planning and service. It is obvious that Joe's profile identifies problem areas that are not likely to be solved even in the best of institutions. As stated earlier it is also obvious that developing a proper post-discharge plan and services cannot be done in the week or two we may have if we wait until Joe is ready to come back to the community. Planning for Joe's return to the community *must* start when he leaves, *not* when he returns.

The cases presented above are intended to be illustrative of the use of the suggested assessment profile. Space does not permit a discussion of all of the different possible profiles. But from these few examples, it should be clear that it is necessary for the counselor to account specifically for each of the identified problem areas in the treatment plan. The presence or absence of a problem area in a profile should be reflected by a difference in the treatment plan.

The assessment scheme does not actually indicate the *cause* of a problem nor does it dictate a "brand" of treatment. It is necessary to return to the supporting explanatory theories for a fuller exploration of why the problem exists. Likewise, the counseling techniques or other interventions to be offered can be drawn from among the approaches described earlier in this book or elsewhere. The purpose of the assessment profile is to provide a vehicle to help the counselor to search more systematically in the pertinent literature and to help him develop goals and approaches in treatment which address specifically *what* is to be planned, and *how* this will deal with problem areas.

A Caveat

It is obvious that the Client Assessment Profile reflects a classification scheme that is neither conceptually nor theoretically elegant. In effect, the scheme is not unidimensional—it mixes the conceptual equivalents of apples, oranges, and pears. Values (I), and personality and self-image (V) are internalized consequences of both physical givens (VI), and social structures such as social institutions and access to them (II), peer groups (III), and family (IV). The state of development in our delinquency and treatment theories does not allow a more sophisticated rendering at this time.

Summary

This chapter represents a beginning attempt to try to systematize our current thinking about delinquency theory, and to make linkages between delinquency types and specific treatments. Much work remains. In particular, we must determine more clearly what the differential effects are when given treatments (e.g., individual counseling, peer group counseling) are applied to different types of cases (e.g., negative value structure, lack of opportunity, poor self-image). We also need to determine which techniques (e.g., confrontation, catharsis, support, etc.) are most effective in given treatment approaches with particular clients.

Questions for Further Inquiry

1. Put yourself in the shoes of Joe, described in this chapter. How does he see himself and his world? Contrast Joe's views of self and world with those of Bill.

2. What within your own personality might help you reach out to a client who had committed a crime against a person? What within your personality might limit your reaching out effectiveness? What internal valuing conflicts might you need to resolve?

3. Review each of the cases presented in this chapter. Which would you describe as "victims?" Why? Would your treatment of those you perceive as "victim" be different in any way.

4. How do the ideas about socialization in the chapter on alienation (Chapter 6) apply to the socialization theory of delinquency in this chapter?

5. Recall the case of John. Is it reasonable to describe him as a "delinquent?" Support your position.

References

Adams, S. Assessment of the psychiatric treatment program, Phase 1: Third interim report. *Research Report No. 21, California Youth Authority,* January, 1961 (mimeographed).

Aichhorn, A. *Wayward youth.* London: Putman, 1936.

Becker, H. S. *Outsiders: Studies in the sociology of deviance.* London: Free Press, 1963.

Bloch, H. W., & Niederhoffer, A. *The gang: A study of adolescent behavior.* New York: Philosophical Library, 1958.

Clark, J. P., & Wenninger, E. P. Social class and delinquency. *American Sociological Review* 1962 *27,* 826–34.

Cloward, R. A., & Ohlin, L. E. *Delinquency and opportunity.* Glencoe, Ill.: Free Press, 1961

Cohen, A. K. *Delinquent boys: The culture of the gang.* Glencoe, Ill.: Free Press, 1955.

Craft, M., Stephenson, G. & Granger, C. A controlled trial of authoritarian and self-governing regimes with adolescent psychopaths. *American Journal of Orthopsychiatry* 1964 *34,* 543–54.

Cressey, Donald R. Organized crime and inner-city youth. *Crime and Delinquency* 1970 *16,* 132–35.

Erikson, E. H. *Childhood and society.* New York: Norton, 1950.

Friedlander, K. *The psycho-analytic approach to delinquency.* New York: International Universities Press, 1947.

General Accounting Office, Comptroller General of the United States. *Learning disabilities: The link to delinquency should be determined, but schools should do more now.* Washington, D. C.: U.S. Government Printing Office, 1976.

Glueck, S., & Glueck, E. *Family environment and delinquency.* Boston: Houghton-Mifflin, 1962.

Glueck, S., & Glueck, E. *Of delinquency and crime: A panorama of years of search and research.* Springfield, Ill.: Charles C. Thomas, 1974.

Gold, M. Undetected delinquent behavior. *Journal of Research In Crime and Delinquency* 1966 *13,* 27–49.

Kobrin, S. The conflict of values in delinquency areas. *American Sociological Review* 1951 *16,* 653–66.

Kvaraceus, W. C., & Miller, W. B. *Delinquent culture: Culture and the individual.* Washington, D.C.: National Education Association, 1959.

Lambo, T. A. Aggressiveness in the human life cycle within different socio-cultural settings. *International Social Science Journal* 1971 *23,* 79–88.

Lemert, E. *Human deviance, social problems and social control.* Englewood Cliffs, N.J.: Prentice-Hall, 1967.

Lombroso, C. *Crime: Its causes and remedies.* Boston: Little, Brown, 1918.

Martinson, Robert. What works—questions and answers about prison reform. *Public Interest 1974, 35,* 22–54.

Merton, R. K. *Social theory and social structure.* Glencoe, Ill.: Free Press, 1949.

Miller, W. B. Lower class culture as a generating milieu of gang delinquency. *Journal of Social Issues* 1958 *14,* 5–19.

Nye, F. I. *Family relationships and delinquent behavior.* New York: Wiley, 1958.

Palmer, T. Martinson revisited. *Journal of Research in Crime and Delinquency* 1975 *12,* 133–52.

Polk, K., & Schafer, W. E. *Schools and delinquency.* Englewood Cliffs, N. J.: Prentice-Hall, 1972.

Reckless, W. C., Dinitz, S., & Murray, E. Self-concept as an insulator against delinquency. *American Sociological Review* 1956 *21,* 744–46.

Redl, F., & Wineman, D. *Children who hate.* Glencoe, Ill.: Free Press, 1956.

Reiss, A. J. Delinquency as the failure of personal and social controls. *American Sociological Review* 1951 *16,* 196–206.

Schoenfield, C. G. A psychoanalytic theory of juvenile delinquency. *Crime and Delinquency* 1971 *17,* 469–81.

Scott, J. W., & Vaz, E. W. A perspective on middle-class delinquency. *Canadian Journal of Economic and Political Science* 1963 *29,* 324–35.

Shaw, C. R., & McKay, H. D. *Juvenile delinquency and urban areas.* Chicago: University of Chicago Press, 1942.

Sheldon, W. H. *Varieties of delinquent youth.* New York: Harper, 1949.

Short, J. Jr., & Strodtbeck, Fred L. *Group process and gang delinquency.* Chicago: University of Chicago Press, 1965.

Sutherland, E. H. *Principles of criminology, (4th ed.)* New York: Lippincott, 1947.

Sykes, G. M., & Matzo, Techniques of neutralization: A theory of delinquency. *American Sociological Review* 1957 *22,* 664–70.

Teeters, N. K., & Reinman, J. O. *The challenge of delinquency.* New York: Prentice-Hall, 1950.

Thorsell, B. A., & Klemke, L. W. The labeling process: Reinforcement or deterrent? *Law and Society Review* 1972 *6,* 393–403.

Thrasher, F. M. *The gang.* Chicago: University of Chicago Press, 1936.

Ullmann, L. P., & Krasmer, L. *A psychological approach to abnormal behavior.* Englewood Cliffs, N. J.: Prentice-Hall, 1969.

Vorrath, H. H., & Brendtro, L. K. *Positive peer culture.* Chicago: Aldine, 1974.

Weeks, H. W. *Youthful offenders at Highfields.* Ann Arbor: University of Michigan Press, 1963.

Whyte, W. F. *Street corner society.* Chicago: University of Chicago Press, 1943.

Yablonsky, L. *The violent gang.* New York: Macmillan, 1963.

Yinger, M. J. Contraculture and subculture. *American Sociological Review* 1960 *25,* 625–35.

Understanding and Overcoming Addictions

17

MARIE BURNETT

Overview

If it is true, as some notable scholars and writers have observed, that the protestant work ethic is dead, and that we are breeding a generation of persons dedicated to instant self-gratification (Albee, 1977; Peele, 1976), then it is likely that counselors and therapists may expect to come in contact with more and more clients who wish to have their problems in living solved by a "fix." The expectation that therapy may be "popped" like a pill is just one aspect of a larger socio-cultural pattern which encourages consumption as a solution to problems that are often experienced as an emptiness within the person. Things, chemicals, pills, and people are consumed hungrily in an effort to incorporate qualities felt lacking within the person. For such persons self-anesthetization is a style of life that works from day to day, warding off the kind of acute pain that motivates people to want to make real and lasting changes. The magic of a mood-altering drug is that it promises an altered consciousness within minutes and has the power to skim the anxiety off the top of any number of problems in living without ever bringing about a lasting solution.

The primary purpose of this chapter is to develop an understanding of the factors that contribute to chemical abuse and addiction, and then to use this understanding as the basis for planning treatment. Included will be discussion of themes such as the differences between abuse and addiction, psychological interpretations of abuse, a review of different kinds of nonalcohol based drugs, and models for treatment.

Understanding Persons Who Abuse Chemical Substances

The Addictive Personality as a Client

While it is not the primary task of this chapter to deal with the problem of the addictive personality, such persons behave in ways that create a need for specific structuring of counseling. The concept holds that addictions reside in the personality, rather than in the particular substance used. (Stanton Peele in *Love and Addiction* makes a good case for asserting that anything, including a loved object, may become an addiction.) Where an individual is lacking in genuine self-esteem, growing out of legitimate accomplishments and successes, he or she may seek magical solutions by the attachment and incorporation of things, chemicals, and/ or persons that provide an illusion of security. The problem is that more and more input is required with a diminishing return of satisfaction. When the supply runs out, the person experiences withdrawal symptoms such as depression, anxiety, and irritability. The addictive person seeks immediate sympton relief rather than problem solutions. The addictive person uses the treatment hour as a "fix," injecting the counselor's ego into his or her psyche, and doing little between sessions to bring about real life changes. Resisting the formulation of treatment goals, they ask, "What can I take from you that will make me feel better now?" rather than, "What can I do now in order to feel better in the future?"

The hallmark of the addictive personality is impatience, impulsivity, the refusal to postpone gratification, and a pessimism with respect to his or her ability to bring about effective changes in his or her environment through activities leading to genuine personal growth. These statements apply to the person addicted to chemicals such as heroin, as well as to the person addicted to alcohol. For people with addictions, the task of the counselor is to help the client set and achieve short-term goals that eventually will build in successes and subsequently provide the client with a more internalized sense of control over his or her life space.

While it may be said that persons who turn to alcohol for symptom relief fall under the general heading of the addictive personality, this conceptualization *alone* has not proved effective or useful enough in bringing about needed change. A more specific formulation is required to meet the special needs of clients with a vulnerability to so powerful an addiction as alcoholism, an addiction that involves a chemical known to be hazardous to health. A more holistic approach must necessarily be taken, one which recognizes the progressive and debilitating nature of this specific addiction. I have found it valuable in counseling alcoholics to keep in mind the possibility that an additional physical vulnerability to alcoholism may exist that has a genetic or constitutional basis. Alcoholics Anonymous has found it useful to conceptualize this vulnerability as a kind of inherited allergy which affects about 10 percent of the population of those who drink. Jellinek (1972) has posited a constitutional tolerance, or nervous tissue adaptation, that encourages the excessive use of alcohol in persons with a psychological vulnerability to alcohol abuse.

Alcohol Abuse vs. Alcohol Addiction

Broadly defined, an alcohol abuser is one who regularly drinks excessively with the *intention* of getting "high" or drunk. He or she is after an effect that may be verbalized as a compensation for feelings of inadequacy, to overcome shyness, inhibitions, tensions, feelings of alienation, impotence, loneliness, depression, anxiety. There is a sense in which the individual feels in control of his or her drinking behavior. In contrast, the alcohol *addict* experiences a compulsion to accelerate drinking once drinking has begun. The intention may be to avoid intoxication; the outcome is inevitably intoxication. The hallmark of an alcohol addict is the loss of control over drinking behavior. The progression from abuse to addiction, however, is rarely so clearly delineated. In the early stages of alcoholism, the client may wish to articulate his or her problems in psychological terms as stemming from marital conflicts, interpersonal difficulties, or career tensions. It is important for the professional helper to distinguish between abuse and addiction. A misdiagnosis at this point could have serious consequences for the client. It is true that most addicts begin as abusers and that not all abusers eventually become addicts, but to be on the safe side, it is best for the counselor to be alerted to early signs of addiction while dealing with all abusers. While younger clients are more often abusers (according to Jellinek [1972], the addictive process takes anywhere from 3 to 15 years to develop), addiction cannot be ruled out on the basis of age alone. Nor can it be assumed that a middle-aged person with a drinking problem is always an alcoholic. Persons who have been social drinkers for most of their lives may become abusers in reaction to a severe ego assault such as the loss of a job or a mate. The counselor must also keep in mind that a maximum of 10 percent of all alcohol users become addicts.

Toward an Understanding of Abuse and Addiction

Alcohol Abuse: A Psychological Interpretation

The male heavy drinker, vulnerable to alcoholism, has been studied intensively by McClelland (1972) and his associates. Their findings are reported in *The Drinking Man* and shall be drawn from heavily in this section. Persons with an interest in the details of research designs, procedures, and cross-cultural data are urged to read their book.

From their research the authors have developed the hypothesis of a "protest masculinity syndrome," more commonly recognized as "machismo." The macho syndrome consists of a cluster of behaviors, including heavy drinking, exploitative sex, and dominance in interpersonal exchanges. Among college students, the syndrome has been described as the "stud cluster" and includes owning and displaying prestige objects, such as sports cars and expensive stereo equipment. The pre-alcoholic male, or what we are terming here the alcohol abuser, is viewed as a person high in the need for and concern over personalized power. He is seen as striving for a feeling of potency, as exemplified by vigorous expansive activity, charisma, and social dominance. He tends to be impulsive and feels unable to acquire legitimate social power through instrumental, goal-oriented behavior requiring the postponement of gratification. He seeks instead a magical transformation to quickly increase his sense of personal power and potency. Drinking provides almost immediately a means of feeling dominant, vigorous, and impactful.

From the research data, the male abuser appears to have developed the belief that the source of all good is outside the self, and that he must take it rather than bring it about through productive activity. Thus he displays the qualities of the addictive personality discussed earlier. Given that the particular "good" he is after is personalized power, his choice is a "fix" of alcohol. A possible physiological basis for the choice might be that the short-term immediate effects of alcohol are to produce "sensations" of increased strength, i.e., a rapid increase of blood sugar and thus available energy, the depression of inhibitory centers thus freeing-up expressivity, stimulation of adrenalin, thus mobilizing the body for action, vaso-dilation which increases sensations of bodily warmth, and finally the blocking of pain sensations. Alcohol produces a "rush" and a pleasant "high."

This exaggerated need for displaying a hyper-masculine facade may be a defense against feelings of weakness, impotence, and social inadequacy. Two possible explanations offered by the researchers to account for these feelings are a too close identification with an overnurturant, overprotective, dominant mother and/or a sociocultural milieu that demands yet frustrates highly assertive behavior from its males. (My own clinical experience is consistent with the first explanation; many male abusers often show a configuration that includes a mother who infantalizes her son, promoting his dependency while undercutting her husband's masculine strivings, thus depriving her son of an adequate model of adult functioning.) In line with the second explanation, cultures in which a man must *prove* his masculine identity seem to promote heavier drinking than those in which a man is well rewarded by virtue of his maleness, (e.g., the Italian and Jewish cultures).

Recognizing that machismo includes an attitude of male superiority with a need to control women and to keep them in their place, the McClelland investigators administered a questionnaire to a group of abstainers and a matched group of alcoholics in a Mexican village with a high incidence of alcoholism, asking whether women should have the same rights as men. Of the alcoholics, 78.6 percent answered no, compared to 44.8 percent of the abstainers. Those who answered negatively expressed a fear of domination by women. Keeping this fact in mind, one could hypothesize that there may be a relationship between sexism and alcohol abuse. Where rigid gender-role stereotyping is promoted, requiring that men exemplify the machismo ideal of masculinity, alcohol may provide a crutch for males in conflict with their gender-identity. For example, men who may be in touch with "feminine" aspects of their character may fear that in a sexist society such traits are unacceptable. Drinking may provide a means of "masculine protest" to compensate for self-doubts regarding manliness. With this in mind, we turn now to a discussion of the female abuser. Here I will rely upon both extrapolation from *The Drinking Man* study and my own clinical experience with female problem drinkers.

In a society which expects women to be nurturant, passive, submissive, unassertive, and dependent, the female alcohol abuser is often hyper-feminine. Sober, she exemplifies the stereotype. She is often "other directed," rigid, and compulsive in her strivings to be feminine. At parties she is often a wall-flower, prim and inhibited—a perfect foil for the macho male. Like the male alcohol abuser, she believes that the source of all good is outside herself, and feels incapable of bringing about significant changes instrumentally through goal-oriented, planned behaviors. Such a woman often has a severe problem asserting angry feelings, standing up for herself and risking rejection. Her felt impotence renders her prone to depression. She has the problem Betty Friedan in the *Feminine Mystique* identified as "the problem that has no name." Drinking provides her with the ability to turn her depression into anger for her condition. Alcohol, by depressing inhibitory centers, initially allows her to be more assertive, comfortable, and sexually uninhibited. She, too, acquires a much sought after illusion of power. The difference between the female heavy drinker and her male counterpart is that while drinking provides a temporary solution for the male who needs to prove his masculinity, for the female, drinking creates a gender-identity conflict fraught with guilt. It is not ladylike to be angry, sexy, or a heavy drinker. Kinsey (1966) found that female alcoholics are in conflict over an internalized acceptance of the traditional female role which results in anxiety and depression. Wilsnak (1973) found that alcoholic women value the maternal role to a hyper-feminine degree and that they wish to be overly adequate. (Once abuse has progressed to an addiction, alcohol provides a means of anesthetizing all feelings.)

While the feminist movement has done much to liberate women from stereotypic roles, there is evidence of an increase in the incidence of female alcoholism among working women. One might hypothesize that the dynamics of female alcohol abuse in the 70s may be essentially the same as the dynamics for men. That is, the expectation for women to be more assertive, aggressive, and competitive may lead some women to turn to alcohol to provide the magical transformation from traditional femininity to powerful liberated women.

Whether the client is male or female, whether traditionally feminine or seeking to be assertive, the *common element* in the etiology of alcohol abuse is *a search for power.* The immediate physiological impact of alcohol is to create an illusion of power.

Drug Abuse (Other Than Alcohol): A Psychological Interpretation

Psychologically defined, an addiction occurs when an abuser's use of any drug becomes obsessive, compulsive, and excludes all other coping mechanisms for warding off unwanted experiences. When that drug is withdrawn, the addict becomes severely disoriented and distressed. Following the completion of the physical symptoms of withdrawal, the desire to seek out a renewed high will motivate the abuser back to the drug experience.

Enslavement to drugs is not wholly chemically based but involves a need that propels the user toward the tyrant again and again. Physical dependency may provide an excuse for the *maintenance* of the drug intake but cannot explain the willingness of the victim to return to the drug after withdrawal from the chemical enslavement has been accomplished.

The specific psychological motivations which attract individuals to abuse certain drugs other than alcohol have not been investigated as thoroughly as motivation for alcohol abuse. We can only infer from what we know of the pharmacological effects of specific drugs and of the experience they produce in the abuser what those motivations might be. The nature of the drug experience is influenced by the user's response to the drug's effects.

To understand drug addiction, therefore, we must explore both the nature of specific drug's highs and the nature of the "straight" experience of those who are susceptible to using drugs addictively. All drugs have the effect of altering consciousness by bringing about changes in the user's perception of self and "the world." The normal organization of the mind is disrupted. The particular effects vary somewhat depending on the class of drugs in question.

In general, all drugs to varying degrees provide the user with an experience of pleasure, of euphoria, of competence, of self-satisfaction, and a sense of omnipotence. Susceptibility to addiction depends in part on the degree to which such feelings are compensatory for feelings of pain, distress, inadequacy, low self-esteem, and impotence.

Addictive Drugs and Their Effects   Those drugs which are said to be addictive in the pharmacological sense (tolerance develops and withdrawal symptoms occur) are the *narcotics or analgesics* which include opium, morphine, codeine, and heroin, and the generalized central nervous system *depressants* which include barbiturates, alcohol, and the minor tranquilizers such as Librium, Valium, and Miltown.

A narcotic high is a perfect, perpetual "cool," which constricts the mind's aperture to the inner and outer world of impinging stimuli—stimuli capable of evoking an unwanted feeling response. The illusion is one of absolute control over one's environment. The heroin user is insulated against all pain to the point of indifference to the inner and outer world. There is grandiosity in the narcotic "high" appealing to persons who experience themselves when "straight" as powerless victims and who at the same time have an appetite for supreme control over their environment. The heroin user is content to achieve the *feeling* of power rather than take the steps and risks required to attain legitimate mastery and with it a reasonable measure of actual power.

To the outside observer, he or she appears to be in a stuporous, benumbed state of withdrawn inactivity. Heroin obliterates all motivation to bring about any change. It has the ability to produce "total drive satiation" (Jaffe, 1970). A perfect homeostasis is experienced. The user experiences no pain, no discomfort, no stress, no wish to change any element of his or her experienced environment. Any drug which can produce this type of experience will be addictive to certain persons —regardless of the chemical structure of the drug or its specific mechanisms for producing that experience. (Peele points out that it has been a fruitless search to discover an analgesic which would produce the desired "experience" without the potential for becoming addictive in susceptible persons. Methadone is being used addictively by ex-addicts.)

While the narcotic drugs are uniquely analgesic, producing a "high" which is characteristically painless, the generalized *depressants* of the central nervous system which we will consider now may be said to produce a "downer" experience characterized as sedating and hypnotic. Since special consideration has been given to alcohol abuse and addiction elsewhere, we will consider only the *barbiturates* in this section. Those commonly abused are the short-acting variety which include Nembutal, Seconal, Amytal, and Tuinal - collectively referred to as "goofballs." The drug abuser uses increasingly large doses of "downers" to produce a quick state of intoxication, or to produce sleep following an extended amphetamine or cocaine high.

"Downers" alter consciousness by dulling awareness and are commonly abused by chronically discontent housewives who may legitimately obtain prescriptions to treat insomnia. Eventually they are used daily as a sedative, and finally as an intoxicant. We may speculate that to some women "pill-popping" may seem more sex-role appropriate than alcohol consumption. Barbiturate addiction is said to be associated often with severe psychotic depressions leading to suicide attempts (Hofmann, 1975). From a psychodynamic point of view we might speculate that "downers" are chosen by isolated persons whose stress tolerance is low to begin with. Barbiturate intoxication is not much fun.

The minor tranquilizers (Miltown, Equanil, Librium, Valium) produce much the same experience as the barbiturates. Designed to relieve anxiety without sedating, their capacity to ameliorate or alter mood contribute to their abuse and addiction in susceptible persons, especially alcoholics and fearful, anxious persons who use them to "calm down," to sleep, to get through stressful situations, and eventually as a crutch for daily coping.

Other Frequently Abused Drugs Several drugs that may not be addictive in the technical sense, are, nevertheless, frequently abused and contribute to significant health and psychological problems. These drugs include *glue, stimulants, cocaine,* and *hallucinogens.* Glue sniffing, another form of "downer" commonly abused by young people, produces a state of giddy intoxication, euphoria, feelings of omnipotence and reckless abandon, and sometimes promotes impulsive, even destructive acts. (Perceptual distortions, delusions of grandeur, and hallucinations are sometimes experienced.) In general, the high is similar to that produced by alcohol abuse and is most probably similarly motivated.

Certain central nervous system stimulants *(amphetamines and methamphetamines)* are abused to produce a drug experience characterized as an "upper." The abuse of "uppers" leads to "speeding," and those who regularly speed are called "speed freaks." Speed freaks may "mainline" large doses of the drug daily, often at two-hour intervals. Adolescents and young adults who speed have been characterized as persons craving action, kicks, and instant pleasure (Hofmann, 1975). The experience of "uppers" provides an illusion of competence, physical and mental omnipotence and provides the needed courage to take risks in certain situations. Unlike the narcotic or barbiturate high, a "speed" high promotes garrulous sociability and explosive outbursts of activity by energizing persons who might otherwise be fearful, withdrawn, or apathetic. The "crash" or hangover from an extended "run" produces a depression which may be so overwhelming as to produce suicidal ideation. An amphetamine high is an exhausting "power trip" which leads eventually to a dreary destination. Experts disagree on whether an amphetamine hangover is a withdrawal syndrome or a physiological outcome to be expected following any protracted period of wakefulness, starvation, and continuous activity. Whether or not physical dependency may be said to develop, the fact is that the amphetamine high easily "hooks" the abuser.

Cocaine ("snow," "coke," "white lady," "lady," "girl") produces effects similar to the amphetamines with the difference that the effects persist for a shorter time. Coke is usually inhaled ("sniffed"), and sometimes injected intravenously. A spree may last for an evening and may require dosages at 20-minute intervals. The experience is said to promote sexuality, and is currently associated with "jetsetters," "the beautiful people," and show business types. Since a "coke" high tends to be expensive, involving elements of conspicuous waste (amphetamines give you more of the same for the money), one aspect in its attraction may be the status and glamor associated with its use.

Each of the drug groups discussed thus far produces a characteristically unique experience which attracts persons seeking those specific effects. What they have in common is the effect of producing a temporary illusion of control over the user's world. The narcotics do this by distancing the user from external and internal stimuli; the depressants dampen the impact of environmental stimuli; the stimulants quiet precautionary internal stimuli. It is the resulting experience of euphoria and control when it is compensatory to feelings of pain, powerlessness, and inadequacy that produces a psychological dependence.

Hallucinogens or "psychedelics" include marihuana ("grass," "pot") which is also mood-altering, mescaline, LSD, and DMT. These are the "mind-blowing" drugs which are said to provide esoteric insights into the nature of self and reality. The psychedelic experience is attractive to creative young nonconforming persons who may use these drugs experimentally, recreationally, episodically, ritualistically, communally, or chronically. The "burn-outs," "pot-heads," and "acid-heads," are those who have become psychically dependent on the experience; (while tolerance to the effects of these drugs has been documented, there is no evidence of a withdrawal syndrome connected to their abuse). The experience of "getting high" on pot is more likely to become a daily "need" than acid "tripping." The mood-altering aspect of the marihuana high may account for its addictive use. An LSD trip is less predictable, longer lasting (from 8–12 hours) and reciprocally inhibiting to almost all normal functioning. (One can go to work or to school "high" on pot.)

The psychedelic experience depends upon the users' willingness to "let it happen," and is influenced by social setting, expectations, previous experiences, and the mood of the user. The effect of LSD is to render the user emotionally labile, and to place him or her in a highly novel and ambiguous world of disorganized sensory data. Judgment can be seriously impaired; success of the trip will therefore depend upon the user's trust of those in the group. Because of increased suggestability, panic and paronoia are common components of a "bad trip." As LSD experimenters have become more knowledgeable of the expected effects of the drug, we are seeing fewer "freak-out" victims than we did in the sixties (Zinberg, 1974).

The marihuana high is individual and variable. In general, a high tends to heighten awareness, especially to the formal and concrete aspects of sensory data, while functional and conceptual aspects of perceptual organization tend to be minimized, producing a heightened aesthetic sensitivity to ordinary everyday objects. For example, one can "get off" on the play of light and dark shadows on drapery folds, or the flickering of candle light. Leaves of a tree lose their usual gestalt so that the observer becomes aware of each individual leaf and twig. This attention to concrete aspects of the environment tends to "stretch" time frames so that an hour is perceived as many hours.

Hallucinogenic properties of marihuana produce mild perceptual distortions and tend to alter responses rather than stimuli, e.g., a straight-forward newscast may be interpreted as hilariously amusing. Loss of self-consciousness may accompany heightened attention to novel details of the environment, resulting in a loss of inhibition and a sense of communality with those who are sharing the experience, in contrast to those outside the group who are "straight." A marihuana high is fun and is most often used recreationally. Since the experience tends to reduce the pressure of achievement motivation and time concern, it is an ideal party drug. When, however, it becomes a daily coping crutch, inhibiting goal-oriented behaviors in young people, it is of serious concern to parents and teachers.

Since marihuana use is more likely to become chronic among troubled adolescents, we will spend the remainder of this section illustrating its progression from use to abuse to psychic dependence. For this purpose, I have chosen to share with the reader excerpts from the diary of a 15-year-old female marihuana abuser. One can observe the progression from the November to January to July entries. The

November journal illustrates the point that susceptibility to drug abuse depends on personality variables, i.e., low self-esteem, concern over peer acceptance, and poor social skills. The January journals illustrate the growing obsession developing around drug use as loss of control becomes apparent. The final July entry demonstrates the deterioration of values, the change in life-style, and the accompanying pain made tolerable only with the help of further drug abuse.

November 26, Wednesday

Went out with the group again. I was so quiet. I don't know, I just felt awful *out* of that group. I never have anything to say. We went outside in the snowy cold (snow began Monday), looking around for guys with some pot. We couldn't find anybody who had some. I was hoping we would so I could come in high and show R and S. But no one had any. I was so quiet. I don't think I said anything. Of course, I don't think they really give a shit about me. P kept giving me glances in a way like wondering what the hell I was doing there. Anyway we went inside of school and smoked cigarettes in a south stairwell. I was quiet then and I mean I felt left out. I couldn't stand it so I left after awhile. I wonder what they all said about me when I left. Probably they said, "Who is that ugly girl—God she's so quiet," or something like that. I hope they didn't think I was ugly. Especially J. He's cutest of all. I wonder how my mother would take it if I ever went with him. His hair is slightly long for her generation. Boy it would be neat to go with him. Anyway, I left the group and went to meet S and R. S was really pissed at me. She says: "T, why did you do *it* again?" I looked at her dumbly and laughed. I told her I didn't have any pot. She didn't believe me but I finally convinced her that I didn't smoke it today. She was pretty cold with me. I don't know why she's so against pot and stuff. I mean, really. Pot is less harmful than cigarettes and if I have it every once in awhile, it cannot possibly hurt. So I don't know why she's so upset about it.

January 26, Monday

There was no school today. D and I slept until 11:30 believe it or not. We sure wasted the day today. We went to my garage and smoked 2 joints (sure was thick joints) then went down Central to look around and then went to N's to remind her not to forget to get me the reefer. We then came home and watched TV for the rest of the time that D was here.

Diary, what is happening to me? I smoke *too* much marihuana. I love it and I don't understand why. Why do I want it so much? I've lost a good relationship with God. I'm afraid. I haven't been praying to him for a while. I guess because I'm always stoned at night. It isn't hurting me is it? Oh Lordy I hope not. I've decided to lay off the stuff for awhile. I really ought to let my poor lungs have a rest. It's a nice feeling to be stoned. I'm planning to get stoned before school tomorrow and then that's it until at least a week. I hope I can do that. Correction: I *must* do that. Since N's getting me Columbian though, I might have a joint with friends Tuesday or Wednesday, or Thursday, or Friday (certainly not all of these days). But is it true that I'm a "burnout?" It's a shame I even started this stuff. A year ago, I never even thought much at all about pot. It just never came to my mind and I never thought about it at all. I never had any urges to try it. It was just that night with L after girl scouts that started all this. I never dreamed I would turn out this way. I could easily give up pot. But I really don't want to at all. I enjoy smoking it which is shit.

I hope I'll never be influenced too much by this stuff, and true honest to goodness research can be done to figure out how harmful marihuana is to the body. I don't smoke that much. I don't think I will ever smoke cigarettes enough to harm me but I'm afraid pot might hurt me sometime later. It's easy to say "but it's not hurting now so let's continue," those later years are far away. But are they far away? Only God can know that one. I love pot and it is something I want to continue smoking. I hope I will go a little more easier on it then I have been lately.

January 27, Tuesday

Got high before going to school. S was kind of disappointed in me when I came to school. "You got high, T, you're such a 'Burnout.' " That's what she said to me. I was quite disappointed with some of the grades I received for exams. . . .

January 28, Wednesday

Got high again this morning. It was fun (kind of). Got a "C" on my dumb English exam. I was super angry about that.

January 29, Thursday

I didn't get high until later tonight. After school, I went over to N's and she gave me the reefer. Wow!

July 15, Thursday

I went down to the beach and drank Southern Comfort with the crowd on the rocks. I really don't know why we did. It just is that I didn't think anything was going to happen to us, because we weren't doing anything. Then the cops tell us to empty our pockets. L was the only one that had anything. They told us we were all under arrest. I was too stoned to think anything was going to happen. They got us down to the station, we sit there listening to their shit, "You're charged for possession of Marihuana and we're calling up your parents." Oh God, fuck these pigs! That's what went through my head. I refused to give him my address because I didn't think I deserved the charge and my parents were having that big party that night and it would've been horrid for my dad to have to come down and pick me up. The cop says: "If you don't give us your address you're going to have to stay in the A. . . Home." I'm staying there then, I said. So, R & I get taken into this office with this ass hole of a juvenile officer. He was so mean. I hated his fuckin' guts. He was *rude rude rude.* I lied about my phone and my address. I didn't want them to get my parents. Unfortunately, he called, found out that wasn't my phone number and he threw me in another room which was a little small room with bars on the windows. When he finally let me out, Mr. A pops in and then my dad. The officer says: "These girls were very uncooperative, they refused to give their names and addresses." Then the Pig told us to wait in the other room. We did. I was too stoned to really know what the fuck was going on. Then they called me out. He tells me I've got to see a probation officer and if I didn't cooperate, I would be sent back to him. Dad takes me home. He didn't believe a fuckin' word I said when I told him I didn't have pot on me, because the stupid pig told our fathers that we had pot on us. I knew I was dead! Grounded for the rest of the summer. Luckily I was burned out so I didn't have to stay up all night crying my eyes out.

Approaches for Helping Clients Overcome Abuse and Addiction

Drugs Other Than Alcohol

While Peele (1977) and other experts emphasize that it is the drug experience that is addictive not the drug, I would emphasize that it is the "straight" experience the addict is avoiding that contributes to the development of an addiction to the experienced "high." Motivation for early use is a critical factor. If you enjoy where you are, you are not likely to go out of your way to repeat the drug experience. If you do not like who you are and feel helpless, escape from your unpleasant reality can be a powerful reinforcer for continued and higher levels of drug use. The job of the counselor is to help the drug dependent person to like who he or she is, where he or she is. You do this by helping to bring about changes in the client's life experience, i.e., helping to provide a new and different meaning for life, new pastimes, a new structure, a more meaningful identity—very much what AA (Alcoholics Anonymous) does for alcoholics.

Helping the client to overcome abuse and addiction is not a simple task. The counselor, therapist, teacher, or parent must help the drug abuser to improve the quality of his or her straight experience. This means showing the client how to gain control over some aspects of experience, while teaching him or her to tolerate the frustration of not being in control of all aspects of the environment. The client must be helped to develop techniques that can be relied upon to alleviate anxiety, depression, boredom, despair, fear, etc.—techniques that grow out of personal efforts rather than the passive ingestion of a chemical.

As the client grows in the ability to take responsibility for personal feelings, there will be less need to escape reality. As the client grows from the position of helpless victim to one of autonomous adult, self-esteem will strengthen. Changing the client's experience from that of a "loser" to that of a "winner" will require a therapeutic milieu. One-to-one counseling alone cannot usually accomplish such a change. Ideally a school might provide special programs designed to enhance achievement by providing immediate and direct rewards for small steps toward effective coping. A peer counseling group might be developed with the goal of resocializing drug abusers who may need to learn social skills for relating to and supporting each other. Family sessions might be scheduled during which parents could be helped to support the developing autonomy of their children. Young people learn to view themselves as their parents view them. Drug abusers often complain of lack of warmth and love in their homes. An absence of parent "stroking" in the home will lead to a low self-image, which contributes to the susceptibility to drug abuse.

Any counseling program must involve resocializing the addict to develop a trust in interpersonal satisfactions. Most substance abusers have learned to manipulate people, to distrust deep interpersonal relationships. They would rather trust a chemical for satisfaction. Addicts are often loners whose intense dependency needs are met by drugs and manipulative interactions with persons. (Some addicts appear to be gregarious). For them there is *safety* in chemical dependency and *risk* in having dependency needs met by people who are viewed as unreliable. When the addicted person attempts to relate to others, the demands placed on the relationship are usually too great because the need is too engulfing. Attempts at controlling the source of security usually leads eventually to rejection thus reinforcing the return to drug addiction—a more dependable and quicker source of gratification. A sensation that is predictable is better than an experience laden with unknowns. A relationship develops in time—the addict is after immediate gratification. (It is interesting that certain antidepressants are rarely abused despite the fact that they are more powerful than the preferred "upper"; the difference is that they must be used regularly over a period of weeks or months before the effects are felt.)

Helping the Problem Drinker: Abuse or Addiction

The distinction between abuse and addiction is more critical when the chemical of choice is alcohol. While an abuser may return to a moderate use of alcohol once the psychological motivation for abuse has been treated, the addict (alcoholic) can rarely return to the moderate use of alcohol without losing control again. It is therefore critical for the counselor to make a differential diagnosis before the goal for treatment is established. My approach is consistent with the view that certain persons may be physically vulnerable as well as psychologically vulnerable to alcohol addiction. Such a nervous sytem vulnerability has not been suggested with respect to other drugs.

The first clue to the formulation of an initial hypothesis about whether a client is an abuser or alcoholic is the manner in which the client presents self. In the case of the *male abuser,* the referral may be made around an incident of acting-out aggressive behavior, often school related. Sometimes it is the mother who makes the original telephone contact. Her son may have flunked out of college or been suspended from high school. Sometimes the referral comes from a community source, such as a juvenile police officer. More usually, the client will call, describing his or her problem as that of having difficulty making social relationships, especially with members of the opposite sex. Rarely will excessive drinking be mentioned initially as the problem.

A male client appearing for his initial appointment will typically present himself as a "macho" young adult between the ages of 19 and 30, dressed in "mod" fashion. His voice well modulated, his verbal style smooth and guarded, he may remain distanced for the first half of the hour. A skilled interviewer can break through this thin façade before the end of the first interview. The client will often then confess to feelings of insecurity. Further probing often reveals that his main concern is that he has never had a girl friend. By this he means that his attempts to "score" have never worked. When questioned about his drinking behavior, he will readily mention that drinking is habitually used as a crutch to shore up his confidence.

The female abuser most often will be self-referred. At the intake level she is more likely to mention, among other complaints, concern over a possible drinking problem. In the past she was more often a housewife and mother; more recently she is likely to be a pink-collar worker. In appearance she presents herself as conventional, inhibited, shy, neat, and somewhat withdrawn. Many of her concerns are work related, e.g., difficulty being supervised, or supervising others, perfectionistic standards, difficulty accepting criticism, inability to express anger. As counseling progresses, she reveals difficulty in establishing intimate relationships. She worries that she is using alcohol habitually to relieve tension. This causes her guilt, especially if she is neglecting sex role-related behaviors.

Alcoholics mostly call because of urgings from a spouse who threatens divorce. It is useful to invite the spouse to accompany the client for the first or second interview. If the client is a single adult, medical problems or employment problems may have promoted the call for help. While alcoholics tend to be typically older than the abuser (somewhere between 30 and 50), remember that a person who has been drinking heavily for as few as three years may very well be at the early stages of alcoholism. While an initial tentative hypothesis may be made on the basis of age and presenting problem, a thorough history must be taken before a final diagnosis can be made. The critical issue is whether or not the client is in control of his or her drinking behavior. The hitch is that alcoholics tend to use denial and rationalization as a defense against the admission that he or she is actually out of control. Evidence for alcoholism must usually be obtained indirectly. Furthermore, counseling success is usually dependent upon the counselor's skill in leading the client to make the final diagnosis. If your suspicion is that the client in your office is most likely an alcoholic, it is safer to proceed as if this were the case.

The position taken here is that alcoholism must be viewed holistically as a psychosomatic social disease with interpersonal and intrapsychic components balanced against somatic components which could be severe enough to result in death. This is the Alcoholics Anonymous approach to the understanding of alcohol addiction. Our aim, therefore, will be to direct the alcoholic client to recovery through AA or an AA-modeled alcoholism treatment facility. Psychological counseling will be offered only if we are certain that the client is free of any signs of addiction, or in the case of alcoholics, only after sobriety has been established, preferably through an AA program.

A Model for Counseling Alcoholics

The single most difficult hurdle the counselor must overcome with the alcoholic client is his or her impaired judgment and defenses (evasions, denials, and rationalizations that often amount to outright delusions). For this reason the drinking history must be taken skillfully in a nonjudgmental manner with a focus on specific, objective information. The aim is to discover whether or not the client is in control of his or her drinking behavior. (For detail of how this is done, the reader is referred to Burnett, 1977).

Once the client has decided that he or she is an alcoholic (and this may require several progressively more confronting interviews, including family members, employers, or school officials), the client is referred to AA or a hospital alcoholism program. Since it is extremely rare that an alcoholic can recover without a powerful group support system such as that provided by AA (Armor, Polick, and Stambul, 1978), it is best to operate on the premise that it cannot be done. This fact needs to be conveyed to the client in objective, factual terms. This, of course, translates to the client that he or she must abstain from drinking altogether. A referral for psychiatric treatment will always be accepted more readily than a referral to AA. A client's claim that AA didn't work, was not enough, etc., must not be accepted by the counselor. It deserves no credibility. If AA cannot succeed, anything less, such as weekly individual therapy sessions, will not be successful. You may have to schedule several appointments to work through the resistance to your recommendation.

Many of the female alcoholics I have seen at the middle stages of alcoholism have recounted to me their histories of having sought help from psychiatrists years earlier who told them that nice girls can't be drunks. In effect, the psychiatrist's unwillingness to see a woman, possibly a mother, as having a drinking problem gave these women the permission they needed from a male authority figure to continue on the road to alcoholism. Female alcoholics, because they tend to be so self-critical and perfectionistic, will often become extremely depressed and suffer a marked reduction in self-esteem once they have accepted the diagnosis. For this reason they may remain resistant to an AA involvement even longer than a male who once accepts that he is an alcoholic. Males who resist AA often resist because they are really not ready to give up drinking; women may be ready, but wish to do it without help. They want to keep their alcoholism a secret.

It is not enough for the counselor to be nonjudgmental; the alcoholic woman needs help in acquiring a nonjudgmental attitude toward herself and other recovering alcoholics before she can benefit from a self-help group. Those who go to AA feeling that they and the others there are "losers" will not fully benefit from the involvement.

What can you do if your client is not ready for AA? There isn't much you can do with the client himself or herself. You have already assured him or her that without the help of AA, he or she will "fall off the wagon." He or she already knows this, or will learn it. In these cases you can often be of help to the family. They may be scared, worried, and doing all the wrong things—from nagging, threatening, yelling, to rescuing and offering chicken soup and sympathy. They may be suffering guilt, shame, taking the responsibility for the alcoholic's problems, or they may be furious and ready to kill him or her if the disease doesn't do it. All of these feelings and behaviors are stressful for the alcoholic and will contribute to the alcoholic's inevitable falling off the wagon. They will provide him or her with an excuse. If children are involved, they will wonder why their parent drinks. They may be feeling neglected, unloved, abandoned, frightened, and more or less responsible. Remember, alcoholism affects the whole family system.

Your task is to help them to share these feelings with you, to share your objective knowledge of alcoholism with them, and when they are ready to do something constructive for the alcoholic in their family, refer them to Al-Anon and/or Al-Ateen.

I have asserted that the counselor working with alcoholics must accept that the AA approach is the only one that works, and that she or he must refuse counseling beyond that of helping the client to diagnose his or her problem, or referring to a group such as AA, and of working through the resistance to treatment. This position is based on both clinical experience and research evidence (Armor, Polick, Stambul, 1978). While such a blanket assertion may seem dogmatic, it is my belief that unless the counselor takes such an authoritative stand, he or she will be manipulated into providing yet another path for the alcoholic to take in avoidance of treatment. AA's critical attitude toward professional services is based on the experiences of thousands of recovering alcoholics who have reported that the unwillingness of psychiatirc workers to recognizo their alcoholism as a powerful addiction was as great as their own wish to deny the reality, and that psychiatric treatment was responsible, in many cases, for the unarrested progression of the addiction.

Eradication of the motive to use alcohol addictively is not as easily accomplished as the detoxification process which cures the addict of physical dependency. So, while theoretically it may be possible for an ex-alcoholic to go back to alcohol use following a period of counseling, or "training," or psychotherapy—the risk is great. Patterns of behavior involving defenses and coping mechanisms that have been well incorporated into a personality structure cannot be easily altered —except possibly for the very young, or highly motivated. (Most recovering alcoholics would prefer not to take the risk; most alcohol counselors are not sure enough of their work to recommend such risk-taking). I don't know any narcotics counselor who would recommend that the client return to moderate heroin use following treatment for heroin addiction.

The AA approach does not ignore character traits and psycho-social factors that contribute to alcohol addiction; they are considered to be a necessary but not sufficient condition for the development of the addiction. Genetic and/or biological explanations do not suggest that alcohol addiction is inevitability based on the biochemical properties of alcohol, only that there is a physical vulnerability among a percentage of the population of those persons who develop a pattern of abusive use of alcohol over a period of time such that those persons will become physically as well as psychologically dependent upon alcohol while others may not. This physical vulnerability remains after the psychological vulnerability has been treated and it constitutes the danger of relapse when normal drinking is attempted.

The return to drinking by the alcoholic may require very little motivational push from within the individual. (Contrary to the situation of a narcotic addict, a person in our society who does not use alcohol is a deviant from the norm). The motivation not to use alcohol must be powerful enough to counteract the pressure from a society that encourages drinking in many settings and that condones drunkenness. A person who seeks an illegal drug probably is more driven away from a painful state of consciousness and toward a pleasurable experience, than a person who learns to engage in alcohol use because it is expected. There is both peer and family approval for alcohol use. For those with a susceptibility to alcohol addiction the return to addictive use following withdrawal is a pattern which requires powerful intervention. Linkage to a support system which can provide an alternative life-style to the prevalent middle-class life-style that involves alcohol use is valuable in maintaining sobriety. (In the case of the narcotic addict, removal from a deviant subculture and integration into the main stream may be a task more easily accomplished.) So while it may not be unequivocally true that the AA approach is the only one that works, it is the only modality that I know of that does report a high degree of success and that is widely accepted by specialists and program directors in the field of alcoholism treatment.

A Model for Counseling Alcohol Abusers

While the model for counseling alcoholics (Burnett, 1977) was specifically designed for those whom one strongly suspects are, in fact, alcoholics, it may be followed with only slight modification during the initial counseling session with alcohol abusers. It will provide education for persons who are statistically speaking, pre-alcoholic. During the history-taking it will become apparent to the counselor if the client is more likely an abuser. A more psychodynamic approach may then be taken. For example, the counselor may listen for issues relating to psychological vulnerabilities related to heavy drinking, especially those relevant to problems around assertive behavior and sex roles. An alcohol abuser will usually at times use alcohol appropriately, and will acknowledge that heavy drinking is more often situational; for a man, at times when he is concerned about displaying masculinity, e.g., at a bar when attempting "to score," or at parties where women are present, or when out with the gang. For women, heavy drinking may take place after a bad day at work or school, or in an anxiety-producing situation where sexual or angry feelings are stirred. Another class of abusers are persons who have recently experienced a severe ego blow such as loss of status, e.g., being fired from a job, the death of a spouse, and/or the loss of a lover. Any situation which renders a person powerless or helpless will stir the need for regaining a feeling of potency through drinking in persons with addictive tendencies.

If alcohol abuse has been going on for several years, the client will often show signs of the beginnings of loss of control. That is, he or she may report frequently drinking more than intended in a situation where, in the past, control was exerted, or getting drunk without intending to, interspersed with more controlled drinking. The unpredictability of the outcome of a given drinking bout may be causing some anxiety. At this stage the denial and rationalization defenses will most likely not yet have been erected, so that the client may be more receptive to abstinence as a necessary step to be taken before the problem gets out of hand. Informing the client that he or she has begun to drink *alcoholically*, and that this is a first step in the direction of alcoholism, may convince the client to abstain from further drinking with or without the help of AA, so long as individual counseling is offered to deal with the psychological motives for drinking.

Having diagnosed the problem, the counselor may now proceed with counseling directed at the underlying problem of alcohol abuse as outlined above. The approach is suitable for: (1) alcohol abusers; (2) for persons in the early stages of addiction who have agreed to abstain from drinking; and (3) for more progressed alcoholics who have established sobriety through AA involvement for a minimum of 6–12 months, and who are continuing their participation in an AA program.

The primary aim of counseling is to reduce the need for personalized power. For men the exaggerated power need appears to be related to doubts about masculinity and to a machismo ideal of manliness. For women the need appears influenced by a sex-role conflict related to assertive behavior. Thus the helping approach will be slightly different depending on the sex of the client. A more general goal is to help the client to shift from a passive-dependent approach to problem-solving to a more active, self-reliant, goal-oriented approach.

My approach to helping is based on a conviction that persons who adhere to an androgynous ego ideal tend to function more flexibly and effectively in all aspects of their lives. The concept of androgyny as developed by Bem (1974, 1975) and her associates holds that traits deemed "masculine" and "feminine" reside in all healthy adults and should be encouraged. Mounting research findings are indicating that healthy successful adults tend to function androgynously despite socio-cultural pressures which would have them conform to sex-role stereotypic patterns. Translated into treatment goals, this means encouraging men to get in touch with nurturant, non-aggressive traits—in the past considered vulnerabilities or cross-sex identities. Helping males to "own" these traits, rather than to compensate for these characteristics through alcohol abuse, could lead to less striving toward an essentially dehumanizing ego ideal. Helping women to accept their assertive active needs as essential to normal adult functioning, rather than as a rejection of her female identity, could reduce the conflict inherent in female alcohol abusers.

Directing assertive behaviors in a direction of realistic goals formulated by the client is the next step. The aim is to shift the client from a wish for immediate magical trasnformation to instrumental behaviors. The client must be helped to gain control over his or her life space as a means to achieving genuine power. This amounts to the substitution of a "fix" for what I call a "process-high". Addictive persons tend to resist working toward long-term goals which involve postponement of gratification and the exercise of self-discipline. It may be necessary to set short-term, easily achievable goals at first. Teach your clients to give themselves "strokes" when they achieve small successes; they will tend to look to the counselor for approval and you may be tempted to oblige.

Since abusers tend to be young adults, they may ask for guidance related to education and career choices. Here, it is useful to keep in mind that their original need for personalized power may still be operating to some extent. That need can be shifted in the direction of social roles which involve an appropriate exercise of authority through the achievement of competence in, for example, a helping profession, or performing art, or an executive or supervisory position. (The success of AA may be attributable to identification with a group from which power emanates, from the role that AA people exercise in helping others to control their drinking behavior, and from the opportunity to tell one's story to a group of interested persons. Alcoholics are notorious exhibitionists.) Despite the shy façade of many female alcohol abusers, they tend to enjoy being the center of attention, and since they tend to be perfectionistic in work situations, they relish the opportunity to run things once they learn to be appropriately assertive.

Another issue which often emerges in counseling young abusers is that of achieving intimacy. Helping male clients to establish nonexploitative relationships with women whom they have tended to fear will sometimes emerge as an important aspect of counseling. For perfectionistic female clients, the problem is that they tend to keep a distance out of fear that self-revelation may lead to criticism and rejection. Counseling will seek to help males to depolarize their views of women, and women to be more open and assertive with respect to their feelings. Consciousness raising and assertiveness training will be important aspects of counseling.

Summary

Persons who use chemical substances to alter reality have in common their dissatisfaction with reality as they experience it. They frequently feel copeless in the face of their daily lives. In instances of alcohol abuse, feelings of powerlessness are common. The effects of drugs other than alcohol vary widely and make it difficult to generalize about the concerns particular individuals may be seeking to overcome.

With persons who abuse chemicals, psychological counseling is indicated. Resolution of personal feelings of inadequacy will remove the need to alter reality with a "fix." Nevertheless, the physiological response of some individuals to alcohol once habituated is so compelling that counseling alone is insufficient. Abstinance from alcohol must be established in cases of alcoholism before counseling is likely to succeed. With certain individuals certain drugs may also react in such a way that abstinance is a prerequisite to effective treatment, though the evidence does not suggest that this is true with all chemicals subject to abusive consumption.

Questions for Further Inquiry

1. What are the factors within our culture which promote addictive lifestyles as opposed to creative/productive lifestyles?

2. If the stress of our times encourages escape, how can those who help others promote more positive alternatives than escape through drugs and alcohol?

3. What kinds of stress does the addicted individual create for the other members of his or her family? What might a counselor do for the other family members?

4. How can mental health professionals prevent therapy from becoming an addiction—a "fix" for a dependent client?

5. Identify the agencies in your community that specialize in treating problems of alcohol and drug abuse, which you might use as referral resources.

References

Albee, G. W. Sex, the protestant ethic, and psychotherapy. *American Psychologist* (February) 1977. 1977.

Armor, D. J., Polick, M. J., & Stambul, H. B. *Alcoholism and treatment.* New York: Wiley, 1978.

Bem, S. L. The measurement of psychological androgyny. *Journal of Contemporary Psychology* 1974 *42,* 155–62.

Bem, S. L. Sex-role adaptability: One consequence of psychological androgyny. *Journal of Personality and Social Psychology* 1975 *31,* 634–43.

Burnett, M. M. Toward a model for counseling alcoholics. *Journal of Contemporary Psychotherapy 1977 8,* 127–35.

Friedan, B. *The feminine mystique.* New York: Norton, 1963.

Hofmann, F. G., & Hofmann, A. D. *A handbook of drug and alcohol abuse: The biomedical aspects.* New York: Oxford University Press, 1975.

Jaffe, J. H. Narcotic analgesics. In L. S. Goodman and A. Gilman (Eds.) *The pharmacological basis of therapeutics.* New York: Macmillan, 1970, pp. 237–75.

Jellinek, E. M. *The disease concept of alcoholism, (5th ed.)* New Haven: College and University Press, 1972.

Kinsey, P. *The female alcoholic: A social psychological study.* Springfield, Ill.: Charles C. Thomas, 1966.

McClelland, D. C., et al. *The drinking man.* New York: Free Press, 1972.

Peele, S. *Love and addiction.* New York: Taplinger, 1976.

Peele, S. Redefining addiction. *International Journal of Health Services* 1977 *7* (*1*), 103–24.

Wilsnack, S. Sex role identity in female alcoholism. *Journal of Abnormal Psychology* 1973 *82(2),* 253–61.

Zinberg, N. E. The search for rational approaches to heroin use. In P. G. Bourne (Ed.), *Addiction.* New York: Academic Press, 1974, pp. 149–74.

About the Authors

Sheldon Eisenberg is an Associate Professor in the Department of Educational Specialists at Cleveland State University, where he teaches courses in counseling theory, group counseling, human behavior, and practicum. He is the senior author of *The Counseling Process, 2nd Edition,* co-author of *The Counseling Process, 1st Edition,* and the author of a number of journal articles, including several on the future as a course of study. His approach to counseling and counselor education emphasizes self-awareness as a base for personal growth, constructive change, improved interpersonal relationships, and personal decision-making. He received his doctorate in 1969 from the University of Illinois (Counselor Education) and taught at Syracuse University before moving to Cleveland State University in 1974. He holds an Ohio Psychologist's license.

Lewis E. Patterson is Professor and Chairperson of the Department of Educational Specialists at the Cleveland State University, teaching in counselor education and managing programs in school administration and supervision, vocational education, and post-secondary education. Educated at the Pennsylvania State University, Dr. Patterson has counseled with adolescents and adults in school, college counseling service, and private practice. He has written about socialization, counselor development, career development, and sexism in education.

About the Contributors

Ernie E. Andrews, M.S.W. is program director of the Family Institute, Cincinnati, Ohio, and maintains a private practice of individual, group, couple, and family psychotherapy. He is Adjunct Assistant Clinical Professor in the Departments of Psychology and Psychiatry, University of Cincinnati, and Visiting Associate Professor, School of Social Work, Ohio State University. A Fellow of the American Group Psychotherapy Association, he is consultant in group and family therapies to clinics, hospitals, agencies and universities in the midwest.

Arthur Blum is Professor of Social Welfare at the School of Applied Social Sciences, Case Western Reserve University. His work experience with delinquent youth includes individual and group therapy in settlements, a child guidance center and residential care institutions. He has been a consultant to youth-outreach gang programs and to the juvenile court. For four years he was Director of the Youth Development Training Center at Case Western Reserve University. The agency was funded by a grant from the President's Committee on Juvenile Delinquency and Youth Crime and included faculty from eight different disciplines who developed training programs in the area of juvenile delinquency.

Gene Bocknek graduated from Boston University with a Ph.D. in Psychology in 1959. He trains students in counseling psychology at Boston University and maintains a private practice as a licensed psychologist. His areas of professional interest focus on adult development, ego psychology, and ego/developmental intervention technology.

Marie Burnett received her doctorate in 1969 from Case Western Reserve University in a combined social and clinical psychology program. She is Chief Psychologist at the Adult and Child Guidance Center of St. Francis Hospital in Evanston, Illinois, and is Director of Alcoholism Outpatient Counseling. Her interest in issues related to traditional sex roles has contributed to her understanding of substance abuse and addiction. She has lectured and published articles both in the areas of feminist psychotherapy and alcoholism.

Diane E. Frey completed her Ph.D. at the University of Illinois and is currently Associate Professor of Counseling at Wright State University in Dayton, Ohio. She writes and consults about conflict management, child abuse, battered women and nonverbal communication. She also maintains private practice as a licensed psychologist.

Eric J. Hatch is Associate Professor and Coordinator of The School Psychology Program at Appalachian State University. He is a licensed psychologist and holds credentials as a secondary school teacher, school psychologist, supervisor of psychological services and marriage counselor. He has been the recipient of several federal grants supporting work with learning disabled children and he has written about the education and placement of learning disabled and educable mentally retarded children.

David W. Johnson is a Professor of Educational Psychology at the University of Minnesota. He holds M.A. and Ed.D. degrees from Columbia University. He is the author of 10 books, including *The Social Psychology of Education, Contemporary Social Psychology, Reaching Out,* and *Human Relations and Your Career.* Dr. Johnson has published over 70 research articles in leading psychological journals, and in 1972 he received a national award for outstanding research from the American Personnel and Guidance Association. For the past 12 years he has served as an organizational consultant to schools and business. He is a practicing psychotherapist.

Donald B. Keat II is Professor and coordinator of the elementary school counseling program at the Pennsylvania State University. Since receiving his Ph.D. from Temple University in 1967, he has practiced child psychology and done teaching and consulting in universities, public and private schools, hospitals, and community agencies. A prolific writer, Dr. Keat has published numerous articles and books, including *Fundamentals of Child Counseling* (1974) and *Multimodal Therapy with Children* (1978). He is currently editor of *Elementary School* and *Guidance and Counseling.*

Laura Kent is a free-lance writer and editor who has collaborated with Nancy Schlossberg on higher education research and projects related to women's issues. She received her M.A. in English from the University of California at Berkeley and has taught at Berkeley, Santa Barbara, and Louisiana State University.

Sophie Freud Loewenstein   is Professor of Social Work at Simmons College in Boston. Since completing her Ph.D. at Brandeis University in 1970, she has completed extensive post-graduate training in group dynamics and has served a post-doctoral internship in group therapy. She has written on female sexuality, feminism and racism in the social work curriculum, and the concept of narcissism. Dr. Loewenstein is the granddaughter of Sigmund Freud.

Janet C. Loxley   is a counseling psychologist at the University of California at Irvine. Since completing doctoral study at Southern Illinois University, she has written and presented papers on assertion training and cognitive-behavioral therapy, divorce and the divorcing family, and moral and community development. She has worked as a therapist with prisoners and institutionalized mental patients.

Milton Matz   is a clinical psychologist in private practice in Cleveland, Ohio. He is also director of the Pastoral Psychology Institute in the Department of Psychiatry at Case Western Reserve University School of Medicine, and he has taught at Case Western Reserve University and Cleveland State University. Formerly a rabbi, Dr. Matz completed his Ph.D. in psychology at the University of Chicago in 1966 and holds an honorary D.D. from Hebrew Union College for his contributions to the prevention of mental illness. Major professional interests are the prevention and treatment of dysfunctional grief and prevention and treatment of dysfunctional marital interaction.

Richard C. Nelson   was educated at Boston University and Ohio University where he received his Ph.D. in 1962. His educational experience includes teaching in public elementary and junior high schools, counseling K-12, teacher education, and counselor education. His writings have had two major thrusts: elementary school guidance and counseling, and choice awareness.

Nancy K. Schlossberg   received a baccalaureate in Sociology from Barnard College and a doctorate in Guidance and Personnel Administration from Teachers College, Columbia University. Now a professor in the Department of Counseling and Personnel Services at the University of Maryland, Dr. Schlossberg also served as the first director of the American Council on Education's Office of Women and has taught at Wayne State University and Howard University.

Dr. Schlossberg's research interests currently center on adult development, with particular emphasis on adaptation to transition. She has written extensively on the problems of women, on sex stereotyping, women, and on age bias. She currently serves on the Board of Trustees of the National Manpower Institute.

James M. Schuerger   is Professor of Psychology at Cleveland State University. In addition to his teaching, he serves as counseling psychologist in the university counseling service, maintains private practice in counseling and industrial assessment, and consults with the juvenile court system. Since completing his doctorate at Kent State University, he has published more than a dozen articles and several books, including *Personality Theory in Action* and *Using Tests and Other Information in Counseling: A Decision Model for Practitioners.*

Edward L. Trembley   completed his professional education in clinical psychology at Ohio University and counselor education at Penn State. Over the last fifteen years he has served as a practicing counseling psychologist, a counseling services and student affairs administrator, and a counselor educator. His interests center on counseling theory and practice and counseling service and academic administration. He is Chairperson of the Department of Counseling and Personnel at Western Michigan University.

Serapio R. Zalba   is Chairman of the Department of Urban Studies and Applied Social Sciences, Case Western Reserve University. He has worked as a recreation worker in Berkeley, California, with delinquent gangs as a neighborhood center group worker in San Francisco, as a juvenile parole officer in Wisconsin, in jails and prisons in California, training gang workers in Los Angeles, and as a trainer and planning consultant to various juvenile courts in Ohio.

Name Index

Subject Index